MODELS FOR EXPOSITORY WRITING

MODELS FOR EXPOSITORY WRITING

MODEL PARAGRAPHS AND ESSAYS

ANTHONY C. WINKLER

JO RAY McCUEN

Glendale College

SCIENCE RESEARCH ASSOCIATES, INC.
Chicago, Henley-on-Thames, Sydney, Toronto
A Subsidiary of IBM

Acquisition Editor	Philip Gerould
Project Editor	Byron Riggan
Production Services	Arthur Kuntz
Text and Cover Designer	Janet Bollow Associates
Cover Photograph	Ernest Braun
Compositor	Allservice Phototypesetting

Library of Congress Cataloging in Publication Data

Main entry under title:

Models for expository writing.

    Includes index.
    1. Exposition (Rhetoric)   2. College readers.
    3. English language—Rhetoric   I. Winkler, Anthony C.
    II. McCuen, Jo Ray, 1929–
    PE1429.M63   1985   808'.0427   84-22137
    ISBN 0-574-22101-8

Acknowledgments

INCIDENT ON A LAKE IN LAUSANNE from Winston Churchill, *A Roving Commission: My Early Life.* Copyright 1930 by Charles Scribner's Sons; copyright renewed (New York: Charles Scribner's Sons, 1930). Reprinted with the permission of Charles Scribner's Sons and the Hamlyn Publishing Group Limited.

THE DEATH OF KING GEORGE VI from *Majesty: Elizabeth II and the House of Windsor,* copyright © 1977 by Robert Lacey. Reprinted by permission of Harcourt Brace Jovanovich, Inc.

THE LOSS OF AN OLD FRIEND Copyright 1979, *Los Angeles Times Syndicate.* Reprinted by permission.

IS ANYBODY LISTENING? Copyright 1979, *Los Angeles Times.* Reprinted by permission.

I THOUGHT MY LAST HOUR HAD COME from *I Saw Tokyo Burning* by Robert Guillain, translated by William R. Byron. Copyright © 1980, 1981 by Doubleday & Company, Inc. Reprinted by permission of Doubleday & Company, Inc.

HE WAS A GOOD LION From "He Was a Good Lion" *West with the Night* Copyright © 1942, 1983 Beryl Markham.

THE TERROR AND LOVE IN LONELINESS from *Loneliness* by Clark E. Moustakas. © 1961 Clark E. Moustakas. Published by Prentice-Hall, Inc., Englewood Cliffs, NJ 07632.

GRADUATION From *I Know Why the Caged Bird Sings* by Maya Angelou. Copyright © 1969 by Maya Angelou. Reprinted by permission of Random House, Inc.

TOO EASY. Reprinted by permission.

(Acknowledgments continue on page 388.)

Preface

This book is a collection of model paragraphs and essays carefully selected to exemplify the nine rhetorical modes most commonly taught in the classroom. These are: narrative, description, definition, example, process, classification, comparison and contrast, causal analysis, and argumentation. A chapter is devoted to each of these modes. In each chapter the examples are arranged in a graduated order of length and difficulty.

Each chapter opens with an introduction that discusses a specific mode of writing. The models that follow consist of two single-paragraph examples, at least three short essays, two long essays, and one student essay—all written in the same rhetorical mode and demonstrating to the student the use of a single organizing principle in material of varying length and complexity.

The apparatus at the end of each chapter focuses attention on the ideas and organizing principles implicit in each essay. Our questions are grouped under two main heads: *Questions for Critical Thinking,* and *Questions on the Writing Process.* There is also a section on *Writing Assignments* and a brief section on *Vocabulary.*

Because students do not write papers only for English classes, essays in this book have been taken from many sources and disciplines, reflecting the new emphasis on writing across the curriculum. The overriding criterion in choosing an essay has been that it must be memorably written. The discipline from which each essay comes is identified in the table of contents. The result, we believe, is a book whose subjects and models reflect an appealing and broad range of interests. We also hope that this mix will teach students that English is not merely a belletristic discipline fussing about grammatical niceties, but one whose skills are indispensable to nearly every subject.

Many people have helped us in preparing this work. But we are especially grateful for the help of Hazel McCuen, whose tastes and editorial skills are reflected throughout the book.

Anthony Winkler
Jo Ray McCuen

Contents

x
CONTENTS

MODELS FOR EXPOSITORY WRITING

THE IDEA OF EXPOSITION

Exposition comes from the past participle of the Latin word for *expound.* When we write an exposition, we write mainly to expound or explain. Expository writing is different from the kind of imaginative or creative writing we find in the works of novelists or dramatists. Few of us will ever write a novel or a play, but nearly all of us at one time or another will write to explain. Therefore, exposition is the kind of writing taught in most English composition courses.

But if you stop to think about it, you will quickly see that there are nearly limitless numbers of occasions that might call for expository writing, ranging from short notes to the milkman to a long letter of explanation to a creditor. No course can possibly teach them all.

Yet there is one teachable principle that is common to all good expository writing: the ability to think logically. The thinking that goes into exposition is classifiable into nine operations (or rhetorical modes): narration, description, definition, example, process, classification, comparison/contrast, causal analysis, and argumentation. Underlying all expository writing is one or a combination of these thinking operations.

Narration explains the occurrence of incidents and events in a definite sequence; description, how a thing looks; definition, what it means. Example is explaining through the use of illustrations and cases. Process explains how an action is done; comparison/contrast, how two things are similar or dissimilar. Classification explains the constituent parts of a larger whole; causal analysis, the causes or effects of an action; and argument, the reasons and evidence behind a certain point of view.

Some essay assignments will call for the exclusive use of one of these operations; some will call for the writer to skillfully blend two of them. And some complicated assignments will require the writer to blend several of these modes into a single essay. Here are some examples of actual essay questions asked in various courses taught at a large West Coast university:

1. Define the elastic-rebound theory (earth science).
2. What were the social, political, and intellectual factors that contributed to the outbreak of the French Revolution (Western civilization)?
3. How were liberalism and nationalism compatible and complementary ideologies? To what degree were they antagonistic (political science)?
4. Point to a place. Can you ever point to that same place again (philosophy)?
5. Write an essay analyzing the major theme behind the short story "Flowering Judas" (English).

The first question requires a definition; the second, an analysis of effect; the third, a comparison/contrast; the fourth, an argument. The fifth will require the writer to blend several of the modes of expository writing into a single essay. In sum, if you master the writing of each of the nine expository modes, you will be able to answer almost any kind of essay question.

Writing is done best when it is done systematically. Yet it is impossible to write an essay systematically if one knows nothing more than the rudiments of syntax and grammar. Grammar is indispensable in organizing and penning a single sentence, but nearly useless in dealing with the larger elements of writing, such as the paragraph, the page, and the whole essay. The techniques of exposition are most useful precisely at this level. They give the writer a general notion of what needs to be done, of how the material must be organized, and of how the larger elements of the essay are created, arranged, and linked.

ONE

NARRATION

Narration is probably the oldest of all the expository modes we will cover in this book, and the one with which nearly everyone will have had at least a glancing acquaintance. In its most basic form, a narrative is a story, and all of us at one time or another have told stories. Narrations may range from the simple two-minute anecdote to the 1000-page biography; in the middle range, there is the police report, the magazine article, and the minutes of a business meeting.

An essential feature of the narrative is the arranging of events and incidents into a tellable sequence. In order to do this, the narrator paces the material. Pacing is the arranging and telling of the story in such a way as to give primary emphasis to its most important parts. Trivial or unimportant sidelights are either omitted or glossed over; the focus of the narrative is unremittingly on its significant incidents. You may have noticed that time does not pass in fiction at the same rate it does in real life—that many a story will signify the passing of a month with a mere sentence such as "A month went by." Yet this same story will linger lovingly over the events of a half an hour, expending pages and pages upon them. This is pacing at work. All time is not treated equally; nor, for that matter, are all events or incidents.

A narrative may be written from the first-person point of view, in which the narrator refers to himself as "I," or from an omniscient point of view, in which the people in the narrative are referred to as "he" or "she" or "they." If you wrote a narrative about your first trip to the dentist you would probably use the first-person point of view; on the other hand, if you wrote a newspaper article for one of the wire services you would most likely use the viewpoint of an omniscient and neutral reporter. In this chapter, "The Death of King George VI" is narrated from an omniscient point of view. "Incident on a Lake in Lausanne," "The Loss of An Old Friend," "Is Anybody Listening?," and "The Terror and Love in Loneliness" are narrated from the first-person point of view. Finally, "I Thought My Last Hour Had Come" combines an omniscient point of view with an embedded eyewitness account narrated in the first person.

If you are not a writer of fiction, most of the narrative writing you do will be from the first-person point of view. And so it should be. This point of view allows the reader immediate and direct entry into the story and the mind of its teller. Care should be taken, however, to focus on the telling of the story rather than on the "I" who tells it. Especial care must also be taken to remain faithful to whatever point of view you choose. If you are writing from the point of view of a child, you must maintain that childlike tone without any inexplicable lapses into adulthood. Without consistency of this kind, the narrative will be unbelievable.

The events in a well-told narrative progress in a climactic way to the conclusion. Nothing in a narrative exists at random; every part contributes to the main point. It has been often said that the art of narration is inherited, not learned, and perhaps this is in large part true. This much, however, can be learned by any storyteller: a story must make a point. Nothing irritates quite as much as the pointless narrative. The point does not have to be weighty: it merely has to be substantial enough to justify the narrative. If the narrative is well-paced, consistent in its point of view, and makes some minor point, the reader, even if not entirely happy with the story, will at least not feel ill-used by it.

INCIDENT ON A LAKE IN LAUSANNE

Winston Churchill

Sir Winston Leonard Spencer Churchill (1874–1965) is widely regarded as one of the greatest statesmen of this century. Born into an aristocratic family, he was educated at Harrow and Sandhurst. During his long lifetime he held a variety of important political posts in various British governments, including prime minister twice (1940–1945, 1951–1955). He is the author of numerous books, among them The Second World War *(6 vol., 1948–53) and* A History of the English-Speaking Peoples *(4 vol., 1956–58). In 1953 he won the Nobel Prize for literature.*

In the summer of 1893 the nineteen-year-old Churchill went rowing on Lake Geneva and nearly drowned. In the paragraph that follows, Churchill tells the story of this incident, which, he writes, brought him as close to death as he had ever been.

My brother and I were sent this summer by our parents for a so-called walking-tour in Switzerland, with a tutor. I need hardly say we travelled by train so far as the money lasted. The tutor and I climbed mountains. We climbed the Wetterhorn and Monte Rosa. The spectacle of the sunrise striking the peaks of the Bernese Oberland is a marvel of light and colour unsurpassed in my experience. I longed to climb the Matterhorn, but this was not only too expensive but held by the tutor to be too dangerous. All this prudence however might easily have been upset by an incident which happened to me in the Lake of Lausanne. I record this incident that it may be a warning to others. I went for a row with another boy a little younger than myself. When we were more than a mile from the shore, we decided to have a swim, pulled off our clothes, jumped into the water and swam about in great delight. When we had had enough, the boat was perhaps 100 yards away. A breeze had begun to stir the waters. The boat had a small red awning over its stern seats. This awning acted as a sail by catching the breeze. As we swam towards the boat, it drifted farther off. After this had happened several times we had perhaps halved the distance. But meanwhile the breeze was freshening and we both, especially my companion, began to be tired. Up to this point no idea of danger had crossed my mind. The sun played upon the sparkling blue waters; the wonderful panorama of mountains and valleys, the gay hotels and villas still smiled. But I now saw Death as near as I believe I have ever seen Him. He was swimming in the water at our side, whispering from time to time in the rising wind which continued to carry the boat away from us at about the same speed we could swim. No help was near. Unaided we could never reach the shore. I was not only an easy, but a fast swimmer, having represented my House at Harrow, when our team defeated all comers. I now swam for life. Twice I reached

7

within a yard of the boat and each time a gust carried it just beyond my reach; but by a supreme effort I caught hold of its side in the nick of time before a still stronger gust bulged the red awning again. I scrambled in, and rowed back for my companion who, though tired, had not apparently realised the dull yellow glare of mortal peril that had so suddenly played around us. I said nothing to the tutor about this serious experience; but I have never forgotten it; and perhaps some of my readers will remember it too.

VOCABULARY

unsurpassed   prudence   panorama

QUESTIONS FOR CRITICAL THINKING

1. Walking tours such as Churchill described played an important part in the education of young English gentlemen. What do you see as the principal value of such tours?
2. How does Churchill's narration of the lake incident fit in with what you know about his character as a man?
3. If you have ever had a near death experience, what effect did it have on your view of life?

QUESTIONS ON THE WRITING PROCESS

1. What lead-in does the author use to introduce his narrative about the incident on Lake Lausanne?
2. How does the author convey the sinister nearness of death in his narrative?
3. In the middle of the narrative about his near drowning, the author intrudes with a description of "the sparkling blue waters" and the "wonderful panorama of mountains and valleys" and "gay hotels and villas." Why does he make a point of mentioning this background scenery? What does it contribute to the narrative?

WRITING ASSIGNMENTS

1. Narrate any exciting or dangerous incident you have ever experienced on water.
2. Write a narration of a trip you have taken.

THE DEATH OF GEORGE VI

Robert Lacey

Robert Lacey (1944–   ), British historian and biographer, was assistant editor of the London Sunday Times *magazine from 1969 to 1973. He is the author of several books, among them* The French Revolution, I: The Fall of the Bastille *(1968);* The French Revolution, II: The Terror *(1968);* The Rise of Napoleon *(1969);* Sir Walter Raleigh *(1973), and* Majesty *(1977).*

Taken from Majesty, *this paragraph narrates the death of George VI (1895–1952), one of Britain's best-loved monarchs and father of the current Queen, Elizabeth II.*

On the morning of 31 January 1952 King George VI waved good-bye to his daughter and son-in-law from the tarmac of London Airport, and then went back up to Sandringham[1] where a small party of friends awaited him. The King had recently learnt the pleasures of tail-end-of-season shoots, rough forays in pursuit of the game left after the conventional shoots had been cropped—coots on the Broads at Hickling, the hare at Sandringham. All the tenants, estate workers, neighbouring small farmers, police, and local worthies would join in to make up a score or more of guns ranging the countryside. The fifth of February was a clear, crisp, late winter day with blue sky, long shadows. The quarry was hare and the King shot cleanly and fast, picking off the animals as they dashed in front of him. Two hundred eighty hare had been bagged by the end of an outing which everyone had enjoyed, and the King retired to his room after dinner that night relaxed and satisfied. A valet brought him a cup of hot chocolate and he read for an hour and a half until about midnight, when a watchman in the garden saw him fastening the latch of his bedroom window that had been newly repaired. He had not entered the 280 hare in his Game Book, and that page has remained vacant, for some time in the small hours of 6 February 1952 the heart of George VI stopped beating.

VOCABULARY

tarmac   forays   quarry

---

[1]Sandringham House, Norfolk, East Anglia. One of the homes of the British royal family.

9

QUESTIONS FOR CRITICAL THINKING

1. What is the significance in the death of a King?
2. What is your attitude toward royalty?
3. The Queen of England has no real constitutional power, which is vested solely in the elected leaders. Yet the British are staunch supporters of their expensive monarchial system. Why? What do you think is the value of royalty to any country?

QUESTIONS ON THE WRITING PROCESS

1. Good narration largely depends on the skillful use of specific detail. What specific detail does the author use in describing the makeup of the King's shooting party?
2. The author compresses seven days in the space of a single paragraph. In pacing the narrative, how does the author manage to convey the passing of time?
3. The author deals with the last days of King George VI in considerable detail, down to mentioning the last person to glimpse the King alive. What do you suppose is the purpose of this kind of painstaking detail?

WRITING ASSIGNMENTS

1. In a single paragraph narrate how you spent an entire week.
2. Write a paragraph about any memorable outdoor experience.

SHORT ESSAYS

THE LOSS OF AN OLD FRIEND

Jim Murray

*Jim Murray (1919–   ) is one of America's most popular sports report-
ers. He began his journalistic career as a reporter for the* New Haven
Register, *and subsequently worked for* Time *magazine and* Sports Illustrated. *Today, his column, syndicated by the* Los Angeles Times, *is
published in approximately 180 newspapers.*

*After entertaining sports fans for two decades, Jim Murray lost the sight
of his one good eye, and in April 1979 he temporarily stopped writing.
The essay below appeared in July of that same year. Despite his blindness, Murray started writing again and continues to produce his column
regularly.*

1   OK, bang the drum slowly, professor. Muffle the cymbals. Kill the laugh
track. You might say the Old Blue Eye is back. But that's as funny as this is
going to get.

2   I feel I owe my friends an explanation as to where I've been all these
weeks. Believe me, I would rather have been in a press box.

3   I lost an old friend the other day. He was blue eyed, impish, he cried a lot
with me, laughed a lot with me, he saw a great many things with me. I don't
know why he left me. Boredom perhaps. We read a lot of books together,
we did a lot of crossword puzzles together, we saw films together. He had a
pretty exciting life. He saw Babe Ruth hit a home run when we were both
12 years old. He saw Willie Mays steal second base, he saw Maury Wills
steal his 104th base. He saw Rocky Marciano get up. I thought he led a
pretty good life.

4   One night a long time ago he saw this pretty lady who laughed a lot and
played the piano, and he couldn't look away from her. Later, he looked on
as I married this pretty lady. He saw her through 34 years—he loved to see
her laugh, he loved to see her happy.

5   You see, the friend I lost was my eye. My good eye. The other eye, the
right one, we've been carrying for years. We just let him tag along like Don
Quixote's nag. It's been a long time since he could read the number on a
halfback or tell whether a ball was fair or foul or even which fighter was
down.

6   So, one blue eye is missing and the other misses a lot.

7   My best friend left me, at least temporarily, in a twilight world where it's
always 8 o'clock on a summer night.

8   He stole away like a thief in the night and he took a lot with him. But
not everything. He left a lot of memories. He couldn't take those with him.
He just took the future with him and the present. He couldn't take the past.

11

9 I don't know why he had to go. I thought we were pals. I thought the things we did together we enjoyed doing together. Sure, we cried together. There were things to cry about.

10 But it was a long, good relationship, a happy one. Went all the way back to the days when we arranged all the marbles in a circle in the dirt in the lots in Connecticut. We played one-old-cat baseball. We saw curveballs together, we tried to hit them or catch them. We looked through a catcher's mask together. We were partners in every sense of the word.

11 He recorded the happy moments, the miracle of children, the beauty of a Pacific sunset, snow-capped mountains, faces on Christmas morning. He allowed me to hit fly balls to young sons in uniforms two sizes too large, to see a pretty daughter march in halftime parades.

12 He allowed me to see most of the major and exciting sports events of our time. I suppose I should be grateful. He didn't drift away when I was 12 or 15 or 27, but stuck around over 50 years, or until we had a vault of memories. Still, I'm only human. I'd like to see again, if possible, a Rocky Marciano with his nose bleeding, behind on points and the other guy coming.

13 I guess I would like to see a Reggie Jackson with the count 3-and-2 and the Series on the line, guessing fastball. I guess I'd like to see a Rod Carew with men on first and second and no place to put him, and the pitcher wishing he were standing in the rain some place reluctant to let go of the baseball.

14 I'd like to see a Stan Musial crouched around a curveball one more time. I'd like to see Don Drysdale trying not to laugh as a young hitter came up there with both feet in the bucket.

15 I'd like to see a Sandy Koufax just once more facing a Willie Mays with a no-hitter on the line. I'd like to see a Maury Wills with a big lead against a pitcher with a good move. I'd like to see a Roberto Clemente with the ball and a guy trying to go from first to third. I'd like to see a Pete Rose sliding into home head-first.

16 I'd like once more to see Henry Aaron standing there with that quiet bat, a study in deadliness. I'd like to see Bob Gibson scowling at a hitter as if he had some nerve just to pick up a bat.

17 I'd like to see Sugar Ray Robinson or Muhammed Ali giving a recital, a ballet, not a fight.

18 Also, to be sure, I'd like to see a sky full of stars, moonlight on the water, and yes, the tips of a royal flush peaking out as I fan out a poker hand, and yes, a straight two-foot putt.

19 Come to think of it, I'm lucky. I saw all of those things. I see them yet.

VOCABULARY

Don Quixote (5)   vault (12)

QUESTIONS FOR CRITICAL THINKING

1. Surveys show that blindness is the affliction most feared by the majority of people. Why do you think this is so?
2. What do you think people expect from the writing of a newspaper columnist? How does Murray fulfill or fall short of that expectation?
3. If you were suddenly afflicted with a serious illness, what memories would you find most consoling?

QUESTIONS ON THE WRITING PROCESS

1. What is the meaning of the expression "bang the drum slowly"? Why is its use appropriate here?
2. Murray is a newspaper columnist. What characteristics can you identify in his writing style, especially in his use of paragraphs, that are obviously geared toward a popular readership?
3. Murray writes about his eye as though it were a living person and not an organ of his body. What is this kind of treatment called?
4. All narratives have a plot. This column also has a plot, although it mainly consists of a catalog of events witnessed by the lost eye. How would you summarize the plot of this column?
5. Murray does not tell us what he has lost until the fifth paragraph, by which time most readers will have already guessed. Why is this an effective technique?
6. Paragraph six consists of a single short sentence. What is its purpose in this essay?

WRITING ASSIGNMENTS

1. Narrate the most exciting sporting event you have either witnessed or played a part in.
2. Write an account of the most serious illness you have ever suffered.

IS ANYBODY LISTENING?

Anonymous

In October 1979, the Los Angeles Times *received the letter reprinted below. It was submitted by a niece of the woman who wrote it on condition that the author remain anonymous. Whether or not the author is still alive is unknown to the editors.*

What follows is a heart-rending plea for society to help make more bearable the lives of old people residing in convalescent hospitals.

1　Hello! Is there anyone out there who will listen to me? How can I convince you that I am a prisoner?

2　For the past five years, I have not seen a park or the ocean or even just a few feet of grass.

3　I am an 84-year-old woman, and the only crime which I have committed is that I have an illness which is called chronic. I have severe arthritis and about five years ago I broke my hip. While I was recuperating in the hospital, I realized that I would need extra help at home. But there was no one. My son died 35 years ago, my husband, 25 years ago. I have a few nieces and nephews who come by to visit once in a while, but I couldn't ask them to take me in, and the few friends I still have are just getting by, themselves. So I wound up at a convalescent hospital in the middle of Los Angeles.

4　All kinds of people are thrown together here. I sit and watch, day after day. As I look around this room, I see the pathetic ones (maybe the lucky ones—who knows?) who have lost their minds, and the poor souls who should be out but nobody comes to get them, and the sick ones who are in pain. We are all locked up together.

5　I have been keeping in touch with the world through the newspaper, my one great luxury. For the last few years I have been reading about the changes in Medicare regulations. All I can see from these improvements is that nurses spend more time writing. For, after all, how do you regulate caring?

6　Most of the nurse's aides who work here are from other countries. Even those who can speak English don't have much in common with us. So they hurry to get their work done as quickly as possible. There are a few caring people who work here, but there are so many of us who are needy for that kind of honest attention.

7　A doctor comes to see me once a month. He spends approximately three to five seconds with me and then a few more minutes writing in the chart or joking with the nurses. (My own doctor doesn't come to convalescent hospitals, so I had to take this one.) I sometimes wonder about how the

14

nurse's aides feel when they work so hard for so little money and then see that the person who spends so little time is the one who is paid the most.

8   I notice that most of the physicians who come here don't even pay attention to things like whether their patient's finger-nails are trimmed or whether their body is foul-smelling. Last week when the doctor came to see me, I hadn't had a bath in 10 days because the nurse's aide took too long on her coffee break. She wrote in the chart that she gave me a shower—anyway, who would check or care? I would be labeled as a complainer or losing my memory, and that would be worse.

9   It is now 8 o'clock. Time to be in bed. I live through each night—and it is a long night—with memories of my childhood. I lived on an apple farm in Washington.

10   I remember how I used to bake, pies and cakes and cookies for friends and neighbors and their children. In the five years I have been here, I have had no choice—no choice of when I want to eat or what I want to eat. It has been so long since I have tasted fruit like mango or cherries.

11   As I write this, I keep wishing I were exaggerating.

12   These last five years feel like the last five hundred of my life.

13   Last year, one of the volunteers here read us a poem. It was by Robert Browning. I think it was called "Rabbi Ben Ezra." It went something like this: "Grow old along with me, the best of life is yet to be." How can I begin to tell you that growing old in America is for me an unbelievable, lonely nightmare?

14   I am writing this because many of you may live to be old like me, and by then it will be too late. You, too, will be stuck here and wonder why nothing is being done, and you, too, will wonder if there is any justice in life. Right now, I pray every night that I may die in my sleep and get this nightmare of what someone has called life over with, if it means living in this prison day after day.

VOCABULARY

chronic (3)   pathetic (4)   convalescent (7)

QUESTIONS FOR CRITICAL THINKING

1. What is your attitude toward the author and her complaint?
2. Some societies honor the elderly and others ignore them. Into which category do you think America falls? Why?
3. What would you do if you found yourself in the author's predicament?
4. What responsibility, if any, does society have toward the elderly?

QUESTIONS ON THE WRITING PROCESS

1. The letter narrates the boredom of the author's life in a convalescent hospital. What other purpose does it have?
2. This piece was originally printed as a Letter to the Editor of a major newspaper. What characteristics identify it as an informal sort of writing such as might be associated with a letter?
3. What comparison does the author develop throughout the essay in order to show what it's like to be confined in a convalescent home? What facts does she present to sustain this comparison?
4. Examine the fourth paragraph of the letter. How do you explain the verb tense in which it is written? Why is the use of this tense rhetorically effective?
5. How is the end of the letter related to its beginning? Why is this an effective ending?

WRITING ASSIGNMENTS

1. Imagine that you are eighty years old. Write a narration describing an ideal day in your life as an elderly person.
2. Since women outlive men by several years, some people have suggested that polygynous marriage—marriage between one man and several women—is the answer to the problem of loneliness among the elderly. Write an essay giving your views on this suggestion.

I THOUGHT MY LAST HOUR HAD COME

Robert Guillain

Robert Guillain (1908–   ) is the permanent Tokyo correspondent for the Paris newspaper Le Monde *and is acknowledged as a world authority on Far Eastern affairs. He is the author of several major books on the Far East, including* The Blue Ants: 6000 Million Chinese Under the Red Flag *(1957),* The Japanese Challenge *(1970),* When China Wakes *(1966), and* I Saw Tokyo Burning *(1981), from which the excerpt below is taken.*

The very word Hiroshima still evokes feelings of terror. The following records an eyewitness account of the famous 1945 atom bomb explosion.

1   Monday, August 6, 1945, in Hiroshima. A few seconds after 8:15 A.M., a flash of light, brighter than a thousand suns, shredded the space over the city's center. A gigantic sphere of fire, a prodigious blast, a formidable pillar of smoke and debris rose into the sky: an entire city annihilated as it was going to work, almost vaporized at the blast's point zero, irradiated to death, crushed and swept away. Its thousands of wooden houses were splintered and soon ablaze, its few stone and brick buildings smashed, its ancient temples destroyed, its schools and barracks incinerated just as classes and drills were beginning, its crowded streetcars upended, their passengers buried under the wreckage of streets and alleys crowded with people going about their daily business. A city of 300,000 inhabitants—more, if its large military population was counted, for Hiroshima was headquarters for the southern Japan command. In a flash, much of its population, especially in the center, was reduced to a mash of burned and bleeding bodies, crawling, writhing on the ground in their death agonies, expiring under the ruins of their houses or, soon, roasted in the fire that was spreading throughout the city—or fleeing, half-mad, with the sudden torrent of nightmare-haunted humanity staggering toward the hills, bodies naked and blackened, flayed alive, with charcoal faces and blind eyes.

2   Is there any way to describe the horror and the pity of that hell? Let a victim tell of it. Among the thousand accounts was this one by a Hiroshima housewife, Mrs. Futaba Kitayama, then aged thirty-three, who was struck down 1900 yards—just over a mile—from the point of impact. We should bear in mind that the horrors she described could be multiplied a hundredfold in the future.

3   "I was in Hiroshima, that morning of August 6. I had joined a team of women who, like me, worked as volunteers in cutting firepaths against

17

incendiary raids by demolishing whole rows of houses. My husband, because of a raid alert the previous night, had stayed at the *Chunichi (Central Japan Journal),* where he worked.

4 "Our group had passed the Tsurumi bridge, Indian-file, when there was an alert; an enemy plane appeared all alone, very high over our heads. Its silver wings shone brightly in the sun. A woman exclaimed, 'Oh, look—a parachute!' I turned toward where she was pointing, and just at that moment a shattering flash filled the whole sky.

5 "Was it the flash that came first, or the sound of the explosion, tearing up my insides? I don't remember. I was thrown to the ground, pinned to the earth, and immediately the world began to collapse around me, on my head, my shoulders. I couldn't see anything. It was completely dark. I thought my last hour had come. I thought of my three children, who had been evacuated to the country to be safe from the raids. I couldn't move; debris kept falling, beams and tiles piled up on top of me.

6 "Finally I did manage to crawl free. There was a terrible smell in the air. Thinking the bomb that hit us might have been a yellow phosphorus incendiary like those that had fallen on so many other cities, I rubbed my nose and mouth hard with a *tenugui* (a kind of towel) I had at my waist. To my horror, I found that the skin of my face had come off in the towel. Oh! The skin on my hands, on my arms, came off too. From elbow to fingertips, all the skin on my right arm had come loose and was hanging grotesquely. The skin of my left hand fell off too, the five fingers, like a glove.

7 "I found myself sitting on the ground, prostrate. Gradually I registered that all my companions had disappeared. What had happened to them? A frantic panic gripped me, I wanted to run, but where? Around me was just debris, wooden framing, beams and roofing tiles; there wasn't a single landmark left.

8 "And what had happened to the sky, so blue a moment ago? Now it was as black as night. Everything seemed vague and fuzzy. It was as though a cloud covered my eyes and I wondered if I had lost my senses. I finally saw the Tsurumi bridge and I ran headlong toward it, jumping over the piles of rubble. What I saw under the bridge then horrified me.

9 "People by the hundreds were flailing in the river. I couldn't tell if they were men or women; they were all in the same state: their faces were puffy and ashen, their hair tangled, they held their hands raised and, groaning with pain, threw themselves into the water. I had a violent impulse to do so myself, because of the pain burning through my whole body. But I can't swim and I held back.

10 "Past the bridge, I looked back to see that the whole Hachobori district had suddenly caught fire, to my surprise, because I thought only the district I was in had been bombed. As I ran, I shouted my children's names. Where was I going? I have no idea, but I can still see the scenes of horror I glimpsed here and there on my way.

11   "A mother, her face and shoulders covered with blood, tried frantically to run into a burning house. A man held her back and she screamed, 'Let me go! Let me go! My son is burning in there!' She was like a mad demon. Under the Kojin bridge, which had half collapsed and had lost its heavy, reinforced-concrete parapets, I saw a lot of bodies floating in the water like dead dogs, almost naked, with their clothes in shreds. At the river's edge, near the bank, a woman lay on her back with her breasts ripped off, bathed in blood. How could such a frightful thing have happened? I thought of the scenes of the Buddhist hell my grandmother had described to me when I was little.

12   "I must have wandered for at least two hours before finding myself on the Eastern military parade ground. My burns were hurting me, but the pain was different from an ordinary burn. It was a dull pain that seemed somehow to come from outside my body. A kind of yellow pus oozed from my hands, and I thought that my face must also be horrible to see.

13   "Around me on the parade ground were a number of grade-school and secondary-school children, boys and girls, writhing in spasms of agony. Like me, they were members of the anti-air raid volunteer corps. I heard them crying 'Mama! Mama!' as though they'd gone crazy. They were so burned and bloody that looking at them was insupportable. I forced myself to do so just the same, and I cried out in rage, 'Why? Why these children?' But there was no one to rage at and I could do nothing but watch them die, one after the other, vainly calling for their mothers.

14   "After lying almost unconscious for a long time on the parade ground, I started walking again. As far as I could see with my failing sight, everything was in flames, as far as the Hiroshima station and the Atago district. It seemed to me that my face was hardening little by little. I cautiously touched my hands to my cheeks. My face felt as though it had doubled in size. I could see less and less clearly. Was I going blind, then? After so much hardship, was I going to die? I kept on walking anyway and I reached a suburban area.

15   "In that district, farther removed from the center, I found my elder sister alive, with only slight injuries to the head and feet. She didn't recognize me at first, then she burst into tears. In a handcart, she wheeled me nearly three miles to the first-aid center at Yaga. It was night when we arrived. I later learned there was a pile of corpses and countless injured there. I spent two nights there, unconscious; my sister told me that in my delirium I kept repeating, 'My children! Take me to my children!'

16   "On August 8, I was carried on a stretcher to a train and transported to the home of relatives in the village of Kasumi. The village doctor said my case was hopeless. My children, recalled from their evacuation refuge, rushed to my side. I could no longer see them; I could recognize them only by smelling their good odor. On August 11, my husband joined us. The children wept with joy as they embraced him.

17   "Our happiness soon ended. My husband, who bore no trace of injury, died suddenly three days later, vomiting blood. We had been married sixteen years and now, because I was at the brink of death myself, I couldn't even rest his head as I should have on the pillow of the dead.

18   "I said to myself, 'My poor children, because of you I don't have the right to die!' And finally, by a miracle, I survived after I had again and again been given up for lost.

19   "My sight returned fairly quickly, and after twenty days I could dimly see my children's features. The burns on my face and hands did not heal so rapidly, and the wounds remained pulpy, like rotten tomatoes. It wasn't until December that I could walk again. When my bandages were removed in January, I knew that my face and hands would always be deformed. My left ear was half its original size. A streak of cheloma, a dark brown swelling as wide as my hand, runs from the side of my head across my mouth to my throat. My right hand is striped with a cheloma two inches wide from the wrist to the little finger. The five fingers on my left hand are now fused at the base. . . ."

VOCABULARY

prodigious (1)	flayed (1)	flailing (9)
debris (1)	incendiary (3)	parapets (11)
vaporized (1)	evacuated (5)	insupportable (13)
irradiated (1)	grotesquely (6)	delirium (15)
incinerated (1)	prostrate (7)	refuge (16)

QUESTIONS FOR CRITICAL THINKING

1.   Which incident described by the narrator moved you the most? Why?
2.   Although the conventional firebombing of Tokyo resulted in more civilian casualties than the atomic bombing of either Hiroshima or Nagasaki, it is the last two cities that have come to symbolize the horrors of modern war. Why?
3.   Over what issue, if any, should the United States be prepared to fight a nuclear war?
4.   Do you believe, as some have said, that nuclear war could destroy all of the world's civilizations? How does this belief affect your life?
5.   Can nuclear war between the superpowers be avoided? How?

QUESTIONS ON THE WRITING PROCESS

1. What is the effect of the opening of this narrative? In what kind of writing would you expect to find such an opening?
2. From what point of view are the first two paragraphs narrated? How does this point of view contrast with the one used by Mrs. Kitayama?
3. What is the effect of having two separate points of view?
4. In pacing her narrative, how does Mrs. Kitayama inform us of the passing of time?
5. In paragraph 4, the narrator tells us that a woman in her group pointed to the sky and exclaimed, "Oh, look—a parachute!" Why does she make a point of sharing this trivial remark with us?
6. In paragraph 18, the narrator recounts her recovery in a mere two sentences. Why does she gloss over this so quickly?

WRITING ASSIGNMENTS

1. In 300 words, recount the most terrifying experience of your life.
2. Write an essay describing your reactions to "I Thought My Last Hour Had Come."

HE WAS A GOOD LION

Beryl Markham

Beryl Markham (1902–   ), an Englishwoman, spent most of her early life on her father's farm in East Africa. At eighteen, she became the first woman in Africa to earn a race horse trainer's license. Later she qualified for a commercial airplane pilot's license and made world headlines as the first person to fly the North Atlantic from England to Cape Breton Island in Nova Scotia. Her only book is an autobiography, West with the Night, *published in 1942.*

In this excerpt, one of the world's great pilots recounts a life-threatening experience with a lion.

1   When I was a child, I spent all my days with the Nandi Murani, hunting barefooted, in the Rongai Valley, or in the cedar forests of the Mau Escarpment.

2   At first I was not permitted to carry a spear, but the Murani depended on nothing else.

3   You cannot hunt an animal with such a weapon unless you know the way of his life. You must know the things he loves, the things he fears, the paths he will follow. You must be sure of the quality of his speed and the measure of his courage. He will know as much about you, and at times make better use of it.

4   But my Murani friends were patient with me.

5   "Amin yut!" one would say, "what but a dik-dik will run like that? Your eyes are filled with clouds today, Lakweit!"

6   That day my eyes were filled with clouds, but they were young enough eyes and they soon cleared. There were other days and other dik-dik. There were so many things.

7   There were dik-dik and leopard, kongoni and warthog, buffalo, lion, and the 'hare that jumps.' There were many thousands of the hare that jumps.

8   And there were wildebeest and antelope. There was the snake that crawls and the snake that climbs. There were birds, and young men like whips of leather, like rainshafts in the sun, like spears before a singiri.

9   "Amin yut!" the young men would say, "that is no buffalo spoor, Lakweit. Here! Bend down and look. Bend down and look at this mark. See how this leaf is crushed. Feel the wetness of this dung. Bend down and look so that you may learn!"

10   And so, in time, I learned. But some things I learned alone.

11   There was a place called Elkington's Farm by Kabete Station. It was near Nairobi on the edge of the Kikuyu Reserve, and my father and I used

to ride there from town on horses or in a buggy, and along the way my father would tell me things about Africa.

12 Sometimes he would tell me stories about the tribal wars—wars between the Masai and the Kikuyu (which the Masai always won), or between the Masai and the Nandi (which neither of them ever won), and about their great leaders and their wild way of life which, to me, seemed much greater fun than our own. He would tell me of Lenana, the brilliant Masai ol-oiboni, who prophesied the coming of the White Man, and of Lenana's tricks and stratagems and victories, and about how his people were unconquerable and unconquered—until, in retaliation against the refusal of the Masai warriors to join the King's African Rifles, the British marched upon the Native villages; how, inadvertently, a Masai woman was killed, and how two Hindu shopkeepers were murdered in reprisal by the Murani. And thus, why it was that the thin, red line of Empire had grown slightly redder.

13 He would tell me old legends sometimes about Mount Kenya, or about the Menegai Crater, called the Mountain of God, or about Kilimanjaro. He would tell me these things and I would ride alongside and ask endless questions, or we would sit together in the jolting buggy and just think about what he had said.

14 One day, when we were riding to Elkington's, my father spoke about lions.

15 "Lions are more intelligent than some men," he said, "and more courageous than most. A lion will fight for what he has and for what he needs; he is contemptuous of cowards and wary of his equals. But he is not afraid. You can always trust a lion to be exactly what he is—and never anything else."

16 "Except," he added, looking more paternally concerned than usual, "that damned lion of Elkington's!"

17 The Elkington lion was famous within a radius of twelve miles in all directions from the farm, because, if you happened to be anywhere inside that circle, you could hear him roar when he was hungry, when he was sad, or when he just felt like roaring. If, in the night, you lay sleepless on your bed and listened to an intermittent sound that began like the bellow of a banshee trapped in the bowels of Kilimanjaro and ended like the sound of that same banshee suddenly at large and arrived at the foot of your bed, you knew (because you had been told) that this was the song of Paddy.

18 Two or three of the settlers in East Africa at that time had caught lion cubs and raised them in cages. But Paddy, the Elkington lion, had never seen a cage.

19 He had grown to full size, tawny, black-maned and muscular, without a worry or a care. He lived on fresh meat, not of his own killing. He spent his waking hours (which coincided with everybody else's sleeping hours) wandering through Elkington's fields and pastures like an affable, if apostrophic, emperor, a-stroll in the gardens of his court.

20   He thrived in solitude. He had no mate, but pretended indifference and walked alone, not toying too much with imaginings of the unattainable. There were no physical barriers to his freedom, but the lions of the plains do not accept into their respected fraternity an individual bearing in his coat the smell of men. So Paddy ate, slept, and roared, and perhaps he sometimes dreamed, but he never left Elkington's. He was a tame lion, Paddy was. He was deaf to the call of the wild.

21   "I'm always careful of that lion," I told my father, "but he's really harmless. I have seen Mrs. Elkington stroke him."

22   "Which proves nothing, said my father. "A domesticated lion is only an unnatural lion—and whatever is unnatural is untrustworthy."

23   Whenever my father made an observation as deeply philosophical as that one, and as inclusive, I knew there was nothing more to be said.

24   I nudged my horse and we broke into a canter covering the remaining distance to Elkington's.

25   It wasn't a big farm as farms went in Africa before the First World War, but it had a very nice house with a large veranda on which my father, Jim Elkington, Mrs. Elkington, and one or two other settlers sat and talked with what to my mind was always unreasonable solemnity.

26   There were drinks, but beyond that there was a tea-table lavishly spread, as only the English can spread them. I have sometimes thought since of the Elkingtons' tea-table—round, capacious, and white, standing with sturdy legs against the green vines of the garden, a thousand miles of Africa receding from its edge.

27   It was a mark of sanity, I suppose, less than of luxury. It was evidence of the double debt England still owes to ancient China for her two gifts that made expansion possible—tea and gunpowder.

28   But cakes and muffins were no fit bribery for me. I had pleasures of my own then, or constant expectations. I made what niggardly salutations I could bring forth from a disinterested memory and left the house at a gait rather faster than a trot.

29   As I scampered past the square hay shed a hundred yards or so behind the Elkington house, I caught sight of Bishon Singh whom my father had sent ahead to tend our horses.

30   I think the Sikh must have been less than forty years old then, but his face was never any indication of his age. On some days he looked thirty and on others he looked fifty, depending on the weather, the time of day, his mood, or the tilt of his turban. If he had ever disengaged his beard from his hair and shaved the one and clipped the other, he might have astonished us all by looking like one of Kipling's elephant boys, but he never did either, and so, to me at least, he remained a man of mystery, without age or youth, but burdened with experience, like the wandering Jew.

31   He raised his arm and greeted me in Swahili as I ran through the Elkington farmyard and out toward the open country.

32   Why I ran at all or with what purpose in mind is beyond my answering,

but when I had no specific destination I always ran as fast as I could in the hope of finding one—and I always found it.

33 I was within twenty yards of the Elkington lion before I saw him. He lay sprawled in the morning sun, huge, black-maned, and gleaming with life. His tail moved slowly, stroking the rough grass like a knotted rope end. His body was sleek and easy, making a mould where he lay, a cool mould, that would be there when he had gone. He was not asleep; he was only idle. He was rusty-red, and soft, like a strokable cat.

34 I stopped and he lifted his head with magnificent ease and stared at me out of yellow eyes.

35 I stood there staring back, scuffling my bare toes in the dust, pursing my lips to make a noiseless whistle—a very small girl who knew about lions.

36 Paddy raised himself then, emitting a little sigh, and began to contemplate me with a kind of quiet premeditation, like that of a slow-witted man fondling an unaccustomed thought.

37 I cannot say that there was any menace in his eyes, because there wasn't, or that his 'frightful jowls' were drooling, because they were handsome jowls and very tidy. He did sniff the air, though, with what impressed me as being close to audible satisfaction. And he did not lie down again.

38 I remembered the rules that one remembers. I did not run. I walked very slowly, and I began to sing a defiant song.

39 "Kali coma Simba sisi," I sang, "Asikari yoti ni udari!—Fierce like the lion are we, Askari all are brave!"

40 I went in a straight line past Paddy when I sang it, seeing his eyes shine in the thick grass, watching his tail beat time to the metre of my ditty.

41 "Twendi, twendi—ku pigana—piga aduoi—piga sana!—Let us go, let us go—to fight—beat down the enemy! Beat hard, beat hard!"

42 What lion would be unimpressed with the marching song of the King's African Rifles?

43 Singing it still, I took up my trot toward the rim of the low hill which might, if I were lucky, have Cape gooseberry bushes on its slopes.

44 The country was grey-green and dry, and the sun lay on it closely, making the ground hot under my bare feet. There was no sound and no wind.

45 Even Paddy made no sound, coming swiftly behind me.

46 What I remember most clearly of the moment that followed are three things—a scream that was barely a whisper, a blow that struck me to the ground, and, as I buried my face in my arms and felt Paddy's teeth close on the flesh of my leg, a fantastically bobbing turban, that was Bishon Singh's turban, appear over the edge of the hill.

47 I remained conscious, but I closed my eyes and tried not to be. It was not so much the pain as it was the sound.

48 The sound of Paddy's roar in my ears will only be duplicated, I think, when the doors of hell slip their wobbly hinges, one day, and give voice and authenticity to the whole panorama of Dante's poetic nightmares. It was an immense roar that encompassed the world and dissolved me in it.

49   I shut my eyes very tight and lay still under the weight of Paddy's paws.

50   Bishon Singh said afterward that he did nothing. He said he had remained by the hay shed for a few minutes after I ran past him, and then, for no explainable reason, had begun to follow me. He admitted, though, that, a little while before, he had seen Paddy go in the direction I had taken.

51   The Sikh called for help, of course, when he saw the lion meant to attack, and a half-dozen of Elkington's syces had come running from the house. Along with them had come Jim Elkington with a rawhide whip.

52   Jim Elkington, even without a rawhide whip, was very impressive. He was one of those enormous men whose girths alone seem to preclude any possibility of normal movement, much less of speed. But Jim had speed—not to be loosely compared with lightning, but rather like the speed of something spherical and smooth and relatively irresistible, like the cannon balls of the Napoleonic Wars. Jim was, without question, a man of considerable courage, but in the case of my Rescue From the Lion, it was, I am told, his momentum rather than his bravery for which I must forever be grateful.

53   It happened like this—as Bishon Singh told it;

54   "I am resting against the walls of the place where hay is kept and first the large lion and then you, Beru, pass me going toward the open field, and a thought comes to me that a lion and a young girl are strange company, so I follow. I follow to the place where the hill that goes up becomes the hill that goes down, and where it goes down deepest I see that you are running without much thought in your head and the lion is running behind you with many thoughts in his head, and I scream for everybody to come very fast.

55   "Everybody comes very fast, but the large lion is faster than anybody, and he jumps on your back and I see you scream but I hear no scream. I only hear the lion, and I begin to run with everybody, and this includes Bwana Elkington, who is saying a great many words I do not know and is carrying a long kiboko which he holds in his hand and is meant for beating the large lion.

56   "Bwana Elkington goes past me the way a man with lighter legs and fewer inches around his stomach might go past me, and he is waving the long kiboko so that it whistles over all of our heads like a very sharp wind, but where we get close to the lion it comes to my mind that that lion is not of the mood to accept a kiboko.

57   "He is standing with the front of himself on your back, Beru, and you are bleeding in three or five places, and he is roaring. I do not believe Bwana Elkington could have thought that that lion at that moment would consent to being beaten, because the lion was not looking the way he had ever looked before when it was necessary for him to be beaten. He was looking as if he did not wish to be disturbed by a kiboko, or the Bwana, or the syces, or Bishon Singh, and he was saying so in a very large voice.

58   "I believe that Bwana Elkington understood this voice when he was still more than several feet from the lion, and I believe the Bwana considered in his mind that it would be the best thing not to beat the lion just then, but the Bwana when he runs very fast is like the trunk of a great baobob tree rolling down a slope, and it seems that because of this it was not possible for him to explain the thought of his mind to the soles of his feet in a sufficient quickness of time to prevent him from rushing much closer to the lion than in his heart he wished to be.

59   "And it was this circumstance, as I am telling it," said Bishon Singh, "which in my considered opinion made it possible for you to be alive, Beru."

60   "Bwana Elkington rushed at the lion then, Bishon Singh?"

61   "The lion, as of the contrary, rushed at Bwana Elkington," said Bishon Singh. "The lion deserted you for the Bwana, Beru. The lion was of the opinion that his master was not in any honest way deserving of a portion of what he, the lion, had accomplished in the matter of fresh meat through no effort by anybody except himself."

62   Bishon Singh offered this extremely reasonable interpretation with impressive gravity, as if he were expounding the Case For the Lion to a chosen jury of Paddy's peers.

63   "Fresh meat" . . . I repeated dreamily, and crossed my fingers.

64   "So then what happened . . . ?"

65   The Sikh lifted his shoulders and let them drop again. "What could happen, Beru? The lion rushed for Bwana Elkington, who in his turn rushed from the lion, and in so rushing did not keep in his hand the long kiboko, but allowed it to fall upon the ground, and in accomplishing this the Bwana was free to ascend a very fortunate tree, which he did."

66   "And you picked me up, Bishon Singh?"

67   He made a little dip with his massive turban. "I was happy with the duty of carrying you back to this very bed, Beru, and of advising your father, who had gone to observe some of Bwana Elkington's horses, that you had been moderately eaten by the large lion. Your father returned very fast, and Bwana Elkington some time later returned very fast, but the large lion has not returned at all."

68   The large lion had not returned at all. That night he killed a horse, and the next night he killed a yearling bullock, and after that a cow fresh for milking.

69   In the end he was caught and finally caged, but brought to no rendezvous with the firing squad at sunrise. He remained for years in his cage, which, had he managed to live in freedom with his inhibitions, he might never have seen at all.

70   It seems characteristic of the mind of man that the repression of what is natural to humans must be abhorred, but that what is natural to an infinitely more natural animal must be confined within the bounds of a rea-

son peculiar only to men—more peculiar sometimes than seems reasonable at all.

71   Paddy lived, people stared at him and he stared back, and this went on until he was an old, old lion. Jim Elkington died, and Mrs. Elkington, who really loved Paddy, was forced, because of circumstances beyond her control or Paddy's, to have him shot by Boy Long, the manager of Lord Delamere's estates.

72   This choice of executioners was, in itself, a tribute to Paddy, for no one loved animals more or understood them better, or could shoot more cleanly than Boy Long.

73   But the result was the same to Paddy. He had lived and died in ways not of his choosing. He was a good lion. He had done what he could about being a tame lion. Who thinks it just to be judged by a single error?

74   I still have the scars of his teeth and claws, but they are very small now and almost forgotten, and I cannot begrudge him his moment.

VOCABULARY

escarpment (1)	apostrophic (19)	Sikh (30)
stratagems (12)	niggardly (28)	syces (51)
reprisal (12)		

QUESTIONS FOR CRITICAL THINKING

1. To a large extent how did the author become educated concerning nature in East Africa? Are there advantages to this method of education? If yes, what are they?

2. What qualities of Paddy, the Elkington lion, might well be admirable in a human society? How would these qualities benefit society?

3. Paragraph 20 states that Paddy was "deaf to the call of the wild." Do you agree with that observation? Why or why not?

4. What is your judgment of the comment (paragraph 22) that "whatever is unnatural is untrustworthy"? Provide specific examples to support your judgment.

5. Why does the author suggest that tea and gunpowder made England's expansion possible? Do you agree with this view? If not, why not?

6. What conclusions about human nature can be drawn from the author's portrait of the lion?

QUESTIONS ON THE WRITING PROCESS

1. Beryl Markham's autobiographical narration is about a childhood experience written from a mature point of view. What does this point of view contribute to the writing?
2. How does the author make the transition from general background of her life in East Africa to the specific experience that taught her something important about animal nature? What sentence functions as the introduction to the specific experience?
3. What purpose does paragraph 30 serve?
4. In paragraphs 44-46 what does the author achieve by describing the lack of any sound?
5. Why does the author choose to have someone other than herself narrate the actual rescue? Do you consider her choice of narrator appropriate for the scene? Why or why not?
6. What definition does the author give to the word *good* when she claims that Paddy was a "good" lion? Does her definition match the dictionary definition?

WRITING ASSIGNMENTS

1. Write a 500-word autobiographical essay in which you describe an incident from your youth when you were in physical danger. Superimpose on the incident some adult comments about life and its meaning as related to the incident.
2. Write a 500-word essay describing your relationship to animals in general or to one animal in particular. Be autobiographical in your point of view.

THE TERROR AND LOVE IN LONELINESS

Clark E. Moustakas

Clark E. Moustakas (1924–   ) has been a psychologist and psycho-therapist with the Merrill-Palmer Institute in Detroit since 1949. His research has involved the areas of creativity and conformity, child and family therapy, and human values associated with learning. Among his best-known books are Loneliness *(1961),* Loneliness and Love *(1972),* Creativity and Conformity *(1967),* Psychotherapy with Children *(1959),* Turning Points *(1977), and* Creative Life *(1977).*

In this selection from Loneliness, *the author examines the nature of loneliness and people's response to it.*

1   I have experienced loneliness many times in my life, but until recently I lived my loneliness without being aware of it. In the past I tried to overcome my sense of isolation by plunging into work projects and entering into social activities. By keeping busy and by committing myself to interesting and challenging work, I never had to face, in any direct or open way, the nature of my own existence as an isolated and solitary individual.

2   I first began to awaken to the meaning of loneliness, to feel loneliness in the center of my consciousness, one terrible day when my wife and I were confronted with the necessity of making a decision. We were told that our five-year-old daughter, Kerry, who had a congenital heart defect, must have immediate surgery. We were warned, gently but firmly, by the cardiologist, that failure to operate would cause continual heart deterioration and premature death. At the same time he informed us that there were many unknown factors in heart surgery and that with Kerry's particular defect there was about a twenty percent chance that she would not survive the operation.

3   What were we to do? We experienced a state of acute worry, followed by a paralyzing indecision that lasted several days.

4   There was no peace or rest for me, anywhere, at this time. I, who had known Kerry as a vigorous, active child, bursting with energy, whether on roller skates, a two-wheel bike, or in the pool, was suddenly forced to view her as handicapped. In spite of her exuberance and her seemingly inexhaustible energy, there in my mind was the report of the X-rays and the catheterization showing a significant perforation and enlargement of her heart.

5   Visions of my daughter were constantly before me. I roamed the streets at night searching for some means, some resource in the universe which would guide me to take the right step. It was during these desperate days

and nights that I first began to think seriously of the inevitable loneliness of life. I was overcome with the pain of having to make a decision, as a parent, which had potentially devastating consequences either way. If I decided on surgery, she might not survive the operation. If I decided against it, the possibility of a premature death would always haunt me. It was a terrible responsibility, being required to make a decision, a life or death decision, for someone else. This awful feeling, this overwhelming sense of responsibility, I could not share with anyone. I felt utterly alone, entirely lost, and frightened; my existence was absorbed in this crisis. No one fully understood my terror or how this terror gave impetus to deep feelings of loneliness and isolation which had lain dormant within me. There at the center of my being, loneliness aroused me to a self-awareness I had never known before.

6   At last a decision was made, primarily by my wife, that we had no choice but to go ahead with the surgery, immediately, while we were both alive and able to give Kerry our strength and love. We explained the problem to Kerry simply. She quickly accepted the idea of the operation with that measureless trust and confidence which a young child feels with parents long before there is any understanding of trust or confidence.

7   The time of waiting during the operation itself was filled with painful anguish, terrifying suspension, and restlessness—but the most terrible loneliness of all occurred several days later.

8   I stood in the dark hallway of the hospital, a place I had repeatedly traversed with restless and weary footsteps. Kerry lay beside me in her wheelcart watching television. The light reflected in her eyes as she watched the program. Momentarily the shots, the tubes, the large incision across her chest were forgotten. I do not know how long I stood beside her. My mind was empty of all thought and feeling. Suddenly she looked at me. There were tears in her eyes. "Daddy, why is that little boy crying?" she asked. I looked for a moment, then I knew; I saw an episode I had witnessed many times in the past week.

9   The boy's eyes were transfixed, glued to the windows, looking below— expectant, watchful, waiting. Waiting for someone to come to protect and comfort him. Waiting for someone to rescue him from abandonment. Waiting. There was no one. He was alone—totally, utterly alone. Outside, people moved rapidly up and down steps and along the walk. Cars hurried down the highway. Inside, the public address blared out doctors' names. Nurse's aides shouted to children to get to sleep. But this child sat up in bed—his small body rigid—his heart breaking. Waiting. I knew in that moment he experienced a crushing loneliness, a feeling of being deserted and forsaken. He was quiet and frightened. Silent tears slipped down his face. What could I say to Kerry? She wept in sympathy. She did not expect an answer.

10   When I could no longer bear his suffering I entered the room. I stood quietly beside him for several minutes. Then the words came, "I know. Right now there's no one. No one at all. Your Mama has left you." He burst into painful, racking sobs and sighs. His grief was momentarily broken. All his silent agony burst into convulsive moans and piercing cries. A nurse entered. She glared at me. She spoke angrily, "Now see what you've done. Why don't you leave him alone?" Then, turning to him, she spoke firmly. "You know your mother isn't here. She left you after supper. She told you she'd be back in the morning. All the crying and shouting you can do will not bring her back. Stop. Stop now. You're keeping the other children awake. Lie down. Go to sleep. Your mother will come tomorrow." I stood by silently; as the nurse left the room, I followed her.

11   Walking beside her, I said, "You can't leave him that way. He is painfully lonely. He feels cut off from all meaningful ties. He will harbor this terror a long time. Go back. Tell him you care. Hold his hand. Say something gentle." She answered, "I can't. I have other duties." I suggested, "Tell him you would like to stay but you have certain duties to finish—that you will look in again soon." Hesitating a few moments, the nurse returned to the child's room. She spoke softly this time, "I'm sorry your mother isn't here with you now when you want her. I must give out medicine to other children but I'll be back. Maybe this will help," and she handed him a sucker.

12   Beside Kerry again, I could see a faint smile cross the child's face as he put the sucker in his mouth. There was a moment of peace. Then the silent tears continued to flow until he slipped into heavy, uncomfortable sleep with the sucker still in his mouth. I knew he would never forget this experience of loneliness just as I would never forget sitting alone in my daughter's room waiting for the slow, restorative process following her heart surgery.

13   For many hours I had been forced to ration to Kerry small cubes of ice—just enough to moisten her lips and mouth—one small piece each half hour. In between Kerry's begging, pleading voice asked for more. I had stated the limit directly and told her why it was necessary. But her lips were dry. She had been without liquids almost forty-eight hours. I felt dry too. I wanted to share this experience with her and had refrained from liquids myself. I felt her extreme thirst and yet worked feverishly to arouse her interest in other matters. Each new thought excited her momentarily but she always returned to the cry for ice, entreating with such urgency that each episode left me feeling the oppressor. The hours passed slowly and finally the glorious moment arrived when a real portion of liquids could be taken. The surgeon ordered a full glass of Coke. She drank it in a frenzy in two or three gulps and within a few minutes fell into a heavy sleep. I was exhausted, feeling her anguish, hearing her distressing cries for ice, exhausted with the effort of distraction and diversion.

It was a peaceful time. I was alone. I felt elated, full—yet empty, and a strange aura of peacefulness settled within me. I stared blankly at the floor. I do not know what forces within me caused me to glance at Kerry, but as I did in an instant an absolute terror overcame me. Suddenly I felt completely desolate and alone. I was aware of being depressed by and conscious of my own solitude. Something vague, hidden, crucial was before me. I could not understand but something seemed wrong in the way she was sleeping.

I noticed a slight tensing, her arms pulled away from her body, the fingers twisted and extended. Her entire body grew rigid. She went into a series of jerky, stretching movements—contortions—convulsions—grotesque and terrifying. Immediately I realized she was having a brain seizure. Her entire being was in a state of extreme agitation. She began biting her tongue. I slipped a pencil in her mouth, shouted for the nurse, and urged that the surgeon be called immediately. The nurse looked in briefly and left. I stroked Kerry's hair and whispered her name, but each time I touched her she moved away with violent, gross movements. I had to hold her body because she twisted and turned so violently there was danger she would fall off the bed. In those moments I experienced indescribable loneliness and fear and shock. In some measure my body writhed with Kerry's. I paced, and stretched, and turned as I witnessed the seizure. The most intolerable feeling was the realization that she was beyond my reach, beyond my voice and touch. She was in a pitiful plight—entirely by herself. She was without anyone or anything. I tried to commune with her. I whispered her name softly, gently, over and over again. "Kerry, Kerry, Kerry, my darling. It's Daddy. I'm here right beside you. I won't leave. Kerry, I'm here. Kerry, Kerry, Kerry." She opened her eyes. A horrible sound issued from her throat—then several more utterances of anguish and pain and fear. She screamed three words as she saw me—three awful words filled with agony and stark terror—words and tones that I shall never forget— *"No You Bad."* I answered, "It's all right, Kerry. It's Daddy. I'm here. I'm beside you." Her entire body was stiff, yet in constant motion. She jerked up and down, flailed her arms and legs at me, and tried to kick me. I was certain she did not recognize me. She was in a state of shock and experiencing a semi-conscious nightmare. In her dim state of awareness she thought I was a doctor who was about to administer a shot. The muscles in her face were tight. The mouth was open and the jaws distended and distorted. The stretching and agitated movement continued as she seemed to be struggling to escape, to find comfort, to find a resting place.

At last the surgeon arrived, took one look, and shouted to the nurse, "Brain edema. I'll have to give her a shot of glucose." The word "shot" struck the center of her terror. She tried to form words to speak, but no sound came; she shook violently in an effort to scream out an alarm. Then came an instinctual cry, emitted from deep within her being, a cry of raving terror followed by excruciating moans. I continued saying her name, whispering softly, gently, trying to offer strength, knowing all the while that she was lost to me, yet knowing also that I alone realized her pain and terror. Her wails were so piercingly effective they reverberated ceaselessly everywhere inside me and in the room. The doctor asked me to leave but I refused; I knew I had to stay whatever happened. Kerry's eyes were wide and fitful. She continued moaning and uttering the weird, painful cries. The nurse pushed me aside to hold Kerry while the shot was being administered. Only a small amount had been injected when Kerry gave such a violent jerk that the nurse let go and the needle fell out. Again the moaning continued and one word rang out distinctly, clearly—a plea, a beseeching, final cry for help. She held the word "Mama" a long, long time and then the moans and furious motions and cries resumed. I held her arms as the surgeon inserted the needle again. She looked at me with utter contempt and hatred. Her eyes were full of pain and accusation. I whispered, "I know how much it hurts." I could feel her pain and terror in my own nerves and bones and tissues and blood, but at the same time I knew in that moment no matter how fervently I lived through it with her, how much I wanted to share it with her, I knew she was alone, beyond my reach. I wanted so much for her to feel my presence, but she could not. She was beyond my call, beyond the call of anyone. It was her situation in a world entirely and solely her own. There was nothing further I could do. Each time she screamed her voice ripped through me, penetrating deeply into my inner being.

17   At last it was finished. The nurse put up the sides of the bed. Then she and the surgeon left. It was dark. Kerry and I were alone again. Kerry's cries and the grotesque, agitated body movements continued. All I could do was stand by. I tried to stroke her forehead but when I touched her she stiffened, screamed in pain, and moved violently away. I wanted her to know I was there, extending my compassion; I wanted her to see I suffered too; I wanted her to realize I had not left her. So I repeated over and over again, "My darling, Kerry. My sweet, Kerry. I'm here. Right here. Daddy is beside you. I won't leave you. Not ever. Not ever."

18   At length, she fell asleep. I left her room and stood outside her door to keep anyone from entering to disturb her. I stood in a frozen position for several hours, not moving at all, completely without feeling, and in a state of total nothingness. I tried in many ways to express this experience immediately afterwards, but I could not. It remained within me, a tremendous constricted mass. Each time I tried to form a word the mass rose within me and I choked and sputtered and the muscles in my body tightened. My mouth closed. The sounds were shut off and the intense experience settled inside me again. There was no way to share this loneliness, this experience

of fear, and shock, and isolation. It was an experience which held its own integrity but was so far-reaching and sharp, so utterly pervasive and gripping, that when I tried to speak only weird and painful cries, like Kerry's, came from me. I distinctly felt that I had failed her and that she had faced this great crisis alone.

19   Later she remembered the doctor who held her while a shot was given her but she did not remember her father who stayed beside her during the terrible ordeal and who suffered along with her, totally isolated and alone. As I dwell upon this experience of mutual loneliness, I realize how completely beyond my most imaginative comprehension is the heart surgery itself, when my daughter lay on the operating table and her heart was removed from her body while a mechanical pump pushed blood through her arteries and veins. Is the horror of this lonely existence perceivable or knowable at all? What does it mean in the life and growth of an individual child?

20   Kerry remained in the hospital two weeks. When we took her home, she was completely recovered physically, but her nightmares and terrors continued for several months after she left the hospital.

21   During the two weeks while she was in the pediatric ward, we never left her side. I had many opportunities to observe children experiencing isolation and loneliness. It was at this time that I felt a strong urge to look into the heart of the lonely experience. Starting with these experiences before and during the hospitalization, I began to discover the meaning of loneliness. I began to see that loneliness is neither good nor bad, but a point of intense and timeless awareness of the Self, a beginning which initiates totally new sensitivities and awareness, and which results in bringing a person deeply in touch with his own existence and in touch with others in a fundamental sense. I began to see that in the deepest experiences the human being can know—the birth of a baby, the prolonged illness or death of a loved relative, the loss of a job, the creation of a poem, a painting, a symphony, the grief of a fire, a flood, an accident—each in its own way touched upon the roots of loneliness. In each of these experiences, in the end, we must go alone.

22   In such experiences, inevitably one is cut off from human companionship. But experiencing a solitary state gives the individual the opportunity to draw upon untouched capacities and resources and to realize himself in an entirely unique manner. It can be a new experience. It may be an experience of exquisite pain, deep fear and terror, an utterly terrible experience, yet it brings into awareness new dimensions of self, new beauty, new power for human compassion, and a reverence for the precious nature of each breathing moment.

VOCABULARY

congenital (2)   convulsive (10)   reverberated (16)
catheterization (4)   restorative (12)   fervently (16)
perforation (4)   entreating (13)   grotesque (17)
impetus (5)   desolate (14)   constricted (18)
dormant (5)   contortions (15)   pervasive (18)
transfixed (9)   distended (15)   perceivable (19)
abandonment (9)   excruciating (16)   pediatric (21)

QUESTIONS FOR CRITICAL THINKING

1. The author writes that loneliness is neither good nor bad. What is your opinion of this view of loneliness?
2. There is a saying about being "lonely in a crowd." How can this saying be reconciled with the definition of loneliness presented in this essay?
3. Is loneliness an inescapable part of the human condition? What can be done about easing feelings of loneliness in oneself or in another?
4. Astronomers often speculate about the loneliness of humankind in a universe possibly empty of other intelligent life. What kind of loneliness do you think they mean? How is the loneliness of an entire species of life different from or similar to the loneliness felt by an individual?
5. In paragraph 10, the author writes about trying to comfort a lonely boy and saying to him, "I know. Right now there's no one. No one at all. Your Mama has left you." Why do you think the author spoke so bluntly to the child?

QUESTIONS ON THE WRITING PROCESS

1. What is the author's definition of loneliness, given in paragraph 21? How is the narrative related to this definition?
2. How is paragraph 7 related to the pacing of the narrative? Why did the author not elaborate on the passing of these several terrifying days?
3. In paragraph 9, the author describes the anguish felt by the small sick boy who is waiting for his mother. How does he emphasize what the boy was doing and must have felt?
4. What is the purpose of paragraph 3, which consists of only two sentences?
5. In paragraph 15, the author writes: "She screamed three words as she saw me—three awful words filled with agony and stark terror—words and tones that I shall never forget." What is the point of the repetition?
6. Examine the opening sentences of paragraphs 6, 16, and 17. What similar transitions does the author use between these paragraphs and the ones that precede them?

WRITING ASSIGNMENTS

1. Narrate any episode in your life in which you were terribly lonely.
2. Write your own definition of the meaning of loneliness and give examples of it.

GRADUATION

Maya Angelou

Maya Angelou (pseudonym for Marguerite Johnson, 1928-   ), is a remarkable American: a singer, dancer, actor, composer, director, writer, teacher, and political activist. She speaks six languages, including two African dialects. Her Black experience has been captured in a four-volume autobiography, the best known part of which is entitled I Know Why the Caged Bird Sings *(1969).*

By describing her own eighth grade graduation, the author sheds light on the endless struggle of all Black people to achieve.

1   The children in Stamps[1] trembled visibly with anticipation. Some adults were excited too, but to be certain the whole young population had come down with graduation epidemic. Large classes were graduating from both the grammar school and the high school. Even those who were years removed from their own day of glorious release were anxious to help with preparations as a kind of dry run. The junior students who were moving into the vacating classes' chairs were tradition-bound to show their talents for leadership and management. They strutted through the school and around the campus exerting pressure on the lower grades. Their authority was so new that occasionally if they pressed a little too hard it had to be overlooked. After all, next term was coming, and it never hurt a sixth grader to have a play sister in the eighth grade, or a tenth-year student to be able to call a twelfth grader Bubba. So all was endured in a spirit of shared understanding. But the graduating classes themselves were the nobility. Like travelers with exotic destinations on their minds, the graduates were remarkably forgetful. They came to school without their books, or tablets or even pencils. Volunteers fell over themselves to secure replacements for the missing equipment. When accepted, the willing workers might or might not be thanked, and it was of no importance to the pregraduation rites. Even teachers were respectful of the now quiet and aging seniors, and tended to speak to them, if not as equals, as beings only slightly lower than themselves. After tests were returned and grades given, the student body, which acted like an extended family, knew who did well, who excelled, and what piteous ones had failed.

2   Unlike the white high school, Lafayette County Training School distinguished itself by having neither lawn, nor hedges, nor tennis court, nor climbing ivy. Its two buildings (main classrooms, the grade school and home economics) were set on a dirt hill with no fence to limit either its boundaries or those of bordering farms. There was a large expanse to the

[1]Town in Arkansas.

left of the school which was used alternately as a baseball diamond or basketball court. Rusty hoops on swaying poles represented the permanent recreational equipment, although bats and balls could be borrowed from the P.E. teacher if the borrower was qualified and if the diamond wasn't occupied.

3   Over this rocky area relieved by a few shady tall persimmon trees the graduating class walked. The girls often held hands and no longer bothered to speak to the lower students. There was a sadness about them, as if this old world was not their home and they were bound for higher ground. The boys, on the other hand, had become more friendly, more outgoing. A decided change from the closed attitude they projected while studying for finals. Now they seemed not ready to give up the old school, the familiar paths and classrooms. Only a small percentage would be continuing on to college—one of the South's A&M (agricultural and mechanical) schools, which trained Negro youths to be carpenters, farmers, handymen, masons, maids, cooks and baby nurses. Their future rode heavily on their shoulders, and blinded them to the collective joy that had pervaded the lives of the boys and girls in the grammar school graduating class.

4   Parents who could afford it had ordered new shoes and ready-made clothes for themselves from Sears and Roebuck or Montgomery Ward. They also engaged the best seamstresses to make the floating graduating dresses and to cut down secondhand pants which would be pressed to a military slickness for the important event.

5   Oh, it was important, all right. Whitefolks would attend the ceremony, and two or three would speak of God and home, and the Southern way of life, and Mrs. Parsons, the principal's wife, would play the graduation march while the lower-grade graduates paraded down the aisles and took their seats below the platform. The high school seniors would wait in empty classrooms to make their dramatic entrance.

6   In the Store I was the person of the moment. The birthday girl. The center. Bailey[2] had graduated the year before, although to do so he had had to forfeit all pleasures to make up for his time lost in Baton Rouge.

7   My class was wearing butter-yellow piqué dresses, and Momma launched out on mine. She smocked the yoke into tiny crisscrossing puckers, then shirred the rest of the bodice. Her dark fingers ducked in and out of the lemony cloth as she embroidered raised daisies around the hem. Before she considered herself finished she had added a crocheted cuff on the puff sleeves, and a pointy crocheted collar.

8   I was going to be lovely. A walking model of all the various styles of fine hand sewing and it didn't worry me that I was only twelve years old and merely graduating from the eighth grade. Besides, many teachers in Arkansas Negro schools had only that diploma and were licensed to impart wisdom.

---

[2]The author's brother.

9   The days had become longer and more noticeable. The faded beige of former times had been replaced with strong and sure colors. I began to see my classmates' clothes, their skin tones, and the dust that waved off pussy willows. Clouds that lazed across the sky were objects of great concern to me. Their shiftier shapes might have held a message that in my new happiness and with a little bit of time I'd soon decipher. During that period I looked at the arch of heaven so religiously my neck kept a steady ache. I had taken to smiling more often, and my jaws hurt from the unaccustomed activity. Between the two physical sore spots, I suppose I could have been uncomfortable, but that was not the case. As a member of the winning team (the graduating class of 1940) I had outdistanced unpleasant sensations by miles. I was headed for the freedom of open fields.

10   Youth and social approval allied themselves with me and we trammeled memories of slights and insults. The wind of our swift passage remodeled my features. Lost tears were pounded to mud and then to dust. Years of withdrawal were brushed aside and left behind, as hanging ropes of parasitic moss.

11   My work alone had awarded me a top place and I was going to be one of the first called in the graduating ceremonies. On the classroom blackboard, as well as on the bulletin board in the auditorium, there were blue stars and white stars and red stars. No absences, no tardinesses, and my academic work was among the best of the year. I could say the preamble to the Constitution even faster than Bailey. We timed ourselves often: 'WethepeopleoftheUnitedStatesinordertoformamoreperfectunion . . ." I had memorized the Presidents of the United States from Washington to Roosevelt in chronological as well as alphabetical order.

12   My hair pleased me too. Gradually the black mass had lengthened and thickened, so that it kept at last to its braided pattern, and I didn't have to yank my scalp off when I tried to comb it.

13   Louise and I had rehearsed the exercises until we tired out ourselves. Henry Reed was class valedictorian. He was a small, very black boy with hooded eyes, a long, broad nose and an oddly shaped head. I had admired him for years because each term he and I vied for the best grades in our class. Most often he bested me, but instead of being disappointed I was pleased that we shared top places between us. Like many Southern Black children, he lived with his grandmother, who was as strict as Momma and as kind as she knew how to be. He was courteous, respectful and soft-spoken to elders, but on the playground he chose to play the roughest games. I admired him. Anyone, I reckoned, sufficiently afraid or sufficiently dull could be polite. But to be able to operate at a top level with both adults and children was admirable.

14   His valedictory speech was entitled "To Be or Not to Be." The rigid tenth-grade teacher had helped him write it. He'd been working on the dramatic stresses for months.

The weeks until graduation were filled with heady activities. A group of small children were to be presented in a play about buttercups and daisies and bunny rabbits. They could be heard throughout the building practicing their hops and their little songs that sounded like silver bells. The older girls (nongraduates, of course) were assigned the task of making refreshments for the night's festivities. A tangy scent of ginger, cinnamon, nutmeg and chocolate wafted around the home economics building as the budding cooks made samples for themselves and their teachers.

6   In every corner of the workshop, axes and saws split fresh timber as the woodshop boys made sets and stage scenery. Only the graduates were left out of the general bustle. We were free to sit in the library at the back of the building or look in quite detachedly, naturally, on the measures being taken for our event.

7   Even the minister preached on graduation the Sunday before. His subject was, "Let your light so shine that men will see your good works and praise your Father, Who is in Heaven." Although the sermon was purported to be addressed to us, he used the occasion to speak to backsliders, gamblers and general ne'er do-wells. But since he had called our names at the beginning of the service we were mollified.

8   Among Negroes the tradition was to give presents to children going only from one grade to another. How much more important this was when the person was graduating at the top of the class. Uncle Willie and Momma had sent away for a Mickey Mouse watch like Bailey's. Louise gave me four embroidered handkerchiefs. (I gave her crocheted doilies.) Mrs. Sneed, the minister's wife, made me an undershirt to wear for graduation, and nearly every customer gave me a nickel or maybe even a dime with the instruction "Keep on moving to higher ground," or some such encouragement.

9   Amazingly the great day finally dawned and I was out of bed before I knew it. I threw open the back door to see it more clearly, but Momma said, "Sister, come away from that door and put your robe on."

10   I hoped the memory of that morning would never leave me. Sunlight was itself young, and the day had none of the insistence maturity would bring it in a few hours. In my robe and barefoot in the backyard, under cover of going to see about my new beans, I gave myself up to the gentle warmth and thanked God that no matter what evil I had done in my life He had allowed me to live to see this day. Somewhere in my fatalism I had expected to die, accidentally, and never have the chance to walk up the stairs in the auditorium and gracefully receive my hard-earned diploma. Out of God's merciful bosom I had won reprieve.

21   Bailey came out in his robe and gave me a box wrapped in Christmas paper. He said he had saved his money for months to pay for it. It felt like a box of chocolates, but I knew Bailey wouldn't save money to buy candy when we had all we could want under our noses.

22   He was as proud of the gift as I. It was a soft-leather-bound copy of a

collection of poems by Edgar Allan Poe, or, as Bailey and I called him, "Eap." I turned to "Annabel Lee" and we walked up and down the garden rows, the cool dirt between our toes, reciting the beautifully sad lines.

23   Momma made a Sunday breakfast although it was only Friday. After we finished the blessing, I opened my eyes to find the watch on my plate. It was a dream of a day. Everything went smoothly and to my credit. I didn't have to be reminded or scolded for anything. Near evening I was too jittery to attend to chores, so Bailey volunteered to do all before his bath.

24   Days before, we had made a sign for the Store, and as we turned out the lights Momma hung the cardboard over the doorknob. It read clearly: CLOSED. GRADUATION.

25   My dress fitted perfectly and everyone said that I looked like a sunbeam in it. On the hill, going toward the school, Bailey walked behind with Uncle Willie, who muttered, "Go on, Ju." He wanted him to walk ahead with us because it embarrassed him to have to walk so slowly. Bailey said he'd let the ladies walk together, and the men would bring up the rear. We all laughed, nicely.

26   Little children dashed by out of the dark like fireflies. Their crepe-paper dresses and butterfly wings were not made for running and we heard more than one rip, dryly, and the regretful "uh uh" that followed.

27   The school blazed without gaiety. The windows seemed cold and unfriendly from the lower hill. A sense of ill-fated timing crept over me, and if Momma hadn't reached for my hand I would have drifted back to Bailey and Uncle Willie, and possibly beyond. She made a few slow jokes about my feet getting cold, and tugged me along to the now-strange building.

28   Around the front steps, assurance came back. There were my fellow "greats," the graduating class. Hair brushed back, legs oiled, new dresses and pressed pleats, fresh pocket handkerchiefs and little handbags, all homesewn. Oh, we were up to snuff, all right. I joined my comrades and didn't even see my family go in to find seats in the crowded auditorium.

29   The school band struck up a march and all classes filed in as had been rehearsed. We stood in front of our seats, as assigned, and on a signal from the choir director, we sat. No sooner had this been accomplished than the band started to play the national anthem. We rose again and sang the song, after which we recited the pledge of allegiance. We remained standing for a brief minute before the choir director and the principal signaled to us, rather desperately I thought, to take our seats. The command was so unusual that our carefully rehearsed and smooth-running machine was thrown off. For a full minute we fumbled for our chairs and bumped into each other awkwardly. Habits change or solidify under pressure, so in our state of nervous tension we had been ready to follow our usual assembly pattern: the American national anthem, then the pledge of allegiance, then the song every Black person I knew called the Negro National Anthem. All done in the same key, with the same passion and most often standing on the same foot.

30   Finding my seat at last, I was overcome with a presentiment of worse things to come. Something unrehearsed, unplanned, was going to happen, and we were going to be made to look bad. I distinctly remember being explicit in the choice of pronoun. It was "we," the graduating class, the unit, that concerned me then.

31   The principal welcomed "parents and friends" and asked the Baptist minister to lead us in prayer. His invocation was brief and punchy, and for a second I thought we were getting on the high road to right action. When the principal came back to the dais, however, his voice had changed. Sounds always affected me profoundly and the principal's voice was one of my favorites. During assembly it melted and lowed weakly into the audience. It had not been in my plan to listen to him, but my curiosity was piqued and I straightened up to give him my attention.

32   He was talking about Booker T. Washington, our "late great leader," who said we can be as close as the fingers on the hand, etc. . . . Then he said a few vague things about friendship and the friendship of kindly people to those less fortunate than themselves. With that his voice nearly faded, thin, away. Like a river diminishing to a stream and then to a trickle. But he cleared his throat and said, "Our speaker tonight, who is also our friend, came from Texarkana to deliver the commencement address, but due to the irregularity of the train schedule, he's going to, as they say, 'speak and run.' " He said that we understood and wanted the man to know that we were most grateful for the time he was able to give us and then something about how we were willing always to adjust to another's program, and without more ado—"I give you Mr. Edward Donleavy."

33   Not one but two white men came through the door off-stage. The shorter one walked to the speaker's platform, and the tall one moved to the center seat and sat down. But that was our principal's seat, and already occupied. The dislodged gentleman bounced around for a long breath or two before the Baptist minister gave him his chair, then with more dignity than the situation deserved, the minister walked off the stage.

34   Donleavy looked at the audience once (on reflection, I'm sure that he wanted only to reassure himself that we were really there), adjusted his glasses and began to read from a sheaf of papers.

35   He was glad "to be here and to see the work going on just as it was in the other schools."

36   At the first "Amen" from the audience I willed the offender to immediate death by choking on the word. But Amens and Yes, sir's began to fall around the room like rain through a ragged umbrella.

37   He told us of the wonderful changes we children in Stamps had in store. The Central School (naturally, the white school was Central) had already been granted improvements that would be in use in the fall. A well-known artist was coming from Little Rock to teach art to them. They were going to have the newest microscopes and chemistry equipment for their laboratory. Mr. Donleavy didn't leave us long in the dark over who made these

improvements available to Central High. Nor were we to be ignored in the general betterment scheme he had in mind.

38   He said that he had pointed out to people at a very high level that one of the first-line football tacklers at Arkansas Agricultural and Mechanical College had graduated from good old Lafayette County Training School. Here fewer Amen's were heard. Those few that did break through lay dully in the air with the heaviness of habit.

39   He went on to praise us. He went on to say how he had bragged that "one of the best basketball players at Fisk sank his first ball right here at Lafayette County Training School."

40   The white kids were going to have a chance to become Galileos and Madame Curies and Edisons and Gauguins, and our boys (the girls weren't even in on it) would try to be Jesse Owenses and Joe Louises.

41   Owens and the Brown Bomber were great heroes in our world, but what school official in the white-goddom of Little Rock had the right to decide that those two men must be our only heroes? Who decided that for Henry Reed to become a scientist he had to work like George Washington Carver, as a bootblack, to buy a lousy microscope? Bailey was obviously always going to be too small to be an athlete, so which concrete angel glued to what country seat had decided that if my brother wanted to become a lawyer he had to first pay penance for his skin by picking cotton and hoeing corn and studying correspondence books at night for twenty years?

42   The man's dead words fell like bricks around the auditorium and too many settled in my belly. Constrained by hard-learning manners I couldn't look behind me, but to my left and right the proud graduating class of 1940 had dropped their heads. Every girl in my row had found something new to do with her handkerchief. Some folded the tiny squares into love knots, some into triangles, but most were wadding them, then pressing them flat on their yellow laps.

43   On the dais, the ancient tragedy was being replayed. Professor Parsons sat, a sculptor's reject, rigid. His large, heavy body seemed devoid of will or willingness, and his eyes said he was no longer with us. The other teachers examined the flag (which was draped stage right) or their notes, or the windows which opened on our now-famous playing diamond.

44   Graduation, the hush-hush magic time of frills and gifts and congratulations and diplomas, was finished for me before my name was called. The accomplishment was nothing. The meticulous maps, drawn in three colors of ink, learning and spelling decasyllabic words, memorizing the whole of *The Rape of Lucrece*[3]—it was for nothing. Donleavy had exposed us.

45   We were maids and farmers, handymen and washerwomen, and anything higher that we aspired to was farcical and presumptuous.

---

[3]Long narrative poem by William Shakespeare.

46   Then I wished that Gabriel Prosser and Nat Turner[4] had killed all whitefolks in their beds and that Abraham Lincoln had been assassinated before the signing of the Emancipation Proclamation, and that Harriet Tubman[5] had been killed by that blow on her head and Christopher Columbus had drowned in the *Santa Maria*.

47   It was awful to be a Negro and have no control over my life. It was brutal to be young and already trained to sit quietly and listen to charges brought against my color with no chance of defense. We should all be dead. I thought I should like to see us all dead, one on top of the other. A pyramid of flesh with the whitefolks on the bottom, as the broad base, then the Indians with their silly tomahawks and teepees and wigwams and treaties, the Negroes with their mops and recipes and cotton sacks and spirituals sticking out of their mouths. The Dutch children should all stumble in their wooden shoes and break their necks. The French should choke to death on the Louisiana Purchase (1803) while silkworms ate all the Chinese with their stupid pigtails. As a species, we were an abomination. All of us.

48   Donleavy was running for election, and assured our parents that if he won we could count on having the only colored paved playing field in that part of Arkansas. Also—he never looked up to acknowledge the grunts of acceptance—also, we were bound to get some new equipment for the home economics building and the workshop.

49   He finished, and since there was no need to give any more than the most perfunctory thank-you's, he nodded to the men on the stage, and the tall white man who was never introduced joined him at the door. They left with the attitude that now they were off to something really important. (The graduation ceremonies at Lafayette County Training School had been a mere preliminary.)

50   The ugliness they left was palpable. An uninvited guest who wouldn't leave. The choir was summoned and sang a modern arrangement of "Onward, Christian Soldiers," with new words pertaining to graduates seeking their place in the world. But it didn't work. Elouise, the daughter of the Baptist minister, recited "Invictus"[6] and I could have cried at the impertinence of "I am the master of my fate, I am the captain of my soul."

51   My name had lost its ring of familiarity and I had to be nudged to go and receive my diploma. All my preparations had fled. I neither marched up to the stage like a conquering Amazon, nor did I look in the audience for Bailey's nod of approval. Marguerite Johnson, I heard the name again, my honors were read, there were noises in the audience of appreciation, and I took my place on the stage as rehearsed.

---

[4]Prosser and Turner were leaders of slave rebellions during the early 1800's in Virginia.

[5]American Black Abolitionist leader.

[6]Poem by William Ernest Henley.

52   I thought about colors I hated: ecru, puce, lavender, beige and black.

53   There was shuffling and rustling around me, then Henry Reed was giving his valedictory address, "To Be or Not to Be." Hadn't he heard the
whitefolks? We couldn't *be,* so the question was a waste of time. Henry's
voice came out clear and strong. I feared to look at him. Hadn't he got the
message? There was no "nobler in the mind" for Negroes because the world
didn't think we had minds, and they let us know it. "Outrageous fortune"?
Now, that was a joke. When the ceremony was over I had to tell Henry
Reed some things. That is, if I still cared. Not "rub," Henry, "erase." "Ah,
there's the erase." Us.

54   Henry had been a good student in elocution. His voice rose on tides of
promise and fell on waves of warnings. The English teacher had helped
him to create a sermon winging through Hamlet's soliloquy. To be a man, a
doer, a builder, a leader, or to be a tool, an unfunny joke, a crusher of funky
toadstools. I marveled that Henry could go through with the speech as if we
had a choice.

55   I had been listening and silently rebutting each sentence with my eyes
closed; then there was a hush, which in an audience warns that something
unplanned is happening. I looked up and saw Henry Reed, the conservative, the proper, the A student, turn his back to the audience and turn to us
(the proud graduating class of 1940) and sing, nearly speaking,

> "Lift ev'ry voice and sing
> Till earth and heaven ring
> Ring with the harmonies of Liberty . . ."

It was the poem written by James Weldon Johnson. It was the music composed by J. Rosamond Johnson. It was the Negro National Anthem. Out of
habit we were singing it.

56   Our mothers and fathers stood in the dark hall and joined the hymn of
encouragement. A kindergarten teacher led the small children onto the
stage and the buttercups and daisies and bunny rabbits marked time and
tried to follow:

> "Stony the road we trod
> Bitter the chastening rod
> Felt in the days when hope, unborn, had died.
> Yet with a steady beat
> Have not our weary feet
> Come to the place for which our fathers sighed?"

Each child I knew had learned that song with his ABC's and along with "Jesus Loves Me This I Know." But I personally had never heard it before. Never heard the words, despite the thousands of times I had sung them. Never thought they had anything to do with me.

On the other hand, the words of Patrick Henry had made such an impression on me that I had been able to stretch myself tall and trembling and say, "I know not what course others may take, but as for me, give me liberty or give me death."

And now I heard, really for the first time:

> "We have come over a way that with tears
> has been watered,
> We have come, treading our path through
> the blood of the slaughtered."

While echoes of the song shivered in the air, Henry Reed bowed his head, said "Thank you," and returned to his place in the line. The tears that slipped down many faces were not wiped away in shame.

We were on top again. As always, again. We survived. The depths had been icy and dark, but now a bright sun spoke to our souls. I was no longer simply a member of the proud graduating class of 1940; I was a proud member of the wonderful, beautiful Negro race.

Oh, Black known and unknown poets, how often have your auctioned pains sustained us? Who will compute the lonely nights made less lonely by your songs, or the empty pots made less tragic by your tales?

If we were a people much given to revealing secrets, we might raise monuments and sacrifice to the memories of our poets, but slavery cured us of that weakness. It may be enough, however, to have it said that we survive in exact relationship to the dedication of our poets (include preachers, musicians and blues singers).

VOCABULARY

smocked (7)	presentiment (3)	decasyllabic (44)
shirred (7)	dais (31)	elocution (54)
lazed (9)		

QUESTIONS FOR CRITICAL THINKING

1. The author makes it obvious that graduation from Lafayette County Training School is an important event. How is this importance conveyed to the reader?
2. What aspects in the principal's introduction of the guest speaker forewarns the author that the graduating class is going to be "made to look bad"?
3. In paragraph 42 the author states: "The man's dead words fell like bricks around the auditorium and too many settled in my belly." Why is the speaker's address so offensive to the author? In your view, how could the speaker have avoided the hostile response from his audience?
4. In paragraph 47 the author damns the whole human race to extinction. What triggers her despair? Is her reaction proportionate to the situation?
5. "Lift Ev'ry Voice and Sing," a poem by the Black poet James Weldon Johnson, is called "the Negro National Anthem" by Angelou. How does singing this anthem effect a change in the author's view of herself and her people?

QUESTIONS ON THE WRITING PROCESS

1. The first five paragraphs are written from an omniscient narrator's point of view whereas the rest of the essay is strictly autobiographical. What reasons can you give for the sudden shift from third to first person?
2. Where in the essay does a foreshadowing effect add suspense to the narration? Cite the specific passage. Evaluate this technique.
3. What do the topics "God," "home," and "Southern way of life" share semantically? See paragraph 5. Suggest some topics that would typically be avoided.
4. Paragraph 10 contains highly poetic language. How would you state this passage in plain English?
5. While most of the essay bears a serious tone, some humor prevails. What two or three humorous passages can you cite?
6. How is the essay organized? List its major parts.

WRITING ASSIGNMENTS

1. In 500 words narrate an experience that changed the direction of your life. Describe the following with clarity: 1) what your life was like before the experience, 2) the experience itself, 3) what you were like after the experience.
2. Write a 500-word essay in which you either support or attack the value of traditional graduation ceremonies.
3. In 500 words describe an event that you had anticipated with joy but that turned out to be a deep disappointment. Be sure to explain what caused the disappointment.

TOO EASY

Cynthia Hale

Although the air was fresh and the sky a crisp deep blue, this was not to be a typical spring morning—not for me. On this day I realized that I, a child of twelve, was capable of easily extinguishing the precious thing known as life.

I was the proud owner of a BB gun. It was a toy many children had, but with it came responsibility. I had to follow one rule, stressed strongly by my parents. I was never, under any circumstances, to shoot at anyone or anything living.

On that day, though, rules seemed unimportant. I was in our backyard, in a mood to rebel. Targets had become boring; shooting at them engendered no excitement. Evil seemed to dwell within me, pounding to get out. I sat quietly beside a thick bush, well concealed. Soon my victim emerged, fluttering down from out of thin air, a small bird similar to a sparrow. He was followed by three smaller comrades. The latter three were of no concern, though, for my eye was drawn to the first. For a sparrow his colors were extravagant, the greys and browns as dark as a moonless night. This bird I chose to be my victim. I waited until the correct moment, never moving. Then the moment arrived. The bird was perched on the limb of a blooming pyracantha shrub, completely still as if to pose, like a model posing for a painting. I took aim ever so carefully so as not to lose my chance. I could feel my heart beating, my breath panting as I aimed to kill. I pulled the trigger ever so gently. Suddenly, a quick shot rang out. A small flurry of feathers flew up and then everything seemed silent. I knew instantly that I had hit my target. Slowly the frail bird started to sway, trying desperately to hang on to his small perch, but to no avail. As if in slow motion, he began to fall, twirling and spinning in midair until he hit the ground, the blow cushioned by his soft body. There he lay for a moment until nerves took over and he began to quiver and shake. This trembling seemed to last forever, sending chills along my spine.

Finally, I ran over for a closer look. The small silver BB had pierced right through the bird's head, smashing the vital brain, and leaving two small holes now covered with blood and dirt. I held this small creature and was amazed that still now, with life extinguished from his body, he remained warm. As I stopped and thought for an instant, it occurred to me that life is too easily extinguished. It had been done in a matter of seconds. What had lived before was now dead. I had planned all along to kill this creature, but now I felt ashamed because killing was too easy.

TWO

DESCRIPTION

The practice of good descriptive writing is rather badly at odds with the popular theories about it. Most of us feel that description is inspired writing that begins and ends with a wondrous gush of feeling. We are convinced that to write a brilliant description we have only to be sufficiently moved by what we see. Yet a study of the writings of the best descriptive writers shows otherwise. The great descriptive poets such as Keats were relentless in their revisions. It is the same with most of the best descriptive novelists and short story writers. They reworked their descriptions endlessly. Some brilliant descriptions no doubt are inspired, and many more may have begun with inspiration. But most owe as much to perspiration as to inspiration.

Good description is selective. It is characterized by focus and intensity. It cannot include everything the author sees or hears, only those things that appeal most to the senses and fit in with the picture the author is trying to draw. The commonplace observation made about vivid descriptions is that they are constructed around a dominant impression—some central theme that the images and details fill out. But to say this is to raise a chicken-and-egg question: which comes first, the dominant impression or the sustaining imagery? Does the author know in advance how he wishes to describe a scene, or does it gradually dawn on him as he labors with the imagery?

The likely answer is both. Some authors no doubt start off with a solid, dominant impression; others grope for images and find them settling around a dominant impression. However it happens, you should write your descriptions around a dominant impression. You must include some appealing images and leave out some appealing images. The description made up of a single, focused impression sustained by a few brilliant images will almost always be better than the one made up of many brilliant images but sustained by no dominant impression. Verbal descriptions, like photographs, are better when they have a theme.

In this chapter we have included a range of descriptions, of people, sounds, places, animals, and events. The single-paragraph examples are a description of the stereotypical woman by Germaine Greer and a vivid rendering by Donald Peattie of the sounds made by frogs in the spring. In the short essays, Alan Devoe paints a vivid portrait of the shrew; and the Count Philippe-Paul de Segur, a lieutenant of Napoleon, portrays the horror of the Grand Army's disastrous retreat from Russia. There is a tale of going under anesthesia by Virginia Woolf; Hillare Belloc writes wittily of a creature.

Imagery—similes, metaphors, and the like—are the stock-in-trade of the descriptive writer. So is the adjective and, to a lesser extent, the adverb. But it is not so much a matter of simply piling on modifiers; as with everything else, quality will be found to count more than quantity. Beginning writers are too apt to paste adjectives and nouns together. Some adjectives may be placed after the nouns they modify; some nouns are better off without an accompanying adjective. Indeed, many of the writers in this chapter manage to be vividly descriptive while using very few adjectives. Consider, for example, the opening sentence of "Marrakech," which evokes the atmosphere of grinding poverty that is the dominant impression of the essay: "As the corpse went past the flies left the restaurant table in a cloud and rushed after it, but they came back a few minutes later." And not an adjective to be found in it.

Selective detail about a person or place, presented with a minimum of flowery language, often results in the most vivid kind of description. This is the kind of description that *shows,* rather than *tells.* The writer shows the picture through the use of detail; he does not try to tell it by force of metaphor and imagery alone. A few writers will try to overwhelm with metaphors and adjectives, but this kind of writing has a tendency to choke on its own richness. Certainly it is not the style of description recommended for the beginner. Better to do as Orwell does—use detail to show the picture; use images and metaphors sparingly to add color.

SINGLE PARAGRAPHS

WOMAN

Germaine Greer

Germaine Greer (1939-   ), a native of Australia, was educated at Cambridge University, England, where she specialized in literature. She is best known for her controversial book The Female Eunuch *(1970), in which she presented her views as a feminist. She is also the author of* The Obstacle Race *(1979), a study of women artists.*

Taken from The Female Eunuch, *this paragraph describes the stereotype of woman as a sex object.*

The sun shines only to burnish her skin and gild her hair; the wind blows only to whip up the color in her cheeks; the sea strives to bathe her; flowers die gladly so that her skin may luxuriate in their essence. She is the crown of creation, the masterpiece. The depths of the sea are ransacked for pearl and coral to deck her; the bowels of the earth are laid open that she might wear gold, sapphires, diamonds and rubies. Baby seals are battered with staves, unborn lambs ripped from their mothers' wombs, millions of moles, muskrats, squirrels, minks, ermines, foxes, beavers, chinchillas, ocelots, lynxes, and other small and lovely creatures die untimely deaths that she might have furs. Egrets, ostriches and peacocks, butterflies and beetles yield her their plumage. Men risk their lives hunting leopards for her coats, and crocodiles for her handbags and shoes. Millions of silkworms offer her their yellow labors; even the seamstresses roll seams and whip lace by hand, so that she might be clad in the best that money can buy.

VOCABULARY

burnish	luxuriate	staves
gild	ransacked	

QUESTIONS FOR CRITICAL THINKING

1. What is a sex object? What fundamental objection do feminists make to the concept of sex objects?
2. What, if any, responsibility should women bear for the things supposedly done in their behalf, such as the killing of animals for fur coats?
3. What, in your view, is the feminist ideal of womanhood?

QUESTIONS ON THE WRITING PROCESS

1. How would you characterize the tone of this piece? What can be inferred from the language about Greer's attitude toward the image of woman she is portraying?
2. Is Greer's description of the stereotype of woman realistic and accurate? In order to portray this stereotype, what obvious device of language does Greer use throughout the paragraph?
3. Description is mainly built around a dominant impression. What dominant impression would you say characterizes this description?

WRITING ASSIGNMENTS

1. Write a paragraph describing "the male" in the same way that the woman is described in Greer's paragraph.
2. Write a description of woman as you imagine feminists would like her to be perceived.

THE QUAVERING OF FROGS

Donald C. Peattie

Donald Culross Peattie (1898–1964) was an American botanist and author. An early popularizer of scientific subjects, Peattie was a roving reporter and writer for Reader's Digest. *Among his many books is* The Road of a Naturalist *(1941).*

Through an accumulation of vivid details, the author creates a disturbing dominant impression of a cold spring day.

On this chill uncertain spring day, toward twilight, I have heard the first frog quaver from the marsh. That is a sound that Pharaoh listened to as it rose from the Nile, and it blended, I suppose, with his discontents and longings, as it does with ours. There is something lonely in that first shaken and uplifted trilling croak. And more than lonely, for I hear a warning in it, as Pharaoh heard the sound of plague. It speaks of the return of life, animal life, to the earth. It tells of all that is most unutterable in evolution—the terrible continuity and fluidity of protoplasm, the irrepressible forces of reproduction—not mythical human love, but the cold batrachian jelly by which we vertebrates are linked to the things that creep and writhe and are blind yet breed and have being. More than that it seems to threaten that when mankind has quite thoroughly shattered and eaten and debauched himself with his own follies, that voice may still be ringing out in the marshes of the Nile and the Thames and the Potomac, unconscious that Pharaoh wept for his son.

VOCABULARY

quaver	fluidity	mythical
trilling	protoplasm	batrachian
unutterable	irrepressible	debauched
continuity		

QUESTIONS FOR CRITICAL THINKING

1. What is your view of the possibility of the eventual extinction of the human race?
2. What implications does a belief in evolution have for religion?
3. What do you find more powerful, love or evolution? Give reasons for your answer.

QUESTIONS ON THE WRITING PROCESS

1. The author makes three references to a certain Pharaoh. Aside from their obvious allusion to the distant past, what do these references contribute to the paragraph?
2. What is the dominant impression around which this paragraph is constructed?
3. The author writes that after man is gone from the earth the voice of the frog may "still be ringing out in the marshes of the Nile and the Thames and the Potomac." What point is he making by mentioning these three widely separate rivers?

WRITING ASSIGNMENTS

1. In one paragraph, describe the view from your window.
2. Write a description of any sound that you find especially delightful or especially hateful.

GAS[1]

Virginia Woolf

Virginia Woolf (1882-1941) was an English writer who courageously departed from traditional modes of fiction. She was in the vanguard of those novelists who try to lead readers inside the consciousness of their characters and to convey the way time is experienced. She was also a superb literary critic. Subject to episodes of mental illness, she died a suicide.

In an unusual approach, the author takes the mundane experience of receiving an anesthetic and turns it into philosophical musings.

1   It is not necessary, perhaps, to dwell upon the circumstances. There can be few people who have not at one time or another had a tooth out under gas. The dentist stands very clean and impersonal in his long white overcoat. He tells one not to cross one's legs and arranges a bit under one's chin. Then the anaesthetist comes in with his bag as clean and impersonal as the dentist and only as black as the other is white. Both seem to wear uniforms and to belong to some separate order of humanity, some third sex. The ordinary conventions lapse, for in ordinary life one does not after shaking hands with an unknown man at once open one's mouth and show him a broken tooth. The new relation with the third sex is stony, statuesque, colourless, but nevertheless humane. These are the people who manage the embarkations and disembarkations of the human spirit; these are they who stand on the border line between life and death forwarding the spirit from one to the other with clean impersonal antiseptic hands. Very well, I resign myself to your charge, one says, uncrossing one's legs; and at your command I cease to breathe through the mouth and breathe through the nose; breathe deep, breathe quietly, and your assurance that one is doing it very nicely is a parting salute, a farewell from the officer who presides over the ritual of disembarkation. Soon one is beyond his care.

2   With each breath one draws in confusion; one draws in darkness, falling, scattering, like a cloud of falling soot flakes. And also one puts out to sea; with every breath one leaves the shore, one cleaves the hot waves of some new sulphurous dark existence in which one flounders without support, attended only by strange relics of old memories, elongated, stretched out, so that they seem to parody the world from which one brought them, with which one tries to keep still in touch by their means; as the curved glass at a fair makes the body seem tapering and then bloated. And as we plunge deeper and deeper away from shore, we seem to be drawn on in the wake of

---

[1]This essay was written in 1929.

some fast flying always disappearing black object, drawn rapidly ahead of us. We become aware of something that we could never see in the other world: something that we have been sent in search of. All the old certainties become smudged and dispersed, because in comparison with this they are unimportant, like old garments crumpled up and dropped in a heap, because one needs to be naked, for this chase, this pursuit: all our most cherished beliefs and certainties and loves become like that. Scudding under a low dark sky we fly on the trail of this truth by which, if we could grasp it, we should be for ever illuminated. And we rush faster and faster and the whole world becomes spiral and like wheels and circles about us, pressing closer and closer until it seems by its pressure to force us through a central hole, very narrow through which it hurts us, squeezing us with its pressure on the head, to pass. Indeed we seem to be crushed between the upper world and the lower world and then suddenly the pressure is lessened; the whole aperture widens up; we pass through a gorge, emerge into daylight, and behold a glass dish and hear a voice saying, "Rinse the mouth. Rinse the mouth," while a trickle of warm blood runs from between the lips. So we are received back by the officials. The truth that was being drawn so fast ahead of us vanishes.

3   Such is a very common experience. Everybody goes through it. But it seems to explain something that one observes very often in a third-class railway carriage for example. For it is impossible not to ask some questions as one looks down the long narrow compartment where so many different people sit facing each other. If they begin originally like that, one muses, looking at a child of three, what is the process that turns them into that? And here one looks at a heavy old man with a despatch box; or at an overdressed red-faced woman. What has made that extraordinary change? What sights, what experiences? For except in some very rare cases it seems as if the passing of sixty or seventy years had inflicted a most terrible punishment on the smooth pink face, had imparted some very strange piece of information, so that, however the features differ, the eyes of old people always have the same expression.

4   And what is that piece of information? one asks. Is it probably that all these people have been several times under gas? Gradually they have been made to think that what passes before them has very little substance. They know that they can be rid of it for a small sum. They can then see another thing, more important, perhaps drawn through the water. But what hardly any of them knows is whether he or she wishes to be rid of it. There they sit, the plumber with his leaden coil, the man with his despatch box, the middle-class woman with her parcel from Selfridges, revolving often unconsciously the question whether there is any meaning in this world compared with the other, and what the truth is that dashed ahead through the water. They woke before they had seized it. And the other world vanished. And

perhaps to forget it, to cover it over, they went to the public house, they went to Oxford Street and bought a hat. As one looks down the third-class carriage, one sees that all the men and women over twenty have often been under gas; it is this that has done more than anything to change the expression of the face. An unchanged face would look almost idiotic. But, of course, there are a few faces which look as if they had caught the thing that dashes through the water.

VOCABULARY

anaesthetist (1)	antiseptic (1)	aperture (2)
statuesque (1)	Scudding (2)	despatch (3)

QUESTIONS FOR CRITICAL THINKING

1. The first half of this essay is a vivid, straightforward description of what happens to a patient when he undergoes an anesthetic in order to have a tooth extracted. After finishing the essay, what other description can the reader ponder? At what point in the essay does the thought shift?
2. What does the author mean when she says that the dentist and anesthetist both seem to belong to "some third sex"? Do you agree or disagree with her assessment? Give reasons for your answer.
3. If you have ever been anesthetized, do you agree with the author's description of the experience? How would *you* describe the feeling of falling asleep under the influence of an anesthetic? Be as concrete as Woolf.
4. In the final paragraph, when Woolf says that "all the men and women over twenty have often been under gas," is she being literal? Support your answer with reasons.

QUESTIONS ON THE WRITING PROCESS

1. Much of the author's description is based on an extended figure of speech. (See paragraph 2) What kind of figure of speech is it? Why is it appropriate to the major point of the essay?
2. Paragraph 4 begins with a question. Is the question ever answered? If so, what is the answer?
3. How do you explain the allusion in the final sentence of the essay?
4. Which part of paragraph 1 could be placed in quotation marks but is not? Why did the author choose not to use direct quotation?

WRITING ASSIGNMENTS

1. Write a one-paragraph description of any experience that slowly caused you to lose touch with reality. Use paragraph 2 of Woolf's essay as a model.
2. Write a 300-word description of a man or woman past the age of seventy. Begin with a dominant impression, such as, "A deep world weariness seems to envelop this old man."

SHREW—THE LITTLEST MAMMAL

Alan Devoe

Alan Devoe (1909–1955) was a naturalist and a prolific writer of essays and books concerning various aspects of nature. Between 1937 and 1953, he wrote a monthly column entitled "Down to Earth" for the American Mercury. *Other magazines with which he was associated are* Audubon Magazine *and* Reader's Digest. *Among his books are* Phudd Hill *(1937),* Down to Earth *(1940),* Lives Around Us *(1942),* Speaking of Animals *(1947), and* This Fascinating Animal World *(1951).*

The essay below, excerpted from Lives Around Us, *offers a touching description of a tiny little mammal that has much in common with humans.*

1   The zoological Class to which we human beings belong is the Mammalia. There has been some dispute as to whether we possess immortal souls and the capacity for a unique kind of intellection, but we do possess unquestionably the ". . . four-chambered heart, double circulatory system, thoracic cavity separated from abdominal cavity by muscular diaphragm, and habit of bearing the young alive and nursing them at the breast" which classically establish our membership in that group of warm-blooded animals which are guessed to have come into being on the planet some hundred-odd million years ago.

2   It is today a large and various group, this mammalian kindred. With some of our fellow-mammals it is not hard to feel relationship: with apes, for instance, or with the small sad-eyed monkeys that we keep for our beguilement as flea-bitten captives in our pet-shops. But with others of the group our tie is less apparent; and the reason, often enough, is disparity of size and shape. It is such disparity, no doubt, that prevents our having much fellow-feeling for the hundred-ton sulphur-bottomed whales that plunge through the deep waters of both Pacific and Atlantic, though whales' blood is warmed as ours is, and the females of their kind have milky teats; and likewise it is doubtless in part because we have two legs and attain to some seventy inches of height that we do not take as much account as otherwise we might of the little animal that is at the opposite end of the mammal size-scale: the little four-footed mammal that is rather smaller than a milkweed pod and not as heavy as a cecropia cocoon.

3   This tiniest of mammals is the minute beast called a shrew. A man need go to no great trouble to look at it, as he must to see a whale; he can find it now in the nearest country woodlot. Despite its tininess a shrew is still after a fashion a relative of ours; and on that account, even if on no other, should merit a little knowing.

61

4   In the narrow twisting earth-burrow dug by a mouse or a mole the least of the mammals is usually born. Its fellows in the litter may number four or five, and they lie together in the warm subterranean darkness of their tiny nest-chamber in a little group whose whole bulk is scarcely that of a walnut. The infant shrew, relative of whales and elephants and us, is no more than a squirming pink speck of warm-fleshed animal aliveness. Totally defenseless and unequipped for life, it can only nuzzle the tiny dugs of its mother, wriggle tightly against its brothers to feel the warmth of the litter, and for many hours of the twenty-four lie asleep in the curled head-to-toes position of a minuscule foetus.

5   The baby shrew remains a long time in the birth-chamber. The size of even an adult shrew is very nearly the smallest possible for mammalian existence, and the young one cannot venture out into the world of adult activity until it has almost completely matured. Until then, therefore, it stays in the warm darkness of the burrow, knowing the universe only as a heat of other little bodies, a pungence of roots and grasses, a periodic sound of tiny chittering squeakings when its mother enters the burrow after foraging-trips, bringing food. She brings in mostly insects—small lady-beetles whose brittle spotted wing-covers must be removed before they can be eaten, soft-bodied caterpillars, ants, and worms. The young shrew, after its weaning has come about, acquires the way of taking this new food between its slim delicate forepaws, fingered like little hands, and in the under-earth darkness nibbles away the wing-covers and chitinous body-shells as adroitly as a squirrel removes the husk from a nut.

6   When at last the time comes for the young shrew to leave its birthplace, it has grown very nearly as large as its mother and has developed all the adult shrew-endowments. It looks, now, not unlike a mouse, save that its muzzle is more sharply pointed, but a mouse reduced in size to extreme miniature. The whole length of its soft-furred little body is only a fraction more than two inches, compared to the four-inch length of even the smallest of the white-footed woods-mice; its tail is less than half as long as a mouse's. The uniquely little body is covered with dense soft hair, sepia above and a paler buffy color underneath—a covering of fur so fine and close that the shrew's ears are nearly invisible in it, and the infinitesimal eyes are scarcely to be discerned. The shrew's hands and feet are white, smaller and more delicate than any other beast's; white also is the underside of the minute furry tail. The whole body, by its softness of coat and coloring and its tininess of bulk, seems far from kinship with the tough strong bodies of the greater mammals. But it is blood-brother to these, all the same; warm blood courses in it; the shrew is as much mammal as a wolf. It sets forth, with its unparalleledly tiny physical equipments, to live as adventurous a life as any of its greater warm-blooded relatives.

7   The life-adventure of Man, "the medium-sized mammal," is shaped by

such diverse motives and impulsions that it is difficult to say what may be the most powerful of the driving urges that direct it. In the life-adventure of the littlest mammal, the shrew, the driving urge is very plain and single: it is hunger. Like hummingbirds, smallest of the *Aves,* this smallest of the mammals lives at a tremendous pitch of nervous intensity. The shrew's little body quite literally quivers with the vibrance of life-force that is in it; from tiny pointed snout to tailtip the shrew is ever in a taut furor of aliveness. Its body-surface, like a hummingbird's, is maximally extensive in relation to its minimal weight; its metabolism must proceed with immense rapidity; to sustain the quivering nervous aliveness of its mite of warm flesh it must contrive a food-intake that is almost constant. It is possible on that account to tell the shrew's life-story almost wholly in terms of its feeding. The shrew's life has other ingredients, of course—the seeking of its small mate, the various rituals of copulating and sleeping and dung-dropping and the rest, that are common to all mammal-lives—but it is the process of feeding that is central and primary, and that is the distinguishing preoccupation of the littlest mammal all its days.

8   The shrew haunts mostly moist thick-growing places, the banks of streams and the undergrowth of damp woods, and it hunts particularly actively at night. Scuttling on its pattery little feet among the fallen leaves, scrabbling in the leaf-mould in a frenzy of tiny investigation, it looks ceaselessly for food. Not a rodent, like a mouse, but an insectivore, it seizes chiefly on such creatures as crickets, grasshoppers, moths, and ants, devouring each victim with nervous eagerness and at once rushing on with quivering haste, tiny muzzle incessantly a-twitch, to look for further provender.

9   Not infrequently the insects discoverable in the shrew's quick scampering little sallies through the darkness are inadequate to nourish it, so quick is its digestion and so intense the nervous energy it must sustain. When this is the case, the shrew widens its diet-range, to include seeds or berries or earthworms or any other sustenance that it can stuff with its little shivering forepaws into its tiny muzzle. It widens its diet to include meat; it becomes a furious and desperate carnivore. It patters through the grass-runways of the meadow-mice, sniffing and quivering; it darts to the nest of a deer-mouse. And presently, finding deer-mouse or meadow-mouse, it plunges into a wild attack on this "prey" that is twice its size. The shrew fights with a kind of mad recklessness; it becomes a leaping, twisting, chittering, squeaking speck of hungering fury. Quite generally, when the battle is over, the shrew has won. Its thirty-two pinpoint teeth are sharp and strong, and the wild fury of its attack takes the victim by surprise. For a little while, after victory, the shrew's relentless body-needs are appeased. For a little while, but only a little; and then the furry speck must go pattering and scuttling forth into the night again, sniffing for food and quivering with need.

10   That is the pattern of shrew-life: a hunting and a hungering that never stops, an endless preoccupied catering to the demands of the kind of metabolism which unique mammalian smallness necessitates. The littlest mammal is a mammal in all ways; it breathes and sleeps and mates and possibly exults, as others do; but chiefly, as the price of unique tininess, it engages in restless never-ending search for something to eat.

11   The way of a shrew's dying is sometimes curious. Sometimes, of course, it dies in battle, when the larger prey which it has tackled proves too strong. Sometimes it dies of starvation; it can starve in a matter of hours. But often it is set upon by one of the big predators—some fox or lynx or man. When that happens, it is usually not the clutch of fingers or the snap of the carnivorous jaws that kills the shrew. The shrew is usually dead before that. At the first instant of a lynx's pounce—at the first touch of a human hand against the shrew's tiny quivering body—the shrew is apt to shiver in a quick violent spasm, and then lie still in death. The littlest of the mammals dies, as often as not, of simple nervous shock.

VOCABULARY

zoological (1)	earth-burrow (4)	infinitesimal (6)
Mammalia (1)	subterranean (4)	*Aves* (7)
intellection (1)	dugs (4)	vibrance (7)
thoracic (1)	minuscule (4)	taut (7)
abdominal (1)	pungence (5)	copulating (7)
beguilement (2)	foraging (5)	insectivore (8)
disparity (2)	chitinous (5)	provender (8)
teats (2)	adroitly (5)	sallies (9)
cecropia (2)	endowments (6)	carnivore (9)
woodlot (3)	sepia (6)	chittering (9)

QUESTIONS FOR CRITICAL THINKING

1. The author says that because the shrew is a member of the same class of animals to which we belong, it merits knowing about. What, if any, is the value of knowing about animals that belong to the same zoological class as humans?

2. The author writes that it is difficult to know which of the many motives and impulses are strongest in humans. Which motives and impulses do you think are strongest in humans?

3. What do you think is the responsibility of humans toward animals?

4. Which animal do you think humans have the kindest feelings toward? Why?

QUESTIONS ON THE WRITING PROCESS

1. The first paragraph contains a passage enclosed within quotation marks. Why? What is the significance of this quotation?
2. What dominating feature characterizes the author's description of the shrew? What synonyms can be found in the essay that also express this feature?
3. In his description of the shrew, what other rhetorical development does the author frequently use throughout the essay? Why?
4. In paragraph 9, why is the word *prey* put in quotation marks?
5. Paragraph 11 contains no new information about either the shrew or its feeding habits. What, then, is its purpose?

WRITING ASSIGNMENTS

1. Write an essay describing your favorite pet.
2. Write an essay about the kind of animal you dislike the most, saying why you dislike it.

NAPOLEON'S RETREAT FROM RUSSIA: THE FIRST SNOWSTORM

Count Philippe-Paul de Segur

Count Philippe-Paul de Segur (1780–1873) was a general and aide-de-camp attached to the personal staff of Napoleon Bonaparte during the Russian campaign. After the fall of Napoleon, de Segur retired to write the history of the Napoleonic invasion of Russia and through this work achieved considerable stature as a historian.

What follows is a dramatic firsthand report of one of history's most famous retreats from battle.

1 On the sixth of November the sky became terrible; its blue disappeared. The army marched along wrapped in a cold mist. Then the mist thickened, and presently from this immense cloud great snowflakes began to sift down on us. It seemed as if the sky had come down and joined with the earth and our enemies to complete our ruin. Everything in sight became vague, unrecognizable. Objects changed their shape; we walked without knowing where we were or what lay ahead, and anything became an obstacle. While the men were struggling to make headway against the icy, cutting blast, the snow driven by the wind was piling up and filling the hollows along the way. Their smooth surfaces hid unsuspected depths which opened up treacherously under our feet. The men were swallowed up, and the weak, unable to struggle out, were buried forever.

2 The soldiers following them turned around, but the tempest whipped their faces with the snow falling from above or swept up from the earth, and seemed fiercely determined to oppose their progress. Russian winter in this new guise attacked them on all sides; it cut through their thin uniforms and worn shoes, their wet clothing froze on them, and this icy shroud molded their bodies and stiffened their limbs. The sharp wind made them gasp for breath, and froze the moisture from their mouths and nostrils into icicles on their beards.

3 Yet the poor wretches dragged themselves along, shivering, with chattering teeth, until the snow packed under the soles of their boots, a bit of debris, a branch, or the body of a fallen comrade tripped them and threw them down. Then their moans for help went unheeded. The snow soon covered them up and only low white mounds showed where they lay. Our road was strewn with these hummocks, like a cemetery. Even the bravest or the most indifferent were deeply moved, and looked away as they hurried by.

4 But in front of them, all around them, everything was snow. The eyes of the men were lost in the immense, dreary uniformity. To their stricken

imagination it was like a great white shroud that Nature was winding about the army. The only objects that stood out were the tall somber firs, grave-yard trees, as we called them, with the funereal verdure, and the gigantic immobility of their black trunks, which completed a picture of universal mourning, a dying army in the midst of a dead nature.

5   Everything turned against the men, even their muskets which they had not used offensively since Malo-Yaroslavetz.[1] Now these became an un-bearable load for their benumbed arms. When they fell down, as they frequently did, their weapons slipped from their grasp and were either broken or lost in the snow. Though never thrown away, they were torn from them by hunger and cold. Many other men had their fingers frozen to the muskets they were holding and which were depriving them of the movement necessary to maintain in their hands a remnant of heat and life.

6   In a short time great numbers of men could be seen wandering over the countryside, either alone or in small groups. These were not cowardly de-serters: cold and starvation had detached them from their columns. In this general and individual struggle, they had got separated from the others, and now they found themselves disarmed, defeated, defenseless, without lead-ers, obeying only the powerful instinct of self-preservation.

7   Most of these stragglers, tempted by the sight of side roads, scattered over the fields in the hope of finding food and shelter from the coming night. But when they had passed that way before, they had left a swath of desolation from fifteen to twenty miles wide. Now they met only armed civilians or Cossacks who fell upon them with ferocious laughter, wounded them, stripped them of everything they had, and left them to perish naked in the snow. These guerrillas, incited by Alexander and Kutuzov,[2] who did not then know how to avenge nobly the country they had been unable to defend, kept abreast of the army on both sides of the road, under cover of the trees. They threw back on the deadly highway the soldiers whom they did not finish off with their spears and axes.

8   Night came on—a night sixteen hours long! But on this waste of snow where were we to stop, where sit down or rest, where find some root to gnaw on, or dry wood for our fires? However, those who had been held together by their own moral and physical strength, and the brave efforts of their officers, were finally halted by fatigue, darkness, and repeated orders. They tried to pitch their camps, but the roaring storm played havoc with their preparations for a bivouac. The firs, coated with ice, stubbornly re-fused to burn. The snow falling in increased fury, and the snow on the ground, melting at the first warmth, put out our fires and dampened our strength and courage.

[1]Site of a bloody clash between the French and Russian armies.

[2]Alexander I (1777–1825), Czar of Russia. Mikhail Ilarionovich Kutuzov (1745–1813), Russian field marshal.

9   When at length we did get some fires burning, officers and soldiers together prepared their wretched meal around them. This consisted of scraps of tough lean meat cut off the horses we had slaughtered, and, for a very few, several spoonfuls of rye flour mixed with snow water. The next morning circular rows of soldiers stretched out stiff in death marked the spots where these fires had burned; and the fields around were strewn with thousands of dead horses.

VOCABULARY

shroud (2)	immobility (4)	Cossacks (7)
unheeded (3)	muskets (5)	ferocious (7)
hummocks (3)	remnant (5)	guerrillas (7)
funereal (4)	swath (7)	havoc (8)
verdure (4)	desolation (7)	bivouac (8)

QUESTIONS FOR CRITICAL THINKING

1. Which part of the description affected you the most? Why?
2. What is the author's attitude toward the suffering soldiers everywhere around him? How can this attitude be detected in this essay?
3. The description is an eyewitness account of a real war. How does this account match up with fictional accounts of battle and war?

QUESTIONS ON THE WRITING PROCESS

1. From whose point of view are most of the descriptions in this essay written? What is the effect of this point of view?
2. What specific detail does the author use in paragraphs 2 and 3 to describe the suffering of the army?
3. Around which of the five senses is the description of paragraph 4 constructed? What is the effect of focusing a description around the impression of a single sense?
4. What single effect of the winter storm does paragraph 5 concentrate on describing?
5. In the final sentence of the sixth paragraph, the author writes: "In this general and individual struggle they [the stragglers] had got separated from the others, and now they found themselves disarmed, defeated, defenseless, without leaders, obeying only the powerful instinct of self-preservation." What technique in the diction of this sentence underscores the hopeless plight of the stragglers?
6. What symbolic meaning can be attached to the fires mentioned in paragraphs 8 and 9?

WRITING ASSIGNMENTS

1. Write a 300-word essay that describes one of the following:
    a. A downpour of rain
    b. A smoggy day in your city
    c. A severe thunderstorm
2. Write an essay describing either a hot summer day or a cold winter day.

ON THEM

Hilaire Belloc

Hilaire Belloc (1870–1953) was a native of France, but became a natural-
ized Englishman. A graduate of Oxford University, he worked as a jour-
nalist and as a member of Parliament. Almost everything he wrote dis-
played his ardent devotion to Roman Catholicism. He is remembered as
a master of English prose, a good writer of light verse, and a great literary
personality. Among his works are The Bad Child's Book of Beasts
(1896), The Path to Rome *(1902),* Marie Antoinette *(1910), and* Napoleon *(1922).*

Will all "Them" lovers please rise to the defense of the creature being
maligned.

1   I do not like Them. It is no good asking me why, though I have plenty of
reasons. I do not like Them. There would be no particular point in saying I
do not like Them if it were not that so many people doted on Them, and
when one hears Them praised, it goads one to expressing one's hatred and
fear of Them.

2   I know very well that They can do one harm, and that They have occult
powers. All the world has known that for a hundred thousand years, more
or less, and every attempt has been made to propitiate Them. James I.
would drown Their mistress or burn her, but *They* were spared. Men
would mummify them in Egypt, and worship the mummies; men would
carve Them in stone in Cyprus, and Crete and Asia Minor, or (more remarkable still) artists, especially in the Western Empire, would leave
Them out altogether; so much was Their influence dreaded. Well, I yield
so far as not to print Their name, and only to call Them "They", but I hate
Them, and I'm not afraid to say so.

3   If you will take a little list of the chief crimes that living beings can
commit you will find that They commit them all. And They are cruel;
cruelty is even in Their tread and expression. They are hatefully cruel. I
saw one of Them catch a mouse the other day (the cat is now out of the
bag), and it was a very much more sickening sight, I fancy, than ordinary
murder. You may imagine that They catch mice to eat them. It is not so.
They catch mice to torture them. And, what is worse, They will teach this
to Their children—Their children who are naturally innocent and fat, and
full of goodness, are deliberately and systematically corrupted by Them;
there is diabolism in it.

4   Other beings (I include mankind) will be gluttonous, but gluttonous
spasmodically, or with a method, or shamefacedly, or, in some way or another that qualifies the vice; not so They. They are gluttonous always and
upon all occasions, and in every place and for ever. It was only last Vigil of

All Fools' Day when, myself fasting, I filled up the saucer seven times with milk and seven times it was emptied, and there went up the most peevish, querulous, vicious complaint and demand for an eighth. They will eat some part of the food of all that are in the house. Now even a child, the most gluttonous one would think of all living creatures, would not do that. It makes a selection, *They* do not. *They* will drink beer. This is not a theory; I know it; I have seen it with my own eyes. They will eat special foods; They will even eat dry bread. Here again I have personal evidence of the fact; They will eat the dog's biscuits, but never upon any occasion will They eat anything that has been poisoned, so utterly lacking are They in simplicity and humility, and so abominably well filled with cunning by whatever demon first brought Their race into existence.

5   They also, alone of all creation, love hateful noises. Some beings indeed (and I count Man among them) cannot help the voice with which they have been endowed, but they know that it is offensive, and are at pains to make it better; others (such as the peacock or the elephant) also know that their cry is unpleasant. They therefore use it sparingly. Others again, the dove, the nightingale, the thrush, know that their voices are very pleasant, and entertain us with them all day and all night long; but They know that Their voices are the most hideous of all the sounds in the world, and, knowing this, They perpetually insist upon thrusting those voices upon us, saying, as it were, "I am giving myself pain, but I am giving you more pain, and therefore I shall go on." And They choose for the place where this pain shall be given, exact and elevated situations, very close to our ears. Is there any need for me to point out that in every city They will begin Their wicked jar just at the time when its inhabitants must sleep? In London you will not hear it till after midnight; in the county towns it begins at ten; in remote villages as early as nine.

6   Their Master also protects Them. They have a charmed life. I have seen one thrown from a great height into a London street, which when It reached it It walked quietly away with the dignity of the Lost World to which It belonged.

7   If one had the time one could watch Them day after day, and never see Them do a single kind or good thing, or be moved by a single virtuous impulse. They have no gesture for the expression of admiration, love, reverence, or ecstasy. They have but one method of expressing content, and They reserve that for moments of physical repletion. The tail, which is in all other animals the signal for joy or for defence, or for mere usefulness, or for a noble anger, is with Them agitated only to express a sullen discontent.

8   All that They do is venomous, and all that They think is evil, and when I take mine away (as I mean to do next week—in a basket), I shall first read in a book of statistics what is the wickedest part of London, and I shall leave It there, for I know of no one even among my neighbours quite so vile as to deserve such a gift.

VOCABULARY

propitiate (2)   querulous (4)   venomous (8)
diabolism (3)   jar (5)

QUESTIONS FOR CRITICAL THINKING

1. What is the tone of this essay? What purpose does the tone serve? How is the title related to the tone?
2. At which point in the essay does all doubt vanish as to what creature the author is describing? At which point in the essay did you recognize the subject?
3. What effect does the author's view of "Them" have on the reader's view of human beings? Do you agree with Belloc's description? Why or why not?
4. Do you think the author really means to do what he threatens in the final paragraph? Give reasons for your answer.

QUESTIONS ON THE WRITING PROCESS

1. What important characteristic of good writing does this essay reveal? How can a student achieve this characteristic in his or her writing?
2. The author delights in attributing to "Them" all the major sins committed by the vilest of human beings. What effect does his portrait have?
3. How is Belloc's essay organized? Is the plan suited to the purpose of the essay?

WRITING ASSIGNMENTS

1. Write a 500-word retort to Belloc's essay in which you defend the honor of cats. If you are so inclined, be humorous.
2. In 500 words describe an animal you find either admirable or loathsome. Be sure to use vivid details as does Belloc.

MARRAKECH

George Orwell

George Orwell (pseudonym of Eric Blair, 1903–1950) was a British author born in India. His books, Animal Farm: A Fairy Story *(1945) and* Nineteen Eighty-Four *(1949), describing fictional totalitarian states are still widely read. A political activist in his youth, Orwell became disillusioned with all politics following service on the losing Republican side in the Spanish Civil War.*

In the essay that follows, Orwell describes the utter squalor and poverty in which a large part of the Moroccan population lives.

1   As the corpse went past the flies left the restaurant table in a cloud and rushed after it, but they came back a few minutes later.

2   The little crowd of mourners—all men and boys, no women—threaded their way across the market-place between the piles of pomegranates and the taxies and the camels, wailing a short chant over and over again. What really appeals to the flies is that the corpses here are never put into coffins, they are merely wrapped in a piece of rag and carried on a rough wooden bier on the shoulders of four friends. When the friends get to the burying-ground they hack an oblong hole a foot or two deep, dump the body in it and fling over it a little of the dried-up, lumpy earth, which is like broken brick. No gravestone, no name, no identifying mark of any kind. The burying-ground is merely a huge waste of hummocky earth, like a derelict building-lot. After a month or two no one can even be certain where his own relatives are buried.

3   When you walk through a town like this—two hundred thousand inhabitants, of whom at least twenty thousand own literally nothing except the rags they stand up in—when you see how the people live, and still more how easily they die, it is always difficult to believe that you are walking among human beings. All colonial empires are in reality founded upon that fact. The people have brown faces—besides, there are so many of them! Are they really the same flesh as yourself? Do they even have names? Or are they merely a kind of undifferentiated brown stuff, about as individual as bees or coral insects? They rise out of the earth, they sweat and starve for a few years, and then they sink back into the nameless mounds of the graveyard and nobody notices that they are gone. And even the graves themselves soon fade back into the soil. Sometimes, out for a walk, as you break your way through the prickly pear, you notice that it is rather bumpy underfoot, and only a certain regularity in the bumps tells you that you are walking over skeletons.

4   I was feeding one of the gazelles in the public gardens.

5   Gazelles are almost the only animals that look good to eat when they are still alive, in fact, one can hardly look at their hindquarters without thinking of mint sauce. The gazelle I was feeding seemed to know that this thought was in my mind, for though it took the piece of bread I was holding out it obviously did not like me. It nibbled rapidly at the bread, then lowered its head and tried to butt me, then took another nibble and then butted again. Probably its idea was that if it could drive me away the bread would somehow remain hanging in mid-air.

6   An Arab navvy working on the path nearby lowered his heavy hoe and sidled slowly towards us. He looked from the gazelle to the bread and from the bread to the gazelle, with a sort of quiet amazement, as though he had never seen anything quite like this before. Finally he said shyly in French:

7   "I could eat some of that bread."

8   I tore off a piece and he stowed it gratefully in some secret place under his rags. This man is an employee of the Municipality.

9   When you go through the Jewish quarters you gather some idea of what the medieval ghettoes were probably like. Under their Moorish rulers the Jews were only allowed to own land in certain restricted areas, and after centuries of this kind of treatment they have ceased to bother about overcrowding. Many of the streets are a good deal less than six feet wide, the houses are completely windowless, and sore-eyed children cluster everywhere in unbelievable numbers, like clouds of flies. Down the center of the street there is generally running a little river of urine.

10 In the bazaar huge families of Jews, all dressed in the long black robe and little black skull-cap, are working in dark fly-infested booths that look like caves. A carpenter sits crosslegged at a prehistoric lathe, turning chair-legs at lightning speed. He works the lathe with a bow in his right hand and guides the chisel with his left foot, and thanks to a lifetime of sitting in this position his left leg is warped out of shape. At his side his grandson, aged six, is already starting on the simpler parts of the job.

11 I was just passing the coppersmith's booths when somebody noticed that I was lighting a cigarette. Instantly, from the dark holes all round, there was a frenzied rush of Jews, many of them old grandfathers with flowing grey beards, all clamoring for a cigarette. Even a blind man somewhere at the back of one of the booths heard a rumor of cigarettes and came crawling out, groping in the air with his hand. In about a minute I had used up the whole packet. None of these people, I suppose, works less than twelve hours a day, and every one of them looks on a cigarette as a more or less impossible luxury.

12 As the Jews live in self-contained communities they follow the same trades as the Arabs, except for agriculture. Fruit-sellers, potters, silversmiths, blacksmiths, butchers, leatherworkers, tailors, water-carriers, beggars, porters—whichever way you look you see nothing but Jews. As a matter of fact there are thirteen thousand of them, all living in the space of

a few acres. A good job Hitler wasn't here. Perhaps he was on his way, however. You hear the usual dark rumors about the Jews, not only from the Arabs but from the poorer Europeans.

13   "Yes, mon vieux, they took my job away from me and gave it to a Jew. The Jews! They're the real rulers of this country, you know. They've got all the money. They control the banks, finance—everything."

14   "But," I said, "isn't it a fact that the average Jew is a laborer working for about a penny an hour?"

15   "Ah, that's only for show! They're all moneylenders really. They're cunning, the Jews."

16   In just the same way, a couple of hundred years ago, poor old women used to be burned for witchcraft when they could not even work enough magic to get themselves a square meal.

17   All people who work with their hands are partly invisible, and the more important the work they do, the less visible they are. Still, a white skin is always fairly conspicuous. In northern Europe, when you see a laborer ploughing a field, you probably give him a second glance. In a hot country, anywhere south of Gibralter or east of the Suez, the chances are that you don't even see him. I have noticed this again and again. In a tropical landscape one's eye takes in everything except the human beings. It takes in the dried-up soil, the prickly pear, the palm tree and the distant mountain, but it always misses the peasant hoeing at his patch. He is the same color as the earth, and a great deal less interesting to look at.

18   It is only because of this that the starved countries of Asia and Africa are accepted as tourist resorts. No one would think of running cheap trips to the Distressed Areas. But where the human beings have brown skins their poverty is simply not noticed. What does Morocco mean to a Frenchman? An orange-grove or a job in Government service. Or to an Englishman? Camels, castles, palm trees, Foreign Legionnaires, brass trays, and bandits. One could probably live there for years without noticing that for nine-tenths of the people the reality of life is an endless, back-breaking struggle to wring a little food out of an eroded soil.

19   Most of Morocco is so desolate that no wild animal bigger than a hare can live on it. Huge areas which were once covered with forest have turned into a treeless waste where the soil is exactly like broken-up brick. Nevertheless a good deal of it is cultivated, with frightful labor. Everything is done by hand. Long lines of women, bent double like inverted capital L's, work their way slowly across the fields, tearing up the prickly weeds with their hands, and the peasant gathering lucerne for fodder pulls it up stalk by stalk instead of reaping it, thus saving an inch or two on each stalk. The plough is a wretched wooden thing, so frail that one can easily carry it on one's shoulder, and fitted underneath with a rough iron spike which stirs the soil to a depth of about four inches. This is as much as the strength of the animals is equal to. It is usual to plough with a cow and a donkey yoked

together. Two donkeys would not be quite strong enough, but on the other hand two cows would cost a little more to feed. The peasants possess no harrows, they merely plough the soil several times over in different directions, finally leaving it in rough furrows, after which the whole field has to be shaped with hoes into small oblong patches to conserve water. Except for a day or two after the rare rainstorms there is never enough water. Along the edges of the fields channels are hacked out to a depth of thirty or forty feet to get at the tiny trickles which run through the subsoil.

20   Every afternoon a file of very old women passes down the road outside my house, each carrying a load of firewood. All of them are mummified with age and the sun, and all of them are tiny. It seems to be generally the case in primitive communities that the women, when they get beyond a certain age, shrink to the size of children. One day a poor old creature who could not have been more than four feet tall crept past me under a vast load of wood. I stopped her and put a five-sou piece (a little more than a farthing) into her hand. She answered with a shrill wail, almost a scream, which was partly gratitude but mainly surprise. I suppose that from her point of view, by taking any notice of her, I seemed almost to be violating a law of nature. She accepted her status as an old woman, that is to say as a beast of burden. When a family is traveling it is quite usual to see a father and a grown-up son riding ahead on donkeys, and an old woman following on foot, carrying the baggage.

21   But what is strange about these people is their invisibility. For several weeks, always at about the same time of day, the file of old women had hobbled past the house with their firewood, and though they had registered themselves on my eyeballs I cannot truly say that I had seen them. Firewood was passing—that was how I saw it. It was only that one day I happened to be walking behind them, and the curious up-and-down motion of a load of wood drew my attention to the human being beneath it. Then for the first time I noticed the poor old earth-colored bodies, bodies reduced to bones and leathery skin, bent double under the crushing weight. Yet I suppose I had not been five minutes on Moroccan soil before I noticed the overloading of the donkeys and was infuriated by it. There is no question that the donkeys are damnably treated. The Moroccan donkey is hardly bigger than a St. Bernard dog, it carries a load which in the British Army would be considered too much for a fifteen-hands mule, and very often its pack-saddle is not taken off its back for weeks together. But what is peculiarly pitiful is that it is the most willing creature on earth, it follows its master like a dog and does not need either bridle or halter. After a dozen years of devoted work it suddenly drops dead, whereupon its master tips it into the ditch and the village dogs have torn its guts out before it is cold.

22   This kind of thing makes one's blood boil, whereas—on the whole—the plight of the human beings does not. I am not commenting, merely pointing

to a fact. People with brown skins are next door to invisible. Anyone can be sorry for the donkey with its galled back, but it is generally owing to some kind of accident if one even notices the old woman under her load of sticks.

23 As the storks flew northward the Negroes were marching southward—a long, dusty column, infantry, screwgun batteries, and then more infantry, four or five thousand men in all, winding up the road with a clumping of boots and a clatter of iron wheels.

24 They were Senegalese, the blackest Negroes in Africa, so black that sometimes it is difficult to see whereabouts on their necks their hair begins. Their splendid bodies were hidden in reach-me-down khaki uniforms, their feet squashed into boots that looked like blocks of wood, and every tin hat seemed to be a couple of sizes too small. It was very hot and the men had marched a long way. They slumped under the weight of their packs and the curiously sensitive black faces were glistening with sweat.

25 As they went past a tall, very young Negro turned and caught my eye. But the look he gave me was not in the least the kind of look you might expect. Not hostile, not contemptuous, not sullen, not even inquisitive. It was the shy, wide-eyed Negro look, which actually is a look of profound respect. I saw how it was. This wretched boy, who is a French citizen and has therefore been dragged from the forest to scrub floors and catch syphilis in garrison towns, actually has feelings of reverence before a white skin. He has been taught that the white race are his masters, and he still believes it.

26 But there is one thought which every white man (and in this connection it doesn't matter twopence if he calls himself a socialist) thinks when he sees a black army marching past. "How much longer can we go on kidding these people? How long before they turn their guns in the other direction?"

27 It was curious, really. Every white man there had this thought stowed somewhere or other in his mind. I had it, so had the other onlookers, so had the officers on their sweating chargers and the white N.C.O.'s marching in the ranks. It was a kind of secret which we all knew and were too clever to tell; only the Negroes didn't know it. And really it was like watching a flock of cattle to see the long column, a mile or two miles of armed men, flowing peacefully up the road, while the great white birds drifted over them in the opposite direction, glittering like scraps of paper.

VOCABULARY

bier (2)	sidled (6)	lucerne (19)
hummocky (2)	frenzied (11)	harrows (19)
derelict (2)	clamoring (11)	galled (22)
navvy (2)	Legionnaires (18)	khaki (24)
gazelles (4)		

QUESTIONS FOR CRITICAL THINKING

1. Given that over half the world's population lives in desperate poverty, what obligation does an affluent nation such as the United States have toward the poorer peoples of the world?

2. Orwell admits that at first he felt sorrier for the donkeys than for the people of Marrakech. How do you explain this? Why do people generally feel sorrier for animals than for their fellow human beings?

3. Why, in your view, are some nations so desperately poor and others so comfortably rich?

4. Some time ago, Haitian boat people crowded the waters off Miami in an effort to escape the grinding poverty of their own country. What should be the policy of the United States toward the citizens of poor countries who wish to come and live here?

5. Orwell implies at the end of his essay that sooner or later the poor will rise up against their masters. What are the chances of such an uprising taking place in the United States?

6. In paragraph 4, Orwell describes the feeding of a gazelle. What is the main point of that scene?

7. Why are the poor countries of Asia and Africa popular as tourist resorts?

8. Why did the old woman scream when the author gave her a coin?

9. What does the author admit infuriated him when he first arrived in Morocco? What is ironic about this admission?

QUESTIONS ON THE WRITING PROCESS

1. Why is the first sentence of this essay set apart as a paragraph? How does this opening fit in with the rest of the essay?

2. How does the author refer to the reader in this essay? What part in the description does this kind of reference play?

3. What is the function of paragraph 4, which consists of a mere eleven words? Why is this sentence written as a paragraph?

4. What verb tense is this essay written in? How does the author use verb tense to heighten his descriptions?

5. In paragraphs 13, 14, and 15, the author records some dialogue with an unnamed someone. What point is the dialogue intended to make? Why doesn't the author simply make the point rather than ask the reader to infer it from the dialogue?

6. The author first describes the squalor of the Jewish ghetto before reporting on the opinions held about Jews by the native and European population. What is the logic of this sequence?

7. In paragraph 20, what other method of development does the author use in describing the burdensome work done by the old women?
8. The entire essay is divisible into five major descriptive scenes. What are these five scenes? Where does each one begin and end?
9. Paragraph 23 describes the storks flying north and the black army marching south. What part does the image of the flying storks play in the end of the essay?

WRITING ASSIGNMENTS

1. Write a description of any city that made a deep impression on you.
2. Describe any aspect of poverty that you have either experienced or witnessed firsthand.

TEACHING A STONE TO TALK

Annie Dillard

Annie Dillard (1945–   ) was born in Pennsylvania and educated at Hollins College, Virginia. She is a teacher of poetry and creative writing at Western Washington State University. She won the Pulitzer Prize in 1974 for Pilgrim at Tinker Creek *(1974). Her latest book,* Living by Fiction *(1982), is, in some aspects, an introduction to the aims and methods of contemporary modernist fiction.*

The essay that follows speaks eloquently about silence and the spiritual power it can engender.

1 The island where I live is peopled with cranks like myself. In a cedar-shake shack on a cliff is a man in his thirties who lives alone with a stone he is trying to teach to talk.

2 Wisecracks on this topic abound, as you might expect, but they are made, as it were, perfunctorily, and mostly by the young. For in fact, almost everyone here respects what Larry is doing, as do I, which is why I am protecting his (or her) privacy, and confusing for you the details. It could be, for instance, a pinch of sand he is teaching to talk, or a prolonged northerly, or any one of a number of waves. But it is, I assure you, a stone. It is—for I have seen it—a palm-sized, oval beach cobble whose dark gray is cut by a band of white which runs around and, presumably, through it; such stones we call "wishing stones," for reasons obscure but not, I think, unimaginable.

3 He keeps it on a shelf. Usually the stone lies protected by a square of untanned leather, like a canary asleep under its cloth. Larry removes the cover for the stone's lessons, or, more accurately, I should say for the ritual or rituals they perform together several times a day.

4 No one knows what goes on at these sessions, least of all myself, for I know Larry but slightly, and that owing only to a mix-up in our mail. I assume that, like any other meaningful effort, the ritual involves sacrifice, the suppression of self-consciousness, and a certain precise tilt of the will, so that the will becomes transparent and hollow, a channel for the work. I wish him well. It is a noble work, and beats, from any angle, selling shoes.

5 Reports differ on precisely what he expects or wants the stone to say. I do not think he expects the stone to speak as we do, and describe for us its long life and many, or few, sensations. I think instead that he is trying to teach it to say a single word, such as "cup," or "uncle." For this purpose he has not, as some have seriously suggested, carved the stone a little mouth, or furnished it in any way with a pocket of air which it might then expel. Rather—and I think he is wise in this—he plans to initiate his son, who is

now an infant living with Larry's estranged wife, into the work, so that it may continue and bear fruit after his death.

6   Nature's silence is its one remark, and every flake of world is a chip off that old mute and immutable block. The Chinese say that we live in the world of the ten thousand things. Each of the ten thousand cries out to us precisely nothing.

7   God used to rage at the Israelites for frequenting sacred groves. I wish I could find one. Martin Buber[1] says, "The crisis of all primitive mankind comes with the discovery of that which is fundamentally not-holy, the a-sacramental, which withstands the methods, and which has no 'hour,' a province which steadily enlarges itself." Now we are no longer primitive; now the whole world seems not-holy. We have drained the light from the boughs in the sacred grove and snuffed it in the high places and along the banks of sacred streams. We as a people have moved from pantheism to panatheism.[2] Silence is not our heritage but our destiny; we live where we want to live.

8   The soul may ask God for anything, and never fail. You may ask God for his presence, or for wisdom, and receive each at his hands. Or you may ask God, in the words of the shopkeeper's little gag sign, that he not go away mad, but just go away. Once, in Israel, an extended family of nomads did that. They heard God's speech and found it too loud. The wilderness generation was at Sinai; it witnessed there the thick darkness where God was: "And all the people saw the thunderings, and the lightnings, and the noise of the trumpet, and the mountain smoking." It scared them witless. Then they asked Moses to beg God, please, never to speak to them directly again. "Let not God speak with us, lest we die." Moses took the message. And God, pitying their fear, agreed. And he added to Moses, "Go say to them, *Get into your tents again.*"

9   It is difficult to undo our own damage, and to recall to our presence that which we have asked to leave. It is hard to desecrate a grove and change your mind. The very holy mountains are keeping mum. We doused the burning bush and cannot rekindle it; we are lighting matches in vain under every green tree. Did the wind once cry, and the hills shout forth praise? Now speech has perished from among the lifeless things of earth, and living things say very little to very few. Birds may crank out sweet gibberish and monkeys howl; horses neigh and pigs say, as you recall, oink oink. But so do cobbles rumble when a wave recedes, and thunders break the air in lightning storms. I call these noises silence. It could be that wherever there is motion there is noise, as when a whale breeches and smacks the water—and wherever there is stillness there is the still small voice, God's speaking from the whirlwind, nature's old song and dance, the show we drove from town.

[1]20th century Austrian existentialist and Judaic scholar.

[2]The absence of God in everything.

At any rate, now it is all we can do, and among our best efforts, to try to teach a given human language, English, to chimpanzees.

10   In the forties an American psychologist and his wife tried to teach a chimp actually to speak. At the end of three years the creature could pronounce, in a hoarse whisper, the words "mama," "papa," and "cup." After another three years of training she could whisper, with difficulty, still only "mama," "papa," and "cup." The more recent successes at teaching chimpanzees American Sign Language are well known. Just the other day a chimp told us, if we can believe that we truly share a vocabulary, that she had been sad in the morning. I'm sorry we asked.

11   What have we been doing all these centuries but trying to call God back to the mountain, or, failing that, raise a peep out of anything that isn't us? What is the difference between a cathedral and a physics lab? Are they not both saying Hello? We spy on whales and on interstellar radio objects; we starve ourselves and pray till we're blue.

12   I have been reading comparative cosmology. At this time most cosmologists favor the picture of the evolving universe described by Lemaître[3] and Gamow.[4] But I prefer a suggestion made years ago by Paul Valéry.[5] He set forth the notion that the universe might be "head-shaped." To what is the head listening, what does it see, of what does it think? Or is the universe and all it contains a snippet of mind?

13   The mountains are great stone bells; they clang together like nuns. Who shushed the stars? A thousand million galaxies are easily seen in the Palomar reflector; collisions between and among them do, of course, occur. But these collisions are very long and silent slides. Billions of stars sift among each other untouched, too distant even to be moved, heedless as always, hushed. The sea pronounces something, over and over, in a hoarse whisper; I can't quite make it out. But God knows I've tried.

14   At a certain point you say to the woods, to the sea, to the mountains, the world, Now I am ready. Now I will stop and be wholly attentive. You empty yourself and wait, listening. After a time you hear it: there is nothing there. There is nothing but those things only, those created objects, discrete, growing or holding, or swaying, being rained on or raining, held, flooding or ebbing, standing, or spread. You feel the world's word as a tension, a hum, a single chorused note everywhere the same. This is it: this hum is the silence. Nature does utter a peep—just this one. The birds and insects, the meadows and swamps and rivers and stones and mountains and clouds: they all do it; they all don't do it. There is a vibrancy to the silence, a suppression, as if someone were gagging the world. But you wait, you give your life's length to listening, and nothing happens. The ice rolls up, the ice

[3]Belgian astrophysicist.

[4]Russian-born American nuclear physicist.

[5]French 19th century poet.

rolls back, and still the single note obtains. The tension, or lack of it, is intolerable. The silence is not actually suppression; instead, it is all there is.

15   We are here to witness. There is nothing else to do with those mute materials we do not need. Until Larry teaches his stone to talk, until God changes his mind, or until the pagan gods slip back to their hilltop groves, all we can do with the whole inhuman array is watch it. We can stage our own act on the planet—build our cities on its plains, dam its rivers, plant its topsoils—but our meaningful activity scarcely covers the terrain. We don't use the songbirds, for instance. We don't eat many of them; we can't befriend them; we can't persuade them to eat more mosquitoes or plant fewer weed seeds. We can only witness them—whoever they are. If we weren't here, they would be songbirds falling in the forest. If we weren't here, material events such as the passage of seasons would lack even the meager meanings we are able to muster for them. The show would play to an empty house, as do all those stars that fall in the daytime. That is why I take walks: to keep an eye on things. And that is why I went to the Galapagos Islands.

16   All of this becomes especially clear on the Galapagos Islands. The Galapagos Islands blew up out of the ocean, some plants blew in on them, some animals drifted aboard and evolved weird forms—and there they all are. The Galapagos are a kind of metaphysics laboratory, almost wholly uncluttered by human culture or history. Whatever happens on those bare volcanic rocks happens in full view, whether anyone is watching or not.

17   What happens there is this, and precious little it is: clouds come and go as well as the round of similar seasons; a pig eats a tortoise or doesn't eat a tortoise; Pacific waves fall up and slide back; a lichen expands; night follows day; an albatross dies and dries on a cliff; a cool current upwells from the ocean floor; fishes multiply, flies swarm, stars rise and fall, and diving birds dive. The news, in other words, breaks on the beaches. And taking it all in are the trees. The palo santo trees crowd the hillsides like any outdoor audience; they face the lagoons, the lava lowlands, and the shores.

18   I have some experience of these palo santo trees. They interest me as emblems of the muteness of the human stance in relation to all that is not human. I see us all as palo santo trees, holy sticks, together watching everything that we watch, and growing in silence.

19   In the Galapagos, I didn't notice the palo santo trees for a long time. Like everyone else, I specialized in sea lions. My shipmates and I liked the sea lions, and envied their lives. Their joy seemed conscious. They were engaged in full-time play. They were all either fat or dead. By day they played in the shallows, alone or together, greeting each other and us with great noises of joy, or they took a turn offshore and body-surfed in the breakers, exultant. By night on the sand they lay in each other's flippers and slept. My shipmates joked, often, that when they "came back," they would just as soon do it all over again as sea lions. I concurred. The sea lion game looked unbeatable.

20   But, a year and a half later, I returned to those unpeopled islands. In the interval my attachment to them had shifted, and my memories of them had altered, the way memories do, like particolored pebbles rolled back and forth over a grating, so that after a time those hard bright ones, the ones you thought you would never lose, have vanished, passed through the grating, and only a few big, unexpected ones remain, no longer unnoticed but now selected out for some meaning, large and unknown.

21   Such were the palo santo trees. Before, I had never given them a thought. They were just miles of half-dead trees on the red lava sea cliffs of some deserted islands. They were only a name in a notebook: "Palo santo—those strange white trees." Look at the sea lions! Look at the flightless cormorants, the penguins, the iguanas, the sunset! But after eighteen months the wonderful cormorants, penguins, iguanas, sunsets, and even the sea lions had dropped from my holey heart. I returned to the Galapagos to see the palo santo trees.

22   They are thin, pale, wispy trees. You walk among them on the lowland deserts, where they grow beside the prickly pear. You see them from the water on the steeps that face the sea, hundreds together small and thin and spread, and so much more pale than their red soils that any black-and-white print of them looks like a negative. Their stands look like blasted orchards. At every season they all seem newly dead, pale and bare as birches drowned in a beaver pond—for at every season they look leafless, paralyzed, and mute. But, in fact, you can see during the rainy months a few meager deciduous leaves here and there on their brittle twigs. And hundreds of lichens always grow on their bark in overlapping explosions which barely enlarge in the course of the decade, lichens pink and orange, lavender, yellow, and green. The palo santo trees bear the lichens effortlessly, unconsciously, the way they bear everything. Their multitudes, transparent as line drawings, crowd the cliffsides like whirling dancers, like empty groves, and look out over cliff-wrecked breakers toward more unpeopled islands, with their freakish lizards and birds, toward the grieving lagoons and the bays where the sea lions wander, and beyond to the clamoring seas.

23   Now I no longer concurred with my shipmates' joke; I no longer wanted to "come back" as a sea lion. For I thought, and I still think, that if I came back to life in the sunlight where everything changes, I would like to come back as a palo santo tree, one of thousands on a cliffside on those godforsaken islands, where a million events occur among the witless, where a splash of rain may drop on a yellow iguana the size of a dachshund, and ten minutes later the iguana may blink. I would like to come back as a palo santo tree on the weather side of an island, so that I could be, myself, a perfect witness, and look, mute, and wave my arms.

24   The silence is all there is. It is the alpha and the omega. It is God's brooding over the face of the waters; it is the blended note of the ten thousand things, the whine of wings. You take a step in the right direction

to pray to this silence, and even to address the prayer to "World." Distinctions blur. Quit your tents. Pray without ceasing.

VOCABULARY

perfunctorily (2)	snippet (12)	holey (21)
immutable (6)	particolored (20)	deciduous (22)
pantheism (7)		

QUESTIONS FOR CRITICAL THINKING

1. What thesis gradually emerges from the author's descriptive writing and philosophical commentary? Try to capture the thesis in one clear sentence.
2. On the surface, teaching a stone to talk seems a foolish waste of time. Why does the author refuse to condemn Larry's efforts? How do *you* react to these efforts?
3. What is the author's attitude toward the science of the cosmos? Evaluate her view and compare or contrast it with your own.
4. On which event, recorded in the Bible, does the author blame God's retreat from man? Do you see a true cause-effect relationship here? Explain your judgment.
5. The author claims that whereas in a next life her friends would like to return as sea lions, she would prefer coming back as a palo santo tree. According to the author, what do the sea lions and palo santo trees symbolize respectively? What aspect of nature do *you* consider emblematic of life's essence? Exclude humans from your choice and supply reasons for your choice.
6. How does the following poem by William Wordsworth complement Annie Dillard's views?

> The World Is Too Much with Us
> The world is too much with us; late and soon,
> Getting and spending, we lay waste our powers;
> Little we see in nature that is ours;
> We have given our hearts away, a sordid boon!
> This sea that bares her bosom to the moon;
> The winds that will be howling at all hours,
> And are up-gathered now like sleeping flowers;
> For this, for everything, we are out of tune;
> It moves us not.—Great God! I'd rather be
> A pagan suckled in a creed outworn;
> So might I, standing on this pleasant lea,
> Have glimpses that would make me less forlorn;
> Have sight of Proteus rising from the sea;
> Or hear old Triton blow his wreathed horn.

QUESTIONS ON THE WRITING PROCESS

1. Annie Dillard has been praised for her poetic style. What evidence of this style have you found in this essay? Supply three or four specific examples.
2. What is the paradox on which much of the essay is based? Where is this paradox best stated?
3. Dillard's essay does not follow a conventional outline. How is the essay organized? Label each section.
4. What poetic device does the author use in describing the palo santo trees? What is the effect?
5. Which part of the essay resembles a minister's sermon? Why?

WRITING ASSIGNMENTS

1. In a 300-word essay, describe your favorite tree. Use Dillard's description of the palo santo trees as a model.
2. In a 300-word essay, describe your favorite animal. Use Dillard's description of the sea lions as a model.
3. Choosing one of the following topics, write a 500-word descriptive essay:
   a. Nature as an agent of spiritual revival.
   b. Nature as an agent of random destruction.

PERINO'S

Robert Vivante

The kitchen at Perino's is an art studio. Every morning at six o'clock, Miguel Olmeda, the great chef, arrives with his assistants to prepare the finest food served in Los Angeles. The kitchen is the core of the restaurant, just as the heart is the core of the body, regulating the constant flow of life. It is divided into stations, resembling the auricles and ventricles of the heart, each individually working to sustain the vitality of the entire organ.

The first section is the cold buffet. Here the exquisitely prepared appetizers will serve as a tantalizing opening gambit for the meal. The delicately cracked crab and tender jumbo shrimp are a delight to the eye as white melts into pink and pink into red to form a subtle color palette. A platter of antipasto lies in the window area, looking like an ornate Chinese fan. Thin salami slices fan out in a geometric pattern and are decorated with glistening black Greek olives, chunks of fresh tuna, provolone cheese rosettes, and mounds of rich caviar.

Next to the pantry are the soups, vegetables, and pastas. These give life and body to the meal, enhancing the main dishes with their vivid color and enchanting aroma. The pungent odor of cooked garlic mixed with baby clams and linguini pervades the entire kitchen.

Center stage is where the main course is prepared. With deft skill and precision, Miguel produces flaming dishes and exotic delicacies that exude an air of excellence. He and his impeccable craftsmen create juicy fillets, tender poached salmon, and succulent veal. Each of these specialties will be drenched in some delicate sauce laced with cognac, sherry, or Grand Marnier. The results are veritable magic.

The bakeshop, tucked away in an alcove, is the paradise of desserts. Here the pastry chef designs fantastical creations of fabulous beauty. Luscious cream puffs, multi-layered tortes, and flaming fruits adorn several sterling silver trays. A baked Alaska takes the form of a floating iceberg, and the dainty strawberry cream soufflés rise like rosebuds blooming on an early spring morning. The bakeshop is a wonderland of seductive charms.

Perino's, after all, is not an ordinary restaurant; it is a place where great maestros display their exquisite and flamboyant culinary arts.

THREE

DEFINITION

The definition essay is written to make clear the meaning of some word, phrase, or term. It may be written to clarify an inexact or obscure meaning or to elaborate on the meaning of a word or phrase that the author intends to use in a special way. "Tonnage," the single-paragraph definition that leads off this chapter, is an example of the first kind of definition. The author's purpose is to tell his readers about an earlier meaning of a common English word.

Most words have at least two meanings—a denotative meaning and a connotative meaning—and this duality is partly responsible for their frequent ambiguity. The denotation of a word is its direct, explicit meaning. It is what the word literally stands for. *Lion,* for example, is a word denoting the mammal that biologists classify as *Panthera leo.* The connotation of a word, on the other hand, consists of the cluster of implications associated with it. To be called a lion is generally accepted as a compliment; to be called a sheep is not. Connotatively, *lion* implies dauntlessness and courage; *sheep* implies passivity and herdlike obedience. Purely for reasons of connotation, anyone in his right mind would therefore rather be called "lionhearted" than "sheephearted."

To ensure that a definition essay will take into account both the denotative and connotative meanings of a word, a number of strategies are commonly used by writers attempting a definition. First, there is an analysis of the etymology of a word—the source from which it sprung. Etymologies are instructive because they tell us how the meaning of the word has shifted over the years. This information, in turn, enables us to understand the word's current meaning. Sometimes the etymology of a word may even turn up a colorful character behind it, as in the case of *spoonerism,* defined in the essay "Will Someone Please Hiccup My Pat?" Here we learn that it was an Oxford don's chronic transposition of syllables in his speech that led to the naming of this kind of mispronunciation. Once we have read this essay, *spoonerism* takes on a new, more vivid meaning for us.

The second strategy used in defining a word or term is to give examples of what it means. Examples of Spooner's transposition of syllables abound in the essay about him. In the essay "I Want a Wife," Judy Syfers gives examples of what a wife is expected to do. In every case the writer is simply amplifying the definition with examples.

A third defining strategy involves an analysis either of cause or of effect. The best example of this strategy is seen in the essay "In Bed," which is actually an extended definition of migraine headaches. The writer analyzes the possible causes of migraines along with their painful effects on her. Such an analysis provides a more substantial meaning of *migraine* than can be found in any dictionary.

Exactly how you should proceed in writing a definition will depend on the complexity of the term you are defining. Abstract words—words that signify concepts and ideas—will require the use of a number of strategies to pinpoint their meanings. Some, such as *freedom,* will prove elusive to any but the most philosophical kind of definition. On the other hand, many concrete words— words that stand for objects and things—may be defined through the use of only one or two defining strategies. In every case, the final criterion of completeness of the definition should be whether or not you have made both the denotative and connotative meanings of the defined term abundantly clear.

SINGLE PARAGRAPHS

"TONNAGE" IN 1492

Samuel Eliot Morison

Samuel Eliot Morison (1887–1976) was an American historian and Harvard professor much admired for his numerous books on history. In 1942 Morison was commissioned by President Franklin Delano Roosevelt to write a history of U.S. naval operations in World War II. This 15-volume work appeared between 1947 and 1962. Two of Morison's other books won Pulitzer prizes: Admiral of the Ocean Sea *(1942), a biography of Christopher Columbus, and* John Paul Jones *(1959).*

Excerpted from the book Admiral of the Ocean Sea, *the following paragraph offers an extended definition of* tonnage.

What did tonnage mean in 1492? Not weight or displacement of the vessel, or her deadweight capacity; tonnage meant simply her cubic capacity in terms of wine tuns. The Castilian *tonelada,* or the Portuguese *tonel* (both of which I translate "ton"), was really a tun of wine, a large cask equivalent in volume to two *pipas* or pipes, the long, tapering hogsheads in which port wine is still sold. As wine was a common cargo, and both pipe and tun of standard dimensions, a vessel's carrying capacity below decks in terms of *toneladas* became a rough-and-ready index of her size; and so a ship's tonnage in 1492 meant the number of tuns or twice the number of pipes of wine she could stow. The tun, *tonelada* or ton being roughly (very roughly) equivalent to 40 cubic feet, this last figure became in the course of time the unit of burthen (or tonnage or capacity) for English vessels, and was so used in America until the Civil War. From the seventeenth century on, it became customary in every country to fix a vessel's official tonnage by a formula composed of her length, breadth and depth, which gave a rough measurement of her capacity. But in 1492 tonnage meant simply the number of tuns of wine that the ship could stow, as estimated by the owner or verified by common report. It was not a constant but a variable.

VOCABULARY

displacement	Castilian	hogsheads
deadweight	cubic	burthen
tun		

QUESTIONS FOR CRITICAL THINKING

1. What historical event does the year 1492 bring to mind?
2. What other units of measurement originated from extremely practical consider-ations? What is their advantage and disadvantage?
3. In your imagination, what kind of ship do you picture sailing the seas in 1492? Describe it as vividly as possible.

QUESTIONS ON THE WRITING PROCESS

1. What technique does the author use first in order to answer the question, "What did tonnage mean in 1492?"
2. Why are the words *tonelada, tonel,* and *pipas* written in italics?
3. Why does the author use the archaic term *burthen* instead of the more modern *burden*?

WRITING ASSIGNMENTS

1. In a brief paragraph, answer the question "What did *silly* mean in Medieval times?"
2. Look up the word *meter* in an unabridged dictionary. Define the word and write a brief paragraph giving its history.

THE SISSY

Geoffrey Gorer

Geoffrey Gorer (1905–   ) is a British author and scholar who has participated in some important anthropological field work in West Africa, the East Indies, and Indochina. He has been on the faculty of Cambridge, Yale, and Columbia universities. His book The American People *(1964), from which the paragraph below is excerpted, is a revealing analysis of American trends and habits.*

Although most Americans are familiar with the word sissy, probably few have seen it so thoroughly defined as in the following paragraph.

This concept of being a sissy is a key concept for the understanding of American character; it has no exact parallel in any other society. It has nowadays become a term of opprobrium which can be applied to anyone, regardless of age or sex; although it is analogous to some English terms of opprobrium (e.g. milksop, cry-baby, nancy, mother's darling) it is more than any of them. Schematically, it means showing more dependence or fear or lack of initiative or passivity than is suitable for the occasion. It can be applied to a gambler hesitant about risking his money, to a mother over-anxious about the pain her child may suffer at the hands of a surgeon, to a boy shy about asking a popular girl for a "date," to stage fright, to overt apprehension about a visit to the dentist, to a little girl crying because her doll is broken, just as well as to occasions which directly elicit courage or initiative or independence and which may be responded to more or less adequately. It is the overriding fear of all American parents that their child will turn into a sissy; it is the overriding fear of all Americans from the moment that they can understand language that they may be taken for a sissy; and a very great deal of American speech and activity, so often misinterpreted by non-Americans, is designed solely to avert this damning judgment. Particularly self-confident Americans may say "I guess I'm just a sissy ..." when they feel quite sure that they are not. When applied to adult males (but only in that case) the term also implies sexual passivity.

VOCABULARY

opprobrium	schematically	passivity
analogous	initiative	elicit

QUESTIONS FOR CRITICAL THINKING

1. Do you agree with Gorer's definition of *sissy*? Does he reflect accurately the way most Americans react to the term? If you agree with the author's definition, then explain why Americans so strongly avoid being sissies.
2. Name some other words currently used to label people. Define each word and explain its connotations.
3. If you have or plan to have children, will you consciously try to keep them from being sissies? Why or why not?

QUESTIONS ON THE WRITING PROCESS

1. What connotations do *milksop, cry-baby, nancy,* and *mother's darling* suggest to you?
2. What examples can you give of the American speech and behavior that are so often "misinterpreted by non-Americans"?
3. Where in the first half of the paragraph is there an example of parallelism?

WRITING ASSIGNMENTS

1. Write a one-paragraph definition of one of the following terms. Begin with a lexical definition and expand your definition by providing examples that explain the term.

    bully   con man   curmudgeon   pollyanna

2. The following terms have been used to describe males and females. Choose one from either column; then define it and give examples to expand your definition.

male	*female*
macho	fox
Milquetoast	sexy
fop	broad

THE PASSION OF *L'AMOUR FOU*

Tom Teepen

Tom Teepen (1935–   ) was born in Nashville, Tennessee. He first attended Ohio University and then Stanford University as a Professional Journalism Fellow. He eventually became Editorial Page editor for the Dayton Daily News in Ohio. Since 1982 he has been Editorial Page editor and popular columnist for the Atlanta Constitution.

All the world loves a lover, but can a lover go too far in the desire to possess and control? The following essay provides the basis for a possible answer and for an evaluation of our society's ability to be committed.

1   I suppose it must be a great burden to Kirk Anderson, this relentless passion of Joyce McKinney's, what with her still dogging him seven years after she kidnapped him and had her way with him. I am afraid, however, that my sympathies run more than they should to Miss McKinney.

2   We must resort to French for the right phrase here. Prim English, and American with its Puritan upbringing, shy from the job. The French call it *l'amour fou*—a crazy love. That is what McKinney has for poor Anderson.

3   This business first hit the public prints in 1977, you may recall. McKinney, who was Miss Wyoming in 1973, met Anderson when they were students at Brigham Young University. Her side of the story—Anderson has been understandably reticent—is that Anderson promised to marry her and then skipped.

4   McKinney hired a private eye, who tracked Anderson to England, where he was doing a turn as a Mormon missionary. McKinney followed and, according to charges later filed against her there, chloroformed him, carried him off to an isolated cottage and chained him to a bed with fur-lined manacles.

5   At the time, I ventured a small commentary on these events. In the circumlocution that newspaper convention demands in delicate matters, I wrote that Miss McKinney, having got Anderson where she wanted him, proceeded for three days to be repeatedly very much nicer to him than would have been proper even with a Unitarian.

6   I kind of liked that line and, as a result, have felt something of a proprietary interest in McKinney and her passion. I have followed their public outcroppings ever since. McKinney bolted from England, which suited Her Majesty's ministers well enough, and a bit later got herself afoul of the U.S. government. She was busted for using a false name to get a passport.

7   Miss McKinney has lately surfaced anew in Salt Lake City, where Anderson now lives. She is said to have been harassing him by spying on him.

She was arrested at the airport and was found to have notebooks filled with details of his activities, including maps she had drawn of his thithering and yonning.

8 McKinney's lawyer has pleaded her innocent—well, not guilty anyway—and says, Hey, she was just gathering material for a book or a movie about her story. I cannot imagine that is much comfort to Anderson.

9 A go-between has since taken Miss McKinney to see Anderson. "I thought it would probably be beneficial for her," the do-gooder said, "to see that this man is married, overweight and has children."

10 Alas, Anderson. Not only was he run to ground in England, mugged with off-beat pleasures and hounded even unto Salt Lake City International Airport. Now he is portrayed by his own defender as an implausible sex object on account of marital status and silhouette.

11 Even so, I can't help but cheer McKinney a little.

12 We live in a time of scant pleasures and superficial satisfactions. This is the era of the hedged bet. Our young are going in numbers for degrees in business. Pragmatism is widely recommended. Commitment is dismissed as passe and spontaneity as a character flaw. Where there was once life, there is lifestyle.

13 Ah, but not with Joyce McKinney. She has crisscrossed the nation for her passion. She has leaped oceans, scammed customs and even, it is said, committed cartography. And it is not, you know, as though she was just *ugly* about it; the manacles, remember, were fur-lined.

14 McKinney, in short, has *l'amour fou*. She has got it in spades. I suppose that must be awful; I suppose it must be wonderful. It is, either way or both ways, grand. It has sweep and rare heedlessness.

15 Our beauty queen, incidentally, is reported to have gone into seclusion pending her trial. It would be only fair if she were to give Anderson a break from now on, but I like to imagine that even in retreat McKinney is steaming and randy with obsession and will one of these days emerge again, undiminished in whatever epic itch it is that impels her. We are overdue for a culture hero.

VOCABULARY

manacles (4)	proprietary (6)	cartography (13)
circumlocution (5)	afoul (6)	randy (15)
Unitarian (5)	Pragmatism (12)	

QUESTIONS FOR CRITICAL THINKING

1. The author ends his essay by stating, "We are overdue for a culture hero." Do you consider McKinney worthy of being called a culture hero? Why or why not?
2. Is Teepen's sole purpose in this essay to convince the reader that McKinney should be cheered on in her attempt to captivate Kirk Anderson? If another purpose underlies the surface one, what is it?
3. What is the English translation for the French expression *l'amour fou*? After reading the essay, how would you define this term in your own words?
4. How would you handle someone who exhibited the traits of *l'amour fou* toward you? What is the opposite of *l'amour fou*?

QUESTIONS ON THE WRITING PROCESS

1. This essay first appeared in *The Atlantic Constitution,* a well-known southern newspaper. What stylistic characteristics are typical of journalism?
2. What is the meaning of the allusion to a "Unitarian" in paragraph 5?
3. What is the tone of paragraphs 10 and 13? What does the tone accomplish?

WRITING ASSIGNMENTS

1. Write a 300-word essay in which you define one of the following terms related to love:

   passion   good will   companionship   friendship
2. Write a letter to Tom Teepen in which you refute his view of the Anderson vs. McKinney case.
3. Write a 300-word essay supporting Teepen's statement, "Where there was once life, there is lifestyle."

IN BED

Joan Didion

Joan Didion (1934–), journalist, novelist, and screenwriter, is a native Californian who lives in Los Angeles with her husband, John Gregory Dunne. Critics quite generally praise her as a stylist and perceptive social critic. She enjoys collaborating with her husband on screenplays; their adaptation of one of her novels, Play It as It Lays *(1970), became a successful movie. Didion is best known for a collection of essays that describe the turmoil of the 1960s,* Slouching Toward Bethlehem *(1968).*

The essay below defines migraine headache, a medical condition that continues to perplex its victims as well as medical science.

1   Three, four, sometimes five times a month, I spend the day in bed with a migraine headache, insensible to the world around me. Almost every day of every month, between these attacks, I feel the sudden irrational irritation and the flush of blood into the cerebral arteries which tell me that migraine is on its way, and I take certain drugs to avert its arrival. If I did not take the drugs, I would be able to function perhaps one day in four. The physiological error called migraine is, in brief, central to the given of my life. When I was 15, 16, even 25, I used to think that I could rid myself of this error by simply denying it, character over chemistry. "Do you have headaches *sometimes? frequently? never?*" the application forms would demand. "Check one." Wary of the trap, wanting whatever it was that the successful circumnavigation of that particular form could bring (a job, a scholarship, the respect of mankind and the grace of God), I would check one. "*Sometimes,*" I would lie. That in fact I spent one or two days a week almost unconscious with pain seemed a shameful secret, evidence not merely of some chemical inferiority but of all my bad attitudes, unpleasant tempers, wrongthink.

2   For I had no brain tumor, no eyestrain, no high blood pressure, nothing wrong with me at all: I simply had migraine headaches, and migraine headaches were, as everyone who did not have them knew, imaginary. I fought migraine then, ignored the warnings it sent, went to school and later to work in spite of it, sat through lectures in Middle English and presentations to advertisers with involuntary tears running down the right side of my face, threw up in washrooms, stumbled home by instinct, emptied ice trays onto my bed and tried to freeze the pain in my right temple, wished only for a neurosurgeon who would do a lobotomy on house call, and cursed my imagination.

3   It was a long time before I began thinking mechanistically enough to accept migraine for what it was: something with which I would be living,

the way some people live with diabetes. Migraine is something more than the fancy of a neurotic imagination. It is an essentially hereditary complex of symptoms, the most frequently noted but by no means the most unpleasant of which is a vascular headache of blinding severity, suffered by a surprising number of women, a fair number of men (Thomas Jefferson had migraine, and so did Ulysses S. Grant, the day he accepted Lee's surrender), and by some unfortunate children as young as two years old. (I had my first when I was eight. It came on during a fire drill at the Columbia School in Colorado Springs, Colorado. I was taken first home and then to the infirmary at Peterson Field, where my father was stationed. The Air Corps doctor prescribed an enema.) Almost anything can trigger a specific attack of migraine: stress, allergy, fatigue, an abrupt change in barometric pressure, a contretemps over a parking ticket. A flashing light. A fire drill. One inherits, of course, only the predisposition. In other words I spent yesterday in bed with a headache not merely because of my bad attitudes, unpleasant tempers and wrongthink, but because both my grandmothers had migraine, my father has migraine and my mother has migraine.

4   No one knows precisely what it is that is inherited. The chemistry of migraine, however, seems to have some connection with the nerve hormone named serotonin, which is naturally present in the brain. The amount of serotonin in the blood falls sharply at the onset of migraine, and one migraine drug, methysergide, or Sansert, seems to have some effect on serotonin. Methysergide is a derivative of lysergic acid (in fact Sandoz Pharmaceuticals first synthesized LSD-25 while looking for a migraine cure), and its use is hemmed about with so many contraindications and side effects that most doctors prescribe it only in the most incapacitating cases. Methysergide, when it is prescribed, is taken daily, as a preventive; another preventive which works for some people is old-fashioned ergotamine tartrate, which helps to constrict the swelling blood vessels during the "aura," the period which in most cases precedes the actual headache.

5   Once an attack is under way, however, no drug touches it. Migraine gives some people mild hallucinations, temporarily blinds others, shows up not only as a headache but as a gastrointestinal disturbance, a painful sensitivity to all sensory stimuli, an abrupt overpowering fatigue, a strokelike aphasia, and a crippling inability to make even the most routine connections. When I am in a migraine aura (for some people the aura lasts fifteen minutes, for others several hours), I will drive through red lights, lose the house keys, spill whatever I am holding, lose the ability to focus my eyes or frame coherent sentences, and generally give the appearance of being on drugs, or drunk. The actual headache, when it comes, brings with it chills, sweating, nausea, a debility that seems to stretch the very limits of endurance. That no one dies of migraine seems, to someone deep into an attack, an ambiguous blessing.

6   My husband also has migraine, which is unfortunate for him but fortunate for me: perhaps nothing so tends to prolong an attack as the accusing eye of someone who has never had a headache. "Why not take a couple of aspirin," the unafflicted will say from the doorway, or "I'd have a headache, too, spending a beautiful day like this inside with all the shades drawn." All of us who have migraine suffer not only from the attacks themselves but from this common conviction that we are perversely refusing to cure ourselves by taking a couple of aspirin, that we are making ourselves sick, that we "bring it on ourselves." And in the most immediate sense, the sense of why we have a headache this Tuesday and not last Thursday, of course we often do. There certainly is what doctors call a "migraine personality," and that personality tends to be ambitious, inward, intolerant of error, rather rigidly organized, perfectionist. "You don't look like a migraine personality," a doctor once said to me. "Your hair's messy. But I suppose you're a compulsive housekeeper." Actually my house is kept even more negligently than my hair, but the doctor was right nonetheless: perfectionism can also take the form of spending most of a week writing and rewriting and not writing a single paragraph.

7   But not all perfectionists have migraine, and not all migrainous people have migraine personalities. We do not escape heredity. I have tried in most of the available ways to escape my own migrainous heredity (at one point I learned to give myself two daily injections of histamine with a hypodermic needle, even though the needle so frightened me that I had to close my eyes when I did it), but I still have migraine. And I have learned now to live with it, learned when to expect it, how to outwit it, even how to regard it, when it does come, as more friend than lodger. We have reached a certain understanding, my migraine and I. It never comes when I am in real trouble. Tell me that my house is burned down, my husband has left me, that there is gunfighting in the streets and panic in the banks, and I will not respond by getting a headache. It comes instead when I am fighting not an open but a guerrilla war with my own life, during weeks of small household confusions, lost laundry, unhappy help, canceled appointments, on days when the telephone rings too much and I get no work done and the wind is coming up. On days like that my friend comes uninvited.

8   And once it comes, now that I am wise in its ways, I no longer fight it. I lie down and let it happen. At first every small apprehension is magnified, every anxiety a pounding terror. Then the pain comes, and I concentrate only on that. Right there is the usefulness of migraine, there in that imposed yoga, the concentration on the pain. For when the pain recedes, ten or twelve hours later, everything goes with it, all the hidden resentments, all the vain anxieties. The migraine has acted as a circuit breaker, and the fuses have emerged intact. There is a pleasant convalescent euphoria. I

open the windows and feel the air, eat gratefully, sleep well. I notice the particular nature of a flower in a glass on the stair landing. I count my blessings.

VOCABULARY

insensible (1)	infirmary (3)	stimuli (5)
cerebral (1)	contretemps (3)	aphasia (5)
avert (1)	predisposition (3)	debility (5)
physiological (1)	hormone (4)	ambiguous (5)
wary (1)	derivative (4)	perversely (6)
circumnavigation (1)	synthesized (4)	guerrilla (7)
involuntary (2)	contraindications (4)	apprehension (8)
lobotomy (2)	incapacitating (4)	yoga (8)
mechanistically (3)	preventive (4)	convalescent (8)
complex (3)	gastrointestinal (5)	euphoria (8)
vascular (3)	sensory (5)	

QUESTIONS FOR CRITICAL THINKING

1. According to Joan Didion, people are filled with numerous misconceptions about migraines. What other diseases have there been common misconceptions about?
2. What is your evaluation of the migraine personality? What is good or bad about it?
3. What remedial action would you take if you had migraine headaches?
4. Although the author states that she has not yet found a cure for migraines, how has she come to terms with the illness?

QUESTIONS ON THE WRITING PROCESS

1. What is the purpose of the opening sentence?
2. In paragraph 3, what is the purpose of the references to Jefferson and Grant?
3. Which paragraph contains the most scientific tone and language? Why?
4. How is the transition from paragraph 4 to paragraph 5 indicated?
5. In the final paragraph, how does the author achieve balance and coherence?
6. What are some of the facts now known about migraines? List them in the order they appear in the essay.

WRITING ASSIGNMENTS

1. Write a 300-word essay in which you define a past illness; describe its symptoms vividly and relate how you were cured.
2. In a 300-word essay define the common cold, describe how it feels to suffer from a cold, and tell how you attempt to cure it.

I WANT A WIFE

Judy Syfer

Judy Syfer is married and has two children. The essay below was published in the preview issue of Ms *magazine in 1972.* Ms *reprinted it in its issue of December 1979, prefaced by the statement that it had become a classic.*

The following essay is a declaration: Wives are so useful that even a wife would want such a companion.

1   I belong to that classification of people known as wives. I am a Wife. And, not altogether incidentally, I am a mother.

2   Not too long ago a male friend of mine appeared on the scene fresh from a recent divorce. He had one child, who is, of course, with his ex-wife. He is obviously looking for another wife. As I thought about him while I was ironing one evening, it suddenly occurred to me that I, too, would like to have a wife. Why do I want a wife?

3   I would like to go back to school so that I can become economically independent, support myself, and, if need be, support those dependent on me. I want a wife who will work and send me to school. And while I am going to school I want a wife to take care of my children. I want a wife to keep track of the children's doctor and dentist appointments. And to keep track of mine, too. I want a wife to make sure that my children eat properly and are kept clean. I want a wife who will wash the children's clothes and keep them mended. I want a wife who is a good nurturant attendant to my children, who arranges for their schooling, makes sure they have an adequate social life with their peers, takes them to the park, the zoo, etc. I want a wife who takes care of the children when they are sick, a wife who arranges to be around when the children need special care, because, of course, I cannot miss classes at school. My wife must arrange to lose time at work and not lose the job. It may mean a small cut in my wife's income from time to time, but I guess I can tolerate that. Needless to say, my wife will arrange and pay for the care of the children while my wife is working.

4   I want a wife who will take care of my physical needs. I want a wife who will keep the house clean. A wife who will pick up after me. I want a wife who will keep my clothes clean, ironed, mended, replaced when need be, and who will see to it that my personal things are kept in their proper place so that I can find what I need the minute I need it. I want a wife who cooks the meals, a wife who is a *good* cook. I want a wife who will plan the menus, do the necessary shopping, prepare the meals, serve them pleasantly, and then do the cleaning up while I do my studying. I want a wife who will care for me when I am sick and sympathize with my pain and loss of time from

103

school. I want a wife to go along when our family takes a vacation so that someone can continue to care for me and my children when I need a rest and change of scene.

5   I want a wife who will not bother me with rambling complaints about a wife's duties. But I want a wife who will listen to me when I feel the need to explain a rather difficult point I have come across in my course of studies. And I want a wife who will type my papers for me when I have written them.

6   I want a wife who will take care of the details of my social life. When my wife and I are invited out by my friends, I want a wife who will take care of the babysitting arrangements. When I meet people at school that I like and want to entertain, I want a wife who will have the house clean, prepare a special meal, serve it to me and my friends, and not interrupt when I talk about the things that interest me and my friends. I want a wife who will have arranged that the children are fed and ready for bed before my guests arrive so that the children do not bother us. I want a wife who takes care of the needs of my guests so that they feel comfortable, who makes sure that they have an ashtray, that they are passed the hors d'oeuvres, that they are offered a second helping of the food, that their wine glasses are replenished when necessary, that their coffee is served to them as they like it.

7   And I want a wife who knows that sometimes I need a night out by myself.

8   I want a wife who is sensitive to my sexual needs, a wife who makes love passionately and eagerly when I feel like it, a wife who makes sure that I am satisfied. And, of course, I want a wife who will not demand sexual attention when I am not in the mood for it. I want a wife who assumes the complete responsibility for birth control, because I do not want more children. I want a wife who will remain sexually faithful to me so that I do not have to clutter up my intellectual life with jealousies. And I want a wife who understands that my sexual needs may entail more than strict adherence to monogamy. I must, after all, be able to relate to people as fully as possible.

9   If, by chance, I find another person more suitable as a wife than the wife I already have, I want the liberty to replace my present wife with another one. Naturally, I will expect a fresh, new life; my wife will take the children and be solely responsible for them so that I am left free.

10   When I am through with school and have a job, I want my wife to quit working and remain at home so that my wife can more fully and completely take care of a wife's duties.

11   My God, who wouldn't want a wife?

VOCABULARY

classification (1)   entail (8)   monogamy (8)
nurturant (3)   adherence (8)

QUESTIONS FOR CRITICAL THINKING

1. How do you feel about the modern trend of dividing household tasks between husband and wife?
2. In your view, how should custody of children in case of a divorce be handled?
3. What is your definition of a good wife? A good husband?
4. What is an ideal marriage partnership? What roles do you see each sex playing?

QUESTIONS ON THE WRITING PROCESS

1. What is the tone of this essay? What produces this tone?
2. What effect is achieved by the constant repetition of the clause "I want . . ."?
3. Why is *my* italicized at the beginning of paragraph 4?
4. What is the effect of the word *naturally* in paragraph 9?
5. What expression in the essay serves to summarize the wife's outrage?

WRITING ASSIGNMENTS

1. Using Judy Syfer's essay as a model, write a 300-word essay entitled "I Want a Husband."
2. Write a 300-word essay defining the term *mother* (or *father*).

WILL SOMEONE PLEASE HICCUP MY PAT?

William Spooner Donald

William Spooner Donald, a nephew of the famous Reverend William Archibald Spooner, who in the early 1900s caused a stir at Oxford's New College with his verbal bloopers, is a retired naval officer living in Cumbria, England. He is the author of several plays and a book on sea adventures, Stand By for Action.

Of the multitude of verbal errors possible in the English language, none produces more laughter than a good spoonerism, which the following essay attempts to define as well as to illustrate.

1   One afternoon nearly a hundred years ago the October wind gusted merrily down Oxford's High Street. Hatless and helpless, a white-haired clergyman with pink cherubic features uttered his plaintive cry for aid. As an athletic youngster chased the spinning topper, other bystanders smiled delightedly—they had just heard at first hand the latest "Spoonerism."

2   My revered relative William Archibald Spooner was born in 1844, the son of a Staffordshire county court judge. As a young man, he was handicapped by a poor physique, a stammer, and weak eyesight; at first, his only possible claim to future fame lay in the fact that he was an albino, with very pale blue eyes and white hair tinged slightly yellow.

3   But nature compensated the weakling by blessing him with a brilliant intellect. By 1868 he had been appointed a lecturer at New College, Oxford. Just then he would have been a caricaturist's dream with his freakish looks, nervous manner, and peculiar mental kink that caused him—in his own words—to "make occasional felicities in verbal diction."

4   Victorian Oxford was a little world of its own where life drifted gently by; a world where splendid intellectuals lived in their ivory towers of Latin, Euclid, and Philosophy; a world where it was always a sunny summer afternoon in a countryside, where Spooner admitted he loved to "pedal gently round on a well-boiled icicle."

5   As the years passed, Spooner grew, probably without himself being aware of the fact, into a "character." A hard worker himself, he detested idleness and is on record as having rent some lazybones with the gem, "You have hissed all my mystery lessons, and completely tasted two whole worms."

6   With his kindly outlook on life, it was almost natural for him to take holy orders; he was ordained a deacon in 1872 and a priest in 1875. His unique idiosyncrasy never caused any serious trouble and merely made him more popular. On one occasion, in New College chapel in 1879, he announced smilingly that the next hymn would be "Number one seven five—

Kinkering Kongs their Titles Take." Other congregations were treated to such jewels as "... Our Lord, we know, is a shoving Leopard ..." and "... All of us have in our hearts a half-warmed fish to lead a better life. ..."

7   Spooner often preached in the little village churches around Oxford and once delivered an eloquent address on the subject of Aristotle. No doubt the sermon contained some surprising information for his rustic congregation. For after Spooner had left the pulpit, an idea seemed to occur to him, and he hopped back up the steps again.

8   "Excuse me, dear brethren," he announced brightly, "I just want to say that in my sermon whenever I mentioned Aristotle, I should have said Saint Paul."

9   By 1885 the word "Spoonerism" was in colloquial use in Oxford circles, and a few years later, in general use all over England. If the dividing line between truth and myth is often only a hairsbreadth, does it really matter? One story that has been told concerns an optician's shop in London. Spooner is reputed to have entered and asked to see a "signifying glass." The optician registered polite bewilderment.

10   "Just an ordinary signifying glass," repeated Spooner, perhaps surprised at the man's obtuseness.

11   "I'm afraid we haven't one in stock, but I'll make inquiries right away, sir," said the shopkeeper, playing for time.

12   "Oh, don't bother, it doesn't magnify, it doesn't magnify," said Spooner airily, and walked out.

13   Fortunately for Spooner, he made the right choice when he met his wife-to-be. He was thirty-four years old when he married Frances Goodwin in 1878. The marriage was a happy one, and they had one son and four daughters. Mrs. Spooner was a tall, good-looking girl, and on one occasion the family went on a short holiday in Switzerland. The "genial Dean," as he was then called, took a keen interest in geology, and in no time at all he had mastered much information and many technical definitions on the subject of glaciers.

14   One day at lunchtime the younger folk were worried because their parents had not returned from a long walk. When Spooner finally appeared with his wife, his explanation was: "We strolled up a long valley, and when we turned a corner we found ourselves completely surrounded by erotic blacks."

15   He was, of course, referring to "erratic blocks," or large boulders left around after the passage of a glacier.

16   In 1903 Spooner was appointed Warden of New College, the highest possible post for a Fellow. One day walking across the quadrangle, he met a certain Mr. Casson, who had just been elected a Fellow of New College.

17   "Do come to dinner tonight," said Spooner, "we are welcoming our new Fellow, Mr. Casson."

18   "But, my dear Warden, I *am* Casson," was the surprised reply.

19   "Never mind, never mind, come along all the same," said Spooner tactfully.

20   On another occasion in later years when his eyesight was really very bad, Spooner found himself seated next to a most elegant lady at dinner. In a casual moment the latter put her lily-white hand onto the polished table, and Spooner, in an even more casual manner, pronged her hand with his fork, remarking genially, "My bread, I think."

21   In 1924 Spooner retired as Warden. He had established an astonishing record of continuous residence at New College for sixty-two years first as undergraduate, then as Fellow, then Dean, and finally as Warden. His death in 1930, at the age of eighty-six, was a blushing crow to collectors of those odd linguistic transpositions known by then throughout the English-speaking world as Spoonerisms.

VOCABULARY

cherubic (1)	felicities (3)	erotic (14)
topper (1)	idiosyncrasy (6)	erratic (15)
albino (2)	colloquial (9)	quadrangle (16)
compensated (3)	obtuseness (10)	linguistic (21)
caricaturist (3)	genial (13)	transpositions (21)

QUESTIONS FOR CRITICAL THINKING

1.   Spoonerisms and other slips of the tongue are of serious concern to psychologists and linguists. Why?
2.   Do you have a favorite spoonerism? If so, share it with the class.
3.   Spoonerisms are only one kind of slip of the tongue. Can you think of other kinds? Give examples.
4.   What is humorous about Spooner's confusing Aristotle with St. Paul in a sermon? (See paragraph 7 and 8.)
5.   Why was it so natural for Spooner to become a clergyman? (See paragraph 5.) Do you consider that a good reason? Why?
6.   What general impressions of the Reverend William Archibald Spooner does the essay convey? How would you describe the man's personality?

QUESTIONS ON THE WRITING PROCESS

1. By what rhetorical means does the author clarify his definition of a spooner-ism? Why?

2. Where in paragraph 3 does the author use a roundabout expression? Why?

3. What is the implication of the rhetorical question asked in paragraph 9? How would you answer the question?

4. How should the title of the essay read if the spoonerism were corrected?

WRITING ASSIGNMENT

Define one of the following terms by providing a lexical definition and some appro-priate examples.

pun   malapropism
hyperbole portmanteau word

LONG ESSAYS

WHAT IS THE BIBLE?

Mary Ellen Chase

Mary Ellen Chase (1887–1973), a professor at Smith College for twenty-five years, also found time to write over forty books. She is perhaps best known as a regionalist, whose novels, for both children and adults, were set in Maine, the state of her birth. But she was also a literary critic and authored a number of books which help, through their logical organization and lucid style, to clarify the Bible.

The essay below serves as the introductory chapter to the author's The Bible and the Common Reader, *a work that has had extraordinary appeal, especially for readers with little previous knowledge of the Bible.**

1   In the derivation of our word, *Bible*, lies its definition. It comes from the Greek word, *biblion*[1] which in its plural *biblia* signifies "little books." The Bible is actually a collection of little books, of every sort and description, written over a long period of time, the very earliest dating, in part at least, as far back as 1200 B.C. or perhaps even earlier; the latest as late as 150 A.D. In its rich and manifold nature it might be called a *library* of Hebrew literature; in its slow production over a period of many centuries it might be termed a *survey* of that literature to be understood as we understand a survey of English literature, in which we become familiar with types of English prose and poetry from Anglo-Saxon times to the twentieth century.

2   The Bible, in the form in which most of us wisely read it, the King James, or Authorized Version, has been called by John Livingston Lowes[2] "the noblest monument of English prose." It is as well the richest monument, for within its covers are to be found all types of literature, both in prose and in poetry. Here are ancient songs, written by unknown hands before the year 1000 B.C., preserved in old collections, now lost, or tenaciously bequeathed by word of mouth to succeeding generations, songs of war and of triumph, such as the famous martial song of Deborah in the 5th chapter of Judges; or in the 10th chapter of the book called by his name the dramatic command of Joshua to the sun and the moon that they should stand still upon Gibeon and in the valley of Ajalon until the Amorites

[1]*Biblos* was the name given to the inner bark of the papyrus; and the word *biblion* meant a papyrus roll, upon which the Bible was originally copied. (Miss Chase's note.)

[2]American scholar and educator, for many years professor of English at Harvard.

should be destroyed; or in Exodus 15 the triumphant song of Miriam, the sister of Moses, who with her women sang "with timbrels and with dances" over the destruction of Pharaoh and his hosts in the Red Sea; the revengeful song of Lamech, boasting to his terrified wives, Adah and Zillah, in the 4th chapter of Genesis; the little song to the well in the 21st chapter of Numbers, a song which the children of Israel sang in the wilderness of the desert when they thirsted for water and which is today in similar form sung by roaming Arabian tribes. Here are riddles, old perhaps as the famous riddle of the Sphinx,[3] such as the riddle in Judges 14 propounded by Samson at his wedding feast about the honey in the carcass of the lion which he had killed with his bare hands; here are fables, exemplified in Judges 9 by Jotham's fable of the talking trees, the olive, the fig tree, the grape vine, and the bramble, and, like all fables, containing in its words a teaching for its time; here are oracles (for the great men of ancient Israel sometimes spoke in oracles as well as did the gods of ancient Greece), the beautiful oracles in Numbers 23 of Balaam, who went astride his wise and talkative ass to confound Balak, king of Moab.

3   These, which are among the oldest pieces of Hebrew literature, existed as folk material long before they were incorporated into the biblical narratives to give added richness to the narratives themselves. And what narratives! For the story-tellers of the Bible have never been surpassed, if equalled, by those of any later age or race, who time and time again have gone to them as to models of the art of narration. The Old Testament teems with stories: legends such as those in Genesis of the creation and of the flood, sagas like the Jacob-Joseph saga in Genesis 27–50, hero tales like those of Gideon, Jephthah, and Samson in the book of Judges, romances like much of the story of David, tragedies like the dark, ironic story of Saul, realistic stories like those many sordid incidents in King David's tempestuous and ill-governed household or in the cruel, designing lives of Ahab and Jezebel. There are short stories in the Bible, the idyllic love story of Ruth and the humorous, ironic story of Jonah sulking under his withering gourd. And there is a novel in the book of Esther, which in plot design and irony of incident has never been surpassed.

4   The story-tellers of the Bible, both in the Old Testament and the New, understood men and women of all sorts and in all conditions. There is literally no type of person whom they have neglected. All are here: the wise and the foolish, the rich and the poor, the faithful and the treacherous, the designing and the generous, the pitiful and the prosperous, the innocent

---

[3]According to ancient legend, the Sphinx, stationed on the road to Thebes, put to death all passers-by who could not solve this riddle: "What is it that, though it has one voice, is four-footed, and two-footed, and three-footed?" Oedipus guessed the answer correctly as man, who crawls on four legs as an infant, walks on two in his prime, and supports himself with a cane when old. Thereupon the Sphinx killed herself.

and the guilty, the spendthrift and the miser, the players of practical jokes and their discomfited victims, the sorry, the tired, the old, the exasperated young, misled and impetuous girls, young men who lusted and young men who loved, friends who counted no cost for friendship, bad-mannered children and children well brought up, a little boy who had a headache in a hay-field, a little servant girl who wanted so much her master's health that she dared to give him good, if unpalatable, advice. Once one discovers such persons as these, still alive after many centuries, they become not only fascinating in themselves but typical of persons whom we know today, just as Mr. Micawber and Fagin are typical of the easy-going and the cruel, or as Robin Hood and Captain Blood[4] typify two different attitudes toward daring and adventure, or as Don Quixote and Parson Adams[5] are typical of men who, although they exist in this world, actually live in a kinder, better, more glorified one.

5   These stories of men and women, old and young, although they occupy a large portion of the Bible, are only one of its many literary forms. There is poetry in the Bible. In addition to the ancient songs already spoken of, there are lyrical love songs, odes, laments, hymns of all kinds, both secular and religious, dramatic monologues, and, above all else, the exalted poetry of the prophets and of the book of Job. And the poets who wrote this biblical poetry, some of them known by name, others unknown, were as distinct and individual in their method of writing and in their ways of thought as were the familiar English poets. Indeed many of them in their manner of expression and in their attitude toward life bear a striking resemblance to other poets whom we know far better than we know the poets of the Bible. Amos, for example, is like Milton in his sonorous, ringing lines; Hosea sounds the sad and minor notes of A. E. Housman; Second-Isaiah is like Shelley in his ecstasy; certain of the Psalmists are like William Blake, or Thomas Traherne, or John Donne.

6   There is at least one great drama in the Bible, that contained in the book of Revelation, with its majestic and awful stage settings, its celestial actors, its solemn acts and scenes. And there are a score of tragedies which, if placed in dramatic form, would rival *Othello* or *Hamlet* on Broadway.

7   There are great biographers among the biblical writers: Baruch, who wrote the biography of the prophet Jeremiah and whose first copy of it was cut in pieces by King Jehoiakim's pen-knife and thrown into the open fire on a cold December day; the unknown, vivid biographer of David, who rivalled Boswell in frankness and detail; the naive, almost childish chronicler, also unknown, who wrote in awed accents of King Solomon's magnificence, how he drank from cups of gold, how he spoke in proverbs, and how

---

[4]Principal character in Rafael Sabatini's novel *Captain Blood*.

[5]Important character in Henry Fielding's novel *Joseph Andrews* (1742).

"he spake of trees"; and, in the New Testament, the biographers of Jesus, especially St. Luke, whose Gospel, to many readers, is more sensitive, more revealing, and more beautiful, than those of the other three writers. And the earliest autobiography of which we have record in ancient literature is that found in Nehemiah's thrilling account of how he left his service as cup-bearer to King Artaxerxes to return to Jerusalem and to rebuild the broken-down walls and gates of his fathers' city.

8   The best letters ever written are in the Bible, and St. Paul is the author of them, a more vivid letter writer than even Horace Walpole or Lord Chesterfield largely because he had far more important things than they to say. St. Paul is never dull. Whether he writes for a room to be made ready for him, or thanks his friends for presents, or gives his opinions on marriage or on the behaviour of women in church, or describes his utter dejection or his astounding faith, or is concerned over the collection of money or the virtue of charity, or rises to impassioned heights over the corruptible and the incorruptible, the terrestrial and the celestial, he is always vibrant with life, and his language in its force and vigour, clarity and beauty, can never be forgotten.

9   There are countless proverbs in the Bible, many contained in the book bearing their name, others scattered elsewhere, maxims and aphorisms, some of great antiquity, some of other origin than Jewish. Proverbs, as all know, are one of the most ancient and perennial forms of literature, reflect-ing the sagacity and common sense of practical men of all ages in their attempts to get on reasonably well in life. They are, in other words, the records of long and sometimes hazardous experience expressed in short sentences. Here in the Bible we have them at their best and, often uncon-scious of their origin, quote them over and over again as Sancho Panza, in his exasperation, quoted ancient Spanish proverbs to Don Quixote.

10   There are two philosophers in the Bible, both of whom give to us in mingled prose and poetry their questions and their conclusions concerning the meaning of life and the ways of God with men. They are the unknown authors of the books of Ecclesiastes and of Job, the one a skeptic, the other a tortured man of faith. Because they dealt, each in his own way, with man's great quest, his search for Reality in life, because they recognized the problems of evil and of pain, and because, like other thoughtful and honest men, they found no sure and certain answers to their questions, the books which they wrote, disparate though they are in both literary and philo-sophical value, are surely among the most deathless of all the books of the Bible.

11   The Bible, then, is a collection, a library of various books, reflecting and illuminating the long life of a small, yet a great people. If it were only that, its value would be imperishable. But it is more. It is, indeed, in its most perfect of translations, the noblest monument of our English prose; and its words and phrases, images and similes have become part and parcel of our

common English speech. Think for a moment how in the course of a single day spent in the homely, necessary details of living, we clarify and illuminate our talk with one another by the often unconscious use of its language. An unwelcome neighbour becomes "gall and wormwood" or "a thorn in the flesh"; a hated task, "a millstone about the neck"; we escape from one thing or another by the "skin of our teeth"; we earn our bread "by the sweat of our faces"; like Martha we become "careful and troubled about many things"; we "strain at gnats and swallow camels"; tired at night, we say that "our spirit is willing but our flesh is weak"; in moments of anger we remember that "a soft answer turneth away wrath"; intrusions upon our sleep are "the pestilence that walketh in darkness"; we warn our children to be "diligent in business" so that they may not "stand before mean men," or prophesy that if "they sow the wind, they shall reap the whirlwind," or puzzle them by knowledge "brought by a bird"; we recall that "the tongue is a little member but boasteth great things"; our pay-days mean "corn in Egypt"; words fitly spoken are "like apples of gold in pictures of silver"; the price of our generous friends is still "far above rubies," they are, in fact, "shining lights" or "the salt of the earth"; we pray that our sons may be brought safely homeward "to the haven where they would be"; we "heap coals of fire" on the heads of recalcitrant children or of harassed wives or husbands; having no servants, we are ourselves "hewers of wood and drawers of water"; we long for the time when men "shall beat their swords into ploughshares and their spears into pruning-hooks"; and, after an irritating session with ration books, we are forced to remember that "better a dinner of herbs where love is than a stalled ox and hatred therewith."

12   The language of the Bible, now simple and direct in its homely vigour, now sonorous and stately in its richness, has placed its indelible stamp upon our best writers from Bacon to Lincoln and even to the present day. Without it there would be no *Paradise Lost,* no *Samson Agonistes,*[6] no *Pilgrim's Progress;* no William Blake, or Whittier, or T. S. Eliot as we know them; no Emerson or Thoreau, no negro Spirituals, no Address at Gettysburg. Without it the words of Burke and Washington, Patrick Henry and Winston Churchill would miss alike their eloquence and their meaning. Without a knowledge of it the best of our literature remains obscure, and many of the characteristic features and qualities of our spoken language are threatened with extinction.

13   The Bible belongs among the noblest and most indispensable of our humanistic and literary traditions. No liberal education is truly liberal without it. Yet in the last fifty years our colleges have, for the most part, abandoned its study as literature, and our schools, for reasons not sufficiently valid, have ceased to teach, or, in many cases, even to read it to their young people. Students of English literature take for granted that a knowledge of

[6]A poetic tragedy by John Milton.

the *Iliad,* the *Odyssey,* the *Aeneid,* and the *Divine Comedy*[7] are necessary not only for the graduate schools but for cultured and civilized life, as, indeed, they are; but most of them remain in comfortable and colossal ignorance of a book which antedates Dante and, in large part, Vergil by many centuries, some of which was written before Homer, and all of which has contributed more to the humanistic civilization of the Western World than have the so-called "Classics."

14   To all English-speaking peoples the Bible is a national as well as a noble monument, for much of their history is securely rooted and anchored within it. In 17th century England it nurtured the Puritan revolt and paved the way for the Bill of Rights. In 17th and 18th century America it supplied not only the names of our ancestors but the stout precepts by which they lived. They walked by its guidance; their rough places were made plain by their trust in its compassionate promises. It was a lamp to their feet and a light to their path, a pillar of cloud by day and of fire by night. It was the source of the convictions that shaped the building of this country, of the faith that endured the first New England winters and later opened up the Great West. It laid the foundations of our educational system, built our earliest colleges, and dictated the training within our homes. In the words alike of Jefferson and Patrick Henry, John Quincy Adams and Franklin it made better and more useful citizens to their country by reminding a man of his individual responsibility, his own dignity, and his equality with his fellow-man. The Bible is, indeed, so imbedded in our American heritage that not to recognize its place there becomes a kind of national apostasy, and not to know and understand it, in these days when we give all for its principles of human worth and human freedom, an act unworthy of us as a people.

15   And, lastly, the Bible in its slow, patient evolution is the noblest record in any language of the hearts and the minds of men. Those who wrote it and those of whom it was written thought and wondered over the eternal questions of life and death, of man's lot upon this earth, and of his ultimate destiny. Amos on the Tekoan hills, the Great Isaiah by the waters of Shiloah and the Second Isaiah by those of Babylon, Job in the dust with his sententious friends, "physicians of no value" to him, St. John on the island of Patmos, Daniel by the river Ulai—these were men of dreams and of visions who struggled with the questions that beset us all. Consumed like Dante "by the Love that moves the sun and the other stars," they were intent upon the possible reaches of man's spirit even in a dry and thirsty land. In the midst of desolation and suffering, of oppression and greed, they saw hope; in war, the ways of peace; in the perennial processes of nature, the treasures of the snow, the former and the latter rain, the waste places of

[7]The great poetic work by the Italian poet Dante, describing the Christian Inferno, Purgatory, and Paradise.

the deep, the singing of the morning stars, they saw the mysterious ways of God with men. Because of their vision, deep calleth unto deep in their pages; and the unanalyzed perception of the meaning and value of three-score years and ten is woven into the very texture of their speech. In their two-fold recognition of wisdom, that moral and ethical code by which a just man lives his life and that intangible and spiritual Power, set up from ever-lasting and possessed by God in the beginning of His way, only by the understanding of which man achieves his triumph, they encompassed all the affairs, small and great, of one's sojourn on this earth.

16   "I myself also am a mortal man, like to all. . . . And when I was born, I drew in the common air, and fell upon the earth, which is of like nature, and the first voice I uttered was crying, as all others do. . . . For all men have one entrance into life, and the like going out. Wherefore I prayed, and understanding was given me; I called upon God, and the spirit of wisdom came to me. I preferred her before sceptres and thrones, and esteemed riches nothing in comparison to her. . . . I loved her above health and beauty, and chose to have her instead of light; for the light that cometh from her never goeth out. All good things together came to me with her, and innumerable riches in her hands. For she is a treasure unto men that never faileth; which they that use become the friends of God."[8]

VOCABULARY

derivation (1)	maxims (9)	illuminating (11)
discomfited (4)	aphorisms (9)	homely (12)
unpalatable (4)	sagacity (9)	indelible (12)
sonorous (5)	disparate (10)	apostasy (14)

QUESTIONS FOR CRITICAL THINKING

1. In addition to defining the Bible, what other purpose does the essay serve? How does the author go about fulfilling this second purpose?
2. Chase begins her essay by supplying a dictionary definition of the Bible, including an etymology of the term. How does this definition help the reader in understanding the Bible? What fallacy does it help to avoid?

---

[8]These words are taken from the seventh chapter of the Wisdom of Solomon from the *Apocrypha*. (Miss Chase's note.)

3. Why is the inclusion of paragraph 11 important? Can you add to the list of examples?

4. In paragraph 2, Chase gives special praise to the King James version of the Bible. Do you agree with her? Or do you find some other translation more attractive and useful? Give reasons for your answer.

5. What point does paragraph 4 support through examples? What other literary characters in addition to Micawber, Fagin, Robin Hood, Captain Blood, Don Quixote, and Parson Adams can you suggest as representing certain human types?

6. What arguments does Chase present to insist that a knowledge of the Bible should become part of a good liberal education? Do you agree or disagree? Give reasons for your view.

QUESTIONS ON THE WRITING PROCESS

1. Many essays have been entitled "What Is . . . ?" What responsibility does such a title place on the author? How does it help the reader?

2. What is the predominant type of development used by the author throughout the essay? Why does she use this development?

3. What method of development is used for paragraph 2? What specific words reinforce that development?

4. In paragraph 9, how does the author define the term *proverb*? Contrast her definition with a dictionary definition. What is the key difference?

5. In paragraph 4, how does the author achieve a rhythmic harmony in her sentence structure? What does this technique add to Chase's style?

6. How well does Chase integrate biblical quotations into paragraph 11? Comment on her technique.

WRITING ASSIGNMENTS

1. Using one of the proverbs listed in paragraph 11 or in the Book of Proverbs itself, write an essay of 500 words in which you prove this proverb to be worth heeding.

2. Write a 500-word essay arguing either for or against the inclusion of a Bible as Literature course in every college curriculum. Begin with a clear statement of your proposition.

3. Choosing one of the following biblical texts, indicate in 500 words how the author dealt with "the eternal questions of life and death, of man's lot upon this earth, and of his ultimate destiny." Begin with a clear thesis and be sure to refer to specific passages from the writer chosen:

     Job   Amos   Isaiah (or Second Isaiah)   St. John

THE AMERICAN SCHOLAR

Ralph Waldo Emerson

Ralph Waldo Emerson (1803–1882) was an American essayist, poet, and lecturer. Though trained as a minister, he spent only a short time in that profession. He became the leader of a group of intellectuals in Concord, Massachusetts, who were influential in the development of American thought. Emerson is recognized today as a literary artist who phrased his thoughts meticulously, and whose poetry was genuinely innovative.

In the address below, delivered to the Phi Beta Kappa chapter at Harvard on August 31, 1837, Emerson probes and defends the meaning of scholarship as a way of life. The essay has been admired for its intellectual depth as well as its literary passion.

1   I greet you on the recommencement of our literary year. Our anniversary is one of hope, and, perhaps, not enough of labor. We do not meet for games of strength or skill, for the recitation of histories, tragedies, and odes, like the ancient Greeks; for parliaments of love and poesy, like the Troubadours; nor for the advancement of science, like our contemporaries in the British and European capitals. Thus far, our holiday has been simply a friendly sign of the survival of the love of letters amongst a people too busy to give to letters any more. As such it is precious as the sign of an indestructible instinct. Perhaps the time is already come when it ought to be, and will be, something else; when the sluggard intellect of this continent will look from under its iron lids and fill the postponed expectation of the world with something better than the exertions of mechanical skill. Our day of dependence, our long apprenticeship to the learning of other lands, draws to a close. The millions that around us are rushing into life, cannot always be fed on the sere remains of foreign harvests. Events, actions arise, that must be sung, that will sing themselves. Who can doubt that poetry will revive and lead in a new age, as the star in the constellation Harp, which now flames in our zenith, astronomers announce shall one day be the polestar for a thousand years?

2   In this hope I accept the topic which not only usage but the nature of our association seem to prescribe to this day,—the American Scholar. Year by year we come up hither to read one more chapter of his biography. Let us inquire what light new days and events have thrown on his character and his hopes.

3   It is one of those fables which out of an unknown antiquity convey an unlooked-for wisdom, that the gods, in the beginning, divided Man into men, that he might be more helpful to himself; just as the hand was divided into fingers, the better to answer its end.

4   The old fable covers a doctrine ever new and sublime; that there is One Man,—present to all particular men only partially, or through one faculty; and that you must take the whole society to find the whole man. Man is not a farmer, or a professor, or an engineer, but he is all. Man is priest, and scholar, and statesman, and producer, and soldier. In the *divided* or social state these functions are parcelled out to individuals, each of whom aims to do his stint of the joint work whilst each other performs his. The fable implies that the individual, to possess himself, must sometimes return from his own labor to embrace all the other laborers. But, unfortunately, this original unit, this fountain of power, has been so distributed to multitudes, has been so minutely subdivided and peddled out, that it is spilled into drops, and cannot be gathered. The state of society is one in which the members have suffered amputation from the trunk, and strut about so many walking monsters,—a good finger, a neck, a stomach, an elbow, but never a man.

5   Man is thus metamorphosed into a thing, into many things. The planter, who is Man sent out into the field to gather food, is seldom cheered by any idea of the true dignity of his ministry. He sees his bushel and his cart, and nothing beyond, and sinks into the farmer, instead of Man on the farm. The tradesman scarcely ever gives an ideal worth to his work, but is ridden by the routine of his craft, and the soul is subject to dollars. The priest becomes a form; the attorney a statute-book; the mechanic a machine; the sailor a rope of the ship.

6   In this distribution of functions the scholar is the delegated intellect. In the right state he is *Man Thinking*. In the degenerate state, when the victim of society, he tends to become a mere thinker, or still worse, the parrot of other men's thinking.

7   In this view of him, as Man Thinking, the theory of his office is contained. Him Nature solicits with all her placid, all her monitory pictures; him the past instructs; him the future invites. Is not indeed every man a student, and do not all things exist for the student's behoof? And, finally, is not the true scholar the only true master? But the old oracle said, "All things have two handles: beware of the wrong one." In life, too often, the scholar errs with mankind and forfeits his privilege. Let us see him in his school, and consider him in reference to the main influences he receives.

8   I. The first in time and the first in importance of the influences upon the mind is that of nature. Every day, the sun; and, after sunset, Night and her stars. Ever the winds blow, ever the grass grows. Every day, men and women, conversing—beholding and beholden. The scholar is he of all men whom this spectacle most engages. He must settle its value in his mind. What is nature to him? There is never a beginning, there is never an end, to the inexplicable continuity of this web of God, but always circular power returning into itself. Therein it resembles his own spirit, whose beginning, whose ending, he never can find,—so entire, so boundless. Far too as her

splendors shine, system on system shooting like rays, upward, downward, without centre, without circumference,—in the mass and in the particle, Nature hastens to render account of herself to the mind. Classification begins. To the young mind every thing is individual, stands by itself. By and by, it finds how to join two things and see in them one nature; then three, then three thousand; and so, tyrannized over by its own unifying instinct, it goes on tying things together, diminishing anomalies, discovering roots running under ground whereby contrary and remote things cohere and flower out from one stem. It presently learns that since the dawn of history there has been a constant accumulation and classifying of facts. But what is classification but the perceiving that these objects are not chaotic, and are not foreign, but have a law which is also a law of the human mind? The astronomer discovers that geometry, a pure abstraction of the human mind, is the measure of planetary motion. The chemist finds proportions and intelligible method throughout matter; and science is nothing but the finding of analogy, identity, in the most remote parts. The ambitious soul sits down before each refractory fact; one after another reduces all strange constitutions, all new powers, to their class and their law, and goes on forever to animate the last fibre of organization, the outskirts of nature, by insight.

9   Thus to him, to this schoolboy under the bending dome of day, is suggested that he and it proceed from one root; one is leaf and one is flower; relation, sympathy, stirring in every vein. And what is that root? Is not that the soul of his soul? A thought too bold; a dream too wild. Yet when this spiritual light shall have revealed the law of more earthly natures,—when he has learned to worship the soul, and to see that the natural philosophy that now is, is only the first gropings of its gigantic hand, he shall look forward to an ever expanding knowledge as to a becoming creator. He shall see that nature is the opposite of the soul, answering to it part for part. One is seal and one is print. Its beauty is the beauty of his own mind. Its laws are the laws of his own mind. Nature then becomes to him the measure of his attainments. So much of nature as he is ignorant of, so much of his own mind does he not yet possess. And, in fine, the ancient precept, "Know thyself," and the modern precept, "Study nature," become at last one maxim.

10   II. The next great influence into the spirit of the scholar is the mind of the Past,—in whatever form, whether of literature, of art, of institutions, that mind is inscribed. Books are the best type of the influence of the past, and perhaps we shall get at the truth,—learn the amount of this influence more conveniently,—by considering their value alone.

11   The theory of books is noble. The scholar of the first age received into him the world around; brooded thereon; gave it the new arrangement of his own mind, and uttered it again. It came into him life; it went out from him truth. It came to him short-lived actions; it went out from him immortal

thoughts. It came to him business; it went from him poetry. It was dead fact; now, it is quick thought. It can stand, and it can go. It now endures, it now flies, it now inspires. Precisely in proportion to the depth of mind from which it issued, so high does it soar, so long does it sing.

12   Or, I might say, it depends on how far the process had gone, of transmuting life into truth. In proportion to the completeness of the distillation, so will the purity and imperishableness of the product be. But none is quite perfect. As no air-pump can by any means make a perfect vacuum, so neither can any artist entirely exclude the conventional, the local, the perishable from his book, or write a book of pure thought, that shall be as efficient, in all respects, to a remote posterity, as to contemporaries, or rather to the second age. Each age, it is found, must write its own books; or rather, each generation for the next succeeding. The books of an older period will not fit this.

13   Yet hence arises a grave mischief. The sacredness which attaches to the act of creation, the act of thought, is transferred to the record. The poet chanting was felt to be a divine man: henceforth the chant is divine also. The writer was a just and wise spirit: henceforward it is settled the book is perfect; as love of the hero corrupts into worship of his statue. Instantly the book becomes noxious: the guide is a tyrant. The sluggish and perverted mind of the multitude, slow to open to the incursions of Reason, having once so opened, having once received this book, stands upon it, and makes an outcry if it is disparaged. Colleges are built on it. Books are written on it by thinkers, not by Man Thinking; by men of talent, that is, who start wrong, who set out from accepted dogmas, not from their own sight of principles. Meek young men grow up in libraries, believing it their duty to accept the view which Cicero, which Locke, which Bacon, have given; forgetful that Cicero, Locke, and Bacon were only young men in libraries when they wrote these books.

14   Hence, instead of Man Thinking, we have the bookworm. Hence the book-learned class, who value books, as such; not as related to nature and the human constitution, but as making a sort of Third Estate with the world and the soul. Hence the restorers of readings, the emendators, the bibliomaniacs of all degrees.

15   Books are the best of things, well used; abused, among the worst. What is the right use? What is the one end which all means go to effect? They are for nothing but to inspire. I had better never see a book than to be warped by its attraction clean out of my own orbit, and made a satellite instead of a system. The one thing in the world, of value, is the active soul. This every man is entitled to; this every man contains within him, although in almost all men obstructed and as yet unborn. The soul active sees absolute truth and utters truth, or creates. In this action it is genius; not the privilege of here and there a favorite, but the sound estate of every man. In its essence it is progressive. The book, the college, the school of art, the

institution of any kind, stop with some past utterance of genius. This is good, say they,—let us hold by this. They pin me down. They look backward and not forward. But genius looks forward: the eyes of man are set in his forehead, not in his hindhead: man hopes: genius creates. Whatever talents may be, if the man create not, the pure efflux of the Deity is not his;—cinders and smoke there may be, but not yet flame. There are creative manners, there are creative actions, and creative words; manners, actions, words, that is, indicative of no custom or authority, but springing spontaneous from the mind's own sense of good and fair.

16   On the other part, instead of being its own seer, let it receive from another mind its truth, though it were in torrents of light, without periods of solitude, inquest, and self-recovery, and a fatal disservice is done. Genius is always sufficiently the enemy of genius by overinfluence. The literature of every nation bears me witness. The English dramatic poets have Shakspearized now for two hundred years.

17   Undoubtedly there is a right way of reading, so it be sternly subordinated. Man Thinking must not be subdued by his instruments. Books are for the scholar's idle times. When he can read God directly the hour is too precious to be wasted in other men's transcripts of their readings. But when the intervals of darkness come, as come they must,—when the sun is hid and the stars withdraw their shining—we repair to the lamps which were kindled by their ray, to guide our steps to the East again, where the dawn is. We hear, that we may speak. The Arabian proverb says, "A fig tree, looking on a fig tree becometh fruitful."

18   It is remarkable, the character of the pleasure we derive from the best books. They impress us with the conviction that one nature wrote and the same reads. We read the verses of one of the great English poets, of Chaucer, of Marvell, of Dryden, with the most modern joy,—with a pleasure, I mean, which is in great part caused by the abstraction of all *time* from their verses. There is some awe mixed with the joy of our surprise, when this poet, who lived in some past world, two or three hundred years ago, says that which lies close to my own soul, that which I also had well-nigh thought and said. But for the evidence thence afforded to the philosophical doctrine of the identity of all minds, we should suppose some preëstablished harmony, some foresight of souls that were to be, and some preparation of stores for their future wants, like the fact observed in insects, who lay up food before death for the young grub they shall never see.

19   I would not be hurried by any love of system, by any exaggeration of instincts, to underrate the Book. We all know, that as the human body can be nourished on any food, though it were boiled grass and the broth of shoes, so the human mind can be fed by any knowledge. And great and heroic men have existed who had almost no other information than by the printed page. I only would say that it needs a strong head to bear that diet. One must be an inventor to read well. As the proverb says, "He that would

bring home the wealth of the Indies, must carry out the wealth of the Indies." There is then creative reading as well as creative writing. When the mind is braced by labor and invention, the page of whatever book we read becomes luminous with manifold allusion. Every sentence is doubly significant, and the sense of our author is as broad as the world. We then see, what is always true, that as the seer's hour of vision is short and rare among heavy days and months, so is its record, perchance, the least part of his volume. The discerning will read, in his Plato or Shakspeare, only that least part,—only the authentic utterances of the oracle;—all the rest he rejects, were it never so many times Plato's and Shakspeare's.

20 Of course there is a portion of reading quite indispensable to a wise man. History and exact science he must learn by laborious reading. Colleges, in like manner, have their indispensable office,—to teach elements. But they can only highly serve us when they aim not to drill, but to create; when they gather from far every ray of various genius to their hospitable halls, and by the concentrated fires, set the hearts of their youth on flame. Thought and knowledge are natures in which apparatus and pretension avail nothing. Gowns and pecuniary foundations, though of towns of gold, can never countervail the least sentence or syllable of wit. Forget this, and our American colleges will recede in their public importance, whilst they grow richer every year.

21 III. There goes in the world a notion that the scholar should be a recluse, a valetudinarian,—as unfit for any handiwork or public labor as a penknife for an axe. The so-called "practical men" sneer at speculative men, as if, because they speculate or *see,* they could do nothing. I have heard it said that the clergy,—who are always, more universally than any other class, the scholars of their day,—are addressed as women; that the rough, spontaneous conversation of men they do not hear, but only a mincing and diluted speech. They are often virtually disfranchised; and indeed there are advocates for their celibacy. As far as this is true of the studious classes, it is not just and wise. Action is with the scholar subordinate, but it is essential. Without it he is not yet man. Without it thought can never ripen into truth. Whilst the world hangs before the eye as a cloud of beauty, we cannot even see its beauty. Inaction is cowardice, but there can be no scholar without the heroic mind. The preamble of thought, the transition through which it passes from the unconscious to the conscious, is action. Only so much do I know, as I have lived. Instantly we know whose words are loaded with life, and whose not.

22 The world,—this shadow of the soul, or *other me,*—lies wide around. Its attractions are the keys which unlock my thoughts and make me acquainted with myself. I run eagerly into this resounding tumult. I grasp the hands of those next me, and take my place in the ring to suffer and to work, taught by an instinct that so shall the dumb abyss be vocal with speech. I pierce its order; I dissipate its fear; I dispose of it within the circuit of my expanding

life. So much only of life as I know by experience, so much of the wilderness have I vanquished and planted, or so far have I extended my being, my dominion. I do not see how any man can afford, for the sake of his nerves and his nap, to spare any action in which he can partake. It is pearls and rubies to his discourse. Drudgery, calamity, exasperation, want, are instructors in eloquence and wisdom. The true scholar grudges every opportunity of action past by, as a loss of power. It is the raw material out of which the intellect moulds her splendid products. A strange process too, this by which experience is converted into thought, as a mulberry leaf is converted into satin. The manufacture goes forward at all hours.

23   The actions and events of our childhood and youth are now matters of calmest observation. They lie like fair pictures in the air. Not so with our recent actions,—with the business which we now have in hand. On this we are quite unable to speculate. Our affections as yet circulate through it. We no more feel or know it than we feel the feet, or the hand, or the brain of our body. The new deed is yet a part of life,—remains for a time immersed in our unconscious life. In some contemplative hour it detaches itself from the life like a ripe fruit, to become a thought of the mind. Instantly it is raised, transfigured; the corruptible has put on incorruption. Henceforth it is an object of beauty, however base its origin and neighborhood. Observe too the impossibility of antedating this act. In its grub state, it cannot fly, it cannot shine, it is a dull grub. But suddenly, without observation, the selfsame thing unfurls beautiful wings, and is an angel of wisdom. So is there no fact, no event, in our private history, which shall not, sooner or later, lose its adhesive, inert form, and astonish us by soaring from our body into the empyrean. Cradle and infancy, school and playground, the fear of boys, and dogs, and ferules, the love of little maids and berries, and many another fact that once filled the whole sky, are gone already; friend and relative, profession and party, town and country, nation and world, must also soar and sing.

24   Of course, he who has put forth his total strength in fit actions has the richest return of wisdom. I will not shut myself out of this globe of action, and transplant an oak into a flowerpot, there to hunger and pine; nor trust the revenue of some single faculty, and exhaust one vein of thought, much like those Savoyards, who, getting their livelihood by carving shepherds, shepherdesses, and smoking Dutchmen, for all Europe, went out one day to the mountain to find stock, and discovered that they had whittled up the last of their pine trees. Authors we have, in numbers, who have written out their vein, and who, moved by a commendable prudence, sail for Greece or Palestine, follow the trapper into the prairie, or ramble round Algiers, to replenish their merchantable stock.

25   If it were only for a vocabulary, the scholar would be covetous of action. Life is our dictionary. Years are well spent in country labors; in town; in the insight into trades and manufactures; in frank intercourse with many men

and women; in science; in art; to the one end of mastering in all their facts a language by which to illustrate and embody our perceptions. I learn immediately from any speaker how much he has already lived, through the poverty or the splendor of his speech. Life lies behind us as the quarry from whence we get tiles and copestones for the masonry of to-day. This is the way to learn grammar. Colleges and books only copy the language which the field and the work-yard made.

26   But the final value of action, like that of books, and better than books, is that it is a resource. The great principle of Undulation in nature, that shows itself in the inspiring and expiring of the breath; in desire and satiety; in the ebb and flow of the sea; in day and night; in heat and cold; and, as yet more deeply ingrained in every atom and every fluid, is known to us under the name of Polarity,—these "fits of easy transmission and reflection," as Newton called them, are the law of nature because they are the law of spirit.

27   The mind now thinks, now acts, and each fit reproduces the other. When the artist has exhausted his materials, when the fancy no longer paints, when thoughts are no longer apprehended and books are a weariness,—he has always the resource *to live*. Character is higher than intellect. Thinking is the function. Living is the functionary. The stream retreats to its source. A great soul will be strong to live, as well as strong to think. Does he lack organ or medium to impart his truths? He can still fall back on this elemental force of living them. This is a total act. Thinking is a partial act. Let the grandeur of justice shine in his affairs. Let the beauty of affection cheer his lowly roof. Those "far from fame," who dwell and act with him, will feel the force of his constitution in the doings and passages of the day better than it can be measured by any public and designed display. Time shall teach him that the scholar loses no hour which the man lives. Herein he unfolds the sacred germ of his instinct, screened from influence. What is lost in seemliness is gained in strength. Not out of those on whom systems of education have exhausted their culture, comes the helpful giant to destroy the old or to build the new, but out of unhandselled savage nature; out of terrible Druids[1] and Berserkers[2] come at last Alfred and Shakspeare.

28   I hear therefore with joy whatever is beginning to be said of the dignity and necessity of labor to every citizen. There is virtue yet in the hoe and the spade, for learned as well as for unlearned hands. And labor is everywhere welcome; always we are invited to work; only be this limitation observed, that a man shall not for the sake of wider activity sacrifice any opinion to the popular judgments and modes of action.

[1]Priests in ancient Gaul and Britain.

[2]Fierce warriors of Norse mythology.

29   I have now spoken of the education of the scholar by nature, by books, and by action. It remains to say somewhat of his duties.

30   They are such as become Man Thinking. They may all be comprised in self-trust. The office of the scholar is to cheer, to raise, and to guide men by showing them facts amidst appearances. He plied the slow, unhonored, and unpaid task of observation. Flamsteed[3] and Herschel,[4] in their glazed observatories, may catalogue the stars with the praise of all men, and the results being splendid and useful, honor is sure. But he, in his private observatory, cataloguing obscure and nebulous stars of the human mind, which as yet no man has thought of as such,—watching days and months sometimes for a few facts correcting still his old records;—must relinquish display and immediate fame. In the long period of his preparation he must betray often an ignorance and shiftlessness in popular arts, incurring the disdain of the able who shoulder him aside. Long he must stammer in his speech; often forego the living for the dead. Worse yet, he must accept—how often!—poverty and solitude. For the ease and pleasure of treading the old road, accepting the fashions, the education, the religion of society, he takes the cross of making his own, and, of course the self-accusation, the faint heart, the frequent uncertainty and loss of time, which are the nettles and tangling vines in the way of the self-relying and self-directed; and the state of virtual hostility in which he seems to stand to society, and especially to educated society. For all this loss and scorn, what offset? He is to find consolation in exercising the highest functions of human nature. He is one who raises himself from private considerations and breathes and lives on public and illustrious thoughts. He is the world's eye. He is the world's heart. He is to resist the vulgar prosperity that retrogrades even to barbarism by preserving and communicating heroic sentiments, noble biographies, melodious verse, and the conclusions of history. Whatsoever oracles the human heart, in all emergencies, in all solemn hours, has uttered as its commentary on the world of actions,—these he shall receive and impart. And whatsoever new verdict Reason from her inviolable seat pronounces on the passing men and events of to-day,—this he shall hear and promulgate.

31   These being his functions, it becomes him to feel all confidence in himself, and to defer never to the popular cry. He and he only knows the world. The world of any moment is the merest appearance. Some great decorum, some fetish of a government, some ephemeral trade or war, or man, is cried up by half mankind and cried down by the other half, as if all depended on this particular up or down. The odds are that the whole question is not worth the poorest thought which the scholar has lost in listening to the controversy. Let him not quit his belief that a popgun is a popgun, though

[3]John Flamsteed, 18th century English astronomer.

[4]Sir William Herschel, 18th century astronomer who discovered Uranus.

the ancient and honorable of the earth affirm it to be the crack of doom. In silence, in steadiness, in severe abstraction, let him hold by himself; add observation to observation, patient of neglect, patient of reproach, and bide his own time,—happy enough if he can satisfy himself alone that this day he has seen something truly. Success treads on every right step. For the instinct is sure, that prompts him to tell his brother what he thinks. He then learns that in going down into the secrets of his own mind he has descended into the secrets of all minds. He learns that he who has mastered any law in his private thoughts, is master to that extent of all men whose language he speaks, and of all into whose language his own can be translated. The poet, in utter solitude remembering his spontaneous thoughts and recording them, is found to have recorded that which men in crowded cities find true for them also. The orator distrusts at first the fitness of his frank confessions, his want of knowledge of the persons he addresses, until he finds that he is the complement of his hearers;—that they drink his words because he fulfils for them their own nature; the deeper he dives into his privatest, secretest presentiment, to his wonder he finds this is the most acceptable, most public, and universally true. The people delight in it; the better part of every man feels, This is my music; this is myself.

32   In self-trust all the virtues are comprehended. Free should the scholar be,—free and brave. Free even to the definition of freedom, "without any hindrance that does not arise out of his own constitution." Brave; for fear is a thing which a scholar by his very function puts behind him. Fear always springs from ignorance. It is a shame to him if his tranquility, amid dangerous times, arise from the presumption that like children and women his is a protected class; or if he seek a temporary peace by the diversion of his thoughts from politics or vexed questions, hiding his head like an ostrich in the flowering bushes, peeping into microscopes, and turning rhymes, as a boy whistles to keep his courage up. So is the danger a danger still; so is the fear worse. Manlike let him turn and face it. Let him look into its eye and search its nature, inspect its origin,—see the whelping of this lion,—which lies no great way back; he will then find in himself a perfect comprehension of its nature and extent; he will have made his hands meet on the other side, and can henceforth defy it and pass on superior. The world is his who can see through its pretension. What deafness, what stone-blind custom, what overgrown error you behold is there only by sufferance,—by your sufferance. See it to be a lie, and you have already dealt it its mortal blow.

33   Yes, we are the cowed,—we the trustless. It is a mischievous notion that we are come late into nature; that the world was finished a long time ago. As the world was plastic and fluid in the hands of God, so it is ever to so much of his attributes as we bring to it. To ignorance and sin, it is flint. They adapt themselves to it as they may; but in proportion as a man has any thing in him divine, the firmament flows before him and takes his signet and form. Not he is great who can alter matter, but he who can alter

my state of mind. They are the kings of the world who give the color of their present thought to all nature and all art, and persuade men by the cheerful serenity of their carrying the matter, that this thing which they do is the apple which the ages have desired to pluck, now at last ripe, and inviting nations to the harvest. The great man makes the great thing. Wherever Macdonald sits, there is the head of the table. Linnaeus makes botany the most alluring of studies, and wins it from the farmer and the herb-woman; Davy, chemistry; and Cuvier, fossils. The day is always his who works in it with serenity and great aims. The unstable estimates of men crowd to him whose mind is filled with a truth, as the heaped waves of the Atlantic follow the moon.

34   For this self-trust, the reason is deeper than can be fathomed,—darker than can be enlightened. I might not carry with me the feeling of my audience in stating my own belief. But I have already shown the ground of my hope, in adverting to the doctrine that man is one. I believe man has been wronged; he has wronged himself. He has almost lost the light that can lead him back to his prerogatives. Men are become of no account. Men in history, men in the world of to-day, are bugs, are spawn, and are called "the mass" and "the herd." In a century, in a millennium, one or two men; that is to say, one or two approximations to the right state of every man. All the rest behold in the hero or the poet their own green and crude being,— ripened; yes, and are content to be less, so *that* may attain to its full stature. What a testimony, full of grandeur, full of pity, is borne to the demands of his own nature, by the poor clansman, the poor partisan, who rejoices in the glory of his chief. The poor and the low find some amends to their immense moral capacity, for their acquiescence in a political and social inferiority. They are content to be brushed like flies from the path of a great person, so that justice shall be done by him to that common nature which it is the dearest desire of all to see enlarged and glorified. They sun themselves in the great man's light, and feel it to be their own element. They cast the dignity of man from their downtrod selves upon the shoulders of a hero, and will perish to add one drop of blood to make that great heart beat, those giant sinews combat and conquer. He lives for us, and we live in him.

35   Men, such as they are, very naturally seek money or power; and power because it is as good as money,—the "spoils," so called, "of office." And why not? for they aspire to the highest, and this, in their sleep-walking, they dream is highest. Wake them and they shall quit the false good and leap to the true, and leave governments to clerks and desks. This revolution is to be wrought by the gradual domestication of the idea of Culture. The main enterprise of the world for splendor, for extent, is the upbuilding of a man. Here are the materials strewn along the ground. The private life of one man shall be a more illustrious monarchy, more formidable to its enemy, more sweet and serene in its influence to its friend, than any kingdom in history. For a man, rightly viewed, comprehendeth the particular natures of

all men. Each philosopher, each bard, each actor has only done for me, as by a delegate, what one day I can do for myself. The books which once we valued more than the apple of the eye, we have quite exhausted. What is that but saying that we have come up with the point of view which the universal mind took through the eyes of one scribe; we have been that man, and have passed on. First, one, then another, we drain all cisterns, and waxing greater by all these supplies, we crave a better and more abundant food. The man has never lived that can feed us ever. The human mind cannot be enshrined in a person who shall set a barrier on any one side to this unbounded, unboundable empire. It is one central fire, which, flaming now out of the lips of Etna, lightens the capes of Sicily, and now out of the throat of Vesuvius, illuminates the towers and vineyards of Naples. It is one light which beams out of a thousand stars. It is one soul which animates all men.

VOCABULARY

sere (1)	bibliomaniacs (14)	empyrean (23)
metamorphosed (5)	efflux (15)	ferules (23)
monitory (7)	luminous (19)	Savoyards (24)
behoof (7)	allusion (19)	copestones (25)
refractory (8)	pecuniary (20)	unhandselled (27)
transmuting (12)	countervail (20)	retrogrades (30)
distillation (12)	valetudinarian (21)	inviolable (30)
noxious (13)	mincing (21)	promulgate (30)
incursions (13)	disfranchised (21)	ephemeral (31)
Third Estate (14)	contemplative (23)	adverting (34)
emendators (14)		

QUESTIONS FOR CRITICAL THINKING

1. What view of scholarship does Emerson present in his lecture? Does he ascribe to it a low or high value? Give reasons for your answers.

2. What dangers, capable of ruining scholarship, does Emerson warn against? Point to specific statements for your answers. Evaluate the author's view. If you disagree, state why.

3. According to the author, as the scholar matures, he acquires the ability to classify. What is the author's definition of classification? (See paragraph 8.) Do you agree with this definition? Supply an example of classification from your own experience.

4. Emerson lists three major resources of the true scholar: nature, books, and action. Do you consider any one of these resources more important than the others? If yes, which one? Why? Has the author neglected a resource you consider important? If yes, which one?

5. Emerson warns scholars against the pitfalls of becoming a book worm. How does one avoid this pitfall? Evaluate Emerson's suggestions and add suggestions of your own.

6. Emerson says that the scholar must also be a man of action or else he tends to become a coward. Do you agree or disagree? Support your answer with reasons and examples. What famous scholars have been men of action? Describe two or three.

7. What does Emerson mean when he says (paragraph 25) that "life is our dictionary"? What does he consider the "final value of action" (paragraph 26)? Why? What value do you attach to action?

QUESTIONS ON THE WRITING PROCESS

1. What rhetorical techniques reveal that this essay was originally delivered as a speech? Point to specific passages.

2. This address by Emerson has often been praised for its memorable single passages. What examples of such passages have you discovered? Point out at least three and interpret each one.

3. What plan has been superimposed on the address? How does Emerson indicate to his audience when he is moving to the next major point?

4. In paragraph 14, the word *hence* is repeated three times. What purpose does this repetition serve? Rewrite the paragraph without the repetition. Has anything been lost?

5. What examples of parallelism can you find in paragraph 30? Cite at least three. What is the purpose of parallelism?

WRITING ASSIGNMENTS

1. In 500 words, write an essay in which you provide your own definition of *scholar*. Be sure to answer the question, "What is a scholar?"

2. Write a 500-word critical analysis of a book that has deeply influenced or changed your life. In writing the essay, do not assume that your reader knows the book.

3. Write a brief essay in which you complete the following statement and use it as your thesis: "The greatest value of action in life is. . . ."

PUNK ROCK

Alexandra Witt

Punk rock is a unique blend of the bizarre, dissonant, violent, and flashy in the realm of rock music. It is not merely a style of music but also a style of dress and thought. It has progressed from a musical fad to a complete way of life.

The punk rock trend was founded in London by the poverty-stricken segment of society. When certain poor wanted to be noticed by all of London, they rebelled by starting this trendy movement. Critics consider it to be anti-hippy; yet it, like the hippy movement, is attempting to stress individuality and nonconformity to roles that society places on people. The main difference between punk rockers and hippies is in the punk rocker's outward expression of short hair, his outrageous display of color, and his bizarre clothing.

There are two main capitals of punk rock in the United States: New York and Los Angeles. The New York mecca for punk rockers is familiarly called The Village. It is here that many of today's punk bands were started and have their greatest concentration of followers. Bands such as XTC, the B52's, the Pretenders, and Devo have all played in The Village at one of the popular rock and roll clubs.

The first American punk rock group to be recognized was the Sex Pistols, whose lead singer, Johnny Rotten, displayed vulgar, repulsive actions during live performances. He played upon the reactions of his audience, and the more people reacted to him, the more he would scream and distort his act on stage.

Today's popular groups have opened up punk rock to more than a select few individuals. In fact, it has become a trendy, diverse, and widely accepted type of music. Punk rockers play in various places, ranging from daytime outdoor park concerts to the chic clubs that come alive with the setting of the sun. The clubs in The Village are geared toward the wealthy and vogue clientele, concentrating on the quality of sound and atmosphere. Most clubs offer a large dance floor in front of the stage which creates a "dance concert" influence on the audience. In general, the performers like the audience to get involved with the music and react in dance-type movements.

Typical dress for punk rockers is as far removed from normal dress as possible. Jumpsuits, tacky jeans with old t-shirts, tight spandex pants, leather, and distorted preppy clothing could all be classified as punk. Usually t-shirts are ripped and torn in strategic places, while the jumpsuits are adorned with rock and roll music buttons. A wide assortment of accessories adorn the outfits, including glasses of bizarre shape and color, bright belts, and chains draped over the body. Boots with spiked heels are a popular accent.

Punk rockers want their movement to accomplish several goals which they feel will benefit those who can understand their school of thought. They want people to "open up their minds and have a good time in life." Most of their tongue-in-cheek phrases and common expressions are used to shock people and provoke out-of-the-ordinary ideas.

Punk rock is a movement which has become popular in the United States and will no doubt last through the 1980s. However, knowing the change of styles and tastes in the past, I believe the next decade is bound to bring an entirely new wave of rock music to the world.

FOUR

EXAMPLE

Examples are so important to writing that most essays use them. Definition uses examples; so do causal analysis and argument. The example essay is taught by itself as a matter of pedagogical emphasis, not to signify any exclusive practice.

Basically, the example essay is an extended illustration of a point. It is an exercise in what is more accurately termed an *extended example.* The writer of an example essay may assemble a collection of facts to clarify a concept. Often, however, the writer uses anecdotes to illustrate a point, as the following excerpt shows.

> Out of all too many comparable cases, I will cite that of a man we may call Tim Kelleher, who worked steadily as a truck driver for forty years, supporting a wife and nine children. In his early sixties, Kelleher found jobs getting scarcer. Now in his late seventies, he has not worked for over a decade. Since his wife died a few years ago he has lived with one or another of his children.
>
> For two years his daughter Kathleen, mother of four, has been caring for him. Because the old man has grown progressively senile and burdensome, Kathleen's husband wants to shift the responsibility to the other children. But they all feel they've done their share.
>
> Mr. Kelleher's future depends on what his family decides to do with him. One of them may still be willing to take care of him, but if not, he will be committed to a state mental hospital. His case will be diagnosed as a "senile psychosis" or something similar. About a third of the patients now in our mental hospitals are such "geriatric" cases. This is how psychiatry meets a purely socioeconomic need.
>
> "What Psychiatry Can and Cannot Do," Thomas S. Szasz, M.D.

It is easy for students to confuse an isolated example with an extended example—to think that introducing a few facts prefaced by "for example" will satisfy the requirements of an example essay. When you are asked to write an essay giving examples of, say, the effects of poverty, it is not enough for you to merely list malnutrition, substandard housing, and cultural deprivation. Each of these effects, if fleshed out into an anecdote with appropriate detail, may indeed serve as the kind of extended example the essay calls for. But each must first be developed in some detail.

The excerpts and essays in this chapter illustrate the use of examples as specific detail in support of an idea or opinion. The examples vary from the anecdotal material found in such essays as "What Psychiatry Can and Cannot Do," "Three Incidents," and "Slang Origins," to the recital of facts, statistics, and cases found in "Getting Dizzy by the Numbers," and "The Stock Market of Literature." Each kind of example—the fact and the anecdote—has its appropriate use, and both share a common function: to make abstract statements more concrete and therefore more understandable.

It is rather a simple matter to introduce and use examples of any kind. What is difficult is to think up appropriate ones that support the idea or concept you are trying to impart. The introduction typically used is the straightforward "for example." But if it is clear from the context of the writing that an example is being given, the introductory phrase or word may easily be omitted.

Some commonsense ideas should guide your use of examples. First, your examples should always be appropriate to the point they are intended to support. Second, the examples should not overshadow the idea of the essay. This is another way of saying that giving too many examples is as bad as giving too few. Sometimes writers who have little to say will resort to padding with examples. But this is a transparent strategy that is easily seen through. Third, your example should be properly introduced, if the context of the writing does not already make it clear that you are giving one. Finally, you should not use the phrase "for example" unless you really intend to give an example. Consider these two sentences taken from an actual student essay: "I don't like history. For example, it bores me." Being bored by history is not an example of why or how one doesn't like it. More accurately, it is either a cause—I don't like history because it bores me—or a consequence—As a result of disliking history, I am bored by it. Neither requires the use of a prefacing "for example."

SINGLE PARAGRAPHS

WOMEN'S LANGUAGE

Robin Lakoff

Robin Lakoff (1942–   ) is a professor of linguistics at the University of California, Berkeley. She has been particularly recognized for her work on linguistic stereotypes and on the language associated with sex roles. Among her books is Language and Women's Place *(1975).*

The following paragraph is excerpted from an essay entitled "You Are What You Say," which appeared in the July 1974 issue of Ms.

"Women's language" shows up in all levels of English. For example, women are encouraged and allowed to make far more precise discriminations in naming colors than men do. Words like *mauve, beige, ecru, aquamarine, lavender,* and so on, are unremarkable in a woman's active vocabulary, but largely absent from that of most men. I know of no evidence suggesting that women actually *see* a wider range of colors than men do. It is simply that fine discriminations of this sort are relevant to women's vocabularies, but not to men's; to men, who control most of the interesting affairs of the world, such distinctions are trivial—irrelevant.

VOCABULARY

discriminations   unremarkable

QUESTIONS FOR CRITICAL THINKING

1. What is implied by the expression "She doesn't talk like a lady"?
2. "She thinks like a man." Do you consider this description complimentary or uncomplimentary? Give reasons for your answer.
3. What are some other examples of expressions that women commonly use but that men shun?

QUESTIONS ON THE WRITING PROCESS

1. What is the topic sentence that controls this paragraph?
2. How does the author notify the reader that she is about to provide supporting details for the topic sentence?
3. What is the antecedent for *it* at the beginning of the final sentence?

WRITING ASSIGNMENTS

1. Write a paragraph in which you provide examples of typical male expressions. Begin with a suitable topic sentence.
2. Write a paragraph in which you analyze the difference in connotation between the words *spinster* and *bachelor.* Begin with a suitable topic sentence.

A LAWYER'S PARAGRAPH

David S. Levine

David Levine received a law degree from the University of California, Berkeley. He practices commercial and general law in Oakland, California. From 1969 to 1978 he worked as a part-time correspondent for Time *magazine.*

A lawyer attributes the archaic and confusing writing style of his profession to the fact that legal language has freely borrowed from multiple sources over centuries.

A lawyer's paragraph may contain words or phrases borrowed from so many sources and centuries that the clashing styles create a kind of grotesque technocratic poetry. Thus, one hardly ever buys "land" without buying "herididaments and tenements" too. There are differences among the three words, but most literate people (and most literate lawyers) would be hard pressed to appreciate them when forced to penetrate an attorney's version of a real estate sales contract. Equally familiar, in the language of wills we leave the "rest, residue, and remainder" of our worldly possessions to our "heirs, successors, and assigns." This "Rule of Threes" has a distinguished ancestry in the law. On the wall of my office, a hand-lettered-on-parchment lease agreement for property located in the City of London, dated 26 August 1842, contains the following:

covenants, conditions and agreements
executors, administrators and assigns
paid, observed and performed
for and during and unto
leave, surrender and yield up
enter and come into and upon
carry on or permit or suffer to be carried on
retain, repossess and enjoy
observing, performing and keeping
have, hold, use, occupy, possess and enjoy
signed, sealed and delivered

Some of these triplets contain words of subtly different meaning; others contain pyramiding words (one contained inside the second, and both contained inside the third); some are inserted because of the form and procedural requirements of a lease agreement; all may be found in twentieth-century legal instruments and guidebooks. This is our verbal heritage.

VOCABULARY

grotesque   pyramiding
technocratic   procedural

QUESTIONS FOR CRITICAL THINKING

1. What is your reaction to most legal language? Do you think the field of law could replace it with clean, concise, straightforward terms?
2. Are there other professions that seem to thrive on murky, confusing language? Give an example.
3. Why do you think legal language tends to be so complex?

QUESTIONS ON THE WRITING PROCESS

1. What transition is used to introduce the first example?
2. What transition announces the second example?
3. Why is the phrase "and most literate lawyers" placed in parentheses?
4. Why is *pyramiding* an excellent word to describe some of the triplets offered as examples?
5. Where is the topic sentence of the paragraph located? Restate it in your own words.
6. How does the author label legal language? What does he mean by such a label?
7. What is the first example offered by the author? Comment on the example.

WRITING ASSIGNMENTS

1. Write a paragraph developing the topic sentence "Slang is forceful but transient" with examples.
2. Write a paragraph in which you offer examples of trite expressions often used in writing. Begin with a topic sentence.

GETTING DIZZY BY THE NUMBERS

Frank Trippett

Frank Trippett (1926–   ) is a senior writer on the staff of Time *magazine. He is also a contributor to* The First Horseman *(1974), a book about the early history of the human race.*

This essay, reprinted from the October 29, 1979, issue of Time, *analyzes modern man's obsession with numbers so large that they cannot be comprehended.*

1   "The very hairs of your head," says *Matthew 10:30,* "are all numbered." There is little reason to doubt it. Increasingly, everything tends to get numbered one way or another, everything that can be counted, measured, averaged, estimated or quantified. Intelligence is gauged by a quotient, the humidity by a ratio, the pollen by its count, and the trends of birth, death, marriage and divorce by rates. In this epoch of runaway demographics, society is as often described and analyzed with statistics as with words. Politics seems more and more a game played with percentages turned up by pollsters, and economics a learned babble of ciphers and indexes that few people can translate and apparently nobody can control. Modern civilization, in sum, has begun to resemble an interminable arithmetic class in which, as Carl Sandburg put it, "numbers fly like pigeons in and out of your head."

2   Most of this numbering is useful, and a good deal of it is indispensable. In any event, the world could hardly have wound up otherwise. Human beings began counting and "falling under the spell of numbers," in H. G. Wells' words, well before they could write. Long ago, the entire species was like some modern aboriginal peoples (the Damara and some Hottentots in Africa, for example) who possess words only for numbers up to three, every larger quantity being simply expressed as "many." A fascination with the multiplicity of things, together with a quenchless scientific yen, pushed the main body of mankind, however, inevitably into its present plight—a time when so many stunning measurements are bandied about that numbers plunge in and out of the brain more like galaxies than pigeons.

3   The trouble is that with everything on earth (and off, too) being quantified, micro and macro, the world is becoming woefully littered with numbers that defy useful comprehension. Biology, for example, estimates that the human brain contains some 1 trillion cells. But can any imagination get a practical hold on such a quantity? It is easy to picture the symbolic numerals: 1,000,000,000,000. Still, who can comprehend that many individual units of anything at one time? The number teases, dazzles the mind and even dizzies it, but that does not add up to understanding. Biology ought to find out what happens to the brain when it tries to visualize 1 trillion.

139

4   Boggling figures of that sort have been popular as curiosities ever since Archimedes tried to calculate how many grains of sand the universe could contain (10^{51}, he said). Today, however, mind-walloping numbers are no longer oddities; they are the stuffing of ordinary news and public discourse. While even the biggest figures no doubt possess meaning, it is impossible not to suspect that many casually circulated numbers might as well be the music of the spheres.

5   Nowadays the commonest statistics about the world and the nation—from the megatonnages of the SALT debate to the dollars of the defense budget—tend to defeat the ordinary imagination. The world's population is supposedly 4.2 billion. The nation's G.N.P. is running at about $2.39 trillion. Washington debates whether defense spending will increase to as much as $122 billion. . . . In truth, far smaller figures can overtax ordinary people, many of whom, after all, have trouble fathoming the weather service's temperature-humidity index.

6   Scientific news is loaded with even more forbidding challenges. Voyager I, it seems, found a hot spot in the vicinity of Jupiter that is 300 million to 400 million degrees centigrade. Later, Voyager II, going almost 45,000 m.p.h., came as close as 404,000 miles to Jupiter's cloud tops on its way to Uranus—some 1.6 billion miles out there. Science now has an electron microscope that can magnify 20 million times and so can photograph a particle with a diameter of about 4 billionths of an inch. Computers can do 80 million calculations a second (and ostensibly 6.9 trillion a day). Other recent news: a suspicion that the proton, a basic natural building block, may be unstable. It may indeed be decaying at such a rate that it would peter out in a million billion billion billion years. The effect of that notion is finally not mathematical but purely poetic.

7   It is not clear at just what magnitude (or diminutude) a number passes beyond the capacity of an ordinary person to grasp—that is, to picture the quantity. Yet obviously a great effort is required even to cope with what is symbolized by a billion. The proof lies in those familiar tormented illustrations that writers cook up in the hope of suggesting the amount of a billion: the 125-mile-high stack of dollar bills that would add up to about a billion, the airplane propeller turning around the clock at 2,400 r.p.m. that would fall short of spinning a billion times in a year, the fact that a billion minutes ago (A.D. 77) the Christian era had scarcely got under way. Still, such efforts to evoke the actuality of a billion are far likelier to give the curious a picture of an extremely tall stack of currency than of the quantity of a billion units. In truth, most mega-numbers (and micro-numbers) that fly by these days paralyze the mind almost as much as a googol.

8   Indeed, the googol might be a good symbol for a time when the world is under the sway of technology, when it has no choice, as Jacques Ellul says

in *The Technological Society,* but to "don mathematical vestments." The googol is the figure 1 followed by 100 zeros. It was made famous, or infamous, in the 1930s by Mathematician Edward Kasner. He also offered the googolplex, which is 1 followed by a googol of zeros—so many zeros, said Kasner, that no matter how tiny they could not all be written on a piece of paper as wide as the visible universe.

9   It could be that the googol's emergence marked the time when mankind's fascination with indigestible numbers slipped beyond the pale. In the same decade that the googol appeared, Sir Arthur Eddington opened his absolutely serious book, *The Philosophy of Physical Science,* with the sentence: "I believe there are 15,747,724,136,275,002,577,605,653,961,181,555,-468,044,717,914,527,116,709,366,231,425,076,185,631,031,296 protons in the universe and the same number of electrons."

10   Plainly, a world that feeds on such impenetrable figures suffers a peculiar compulsion that might be called googolmania. The hunger is, whatever else, a marvel to behold, providing the spectacle of a species unable to solve a 13% inflation rate, yet eager to be informed by the *Guinness Book of World Records* that the world weighs 6,585,600,000,000,000,000,000 tons.

11   The human craving for numbers tells a good deal about mankind. It is both sign and cause of man's long trek from the days of one, two, three, many. It can be taken as a symptom of exuberant joy in the quantity and multiplicity of things. Still, the dizzy acceptance of those truly incomprehensible figures might also be construed as a vicarious variation of the old Faustian game: the yearning to know the unknowable.

12   So far, the game has not cost the species its unquantifiable soul. Enough of that remains to nurture widespread excitement over, let us say, a World Series. A googol may not tell us much about where we stand today, but even Edward Kasner would have appreciated the true human relevance of 4–3 Pirates.

VOCABULARY

quantified (1)	macro (3)	pale (9)
gauged (1)	curiosities (4)	impenetrable (10)
quotient (1)	discourse (4)	exuberant (11)
demographics (1)	megatonnages (5)	multiplicity (11)
interminable (1)	G.N.P. (5)	incomprehensible (11)
aboriginal (2)	diminutude (7)	Faustian (11)
micro (3)	indigestible (9)	

QUESTIONS FOR CRITICAL THINKING

1. Before reading this essay, were you aware of the frequency with which large numbers are used in our society? If so, can you name some of the fields in which large numbers are used?
2. The spread of huge numbers is a sign of the complexity of modern society. What other signs can you cite?
3. Trippett states that man's soul is "unquantifiable." What does he mean? Do you agree? Explain your view of man's soul, if you believe man has one.
4. Surely incomprehensible numbers are not the only forbidding challenge connected with scientific news. What other forbidding challenges are there? What is your response?

QUESTIONS ON THE WRITING PROCESS

1. What is the purpose of the Biblical quotation at the beginning of the essay?
2. In paragraph 3, how does the author emphasize the effect of large numbers on the mind? What contrast follows?
3. What is the effect of placing *diminutude* in parentheses (see paragraph 7)?
4. In paragraph 8, why does the author quote Jacques Ellul?
5. What is the tone of the final paragraph? What purpose does it serve?

WRITING ASSIGNMENTS

1. Write a 300-word essay in which you argue that modern life has been spoiled by too much technology. Provide at least three examples.
2. Write a 300-word essay in which you argue for the usefulness of numbers. Provide some appropriate examples.
3. Write a 300-word essay telling how a knowledge of mathematics has helped you (or how the lack of knowledge of mathematics has hindered you) in the past. Provide some appropriate examples.

THREE INCIDENTS

The Talk of the Town

"The Talk of the Town," an editorial column written by staff members, appears in each issue of The New Yorker.

The essay that follows appeared in the September 15, 1980, issue of The New Yorker. *In it the writer charmingly portrays three examples of nature as a bungler remindful of human beings.*

1 A friend who lives in the country writes:

2 I am fully aware that anecdotal evidence is no longer, if it ever was, in good scientific repute. Nevertheless, in the course of the past few months I have been witness to three aberrations of nature that seem to me to be worth noting. They suggest, if nothing else, that, contrary to much received understanding, man is not the only form of life that is capable of making a fool of itself. The first of these incidents occurred in the spring, just under the eaves in our front veranda. There is a fixture up there, a galvanized-iron box about the size and shape of a thick paperback book (it has something to do with the outdoor lights), that forms a kind of shelf. I came out on the veranda one morning in time to see a bird—a little red-breasted house finch—make a landing there on the top of the box and deposit a beakful of grass. I stood on tiptoe and craned my neck, and saw the beginnings of a nest. It was in many ways an excellent nesting site—dry, airy, nicely sheltered. But it was also as slippery as glass. And, as I watched, a gust of breeze came along and the nest slid off and blew away in pieces. Well, that, I thought, is that. The bird, however, thought differently. It went to work again, retrieving the scattered grasses, and started another nest. Another doomed nest, I should say. Because another little breeze came along and scattered that nest, too. But the finch was undismayed. I watched it start still another nest, and I watched that nest blow away. That was enough for me. I went on with my own affairs. But every now and then through the rest of the day I went over to the door or the window and looked out. The finch was always there—sitting on the box, fluttering away, swooping back with a wisp of grass. And there was still nothing more than the pathetic beginnings of a nest.

3 The second incident occurred in the house, in the attic. I went up there a couple of weeks ago to look for something or other. I was feeling my way toward an old chest of drawers when something odd caught my eye. It was a strand of ivy espaliered on the wall above the little end window. It was two or three feet long, its leaves were a sickly yellowy green, and it had forced itself, at God knows what exertion, through a tiny crack in the window frame from the life-giving sunlight into the deadly dusk of the attic.

143

4   And then, just the other day, I was out weeding the garden and sat down on the bench to rest and noticed an anthill at my feet. There was much coming and going around the hole—a stream of foraging workers. I leaned down and watched a worker emerge from the hole, race away through the grass, pounce on a tiny something—a seed, maybe, or an egg or a minuscule creature—and head quickly back toward the hole. Only, it headed in the wrong direction. It raced this way and that, back and forth, farther and farther away from home. I had to get up from the bench to follow it. I finally lost it, in a weedy jungle, a good eight feet (the equivalent, perhaps, of a couple of miles) from where it wanted to be. I went back to the bench and sat down again and wondered. It might be possible, I thought, to somehow see the strivings of the finch as an example of determination, an iron procreative perseverance. And the ivy: its suicidal floundering, too, might be explained—as an evolutionary thrust, an urge (like that of some aquatic organism feeling its way up a beach) to try a new environment. But the ant! There was no way of rationalizing that: the phenomenon of a worker ant— an ant bred exclusively to forage for its queen—unable to find its way home. It shook and shattered the concept of a knowing and nurturing instinct, of a computerized infallibility, in nature. I felt a tug of something like sympathy for that errant ant. And also for the finch and the ivy. They gave me a new vision of nature: a nature unmechanized, a nature vulnerable, a nature appealingly natural.

VOCABULARY

anecdotal (2)	undismayed (2)	phenomenon (4)
repute (2)	espaliered (3)	nurturing (4)
aberrations (2)	foraging (4)	infallibility (4)
galvanized (2)	minuscule (4)	errant (4)
retrieving (2)	procreative (4)	

QUESTIONS FOR CRITICAL THINKING

1.   What examples can you present to prove that nature is unerring?
2.   Nature can be both benevolent and cruel. What examples can you present to illustrate either the benevolence or the cruelty of nature?
3.   What other adjectives suggest certain aspects of nature? Provide examples to prove your choice.

QUESTIONS ON THE WRITING PROCESS

1. How is the essay organized? Does the organization evolve naturally or is it artificially imposed?
2. The thesis statement does not appear in its traditional spot either at the beginning or at the end of the first paragraph. How, then, can the reader recognize the thesis?
3. In addition to setting each example in a separate paragraph, what transitions are used to indicate that the writer is moving from one example to the next?

WRITING ASSIGNMENTS

1. Write a 300-word essay in which you give three illustrations of nature as kind or beautiful. Use one paragraph for each illustration. Begin with a thesis.
2. Write a 300-word essay in which you give three illustrations of nature as ugly or cruel. Use one paragraph for each illustration. Begin with a clear thesis.
3. Beginning with a clear thesis and supplying appropriate examples, write a 300-word essay in which you prove that nature is often lavish (or miserly, if you prefer).

SLANG ORIGINS

Woody Allen

Woody Allen (1934–   ) began writing jokes for columnists and celebrities while still in high school. Extremely versatile, he not only writes successful books, short stories, plays, and screen plays, but also directs and stars in his own movies. His books include Getting Even *(1971) and* Without Feathers *(1975).*

"Slang Origins" is a satiric essay claiming to explain the origins of certain expressions in our language.

1   How many of you have ever wondered where certain slang expressions come from? Like "She's the cat's pajamas," or to "take it on the lam." Neither have I. And yet for those who are interested in this sort of thing I have provided a brief guide to a few of the more interesting origins.

2   Unfortunately, time did not permit consulting any of the established works on the subject, and I was forced to either obtain the information from friends or fill in certain gaps by using my own common sense.

3   Take, for instance, the expression "to eat humble pie." During the reign of Louis the Fat, the culinary arts flourished in France to a degree unequaled anywhere. So obese was the French monarch that he had to be lowered onto the throne with a winch and packed into the seat itself with a large spatula. A typical dinner (according to DeRochet) consisted of a thin crepe appetizer, some parsley, an ox, and custard. Food became the court obsession, and no other subject could be discussed under penalty of death. Members of a decadent aristocracy consumed incredible meals and even dressed as foods. DeRochet tells us that M. Monsant showed up at the coronation as a weiner, and Etienne Tisserant received papal dispensation to wed his favorite codfish. Desserts grew more and more elaborate and pies grew larger and larger until the minister of justice suffocated trying to eat a seven-foot "Jumbo Pie." *Jumbo* pie soon became *jumble* pie and "to eat a jumble pie" referred to any kind of humiliating act. When the Spanish seamen heard the word *jumble,* they pronounced it "humble," although many preferred to say nothing and simply grin.

4   Now, while "humble pie" goes back to the French, "take it on the lam" is English in origin. Years ago, in England, "lamming" was a game played with dice and a large tube of ointment. Each player in turn threw dice and then skipped around the room until he hemorrhaged. If a person threw seven or under he would say the word "quintz" and proceed to twirl in a frenzy. If he threw over seven, he was forced to give every player a portion of his feathers and was given a good "lamming." Three "lammings" and a player was "kwirled" or declared a moral bankrupt. Gradually any game with feathers was called "lamming" and feathers became "lams." To "take it

on the lam" meant to put on feathers and later, to escape, although the transition is unclear.

5   Incidentally, if two of the players disagreed on the rules, we might say they "got into a beef." This term goes back to the Renaissance when a man would court a woman by stroking the side of her head with a slab of meat. If she pulled away, it meant she was spoken for. If, however, she assisted by clamping the meat to her face and pushing it all over her head, it meant she would marry him. The meat was kept by the bride's parents and worn as a hat on special occasions. If, however, the husband took another lover, the wife could dissolve the marriage by running with the meat to the town square and yelling, "With thine own beef, I do reject thee. Aroo! Aroo!" If a couple "took to the beef" or "had a beef" it meant they were quarreling.

6   Another marital custom gives us that eloquent and colorful expression of disdain, "to look down one's nose." In Persia it was considered a mark of great beauty for a woman to have a long nose. In fact, the longer the nose, the more desirable the female, up to a certain point. Then it became funny. When a man proposed to a beautiful woman he awaited her decision on bended knee as she "looked down her nose at him." If her nostrils twitched, he was accepted, but if she sharpened her nose with pumice and began pecking him on the neck and shoulders, it meant she loved another.

7   Now, we all know when someone is very dressed up, we say he looks "spiffy." The term owes its origin to Sir Oswald Spiffy, perhaps the most renowned fop of Victorian England. Heir to treacle millions, Spiffy squandered his money on clothes. It was said that at one time he owned enough handkerchiefs for all the men, women and children in Asia to blow their noses for seven years without stopping. Spiffy's sartorial innovations were legend, and he was the first man ever to wear gloves on his head. Because of extra-sensitive skin, Spiffy's underwear had to be made of the finest Nova Scotia salmon, carefully sliced by one particular tailor. His libertine attitudes involved him in several notorious scandals, and he eventually sued the government over the right to wear earmuffs while fondling a dwarf. In the end, Spiffy died a broken man in Chichester, his total wardrobe reduced to kneepads and a sombrero.

8   Looking "spiffy," then, is quite a compliment, and one who does is liable to be dressed "to beat the band," a turn-of-the-century expression that originated from the custom of attacking with clubs any symphony orchestra whose conductor smiled during Berlioz. "Beating the band" soon became a popular evening out, and people dressed up in their finest clothes, carrying with them sticks and rocks. The practice was finally abandoned during a performance of the *Symphonie fantastique* in New York when the entire string section suddenly stopped playing and exchanged gunfire with the first ten rows. Police ended the melee but not before a relative of J. P. Morgan's was wounded in the soft palate. After that, for a while at least, nobody dressed "to beat the band."

9   If you think some of the above derivations questionable, you might throw up your hands and say, "Fiddlesticks." This marvelous expression originated in Austria many years ago. Whenever a man in the banking profession announced his marriage to a circus pinhead, it was the custom for friends to present him with a bellows and a three-year supply of wax fruit. Legend has it that when Leo Rothschild made known his betrothal, a box of cello bows was delivered to him by mistake. When it was opened and found not to contain the traditional gift, he exclaimed, "What are these? Where are my bellows and fruit? Eh? All I rate is fiddlesticks!" The term "fiddlesticks" became a joke overnight in the taverns amongst the lower classes, who hated Leo Rothschild for never removing the comb from his hair after combing it. Eventually "fiddlesticks" meant any foolishness.

10   Well, I hope you've enjoyed some of these slang origins and that they stimulate you to investigate some on your own. And in case you were wondering about the term used to open this study, "the cat's pajamas," it goes back to an old burlesque routine of Chase and Rowe's, the two nutsy German professors. Dressed in oversized tails, Bill Rowe stole some poor victim's pajamas. Dave Chase, who got great mileage out of his "hard of hearing" specialty, would ask him:

CHASE: Ach, Herr Professor. Vot is dot bulge under your pocket?
ROWE: Dot? Dot's de chap's pajamas.
CHASE: The cat's pajamas? Ut mein Gott?

11   Audiences were convulsed by this sort of repartee and only a premature death of the team by strangulation kept them from stardom.

VOCABULARY

culinary (3)	pumice (6)	melee (8)
winch (3)	fop (7)	J. P. Morgan (8)
crepe (3)	treacle (7)	derivations (9)
decadent (3)	sartorial (7)	bellows (9)
papal (3)	libertine (7)	Leo Rothschild (9)
dispensation (3)	notorious (7)	burlesque (10)
hemorrhaged (4)	sombrero (7)	repartee (11)
disdain (6)	Berlioz (8)	strangulation (11)

QUESTIONS FOR CRITICAL THINKING

1. What is Woody Allen's purported purpose? Where is it stated?
2. At what point does the reader realize that the essay cannot possibly be accurate or scholarly?
3. What effect does the accumulation of examples produce? What is your personal reaction to them?
4. Which example do you find the funniest? Why?

QUESTIONS ON THE WRITING PROCESS

1. How does Woody Allen pretend to be a linguistic scholar? Cite examples from the essay.
2. What makes Woody Allen's humor so effective? Cite some examples.
3. How does the author turn the opening question into humor?
4. What is the purpose of directly addressing the reader in paragraph 9?
5. What effect does the accumulation of examples produce? What is your personal reaction to them?
6. Which example do you find the funniest? Why?

WRITING ASSIGNMENTS

1. Using Woody Allen's essay as a model, write a 300-word essay creating your own humorous "origins" of slang expressions commonly used today.
2. Using Woody Allen's essay as a model for form only, write a 300-word essay tracing the real origins of three to five interesting words, phrases, or expressions in the English language. The following library reference works will be of help.

   Morris, William, and Mary Morris. *Dictionary of Word and Phrase Origins.* 3 vols. New York: Harper & Row, 1971.

   Partridge, Eric. *Dictionary of Slang and Unconventional English.* 7th ed. New York: Macmillan, 1970.
3. Write a 300-word essay to prove that certain television shows are truly funny. Provide appropriate examples to prove your thesis.

OF WHAT USE?

Isaac Asimov

Isaac Asimov (1920–   ), sometimes pseudonymously Paul French or Dr. "A," was born in the U.S.S.R. but was brought to the United States at the age of three. A professor of biochemistry at Boston University, he writes respected books in scientific fields and has written on Shakespeare and the Bible; however, he is best known as the author of science fiction stories such as I, Robot *(1950),* The Caves of Steel *(1954), and* The Gods Themselves *(1973). A prolific talent, he is said to have produced an average of one book every six weeks over the last thirty years. His science fiction story "Nightfall," written when he was twenty-one, is still considered a model.*

Although originally appearing as an introduction to a book on modern research, entitled The Greatest Adventure, *the following piece stands as an independent essay, making a significant statement about knowledge and its practical use.*

1 It is the fate of the scientist to face the constant demand that he show his learning to have some "practical use." Yet it may not be of any interest to him to have such a "practical use" exist; he may feel that the delight of learning, of understanding, of probing the Universe is its own reward entirely. In that case, he might even allow himself the indulgence of contempt for anyone who asks more.

2 There is a famous story of a student who asked the Greek philosopher Plato, about 370 B.C., of what use were the elaborate and abstract theorems he was being taught. Plato at once ordered a slave to give the student a small coin so that he might not think he had gained knowledge for nothing, then had him dismissed from the school.

3 The student need not have asked, and Plato need not have scorned. Who would today doubt that mathematics has its uses? Mathematical theorems which seem unbearably refined and remote from anything a sensible man can have any interest in turn out to be absolutely necessary to such highly essential parts of our modern life as, for instance, the telephone network that knits the world together.

4 This story of Plato, famous for two thousand years, has not made the matter plainer to most people. Unless the application of a new discovery is clear and present, most are dubious of its value.

5 There is a story of the English scientist Michael Faraday that illustrates this. He was in his time an enormously popular lecturer as well as a physicist and chemist of the first rank. In one of his lectures in the 1840s, he illustrated the peculiar behavior of a magnet and a spiral coil of wire which

150

was connected to a galvanometer that would record the presence of an electric current.

6 There was no current in the wire to begin with, but when the magnet was thrust into the hollow center of the spiral coil, the needle of the galvanometer moved to one side of the scale, showing that a current was flowing. When the magnet was withdrawn from the coil, the needle flipped in the other direction, showing that the current was now flowing the other way. When the magnet was held motionless in any position within the coil, there was no current at all, and the needle was motionless.

7 At the conclusion of the lecture, one member of the audience approached Faraday and said, "Mr. Faraday, the behavior of the magnet and the coil of wire was interesting, but of what possible use can it be?"

8 And Faraday answered politely, "Sir, of what use is a newborn baby?"

9 It was precisely the phenomenon whose use was questioned so peremptorily by one of the audience which Faraday made use of to develop the electric generator, which, for the first time, made it possible to produce electricity cheaply and in quantity. That, in turn, made it possible to build the electrified technology that surrounds us today and without which life, in the modern sense, is inconceivable. Faraday's demonstration was a newborn baby that grew into a giant.

10 Even the shewdest of men cannot always judge what is useful and what is not. There never was a man so ingeniously practical in judging the useful as Thomas Alva Edison, surely the greatest inventor who ever lived, and we can take him as our example.

11 In 1868, he patented his first invention. It was a device to record votes mechanically. By using it, congressmen could press a button and all their votes would be instantly recorded and totaled. There was no question but that the invention worked; it remained only to sell it. A congressman whom Edison consulted, however, told him, with mingled amusement and horror, that there wasn't a chance of the invention's being accepted, however unfailingly it might work.

12 A slow vote, it seemed, was sometimes a political necessity. Some congressmen might have their opinions changed in the course of a slow vote where a quick vote might, in a moment of emotion, commit Congress to something undesirable.

13 Edison, chagrined, learned his lesson. After that, he decided never to invent anything unless he was sure it would be needed and wanted and not merely because it worked.

14 He stuck to that. Before he died, he had obtained nearly 1300 patents— 300 of them over a four-year stretch, or one every five days, on the average. Always, he was guided by his notion of the useful and the practical.

15 On October 21, 1879, he produced the first practical electric light, perhaps the most astonishing of all his inventions. (We need only sit by can-

dlelight for a while during a power breakdown to discover how much we accept, and take for granted, the electric light.)

16 In succeeding years, Edison labored to improve the electric light and, mainly, to find ways of making the glowing filament last longer before breaking. As was usual with him, he tried everything he could think of. One of his hit-and-miss efforts was to seal a metal wire into the evacuated electric light bulb, near the filament but not touching it. The two were separated by a small gap of vacuum.

17 Edison then turned on the electric current to see if the presence of a metal wire would somehow preserve the life of the glowing filament. It didn't and Edison abandoned the approach. However, he could not help noticing that an electric current seemed to flow from the filament to the wire across that vacuum gap.

18 Nothing in Edison's vast practical knowledge of electricity explained that, and all Edison could do was to observe it, write it up in his notebooks, and, in 1884 (being Edison), patent it. The phenomenon was called the "Edison effect" and it was Edison's only discovery in pure science.

19 Edison could see no use for it. He therefore pursued the matter no further and let it go, while he continued the chase for what he considered the useful and practical.

20 In the 1880s and 1890s, however, scientists who pursued "useless" knowledge for its own sake discovered that subatomic particles (eventually called "electrons") existed, and that the electric current was accompanied by a flow of electrons. The Edison effect was the result of the ability of electrons, under certain conditions, to travel, unimpeded, through a vacuum.

21 In 1904, the English electrical engineer John Ambrose Fleming (who had worked in Edison's London office in the 1880s in connection with the developing electric light industry) made use of the Edison effect and of the new understanding which the electron theory had brought, and devised an evacuated glass bulb with a filament and wire which would let current pass through in one direction and not in the other. The result was a "current rectifier."

22 In 1906, the American inventor Lee De Forest made a further elaboration of Fleming's device, introducing a metal plate which enabled it to amplify electric current as well as rectify it. The result is called a "radio tube" by Americans.

23 It is called that because it was only such a device that could handle an electric current with sufficient rapidity and delicacy to make the radio a practical device for receiving and transmitting sound carried by the fluctuating amplitude of radio waves.

24 In fact, the radio tube made all of our modern electronic devices possible, including television.

25 The Edison effect, then, which the practical Edison shrugged off as interesting but useless, turned out to have more astonishing results than

any of his practical devices. In a power breakdown, candles and kerosene lamps can substitute (however poorly) for the electric light, but what substitute is there for a television screen? We can live without it (if we consider it only an entertainment device, which does it wrong), but not many people seem to want to.

26   In fact, the problem isn't a matter of showing that pure science can be useful. It is much more difficult a problem to find some branch of science that *isn't* useful. Between 1900 and 1930, for instance, theoretical physics underwent a revolution. The theory of relativity and the development of quantum mechanics led to a new and more subtle understanding of the basic laws of the universe and of the behavior of the inner components of the atom.

27   None of it seemed to have the slightest use to mankind, and the scientists involved, a brilliant group of young men, had apparently found an ivory tower for themselves which nothing could disturb. Those who survived into later decades looked back on that happy time of abstraction and impracticality as a Garden of Eden out of which they had been evicted.

28   For out of that abstract work, there unexpectedly came the nuclear bomb, and a world that lives in terror, now, of a possible war that could destroy mankind in a day.

29   But it did not bring only terror. Out of that work, there came radio-isotopes which have made it possible to probe the workings of living tissue with a delicacy otherwise quite impossible, and whose findings have revolutionized medicine in a thousand ways. There are also nuclear power stations which, at present and in the future, offer mankind the brightest hope of ample energy during all his future existence on Earth.

30   There is nothing, it turns out, that is more practical, more downright important to the average man, whether for good or for evil, than the ivory tower researches of the young men of the early twentieth century who could see no use in what they were doing and were glad of it, for they wanted only to revel in knowledge for its own sake.

31   The point is, we cannot foresee the consequences in detail. Plato, in demonstrating the theorems of geometry, did not envisage a computerized society. Faraday knew that his magnet-born electric current was a newborn baby, but he surely did not foresee our electrified technology. Edison certainly didn't foresee a television set when he puzzled over the electric current that leaped the vacuum, and Einstein, when he worked out the equation $E = mc^2$ from purely theoretical considerations in 1905, did not sense the mushroom cloud as he did so.

32   We can only make the general rule that through all of history, an increased understanding of the Universe, however out-of-the-way a particular bit of new understanding may seem, however ethereal, however abstract, however useless, has always ended in some practical application (even if sometimes only indirectly).

33   It cannot be predicted what the application will be in advance, but we can be sure that it will have both its beneficial and its uncomfortable aspects. (The discovery of the germ theory of disease by Louis Pasteur in the 1860s was the greatest single advance ever made in medicine and led to the saving of countless millions of lives. Who can quarrel with that? Yet it has also led, in great measure, to the dangerous population explosion of today.)

34   It remains for the wisdom of mankind to make the decisions by which advancing knowledge will be used well and not ill, but all the wisdom of mankind will never improve the material lot of man unless advancing knowledge presents it with the matters over which it can make those decisions. And when, despite the most careful decisions, there come dangerous side effects of the new knowledge—it is only still further advances in knowledge that will offer hope for correction.

35   And now we stand in the closing decades of the twentieth century, with science advancing as never before in all sorts of odd, and sometimes apparently useless, ways. We've discovered quasars and pulsars in the distant heavens. Of what use are they to the average man? Astronauts have brought back Moon rocks at great expense. So what? Scientists discover new compounds, develop new theories, work out new mathematical complexities. What for? What's in it for you?

36   No one knows what's in it for you right now, any more than Plato knew in his time, or Faraday knew, or Edison knew, or Einstein knew.

37   But you will know if you live long enough; and if not, your children or grandchildren will know. And they will smile at those who say, "But what is the use of sending rockets into space?" just as we now smile at the person who asked Faraday the use of his demonstration.

38   In fact, unless we continue with science and gather knowledge, whether it is seemingly useful on the spot or not, we will be buried under our problems and find no way out.

39   It is up to you, then, and up to everyone, to support science and, where possible, to keep abreast of it, for today's science is tomorrow's solution— and tomorrow's problems, too—and most of all, mankind's greatest adventure, now and forever.

VOCABULARY

peremptorily (9)	envisage (31)	quasars (35)
chagrined (13)	ethereal (32)	pulsars (35)
amplitude (23)		

QUESTIONS FOR CRITICAL THINKING

1. How does the author answer the question posed in the title of the essay? What makes his answer convincing?
2. The author indicates clearly his awareness of both the advantages and disadvantages imbedded in pure science. How does he reconcile the paradox? Do you agree with his view? Why or why not?
3. In paragraph 35, the author mentions the recent discoveries made by astronomers and astronauts delving into the vastness of space. What is your opinion of the value of this research, which has cost billions of dollars but so far has yielded few practical results?
4. Most students have taken college classes where the knowledge disseminated at first seemed utterly useless but later on revealed a useful application. What useful application can you foresee for certain abstract, ethereal, or impractical knowledge you have been asked to pursue in college? Cite one or two specific examples.

QUESTIONS ON THE WRITING PROCESS

1. What pattern of organization does the author use in presenting his examples? What advantage, if any, is gained by using this pattern?
2. In paragraph 36, the author makes a sudden shift in point of view. What is the shift and what purpose does it achieve?
3. In paragraph 27, what is the meaning of the "ivory tower" metaphor and the allusion to the Garden of Eden? Explain both.
4. In what paragraph does it become clear that the author's motive is to persuade as well as to inform? What is your response?

WRITING ASSIGNMENTS

1. Write a 500-word essay in which you list at least three examples of the most useful inventions in the history of mankind. Begin with a clear thesis.
2. In 500 words speculate on what practical benefits the vast sums of money presently spent on astronomical research may yield for the future.
3. Write a persuasive essay either attacking or defending the government's budget for space exploration.

WHAT PSYCHIATRY CAN AND CANNOT DO

Thomas S. Szasz, M.D.

Thomas Szasz (1920–   ), psychiatrist and author, came to the United States from Hungary in 1938. Throughout his writing, which includes eleven books, he has waged a war against psychiatry as generally practiced in the United States. Dr. Szasz believes that the label "mental illness" too often hides the existence of real problems of living. Law, Liberty, and Psychiatry (1963) forcefully argues Dr. Szasz's position.

The following essay, reprinted from the February 1964 issue of Harper's magazine, provides some telling examples to prove the thesis that although eccentrics and social misfits may be a burden to their families and a nuisance to the public, usually they are not "mentally ill" and hospitalizing them may do more harm than good.

1   Psychiatry today is in the curious position of being viewed simultaneously with too much reverence and with undue contempt. Indeed thoughtful Americans can be roughly divided between those who dismiss all forms of psychiatric practice as worthless or harmful and those who regard it as a panacea for crime, unhappiness, political fanaticism, promiscuity, juvenile delinquency—and virtually every other moral, personal, and social ill of our time.

2   The adherents of this exaggerated faith are, I believe, the larger and certainly the more influential group in shaping contemporary social policy. It is they who beat the drums for large-scale mental-health programs and who use the prestige and the services of a massive psychiatric establishment as a shield of illusion, concealing some ugly realities we would rather not face. Thus when we read in the paper that the alcoholic, the rapist, or the vandal needs or will be given "psychiatric care," we are reassured that the problem is being solved or, in any event, effectively dealt with, and we dismiss it from our minds.

3   I contend that we have no right to this easy absolution from responsibility. In saying this I do not, as a practicing psychiatrist, intend to belittle the help which my profession can give to some troubled individuals. We have made significant progress since the pre-Freudian era when psychiatry was a purely medical and custodial enterprise. In contemporary America, much of psychiatric practice consists of psychotherapy, and much of psychiatric theory is psychological and social, rather than biological and medical.

4   Our refusal to recognize this difference—that is, between deviations from biological norms which we usually call "illness," and deviations from social norms which we call "mental illness" (or crime, delinquency, etc.)—has made it possible to popularize the simplistic clichés of current mental-

health propaganda. One of these, for instance, is the deceptive slogan, "Mental illness is like any other illness." This is not true; psychiatric and medical problems are not fundamentally similar. In curing a disease like syphilis or pneumonia, the physician benefits both the patient and society. Can the psychiatrist who "cures" a "neurosis" make the same claim? Often he cannot, for in "mental illness" we find the individual *in conflict* with those about him—his family, his friends, his employer, perhaps his whole society. Do we expect psychiatry to help the individual—or society? If the interests of the two conflict, as they often do, the psychiatrist can help one only by harming the other.

5   Let us, for example, examine the case of a man I will call Victor Clauson. He is a junior executive with a promising future, a wife who loves him, and two healthy children. Nevertheless he is anxious and unhappy. He is bored with his job, which he believes saps his initiative and destroys his integrity; he is also dissatisfied with his wife, and convinced he never loved her. Feeling like a slave to his company, his wife, and his children, Clauson realizes that he has lost control over the conduct of his life.

6   Is this man "sick"? And if so, what can be done about it? At least half a dozen alternatives are open to him. He could throw himself into his present work or change jobs or have an affair or get a divorce. Or he could develop a psychosomatic symptom such as headaches and consult a doctor. Or, as still another alternative, he could seek out a psychotherapist. Which of these alternatives is the *right* one for him? The answer is not easy.

7   For in fact, hard work, an affair, a divorce, a new job may all "help" him; and so may psychotherapy. But "treatment" cannot change his external, social situation; only he can do that. What psychoanalysis (and some other therapies) *can* offer him is a better knowledge of himself, which may enable him to make *new choices* in the conduct of his life.

8   Is Clauson "mentally sick"? If we so label him, what then is he to be cured of? Unhappiness? Indecision? The consequences of earlier unwise decisions?

9   These are problems in living, not diseases. And by and large it is such problems that are brought to the psychiatrist's office. To ameliorate them he offers not treatment or cure but psychological counseling. To be of any avail this process requires a consenting, cooperative client. There is, indeed, no way to "help" an individual who does not want to be a psychiatric patient. When treatment is *imposed* on a person, inevitably he sees it as serving not his own best interests, but the interests of those who brought him to the psychiatrist (and who often pay him).

10   Take the case of an elderly widow I will call Mrs. Rachel Abelson. Her husband was a successful businessman who died five years ago, bequeathing part of his estate of $4 million to his children and grandchildren, part to charities, and one-third to his wife. Mrs. Abelson had always been a frugal woman, whose life revolved around her husband. After he died, however,

she changed. She began to give her money away—to her widowed sister, to charities, and finally to distant relatives abroad.

11   After a few years, Mrs. Abelson's children remonstrated, urging her to treat herself better instead of wasting her money on people who had long managed by themselves. But Mrs. Abelson persisted in doing what she felt was "the right thing." Her children were wealthy; she enjoyed helping others.

12   Finally, the Abelson children consulted the family attorney. He was equally dismayed by the prospect that Mrs. Abelson might spend all the money she controlled in this fashion. Like the children, he reasoned that if Mr. Abelson had wanted to help his third cousin's poverty-stricken daughters in Romania, he could have done so himself; but he never did. Convinced they ought to carry out the essence of their father's intention and keep the money in the family, the Abelson children petitioned to have their mother declared mentally incompetent to manage her affairs. Thereafter Mrs. Abelson became inconsolable. Her bitter accusations and the painful scenes that resulted only convinced her children that she really was mentally abnormal. When she refused to enter a private sanitarium voluntarily, she was committed by court order. She died two years later, and her will—leaving most of her assets to distant relatives—was easily broken on psychiatric grounds.

13   Like thousands of other involuntary mental patients, Mrs. Abelson was given psychiatric care in the hope of changing behavior offensive to others. Indeed, what was Mrs. Abelson's illness? Spending her money unwisely? Disinheriting her sons? In effect, recourse to psychiatry provided Mrs. Abelson's children with a socially acceptable solution for their dilemma, not hers. To an appalling degree state mental hospitals perform a like function for the less affluent members of our society.

14   Out of all too many comparable cases, I will cite that of a man we may call Tim Kelleher, who worked steadily as a truck driver for forty years, supporting a wife and nine children. In his early sixties, Kelleher found jobs getting scarcer. Now in his late seventies, he has not worked for over a decade. Since his wife died a few years ago he has lived with one or another of his children.

15   For two years his daughter Kathleen, mother of four, has been caring for him. Because the old man has grown progressively senile and burdensome, Kathleen's husband wants to shift the responsibility to the other children. But they all feel they've done their share.

16   Mr. Kelleher's future depends on what his family decides to do with him. One of them may still be willing to take care of him, but if not, he will be committed to a state mental hospital. His case will be diagnosed as a "senile psychosis" or something similar. About a third of the patients now in our mental hospitals are such "geriatric" cases. This is how psychiatry meets a purely socioeconomic need.

17   If Mr. Kelleher or one of his children were even moderately wealthy, they could hire a companion or nurse to care for him at home or they could place him in a private nursing home. There would be no need to label him a "mental patient" and confine him to a building he will never again leave, and where he will doubtless die within a year.

18   But for the poor, the public mental hospital is often the only way. Such is the plight of Mrs. Anna Tarranti (this is not her real name). At thirty-two— but looking ten years older—she has just been delivered of her seventh child. Her husband is a construction worker, sporadically employed, and a heavy drinker. After each of the last three babies was born, Mrs. Tarranti was so "depressed" that she had to stay in the hospital an extra week or more. Now she complains of exhaustion, cannot eat or sleep, and does not want to see her baby. At the same time she feels guilty for not being a good mother and says she ought to die.

19   The fact is that Mrs. Tarranti is overwhelmed. She has more children than she wants, a husband who earns only a marginal living, and religious beliefs that virtually prohibit birth control. What should she do? She knows that if she goes home, she'll soon be pregnant again, a prospect she cannot tolerate. She would like to stay in the hospital, but the obstetrical ward is too busy to keep her long without a bona fide obstetrical illness.

20   Again, psychiatry comes to the rescue. Mrs. Tarranti's condition is diagnosed as a "post-partum depression" and she is committed to the state hospital. As in the case of Mr. Kelleher, society has found no more decent solution to a human problem than involuntary confinement in a mental hospital.

21   In effect psychiatry has accepted the job of warehousing society's undesirables. Such, alas, has long been its role. More than a hundred years ago, the great French psychiatrist Philippe Pinel observed that "public asylums for maniacs have been regarded as places of confinement for such of its members as have become dangerous to the peace of society."

22   Nor have we any right to comfort ourselves with the belief that in our enlightened age confinement in a mental institution is really the same as any other kind of hospitalization. For even though we show more compassion and understanding toward the insane than some of our forebears, the fact is that the person diagnosed as mentally ill is stigmatized—particularly if he has been confined in a public mental hospital. These stigmata cannot be removed by mental-health "education," for the root of the matter is our intolerance of certain kinds of behavior.

23   Most people who are considered mentally sick (especially those confined involuntarily) are so defined by their relatives, friends, employers, or perhaps the police—*not* by themselves. These people have upset the social order—by disregarding the conventions of polite society or by violating laws—so we label them "mentally ill" and punish them by commitment to a mental institution.

24   The patient knows that he is deprived of freedom because he has annoyed others, not because he is sick. And in the mental hospital, he learns that until he alters his behavior, he will be segregated from society. But even if he changes and is permitted to leave, his record of confinement goes with him. And the practical consequences are more those of a prison than a hospital record. The psychological and social damage thus incurred often far outweighs the benefits of any psychiatric therapy.

25   Consider, for example, the case of a young nurse I will call Emily Silverman who works in a general hospital in a small city. Unmarried and lonely, she worries about the future. Will she find a husband? Will she have to go on supporting herself in a job that has become drudgery? She feels depressed, sleeps poorly, loses weight. Finally, she consults an internist at the hospital and is referred to a psychiatrist. He diagnoses her trouble as a case of "depression" and prescribes "antidepressant" drugs. Emily takes the pills and visits the psychiatrist weekly, but she remains depressed and begins to think about suicide. This alarms the psychiatrist, who recommends hospitalization. Since there is no private mental hospital in the city, Emily seeks admission to the state hospital nearby. There, after a few months, she realizes that the "treatment" the hospital offers cannot help her solve her problems. She then "recovers" and is discharged.

26   From now, Emily is no longer just a nurse; she is a nurse with a "record" of confinement in a state mental hospital. When she tries to return to her job, she will probably find it filled and that there are no openings. Indeed, as an ex-mental patient she may find it impossible to obtain any employment in nursing. This is a heavy price to pay for ignorance, yet no one warned her of the hazards involved before she decided to enter the hospital for her "depression."

27   Because the therapeutic potentialities of psychiatry are consistently exaggerated and its punitive functions minimized or even denied, a distorted relationship between psychiatry and the law has evolved in our time.

28   Years ago some people accused of serious crimes pleaded "insanity." Today they are often charged with it. Instead of receiving a brief jail sentence, a defendant may be branded "insane" and incarcerated *for life* in a psychiatric institution.

29   This is what happened, for example, to a filling-station operator I will call Joe Skulski. When he was told to move his business to make way for a new shopping center, he stubbornly resisted eviction. Finally the police were summoned. Joe greeted them with a warning shot in the air. He was taken into custody and denied bail, because the police considered his protest peculiar and thought he must be crazy. The district attorney requested a pretrial psychiatric examination of the accused. Mr. Skulski was examined, pronounced mentally unfit to stand trial, and confined in the state hospital for the criminally insane. Through it all, he pleaded for the right to be tried for his offense. Now in the mental hospital he will spend years of

fruitless effort to prove that he is sane enough to stand trial. If convicted, his prison sentence would have been shorter than the term he has already served in the hospital.

30   Joe, like most patients in public mental hospitals, is a victim of social injustice. A wealthy and important man would have a chance, and the means, to rebut the charge of mental illness—as indeed happened when the government last year tried to handle the incident of General Edwin Walker in this fashion.

31   All this is not to say that our public mental hospitals serve no socially necessary purpose. They do, in fact, perform two essential—and very different—functions. On the one hand, they help *patients* recover from personal difficulties by providing them with room, board, and a medically approved escape from everyday responsibilities. On the other hand, they help *families* (and society) care for those who annoy or burden them unduly. It is important that we sort out these very different services, for unfortunately their goals are not the same. To relieve people annoyed by the eccentricities, failings, or outright meanness of so-called mentally disturbed persons requires that something be done *to* mental patients, not *for* them. The aim here is to safeguard the sensibilities not of the patient, but of those he upsets. This is a moral and social, not a medical, problem. How, for example, do you weigh the right of Mr. Kelleher to spend his declining years in freedom and dignity rather than as a psychiatric prisoner, against the right of his children to lead a "life of their own" unburdened by a senile father? Or the right of Mrs. Tarranti to repudiate overwhelming responsibilities against her husband's and children's need for the services of a full-time wife and mother? Or the right of Mrs. Abelson to give away her money to poor relatives, against her children's claim on their father's fortune?

32   Granting that there can often be no happy resolution to such conflicts, there is no reason to feel that we are as yet on the right road. For one thing—we still tolerate appalling inequities between our treatment of the rich and the poor. Though it may be no more than a dimly grasped ideal, both medicine and law strive to treat all people equally. In psychiatry, however, we not only fail to approximate this goal in our practice; we do not even value it as an ideal.

33   We regard the rich and influential psychiatric patient as a self-governing, responsible client—free to decide whether or not to be a patient. But we look upon the poor and the aged patient as a ward of the state—too ignorant or too "mentally sick" to know what is best for him. The paternalistic psychiatrist, as an agent of the family or the state, assumes "responsibility" for him, defines him as a "patient" against his will, and subjects him to "treatment" deemed best for him, with or without his consent.

34   Do we really need more of this kind of psychiatry?

VOCABULARY

panacea (1)
adherents (2)
custodial (3)
psychosomatic (6)
ameliorate (9)
remonstrated (11)
inconsolable (12)
appalling (13)

geriatric (16)
sporadically (18)
marginal (19)
stigmatized (22)
incurred (24)
therapeutic (27)
potentialities (27)

punitive (27)
incarcerated (28)
rebut (30)
eccentricities (31)
safeguard (31)
inequities (32)
paternalistic (33)

QUESTIONS FOR CRITICAL THINKING

1. What is your personal answer to the rhetorical question posed at the end of the essay? Comment on your point of view.
2. What is your opinion of psychiatry? Do you find it helpful or harmful? Give examples to support your answer.
3. How would you answer each question posed in the last half of paragraph 31?
4. What factor, if any, has retarded the progress of proper psychiatric treatment in our society?
5. If you do not trust psychiatry, what alternate treatment would you suggest for people with mental or emotional problems? Why do you suggest this alternate method?

QUESTIONS ON THE WRITING PROCESS

1. Psychiatrists, psychologists, and social workers have a special name to describe the kinds of examples used in this essay. What is it?
2. How does the author make sure that his readers will know when he is giving an example?
3. This essay does not contain a one-sentence thesis to which we can readily point. Nevertheless, the reader is not left in doubt as to the author's purpose. How is the purpose revealed?
4. What purpose does the quotation (paragraph 21) by Philippe Pinel serve?
5. In paragraph 31, what is the antecedent of *this* in the opening sentence beginning "All *this* . . . ."?
6. Why is the presentation of examples an effective method of proving a point such as the one made by Dr. Szasz?

WRITING ASSIGNMENTS

1. Write a 500-word theme in which you take the position that psychiatry is of great benefit to our present society. Use appropriate examples to bolster your position.

2. Write a 500-word essay giving examples to demonstrate that religious faith helps people with emotional and mental problems. Offer appropriate examples to support your view.

3. Write a 500-word essay citing examples of mental institutions as hideous prisons.

HOMO MONSTROSUS

Annemarie de Waal Malefijt

Annemarie de Waal Malefijt (1914–   ) was born in the Netherlands but came to the United States in 1951 to study anthropology at Columbia University in New York. Presently she teaches anthropology at Hunter College (City of New York University), where her area of concentration is the history of anthropology.

The essay that follows is the result of the author's library research on how throughout history the idea of manlike creatures with weird characteristics has prevailed. However, her study also reaches into the area of modern-day prejudice toward people who are "different."

1   When Carl von Linné (Linnaeus) worked out his monumental classification of natural things in the 18th century, he included the species *Homo monstrosus*. By *Homo monstrosus* he meant a species related to *Homo sapiens* but markedly different in physical appearance. To do Linnaeus full justice, he was quite aware that there were men on all continents who belonged to the species *Homo sapiens*. He nonetheless believed, as many of his contemporaries and predecessors did, that in remote areas there were manlike creatures with weird characteristics.

2   The belief in the existence of monstrous races had endured in the Western world for at least 2,000 years. During that time a rich assortment of semihuman creatures were described by explorers and travelers, whose accounts were probably based largely on malformed individuals and the desire to enhance their own fame at home. No part of the human body was neglected; each was conceived as having elaborate variations. There were, for example, peoples with tiny heads, with gigantic heads, with pointed heads, with no heads, with detachable heads, with dog heads, with horse heads, with pig snouts and with bird beaks. In the absence of knowledge about faraway places (and about the limits of human variation) men populated them with creatures of their imagination.

3   At the same time there were efforts to explain how such strange beings could have originated and what was responsible for their extraordinary characteristics. Thus in the rise and decline of *Homo monstrosus* encounters ideas and attitudes that hold much interest for the modern anthropologist. The credulousness of those who accepted the reality of monstrous peoples is not so very different from the unfounded prejudices that human groups often harbor toward one another today, and one of the major tasks of anthropology is to clear away misinformation that may lead to such misunderstanding.

4   Among the earlier writers on fabulous peoples was the Greek historian Herodotus. In the fifth century B.C. he traveled widely in the world that was known to him. He was fairly objective in his accounts of the nearby Egyptians and Persians, and he certainly did not believe everything he was told. In lands far from home, however, people and their habits often appear more unusual; as Herodotus wrote, "The ends of the earth produce the things that we think most fair and rare." Thus he reports that in Ethiopia near the Egyptian border a tribe called the Troglodytes live underground. They eat snakes and lizards, and their language resembles the screeching of bats. Near the Atlas Mountains live the Atlantes, who are unable to dream. The Indian Padaei consume their fellow men as soon as they show the slightest sign of illness; the Libyan Adyrmachidae, after catching a flea on their person, give it bite for bite before throwing it away.

5   If human habits could be so strange, it was perhaps not surprising that physical differences also existed. Herodotus reports that the Agrippaei across the River Don are totally bald. In the mountains of the same region, so the bald men told him, are a goat-footed race of men and another group that sleeps six months of the year, hibernating like bears.

6   "I don't believe it," Herodotus comments, yet he continues. He describes the Arimaspi, who have only one eye situated in the middle of their forehead, and the griffins (half-lion, half-eagle) that guard hoards of gold. He writes that, according to the Libyans, their region has dog-headed men, headless people with eyes in their chest, wild men and wild women and many other monstrous races.

7   It may be that Herodotus actually heard such stories in his travels, but it should be noted that other Greeks of his time were acquainted with similar fabulous tales. Several centuries before Herodotus the poet Hesiod had mentioned one-eyed, dog-headed and breast-eyed tribes. Homer wrote about the one-eyed Cyclops and about giants and pygmies; the epic poet Aristeas spoke of the one-eyed Arimaspi. Herodotus thus did not invent the monsters; he was rather the first to locate them in actual geographic areas.

8   The Greeks knew that surrounding them were people with cultures quite different from their own. This may have made it easier for them to accept the monstrous races as a reality. There was at least one Greek theory of evolution that could account for the existence of hybrid creatures. Empedocles, a contemporary of Herodotus, held that parts of men and animals arose separately and independently. Hands wandered without arms, feet without legs and heads without trunks. These isolated parts combined at random, so that there could be animals with human heads or manlike creatures with the features of animals. Although in time only favorable combinations survived, peculiar ones could still be found.

9   Soon after the death of Herodotus reports about India added to the credibility of monstrous races. At the beginning of the fourth century B.C.

Ktesias, who had once been a physician at the Persian court, wrote that India was populated by many wondrous tribes. He described the Sciapodes, who had a single large foot on which they could hop faster than any biped. They made further use of this appendage by employing it as a kind of umbrella, holding it over their head for protection against the rain or the heat of the sun. The Cynocephali, or dog-headed ones, were said to bark rather than to use words; the Blemmyae were headless, with their face between their shoulders. There were people with ears so long they covered their arms as far as the elbow; others had long and very hairy tails; still others had eight fingers on each hand and eight toes on each foot.

10   Similar reports about India came from Megasthenes, the learned ambassador of the Babylonian king Seleucus I. Having served at the Indian court of Chandragupta, he added some new examples to the older ones and was the first to give currency to the tale of certain Indian nomads who had no nose but only small holes for nostrils. He also spoke of Sciapodes whose feet pointed backward, and of the happy Hyborians, whose lifespan was 1,000 years. The Phanesians, he said, had ears so long they slept in them, with one ear serving as a mattress and the other as a blanket. There were also Indian tribes that had dog ears or had an upper lip extending below their chin or had no mouth. The last, being unable to eat (or to speak), subsisted on the odor of roast meat and fruit and the perfume of flowers.

11   The invasion of India by Alexander the Great in 326 B.C. probably gave rise to similar reports. With Alexander's army were scholars charged with describing the countries through which they passed. Most of these writings have been lost, but the *Romance of Alexander* (which some scholars date back to 200 B.C.) was translated into many languages in the early Middle Ages. Together with the works of Megasthenes it was for centuries an important source of knowledge about the real and imaginary inhabitants of India.

12   A number of learned Greeks challenged the stories about monsters. The geographer Strabo, who lived at about the time of the birth of Christ, did not hesitate to call such tales mere superstition. Nonetheless, the tradition remained vigorously alive.

13   In the first century A.D. the Roman naturalist Pliny the Elder devoted several volumes of his encyclopedic *Historia Naturalis (Natural History)* to descriptions of the physical nature and manners of mankind. Asserting that he had read more than 2,000 books, Pliny repeated in a systematic manner all that had been said about monsters; he also added a few embellishments of his own. Some later commentators remarked that a more appropriate title for these writings would have been "Unnatural History." Pliny's contributions included the cannibal Scythians, who used skulls for drinking vessels; the Thibii, who had a double pupil in one eye and the image of a horse in the other, and the solitary Essenes, who lived without women and yet propagated. Other Roman writers, such as Pomponius Mela (first cen-

tury A.D.) and Caius Julius Solinus (third century), elaborated on Pliny. The ears of the Phanesians and the feet of the Sciapodes grew larger and larger; in the land of the Neuers the men were transformed into wolves in summer and regained human form in winter. These writers were important sources for the medieval acquaintance with monsters. Belief in their reliability was bolstered by reports of travelers and missionaries that were written with apparent sincerity and conviction.

14   Monstrous races presented a problem for the early church fathers. It was difficult to deny the reality of such creatures, not only because of the missionaries' reports but also because of the Bible. The Book of Genesis refers to races of giants. A passage in St. Jerome's translation of Isaiah reads: "And the hairy ones shall dance there." St. Jerome's own commentary explained that "the hairy ones" might be wild men.

15   In *The City of God* St. Augustine dealt with the question of the reality of such beings. If, he wrote, the stories about monsters are not plain lies, such beings either are not men at all or, if they are men, they are, like other men, descendants of Adam. St. Augustine tended to favor the last possibility. He argued that individual monstrous births do occur and are clearly descended from Adam. Monstrous races might therefore exist and be human.

16   Later medieval scholars asked themselves how such transformations could have taken place. A common answer was that the devil had so perverted the souls of some pagans that their appearance had also degenerated. Scripture could be invoked to prove that such changes were possible. The evil king Nebuchadnezzar had been transformed from a man into a beast-like creature; his hair grew like an eagle's feathers, his nails were like a bird's claws and he ate grass.

17   Other commentators who were less strict about the concept that man— monstrous or otherwise—had a single origin advanced the idea that monsters might have been separately created by the devil in an effort to confound God's creation, man. It was also deemed possible that monsters were creatures of the Antipodes who had managed to climb up over the edges of the (flat) world.

18   Meanwhile medieval travelers steadily made the monsters more monstrous. There were peoples with one eye, three eyes or five eyes, with eyes in the back of their head, with four or more arms and legs or with enormously long teeth. There were others without nostrils, without eyes, without a mouth or with a mouth so small they could only drink through a straw. Some had ears so long they hindered walking and had to be knotted together behind the back or wound around the arms; some had ears shaped like large fans. Some walked on all fours or had legs that were mere leather strips to that they could only crawl; some had spider legs or goat feet or bird claws. Some were entirely bald or exceedingly hairy; some had tails or had the neck as well as the head of horses or mice. There was also a tribe of creatures that had only a head; the rest of the body was lacking.

19   It was understood that monsters had monstrous habits; they were naked, lascivious, promiscuous and filthy; they had a bad smell and no religion. They ate snakes, lizards, dogs, mice, fleas and flies; they ate their parents or (after fattening them for years) their children.

20   The celebrated myth of Prester John lent further credence to fabulous creatures. In the 12th century there appeared the Latin text of a letter addressed to the Byzantine emperor Manuel Comnenus and purportedly written by Prester John, ruler of a realm in the East. Prester John professed to be a devout Christian whose land was enormously wealthy, harboring not only rich mineral resources but also the fountain of perpetual youth. The inhabitants of the region included, in addition to a normal human population, nearly all the marvelous and monstrous creatures ever described: wild men, men with horns, one-eyed men, pygmies, giants 40 ells (about 90 feet) tall, centaurs, fauns and so on.

21   The letter was widely accepted as being genuine. European monarchs were eager to discover Prester John's realm, if only to enlist a powerful ally in their struggle with Islam. Pope Alexander III wrote a letter to Prester John and entrusted it to his physician for personal delivery. The physician never returned. Many travelers who later set out to discover this earthly paradise did return, and they gave "eyewitness" accounts. As late as 1590 an English traveler by the name of Edward Webbe reported that he had visited Prester John's court and had seen a monster there. It was kept chained to prevent it from devouring human beings, but after executions it was fed human flesh. The geographic location of Prester John's country was variously conceived. At first it was usually in or near India; later it was in Abyssinia. The discovery of the Cape of Good Hope was due in part to the efforts of the Portuguese to find Prester John's country. Columbus believed he had passed near it.

22   Apart from the Prester John myth and the fictitious accounts of travelers, there were many literary sources dealing with monsters. One of the earliest encyclopedic works was *Etymologies,* written by Isidore of Seville in the seventh century A.D. Isidore attempted single-handedly to summarize all knowledge; he devoted a volume to "men and monsters," and he placed the monsters in definite geographic areas. This immensely popular work was translated into several languages and was often imitated. In the 13th century a similar work explicitly directed to unlearned people (*On the Properties of Things,* by Bartholomaeus Anglicus) was translated into six European languages; with the invention of the printing press it reached 46 editions. The popularity of monsters is further attested by the fact that printed pictures of them were often sold at country fairs.

23   Monstrous men are also depicted on the medieval *mappa mundi,* maps of the world. In earlier editions the fabulous races were drawn on the maps themselves, indicating their supposed geographic distribution. On a late-13th-century map in Hereford Cathedral the Sciapodes, pygmies and giants

are found in India, horse-hoofed and long-eared tribes in Scythia, and tailed satyrs and the Blemmyae in Abyssinia. On later maps the creatures often appear as border decorations, suggesting the direction in which they might be found.

24   In the Middle Ages monsters were cited to teach moral lessons. According to one 13th-century source, pygmies denoted humility, giants pride and Cynocephali harshness of temper. The long-lipped races were gossips and mischief-makers. In the widely translated *Gesta Romanorum,* a late-medieval collection of moral tales, the symbolism had changed. Long-lipped people now signified justice; long-eared ones were devout. (They were listening to the word of God.) The dog-headed people were humble. (They were said to be a model for priests.) The headless Blemmyae also represented humility.

25   The question St. Augustine had raised—Are the monstrous races human?— became a matter of practical concern with the discovery of the New World and its inhabitants. Columbus (convinced to the day of his death that he had found the sea route to India) wrote quite objectively about the Indians of Hispaniola (today Haiti and the Dominican Republic). They were, he said, well-made men who were so generous with their possessions that they never refused anything that was requested. He described the Carib Indians as being handsome of face and figure and intelligent. Nonetheless, Columbus also mentioned the existence of races that were hairless, tailed or dog-headed.

26   Later explorers less restrained than Columbus maintained that they had personally met Indians who were monstrous both in appearance and habits. It was necessary for Pope Paul II to declare explicitly (in his Papal Bull of 1537) that American Indians were fully human and in possession of an immortal soul.

27   Many Europeans had the opportunity to examine human representatives of the New World. Captured "specimens" where shipped to Europe and placed on public display; some of them, dressed in tiger skins and fed raw meat, were exhibited in cages. Even so, it must have been a disappointment to many onlookers that they had no tail, were not very hirsute and had only two eyes, two arms and normal-sized ears.

28   The character Caliban in *The Tempest* no doubt reflects attitudes toward the peoples of the New World in Shakespeare's time. Caliban is "as disproportion'd in his manners as in his shape," "a thing most brutish," a member of a "vile race," a "monster of the isle with four legs." He is filthy and smells like a fish, and one of the European sailors shipwrecked on his island at first mistakes him for a devil. Another sailor calls him a puppy-headed monster. Caliban is said to use the language taught him by his master, but only to curse. He has no capacity for abstraction and understands neither music nor love. "A devil, a born devil, on whose nature nurture can never stick. . . ."

29   The name Caliban is an anagram of *canibal* and this Spanish word is itself a corruption of *Caribal,* an inhabitant of the Caribbean islands. *Canibal* in turn suggests *canino,* Spanish for "dog." The Cynocephali come readily to mind, the more so because of the term "puppy-headed monster." Shakespeare thus equated the monstrous Caliban with inhabitants of the New World. A further indication that he was thinking of the New World in *The Tempest* is his mention of "vex'd Bermoothes" (Bermuda).

30   With the development of modern science in the 17th century, emphasis was placed on systematic study by direct observation; this method was also applied to the study of monsters. The only monsters available for examination, however, were those resulting from abnormal births. In the absence of detailed knowledge of embryology, endocrine glands and hormones the cause of such births were little understood. Most of the scholarly works dealing with them were a mixture of science and credulousness; congenital abnormalities were discussed on the same level as the fictitious monstrous races. In his book *De Monstris* (1665) Fortunio Liceti added an elephant-headed creature to the lengthy catalogue of composite beings. Other students of teratology (the study of monstrous living forms) occupied themselves with classification; they grouped fabulous tribes according to the part of the body that was abnormal. Moral lessons were not lacking: monstrous births were seen as punishment for deviation from accepted customs, most particularly for incest or promiscuity but also for a variety of other transgressions.

31   In the 17th century, as increasing numbers of animal and plant species were being discovered, efforts were made to arrange the species in an orderly array. In some of the earlier systems of classification the monsters presented no problem: they were simply left out (together with man himself). Linnaeus, however, proposed to classify everything in nature. In the first edition of his *System of Nature,* which appeared in 1735, he boldly classified man as a quadruped, placing him in the same order as the sloth and the ape. At that time Linnaeus had not yet introduced his binomial system of nomenclature (genus and species); he simply noted that satyrs (described as being tailed, hairy and bearded and having a human body) and tailed men were ape species.

32   In the 10th edition of Linnaeus (1758) man was given the name *Homo sapiens,* and the separate species *Homo monstrosus* was also listed. Linnaeus considered the satyrs and the pygmies to be closer to the apes, as is indicated by their names: *Simia satyrus* and *Simia sylvanus.* He described a somewhat more human species believed to live in Abyssinia and on Java. They are, he said, nocturnal, they walk erect, they have frizzled white hair, they speak in a hiss, they are able to think and they believe the world was made for them.

33   Linnaeus granted that it was extremely difficult to distinguish such crea-

tures from man. He was of course severely handicapped; not only were there no specimens of monsters but also he had not seen many apes. The only ape he mentioned as being accessible to him for examination was an immature chimpanzee.

34   At least two followers of Linnaeus continued to classify fabulous tribes in a scientific manner. C. E. Hoppius, a pupil of Linnaeus', ranked *Homo troglodytus* closest to man. Next came *Homo luciferus,* as Hoppius named human creatures with tails; he was followed by *Homo satyrus* and *Homo pygmaeus.* A German physician named Martinus contended that there were two races of *Homo sylvestris,* the members of one race being smaller than those of the other.

35   Nonetheless, the end of *Homo monstrosus* and his like was approaching. With increased knowledge of anatomy, in particular the anatomy of the great apes, it was realized that the stories about satyrs and men with tails, if they were not fantasies, came from faulty observations of apes and monkeys. Although many a 19th-century traveler wrote about tailed men, such reports eventually became rare.

36   The puzzling similarities and differences between men and apes were clarified by Darwin's theory of evolution, but the theory did not solve the problem of man's specific ancestry. The erroneous idea that the lineage of man could be traced to know ape species spurred the search for a "missing link," a creature half-ape, half-man. Eugène Dubois believed that (in the fossil remains of *Pithecanthropus erectus,* or Java man) he had found such a link, a belief many people shared until the discovery of other human fossils changed the picture. With the knowledge that the ancestors of man are not represented among contemporary ape species, the search for links between men and apes ended.

37   Curiously, however, *Homo monstrosus* is not quite dead. Reports of an "abominable snowman" living in hidden fastnesses of the Himalayas are still in circulation. Speculation about life on other planets gives rise to new monsters with pointed heads and strange appendages. These fanciful beings are mostly invented in a spirit of fun, but the lesson is the same: When men can conceive of some remote place where other men or manlike creatures might exist, he is profoundly motivated to populate the unknown with creatures of his imagination.

VOCABULARY

Homo sapiens (1)	lascivious (19)	hirsute (27)
credulousness (3)	centaurs (20)	anagram (29)
propagated (13)	fauns (20)	binomial (31)
Antipodes (17)	satyrs (23)	nomenclature (31)

QUESTIONS FOR CRITICAL THINKING

1. What keeps Malefijt's essay from falling into the category of science fiction, fantasy, or myth?

2. The author claims in paragraph 3 that the "credulousness of those who accepted the reality of monstrous peoples is not so very different from the unfounded prejudices that human groups often harbor toward one another today." Do you agree with her claim? Supply examples of such prejudices in our society. What is the best way to overcome the prejudice?

3. In your view, has the fascination with monsters disappeared with the advance of scientific knowledge? Give reasons for your answer.

4. The author hopes that anthropology will help clear away misinformation that leads to misunderstanding about various people (paragraph 3). What is your view of the benefits derived from anthropology? Be specific.

5. How do the looks of characters such as Cyrano de Bergerac, the Hunchback of Notre Dame, or Elephant Man contribute to the literature in which these disfigured men appear? How do you feel toward these characters?

6. What is your reaction to the medieval idea that monsters were produced by the Devil in order to help confuse and destroy man? Is that idea still prevalent among some people today? What experience, if any, have you had with individuals or groups who hold this view?

QUESTIONS ON THE WRITING PROCESS

1. What is the purpose of Malefijt's study? Where is her purpose stated? What method of development does she use to achieve her purpose? Why is the method effective?

2. How does the writer make a transition from Ktesias's view of India (paragraph 9) to the view of Megathenes (paragraph 10)? What does this transition provide?

3. How does the author indicate the passage of time? Refer to specific examples.

4. How does the author's allusion to the "abominable snowman" of the Himalayas help draw the author's conclusion?

WRITING ASSIGNMENTS

1. Write a 500-word essay in which you provide examples from our society or from history to prove that people are often prejudiced against other people who look and act contrary to the norm.

2. Write an essay in which you provide three extended examples of historical or literary characters who are admirable or lovable even though they are physically ugly.

3. In 500 words express your views of what makes a person truly beautiful. Supply vivid examples from literature or history to enhance your essay.

4. Choosing one of the creatures listed below, write a 500-word essay on its contribution to literature:

Satyrs	Griffins	The Grecian sphinx
Fauns	The phoenix bird	The Medusa
Centaurs		

MY BRÜNNHILDE

Bradley Sheklian

My idea of a beautiful woman is a big buxom German opera singer. Let me illustrate what I mean.

To start with, my beauty's face must reflect strength and pride. She must have big blue eyes like cool, crisp winterland skies. She must have golden hair like a lion's flowing mane. Her nose will jut out like a proud alabaster ornament handed down from generation to generation. Furthermore, this beauty must have lips as red as the blood of ancient Rome, vanquished by her ancestors, hordes of fearless Germanic barbarians.

Next, my beauty's body must resemble an imperious statue of the kind found in many ancient Nordic city squares. For instance, she must have arms that could squeeze the wind out of a bear. She must have swelling bosoms—firm, round, and taut—to bury my face in. She must have marble-smooth skin that is milk white. When casually striding along, she will resemble the Valkyries draped in white ceremonial gowns to lead a procession in Valhalla. Naturally, another requirement is generous hips, capable of bringing forth many a big strong healthy son into the world.

Last but most important, this bombastic beauty must have a magic voice, a voice so mighty as to topple the greatest mountains yet so sweet that it could force the sirens of ancient Greece to hang their heads in shame. Her voice must sound forth majestically, but with such holiness that it could part the clouds and make the herald angels sing in harmony, sending the Devil, tormented and spitting fire and damnations, all the way back to hell.

Daily I pray to the great god Odin to send me a woman such as this.

FIVE

PROCESS

The process essay is a step-by-step explanation of how an act is performed. It is considered the simplest of all the expository modes to write because it is the least abstract. Yet for reasons that defy explanation good process writing is rare, as anyone who has ever struggled to assemble a child's toy according to its accompanying instructions can attest. Something is always left out of the process; simple procedures are made unnecessarily complex; parts and pieces are improperly labeled or described. Even cookbook recipes have been ruined by bad process writing.

The collection of process excerpts in this chapter deals with a variety of subjects. Lee Strout White explains how to start a Model T and H. A. Calahan, how to hoist sails. The essays tell us how dictionaries are made, how to read faster, and how to scribble our impressions in the margins of a book as we read it. One of the short essays takes us step by step through the procedures involved in abdominal surgery.

Process writing is primarily an exercise in common sense and therefore nearly impossible to teach. Many teachers do not even assign the process essay in the classroom. Nevertheless, some basic prescriptions can be given for explaining a process.

First, you should not try to explain any process that you do not understand. Poor understanding inevitably leads to bad explanations. Second, you should make clear at the outset what process you are explaining. Third, you should make the essay just as long or as short as it needs to be. An overexplained process is just as hard to fathom as one that is not explained enough. Fourth, you should cover the sequence of steps in their most logical order, using transitions such as "first," "then," "next," and "last" so that your reader can follow your explanations. Finally, even if it involves a great deal of repetition, you should call a thing or step by the same name throughout your entire explanation. Indeed, repetition is often useful in explaining how any process, simple or complex, is carried out.

STARTING A MODEL T

Lee Strout White

Lee Strout White is an expert on the origin and history of the Model T. His book Farewell to Model T *(1936) evokes nostalgia for a bygone era, when buying gadgets to enhance one's Model T was a way of life for many people.*

The paragraph below outlines the steps involved in starting a Model T with confidence and style.

During my association with Model T's, self-starters were not a prevalent accessory. They were expensive and under suspicion. Your car came equipped with a serviceable crank, and the first thing you learned was how to Get Results. It was a special trick, and until you learned it (usually from another Ford owner, but sometimes by a period of appalling experimentation) you might as well have been winding up an awning. The trick was to leave the ignition switch off, proceed to the animal's head, pull the choke (which was a little wire protruding through the radiator), and give the crank two or three nonchalant upward lifts. Then, whistling as though thinking about something else, you would saunter back to the driver's cabin, turn the ignition on, return to the crank, and this time, catching it on the down stroke, give it a quick spin with plenty of That. If this procedure was followed, the engine almost always responded—first with a few scattered explosions, then with a tumultuous gunfire, which you checked by racing around to the driver's seat and retarding the throttle. Often, if the emergency brake hadn't been pulled all the way back, the car advanced on you the instant the first explosion occurred and you would hold it back by leaning your weight against it. I can still feel my old Ford nuzzling me at the curb, as though looking for an apple in my pocket.

VOCABULARY

prevalent	appalling	saunter
accessory	protruding	tumultuous
serviceable	nonchalant	retarding

QUESTIONS FOR CRITICAL THINKING

1. Can you think of car accessories today that are expensive and under suspicion by the average driver? Describe them and state how you feel about them.
2. Do car owners today reveal their personalities in the kind of car they buy? How? Give some specific examples.
3. What are the advantages of owning a "spiffy" car? What are the disadvantages?

QUESTIONS ON THE WRITING PROCESS

1. From what point of view is the process described? What is the effect?
2. What combined purpose do the words *whistling* and *saunter* serve?
3. What figure of speech is used in the final sentence? Interpret it.

WRITING ASSIGNMENTS

1. In a single paragraph, describe the steps involved in starting a stick-shift car today.
2. In a single paragraph, describe one of the following processes:
    a. changing a tire
    b. washing a car
    c. parking a car in a parallel parking space
    Be sure to delineate each step carefully.

HOW TO HOIST SAILS

H. A. Calahan

H. A. Calahan, a writer of many books on sailing, is also the author of Back to Treasure Island *(1935),* So You're Going to Buy a Boat *(1939), and* What Makes a War End? *(1944).*

The paragraph that follows gives explicit instructions on how to hoist sails.

Let's send 'em up. Always hoist the aftermost sail first, the mainsail in a sloop, cutter, or two-masted schooner, the mizzen in a yawl or ketch. Do not hoist your headsails until just before you let go your mooring or break out the anchor. The sails are lowered in the reverse order. The first step in hoisting a sail is to take the weight of the boom on the topping-lift. We will find the boom probably resting in a boom crutch or gallows. Free the main sheet so that it is perfectly clear to run off freely and without fouling. Now hoist on the topping-lift to top the boom out of the crutch or gallows. . . . If you have no topping-lift on your boat—and many small boats lack them— leave the boom in the crutch or hold it up by hand until the sail is hoisted. With the boom topped up, we will stow away the boom crutch or gallows and go to work on the halyard. If the boat is rigged with running backstays, or "runners" or "preventers" as they are variously called, it is wise to pull them forward to avoid fouling the battens.

VOCABULARY

hoist (title)	yawl	sheet
aftermost	ketch	fouling
mainsail	headsails	halyard
sloop	mooring	rigged
cutter	boom	backstays
schooner	crutch	battens
mizzen	gallows	

QUESTIONS FOR CRITICAL THINKING

1. Why does sailing have a specialized vocabulary? Can you think of some other sports that involve a specialized vocabulary? Give examples.
2. Since sailing appears to be considerable work, why do you think so many people like to sail?
3. If money were no object, what kind of vessel would you like to own? Why?

QUESTIONS ON THE WRITING PROCESS

1. Why does the author open his paragraph with "Let's send 'em up" rather than "Let's hoist the sails"?
2. What purpose does the opening sentence serve?
3. What two points of view does the author use in the paragraph? How does he maintain clarity?
4. How does the reader know when the first step is to be described?
5. What other transitions are used to clarify steps?

WRITING ASSIGNMENTS

1. In a single paragraph delineate the steps involved in one aspect of a sport at which you excel. For instance, describe strapping on a pair of snow skis, serving a tennis ball, or performing a certain dive.
2. In a single paragraph explain the process of preparing for a history quiz on one chapter of your textbook.

THE KNIFE

Richard Selzer, M.D.

Richard Selzer (1928–   ), surgeon and author, is associate professor of surgery at Yale University. His articles on various aspects of medicine have appeared in Harper's, Esquire, Mademoiselle, *and* Redbook. *Among his books are* Rituals of Surgery *(1974) and* Mortal Lessons *(1977). The author is currently at work on a mythological treatment of the Civil War.*

In this essay reprinted from Mortal Lessons, *Selzer uses poetic language to describe the steps of the surgical process.*

1   One holds the knife as one holds the bow of a cello or a tulip—by the stem. Not palmed nor gripped nor grasped, but lightly, with the tips of the fingers. The knife is not for pressing. It is for drawing across the field of skin. Like a slender fish, it waits, at the ready, then, go! It darts, followed by a fine wake of red. The flesh parts, falling away to yellow globules of fat. Even now, after so many times, I still marvel at its power—cold, gleaming, silent. More, I am still struck with a kind of dread that it is I in whose hand the blade travels, that my hand is its vehicle, that yet again this terrible steel-bellied thing and I have conspired for a most unnatural purpose, the laying open of the body of a human being.

2   A stillness settles in my heart and is carried to my hand. It is the quietude of resolve layered over fear. And it is this resolve that lowers us, my knife and me, deeper and deeper into the person beneath. It is an entry into the body that is nothing like a caress; still it is among the gentlest of acts. Then stroke and stroke again, and we are joined by other instruments, hemostats and forceps, until the wound blooms with strange flowers whose looped handles fall to the sides in steely array.

3   There is sound, the tight click of clamps fixing teeth into severed blood vessels, the snuffle and gargle of the suction machine clearing the field of blood for the next stroke, the litany of monosyllables with which one prays his way down and in: *clamp, sponge, suture, tie, cut.* And there is color. The green of the cloth, the white of the sponges, the red and yellow of the body. Beneath the fat lies the fascia, the tough fibrous sheet encasing the muscles. It must be sliced and the red beef of the muscles separated. Now there are retractors to hold apart the wound. Hands move together, part, weave. We are fully engaged, like children absorbed in a game or the craftsmen of some place like Damascus.

4   Deeper still. The peritoneum, pink and gleaming and membranous, bulges into the wound. It is grasped with forceps, and opened. For the first time we can see into the cavity of the abdomen. Such a primitive place.

180

One expects to find drawings of buffalo on the walls. The sense of trespassing is keener now, heightened by the world's light illuminating the organs, their secret colors revealed—maroon and salmon and yellow. The vista is sweetly vulnerable at this moment, a kind of welcoming. An arc of the liver shines high and on the right, like a dark sun. It laps over the pink sweep of the stomach, from whose lower border the gauzy omentum is draped, and through which veil one sees, sinuous, slow as just-fed snakes, the indolent coils of the intestine.

5   You turn aside to wash your gloves. It is a ritual cleansing. One enters this temple doubly washed. Here is man as microcosm, representing in all his parts the earth, perhaps the universe.

6   I must confess that the priestliness of my profession has ever been impressed on me. In the beginning there are vows, taken with all solemnity. Then there is the endless harsh novitiate of training, much fatigue, much sacrifice. At last one emerges as celebrant, standing close to the truth lying curtained in the Ark of the body. Not surplice and cassock but mask and gown are your regalia. You hold no chalice, but a knife. There is no wine, no wafer. There are only the facts of blood and flesh.

7   And if the surgeon is like a poet, then the scars you have made on countless bodies are like verses into the fashioning of which you have poured your soul. I think that if years later I were to see the trace from an old incision of mine, I should know it at once, as one recognizes his pet expressions.

8   But mostly you are a traveler in a dangerous country, advancing into the moist and jungly cleft your hands have made. Eyes and ears are shuttered from the land you left behind; mind empties itself of all other thought. You are the root of groping fingers. It is a fine hour for the fingers, their sense of touch so enhanced. The blind must know this feeling. Oh, there is risk everywhere. One goes lightly. The spleen. No! No! Do not touch the spleen that lurks below the left leaf of the diaphragm, a manta ray in a coral cave, its bloody tongue protruding. One poke and it might rupture, exploding with sudden hemorrhage. The filmy omentum must not be torn, the intestine scraped or denuded. The hand finds the liver, palms it, fingers running along its sharp lower edge, admiring. Here are the twin mounds of the kidneys, the apron of the omentum hanging in front of the intestinal coils. One lifts it aside and the fingers dip among the loops, searching, mapping territory, establishing boundaries. Deeper still, and the womb is touched, then held like a small muscular bottle—the womb and its earlike appendages, the ovaries. How they do nestle in the cup of a man's hand, their power all dormant. They are frailty itself.

9   There is a hush in the room. Speech stops. The hands of the others, assistants and nurses, are still. Only the voice of the patient's respiration remains. It is the rhythm of a quiet sea, the sound of waiting. Then you speak, slowly, the terse entries of a Himalayan climber reporting back.

10   "The stomach is okay. Greater curvature clean. No sign of ulcer. Pylorus, duodenum fine. Now comes the gallbladder. No stones. Right kidney, left, all right. Liver . . . uh-oh."

11   Your speech lowers to a whisper, falters, stops for a long, long moment, then picks up again at the end of a sigh that comes through your mask like a last exhalation.

12   "Three big hard ones in the left lobe, one on the right. Metastatic deposits. Bad, bad. Where's the primary? Got to be coming from somewhere."

13   The arm shifts direction and the fingers drop lower and lower into the pelvis—the body impaled now upon the arm of the surgeon to the hilt of the elbow.

14   "Here it is."

15   The voice goes flat, all business now.

16   "Tumor in the sigmoid colon, wrapped all around it, pretty tight. We'll take out a sleeve of the bowel. No colostomy. Not that, anyway. But, God, there's a lot of it down there. Here, you take a feel."

17   You step back from the table, and lean into a sterile basin of water, resting on stiff arms, while the others locate the cancer. . . .

VOCABULARY

globules (1)	vista (4)	protruding (8)
vehicle (1)	arc (4)	denuded (8)
conspired (1)	omentum (4)	appendages (8)
quietude (2)	sinuous (4)	dormant (8)
hemostats (2)	indolent (4)	respiration (9)
forceps (2)	microcosm (5)	terse (9)
snuffle (3)	priestliness (6)	Himalayan (9)
litany (3)	novitiate (6)	curvature (10)
monosyllables (3)	celebrant (6)	pylorus (10)
suture (3)	Ark (6)	duodenum (10)
fascia (3)	surplice (6)	exhalation (11)
fibrous (3)	cassock (6)	metastatic (12)
retractors (3)	regalia (6)	primary (12)
Damascus (3)	chalice (6)	pelvis (13)
peritoneum (4)	cleft (8)	impaled (13)
membranous (4)	enhanced (8)	tumor (16)
abdomen (4)	manta ray (8)	sigmoid colon (16)
illuminating (4)		

QUESTIONS FOR CRITICAL THINKING

1. After reading this essay, how would you feel about observing a similar surgical process firsthand?
2. What do you think are the most important qualities required of a surgeon? List them in order of importance if they are not all equally important.
3. Do you think Richard Selzer represents a typical surgeon? Give reasons for your answer.
4. What difference do you think exists between a surgeon's view of surgery and a nurse's view? Comment on the difference if you see any.

QUESTIONS ON THE WRITING PROCESS

1. Into what major steps is the process of surgery divided? What paragraphs are involved in each step?
2. What three analogies does the author use to clarify the role of the surgeon? (See paragraphs 5–8.)
3. What is the meaning of the reference to Damascus in paragraph 3? Explain.
4. What is the meaning of the phrase "their power all dormant" in paragraph 8?
5. Paragraphs 10–17 are shorter than most of the other paragraphs. What effect does their brevity produce?
6. Why are most of the sentences in paragraph 10 incomplete?

WRITING ASSIGNMENTS

1. If you have ever had surgery, write a brief essay in which you recreate the procedures you went through before you were anesthetized. List the steps chronologically.
2. Describe, as best you remember, the steps involved in having a filling placed in your tooth.
3. In a 300-word essay, describe any process conducive to good health. (Examples: aerobic exercise, balanced breakfast, spiritual meditation.)
4. Write a 300-word essay in which you list the steps involved in curing a common cold.

HOW TO READ BETTER AND FASTER

Dennis Mark Doyle

Dennis Mark Doyle (1952–   ) is a reading specialist at Glendale Community College in California. He has written numerous articles aimed at helping students achieve better reading skills.

The essay that follows provides some practical advice on how to read faster and at the same time get more out of the reading.

1   Not everyone can compete with Evelyn Wood in rapid reading, but many of us can read much faster than we presently do. Often we have acquired through the years habits which slow us down and tend to rob us of some of the enjoyment of reading. Efficient readers, who know when to slow down and when to speed up, experience reading as "viewing a panorama of ideas" rather than slowly slogging their way through the text word for word.

2   How can you get more out of your reading at a faster rate? Try these tips:

3   1. *Read Actively*—Don't read in the same passive way that you watch television. Reading takes effort! You must pay a price or you get nothing out of it! Before you read anything, preview the passage. Look at the title, the pictures, and major headings. Read the first and last paragraph and skim through the text. Get a general idea of what the whole thing is about. Remember that a real person actually wrote this passage which you are about to read. Disagree with the author. Get emotionally involved. Make up some questions in your mind which you'd want to ask him as you go along in the reading. As you read, actively seek the answers to your questions.

4   2. *Avoid Regressions*—When you read, do you find yourself reading and re-reading and re-reading the same passage over and over again? This is called regression and shows a lack of confidence with the material. Don't slow yourself by constantly re-reading. Learn to catch the meaning the first time through. If you are reading actively, you will find that you remember as much after a single reading as you did during repeated re-readings at your old passive rate.

5   How do you avoid regressions? Force yourself to go faster. Time yourself when you are reading moderately easy material. Cover the portion of the book which you have read with a white card and push that card slowly but evenly down the page. Try to read the page quickly before the card covers the print. Special reading machines which are available in learning centers, such as the Controlled Reader, Combo-8, Craig Reader, and SRA Reading Pacer, may also be of use because they force you to read at a steady pace

and don't permit you to look back. This well-worn habit dies slowly, but it will succumb eventually with practice.

6   3. *Stop Talking to Yourself as You Read*—Remember when you learned how to read in first grade? It was often in a "Round-Robin" style in which you had to stand up in a small circle and read out loud for the teacher. Reading began for most of us as an activity in which we had to move our lips and speak; many people still read that way. They don't read as slowly as they did in primary school, yet they still find it necessary to move their lips and tongue as they scan the text. This habit slows reading down unnecessarily because it ties the speed of reading to the speed of speech. Few people speak faster than 300 words per minute, hence their reading speed is limited to that slow level. Moving your lips as you read is called "vocalization."

7   There is another problem, however, which is much more common than vocalization. Early in grammar school, most of us rid ourselves of the habit of actually mouthing the words as we read, but the habit often continues in a more subtle way. When you read, do you hear yourself "telling yourself the words in your head"? Is it as if one part of your head is talking to another part? This is called subvocalization, and also results in slow reading because it is still binding reading speed to the level of speech. Many of us begin to feel that we are not actually "comprehending" unless we hear that persistent voice in our head.

8   The fact is, we can and do comprehend faster than vocal speech. We often hear in the media about the wonderful capacity of the human brain. We need not fear loss of comprehension when we don't vocalize or subvocalize. Reading, rather, should be an affair between the eyes and the brain, which doesn't involve the muscles in the throat or mouth. Even during subvocalization when no external facial movement is apparent, it has been found that the vocal cords make subtle imperceptible vibrations mimicking oral speech.

9   How do you combat subvocalization? Force yourself to go faster. Go beyond the point where you can comfortably talk to yourself as you read. Your comprehension will drop at first as your confidence falters, but soon you will find that you *are* understanding what you read and you will wonder why you ever went so slowly before.

10   4. *Read in Thought Groups*—When I listen to primary school children read, I notice that sometimes a child will read the words of a sentence one by one, as if they had no relationship to each other. It sounds as if he were reading a list of words. When that happens, I know that the child is not understanding the text. He is not getting the "thought" behind the passage because understanding the text involves more than just reading individual words: He must see the *relationship* between the words and also notice the *order of the words in groups* so as to discover the meaning. Meaning, after all, is what reading is all about.

11   When you read, meaning must be your main objective also. This is best done if you wean yourself away from reading the words one by one and seek to read whole phrases or even sentences at a time. Words by themselves really have little meaning. It is only in the context of a sentence that meaning becomes apparent.

12   5. *Be Flexible in Your Reading Rate*—Some things written were simply not meant to be read rapidly. You cannot speed-read through a Shakespearean play or through a poem by Keats or Shelley. Difficult material of a highly technical or philosophical nature should not be read rapidly. Reading poetry quickly is like chug-a-lugging fine wine. The words should be formed on the tongue and savored carefully. You should listen to the sounds of the words as you speak them out loud.

13   Yet we needn't show the same reverence for a fashion magazine, the newspaper, or most things which we read during the day. The average American reads at about an eighth grade level, so most of the printed media rarely exceed that low level. Speed-reading techniques are justifiably used to quickly dispose of much of the volume of low-level written material which fills our time.

14   Go fast when you are confronted with light or familiar material, but don't be reluctant to shift gears into a slower speed for more difficult passages. Above all, adjust your speed to match the reading matter.

VOCABULARY

panorama (1)	imperceptible (8)	Shelley (12)
slogging (1)	wean (11)	justifiably (13)
moderately (5)	context (11)	reluctant (14)
succumb (5)	Keats (12)	

QUESTIONS FOR CRITICAL THINKING

1. Do you find yourself vocalizing or subvocalizing while reading? Before reading this essay, were you aware of the fact that you had this habit? Do you agree with the author's view on how to get rid of this habit?
2. What disadvantage would a foreign student have in attempting to improve his reading speed in English?
3. What specific book or magazine would you suggest to a student who wants to learn to speed-read?
4. What poem can you recall reading without understanding until you had read it slowly and pondered it? Discuss the poem and its meaning with the class.

QUESTIONS ON THE WRITING PROCESS

1. How are the rules about correct reading made unmistakably clear? Why is this technique helpful to the reader?
2. What is the purpose of the question at the beginning of paragraph 9?
3. What simile does the author use in order to clarify why poetry should be read slowly?
4. What is the purpose of the final paragraph?

WRITING ASSIGNMENTS

1. Write a 300-word essay in which you outline a step-by-step process for the improvement of some aspect of your life. Here are some possible subjects:
   a. Keeping your room tidy
   b. Going on a reducing diet
   c. Starting an exercise program
   d. Getting acquainted with a person who interests you
2. Write a 300-word essay in which you suggest an efficient process for studying for final exams. Use a format similar to Dennis Doyle's.
3. Write a brief essay in which you suggest some practical steps for reducing feelings of guilt (or anger, if you prefer).

HOW DICTIONARIES ARE MADE

S. I. Hayakawa

S. I. Hayakawa (1906–   ) is a senator as well as an educator. Before being elected to the U.S. Senate as a representative from California, he was well known as the president of California State University, San Francisco, and as a semanticist whose book Language in Thought and Action *(1964) is still considered a major work in the field.*

The essay that follows offers some interesting insights into the laborious process of assembling a dictionary.

1   It is widely believed that every word has a correct meaning, that we learn these meanings principally from teachers and grammarians (except that most of the time we don't bother to, so that we ordinarily speak "sloppy English"), and that dictionaries and grammars are the supreme authority in matters of meaning and usage. Few people ask by what authority the writers of dictionaries and grammars say what they say. I once got into a dispute with an English woman over the pronunciation of a word and offered to look it up in the dictionary. The English woman said firmly, "What for? I am English. I was born and brought up in England. The way I speak *is* English." Such self-assurance about one's own language is not uncommon among the English. In the United States, however, anyone who is willing to quarrel with the dictionary is regarded as either eccentric or mad.

2   Let us see how dictionaries are made and how the editors arrive at definitions. What follows applies, incidentally, only to those dictionary offices where first-hand, original research goes on—not those in which editors simply copy existing dictionaries. The task of writing a dictionary begins with the reading of vast amounts of the literature of the period or subject that the dictionary is to cover. As the editors read, they copy on cards every interesting or rare word, every unusual or peculiar occurrence of a common word, a large number of common words in their ordinary uses, and also the sentences in which each of these words appears, thus:

> pail
> The dairy *pails* bring home increase of milk
> Keats, *Endymion*
> I, 44–45

3   That is to say, the context of each word is collected, along with the word itself. For a really big job of dictionary writing, such as the *Oxford English Dictionary* (usually bound in about twenty-five volumes), millions of such cards are collected, and the task of editing occupies decades. As the cards are collected, they are alphabetized and sorted. When the sorting is completed, there will be for each word anywhere from two or three to several hundred illustrative quotations, each on its card.

4   To define a word, then, the dictionary editor places before him the stack of cards illustrating that word; each of the cards represents an actual use of the word by a writer of some literary or historical importance. He reads the cards carefully, discards some, re-reads the rest, and divides up the stack according to what he thinks are the several senses of the word. Finally, he writes his definitions, following the hard-and-fast rule that each definition *must* be based on what the quotations in front of him reveal about the meaning of the word. The editor cannot be influenced by what *he* thinks a given word *ought* to mean. He must work according to the cards, or not at all.

5   The writing of a dictionary, therefore, is not a task of setting up authoritative statements about the "true meanings" of words, but a task of *recording,* to the best of one's ability, what various words have *meant* to authors in the distant or immediate past. *The writer of a dictionary is a historian, not a lawgiver.* If, for example, we had been writing a dictionary in 1890, or even as late as 1919, we could have said that the word "broadcast" means "to scatter" (seed, for example), but we could not have decreed that from 1921 on, the most common meaning of the word should become "to disseminate audible messages, etc., by radio transmission." To regard the dictionary as an "authority," therefore, is to credit the dictionary writer with gifts of prophecy which neither he nor anyone else possesses. In choosing our words when we speak or write, we can be *guided* by the historical record afforded us by the dictionary, but we cannot be *bound* by it, because new situations, new experiences, new inventions, new feelings, are always compelling us to give new uses to old words. Looking under a "hood," we should ordinarily have found, five hundred years ago, a monk; today, we find a motorcar engine.

VOCABULARY

occurrence (2)	authoritative (5)	telephony (5)
context (3)	decreed (5)	prophecy (5)
illustrative (3)	disseminate (5)	afforded (5)
literary (4)	audible (5)	compelling (5)

QUESTIONS FOR CRITICAL THINKING

1. What words exist in our vocabulary today that did not exist one hundred years ago?
2. The author suggests that perhaps people ought to challenge dictionaries more often. Do you agree? Why or why not?
3. What word not now in the dictionary would you like to see included if you were a dictionary maker? (Consider even slang.)

QUESTIONS ON THE WRITING PROCESS

1. How does the author announce that he is now beginning his process analysis?
2. In paragraph 4, what two transitions are used to help the coherence of the paragraph?
3. What transition is used to indicate that the process analysis has ended and that the author will now draw some conclusions?
4. In paragraph 5, what transition is used to indicate that an illustration follows?
5. In paragraph 5, what word is repeated five times? Why?

WRITING ASSIGNMENTS

1. Write a 300-word essay in which you develop one of the following theses:
   a. What the world needs is a universal language.
   b. Sloppy language reveals sloppy thinking.
   c. College students today have limited vocabularies.
2. Write a 300-word essay in which you suggest a plan for increasing a student's vocabulary.

CAMPING OUT

Ernest Hemingway

Ernest Hemingway (1899–1961) is regarded as one of the great American short story writers and novelists of the 20th century. Born in Oak Park, Illinois, Hemingway was first lauded for a writing style of stunning simplicity. His many novels include The Sun Also Rises *(1926),* A Farewell to Arms *(1929), and* For Whom The Bell Tolls *(1940). He was awarded the Nobel Prize for Literature in 1954. Hemingway died from a self-inflicted gunshot wound in 1961.*

The following essay, written for the Toronto Star *in the early 1920's before Hemingway became the literary star of his generation, exhibits the famous Hemingway strong but laconic style as it explains the processes a camper must follow to live comfortably in the woods.*

1 Thousands of people will go into the bush this summer to cut the high cost of living. A man who gets his two weeks' salary while he is on vacation should be able to put those two weeks in fishing and camping and be able to save one week's salary clear. He ought to be able to sleep comfortably every night, to eat well every day and to return to the city rested and in good condition.

2 But if he goes into the woods with a frying pan, an ignorance of black flies and mosquitoes, and a great and abiding lack of knowledge about cookery the chances are that his return will be very different. He will come back with enough mosquito bites to make the back of his neck look like a relief map of the Caucasus. His digestion will be wrecked after a valiant battle to assimilate half-cooked or charred grub. And he won't have had a decent night's sleep while he has been gone.

3 He will solemnly raise his right hand and inform you that he has joined the grand army of never-agains. The call of the wild may be all right, but it's a dog's life. He's heard the call of the tame with both ears. Waiter, bring him an order of milk toast.

4 In the first place he overlooked the insects. Black flies, no-see-ums, deer flies, gnats and mosquitoes were instituted by the devil to force people to live in cities where he could get at them better. If it weren't for them everybody would live in the bush and he would be out of work. It was a rather successful invention.

5 But there are lots of dopes that will counteract the pests. The simplest perhaps is oil of citronella. Two bits' worth of this purchased at any pharmacist's will be enough to last for two weeks in the worst fly and mosquito-ridden country.

6   Rub a little on the back of your neck, your forehead and your wrists before you start fishing, and the blacks and skeeters will shun you. The odor of citronella is not offensive to people. It smells like gun oil. But the bugs do hate it.

7   Oil of pennyroyal and eucalyptol are also much hated by mosquitoes, and with citronella they form the basis for many proprietary preparations. But it is cheaper and better to buy the straight citronella. Put a little on the mosquito netting that covers the front of your pup tent or canoe tent at night, and you won't be bothered.

8   To be really rested and get any benefit out of a vacation a man must get a good night's sleep every night. The first requisite for this is to have plenty of cover. It is twice as cold as you expect it will be in the bush four nights out of five, and a good plan is to take just double the bedding that you think you will need. An old quilt that you can wrap up in is as warm as two blankets.

9   Nearly all outdoor writers rhapsodize over the browse bed. It is all right for the man who knows how to make one and has plenty of time. But in a succession of one-night camps on a canoe trip all you need is level ground for your tent floor and you will sleep all right if you have plenty of covers under you. Take twice as much cover as you think that you will need, and then put two-thirds of it under you. You will sleep warm and get your rest.

10   When it is clear weather you don't need to pitch your tent if you are only stopping for the night. Drive four stakes at the head of your made-up bed and drape your mosquito bar over that, then you can sleep like a log and laugh at the mosquitoes.

11   Outside of insects and bum sleeping the rock that wrecks most camping trips is cooking. The average tyro's idea of cooking is to fry everything and fry it good and plenty. Now, a frying pan is a most necessary thing to any trip, but you also need the old stew kettle and the folding reflector baker.

12   A pan of fried trout can't be bettered and they don't cost any more than ever. But there is a good and bad way of frying them.

13   The beginner puts his trout and his bacon in and over a brightly burning fire the bacon curls up and dries into a dry tasteless cinder and the trout is burned outside while it is still raw inside. He eats them and it is all right if he is only out for the day and going home to a good meal at night. But if he is going to face more trout and bacon the next morning and other equally well-cooked dishes for the remainder of two weeks he is on the pathway to nervous dyspepsia.

14   The proper way is to cook over coals. Have several cans of Crisco or Cotosuet or one of the vegetable shortenings along that are as good as lard and excellent for all kinds of shortening. Put the bacon in and when it is about half cooked lay the trout in the hot grease, dipping them in corn meal first. Then put the bacon on top of the trout and it will baste them as it slowly cooks.

15   The coffee can be boiling at the same time and in a smaller skillet pancakes being made that are satisfying the other campers while they are waiting for the trout.

16   With the prepared pancake flours you take a cupful of pancake flour and add a cup of water. Mix the water and flour and as soon as the lumps are out it is ready for cooking. Have the skillet hot and keep it well greased. Drop the batter in and as soon as it is done on one side loosen it in the skillet and flip it over. Apple butter, syrup or cinnamon and sugar go well with the cakes.

17   While the crowd have taken the edge from their appetites with flapjacks the trout have been cooked and they and the bacon are ready to serve. The trout are crisp outside and firm and pink inside and the bacon is well done—but not too done. If there is anything better than that combination the writer has yet to taste it in a lifetime devoted largely and studiously to eating.

18   The stew kettle will cook you dried apricots when they have resumed their predried plumpness after a night of soaking, it will serve to concoct a mulligan in, and it will cook macaroni. When you are not using it, it should be boiling water for the dishes.

19   In the baker, mere man comes into his own, for he can make a pie that to his bush appetite will have it all over the product that mother used to make, like a tent. Men have always believed that there was something mysterious and difficult about making a pie. Here is a great secret. There is nothing to it. We've been kidded for years. Any man of average office intelligence can make at least as good a pie as his wife.

20   All there is to a pie is a cup and a half of flour, one-half teaspoonful of salt, one-half cup of lard and cold water. That will make pie crust that will bring tears of joy into your camping partner's eyes.

21   Mix the salt with the flour, work the lard into the flour, make it up into a good workmanlike dough with cold water. Spread some flour on the back of a box or something flat, and pat the dough around a while. Then roll it out with whatever kind of round bottle you prefer. Put a little more lard on the surface of the sheet of dough and then slosh a little flour on and roll it up and then roll it out again with the bottle.

22   Cut out a piece of the rolled out dough big enough to line a pie tin. I like the kind with holes in the bottom. Then put in your dried apples that have soaked all night and been sweetened, or your apricots, or your blueberries, and then take another sheet of the dough and drape it gracefully over the top, soldering it down at the edges with your fingers. Cut a couple of slits in the top dough sheet and prick it a few times with a fork in an artistic manner.

23   Put it in the baker with a good slow fire for forty-five minutes and then take it out and if your pals are Frenchmen they will kiss you. The penalty for knowing how to cook is that the others will make you do all the cooking.

24   It is all right to talk about roughing it in the woods. But the real woods-
man is the man who can be really comfortable in the bush.

VOCABULARY

assimilate (2)   rhapsodize (9)   dyspepsia (13)
requisite (8)   tyro (11)

QUESTIONS FOR CRITICAL THINKING

1. Although the author uses "he" to refer to his example of the unprepared
    camper whom he is instructing in the way of the woods, his advice obviously
    applies to campers of either sex. What is your attitude towards this use of "he"
    as a generalized third-person pronoun?
2. Hemingway became known later in his life as the prototype of the macho male.
    What early evidence of this attitude can you find in this essay?
3. What stereotypes are evident in this essay?
4. What does the phrase "back to nature" mean to you? How do you regard
    nature: as a place or as a process?

QUESTIONS ON THE WRITING PROCESS

1. What three major how-to topics does this article discuss and in what order?
    What is the logic of this arrangement?
2. Hemingway would later gain international fame for his distinctive writing style.
    Based on this article, what are the characteristics of this style?
3. What is the purpose of paragraph 12?
4. How does the author give the impression that he is a seasoned veteran of the
    woods who knows whereof he speaks?

WRITING ASSIGNMENTS

1. Write an essay explaining in detail how to set up a tent, build a camp fire, or do
    any of the many other housekeeping chores of camping out.
2. In an essay discuss the benefits of camping as recreation.
3. Have you ever taken a memorable camping trip? Write a narrative essay telling
    about it.

THE PHYSICAL

Noel Coward

Sir Noel Coward (1899–1973) was an English playwright, actor, composer, and director. He was born in Teddington, England, and first appeared on stage at the age of 12. In the 1920's he was celebrated as the most successful playwright of his time, enjoying five simultaneous hits in 1925. His plays usually feature characters who are sophisticated, witty and rich. Among them are Fallen Angels *(1925),* Private Lives *(1930), and* Blithe Spirit *(1941). Coward also wrote short stories, songs, a novel, and acted in films. On 26th March, 1973 Coward died at Firefly, his home near Port Maria, Jamaica, where he is buried.*

The following excerpt from Coward's posthumously published journal The Noel Coward Diaries *(1982), follows the process of a three-day physical Coward underwent at a Chicago hospital on July 12, 1955. It is a humorous treatment from a how-it-is-done perspective of a process through which many of us will eventually have to suffer, if we haven't already.*

Tuesday 12 July   Chicago

1   Here I am, in the Passevant Hospital, for a three-day check-up. I arrived last night under the assumed name of Nicholas Cole. Coley[1] unpacked for me and then he and Alfred[2] departed for Genesee Depot, leaving me weary but cheerful enough in a small green room with a functional bed. The curtains refuse to draw completely, the waste plug in the lavatory basin doesn't work, and outside in the warm humid Chicago air the Shriners are holding their Annual Convention. This consists of many thousand old men and young men dressed in fancy clothes marching about to a series of excruciating brass bands. A pleasant doctor (Walters) came to see me and extracted my life's history, after which he examined me with the utmost thoroughness even to tickling my balls and, after giving me a sleeping-pill, left.

2   This morning I woke at seven owing to the light striking my eyes like a sword through the non-drawing curtains. A series of different ladies appeared from time to time, some on errands, some apparently vaguely as though they had nowhere else to go. One of these latter said 'How ya comin?' I replied that in my present mood I saw little hope of such a contingency arising, whereupon she looked at me blankly, said 'Okay' and went away.

[1]Cole Lesley (1911–1980), valet to Noel Coward since 1936 and co-inheritor of his estate.

[2]Alfred Lunt (1892–1977), well-known American stage actor.

3   Another lady arrived and, having stuck a large syringe into one of my arm veins, extracted a lot of my blood and also went away. She was followed by a big, moist William Bendix[3] character who, with almost maternal sympathy, rammed an enema up my bottom and that was that. Presently some cereal was brought to me, and a cup of coffee. While I was enjoying this, a very ramshackle man arrived with a ladder to fix the curtains while the Shriners struck up 'God Bless America'. Presently Dr. Bigg himself arrived looking very like Michel St. Denis,[4] and we had a purposeful little chat. Following on his visit, two men came in to fix the wash-basin, which they failed to do, then a few other ladies bounced in and out for no apparent reason. At about 10:30 I was taken down in the elevator by a personable young Jew called Tony. Here I was led into a small lavatory and told to take off my dressing-gown and pyjamas and put on a strange garment which tied at the side and made me look like a rather skittish Roman matron. In this I was led into a large, depressing room and laid on a slab. Over me and all round me were vast machines. Two men appeared and proceeded to administer a barium enema, a very unpleasant procedure indeed. One of them inserted a tube into my arse while the Shriners, slightly muffled by distance, struck up 'The Darktown Strutters Ball'. Then, in the pitch dark, accompanied by whirrings and whizzings, I was blown up with barium until I thought I should burst. Meanwhile the whizzings and whirrings were photographing what was going on. One of the men massaged my stomach and genitals rather hard, which was painful. At long last it was over and I was allowed to retire to the loo and sit on it until most of my inside had dropped out. Dr. Walters appeared and gave me a cigarette. After half an hour or so I was taken to another room and my chest was x-rayed.

4   Then I was led back to my room and allowed to relax for a few minutes until yet another very brisk lady came in with an electric apparatus. She proceeded to sandpaper different parts of my skin until it glowed like an ember and clamped electric things on to me and switched on the current. It was quite painless and apparently took a movie of my heart. When she had gone a grey woman arrived with a menu. I chose and marked devilled-egg salad, cheese, rye bread, French dressing and iced tea. An hour or so later a tray was brought me on which was a cup of vegetable soup, a pear in a bed of lettuce with mayonnaise, a hunk of hamburger covered in ketchup accompanied by two moist boiled potatoes, a corn on the cob which I didn't attempt on account of my teeth, and a pistachio ice-cream which tasted like brilliantine. I ate very little of all this ambrosia, but enjoyed the coffee which came instead of the iced tea. So far that is all that has happened to

[3]William Bendix (1906-1964), American film and television star who often played kindly but dim characters.

[4]French theatre director.

me today, and thank God the Shriners have at last moved off in ragged formation to lacerate the nerves of the rest of Chicago.

Wednesday 13 July

5 This has not been a good day. Whatever I write of it will be prejudiced by nervous exhaustion, physical exhaustion and quivering exasperation. First of all, let me state unequivocally that I do not think American women make good nurses. With one or two exceptions those I have encountered in this hospital are smart, bossy and overwhelmingly pleased with themselves. They represent the dominant sex all right in this country and they bloody well know it. The male orderlies are kind, gentle and cowed. Last night, after a meal of fruit only and a pleasant conversation with Dr. Bigg, who is obviously a wise man and a first-rate doctor, I retired to sleep at 11:30 with a sleeping pill. I have been moved into a much nicer room which overlooks the lake (it also overlooks a parking lot in process of construction, a fact that was withheld from me until this morning when the hydraulic drills began at 7:30). At 3:30 a.m. I was torn from a deep sleep by a light being flashed in my eyes and a brisk nurse saying, 'I'm only checking up; go to sleep again.'

6 From that moment I was done for and never closed an eye until 5:30, when I gave up trying and read Tolstoy's *War and Peace* which has saved my reason. From 5:30 until 9:30 I waited without breakfast because I was to have barium for further x-rays. During this time the drills went on outside, while inside different nurses bounced in and out for no apparent reason. After I had returned from the second x-ray jaunt at 2:30 I was allowed breakfast. I ordered poached eggs, bacon and coffee, but when the tray finally arrived the eggs were lying sullenly in the water they'd been poached in, which was not very appetizing. By mid-afternoon I began to feel really beastly and the slight infection in my urinary tract started to give me trouble. Dr. Bigg appeared and, to my intense relief, all my organs are healthy: liver, prostate and heart particularly so. He was wise and comforting and of course the main cause for jubilation is that I am neither festooned with ulcers nor riddled with cancer. Finally, after he had given me a belladonna and opium suppository to ease my discomfort, he went.

Friday 15 July   Wisconsin

7 Yesterday was fairly restful except for the hydraulic drills which happily stopped at 4:30 p.m., having been going since 7:30 a.m. At about five o'clock I had a long talk to Dr. Bigg. He lectured me firmly about my future health, with emphasis on my 'nervous' stomach. He said nothing organic was wrong with me, except a slight curving of the spine which can be remedied or at least prevented from curving more by watching my posture and walking and sitting with more care, but that I must remember that I am fifty-five and not twenty-five, and live sensibly and moderately and *not* give myself so much to other people and their problems. He also said that I should create more and perform less and, for the rest of my life, drink as

little alcohol as socially possible. He also told me not to be fussy about my diet, but to eat little and well. He specified that roughage was bad for my colon, which apparently is over-sensitive, like so many of my friends. He said that all the old wives' tales about cooked green vegetables being good for me was nonsense and that meat and fish, eggs, potatoes, bread and sugar were much better! He advised the latter in moderation on account of my figure. In face he advised moderation in everything. We then got into a long discussion of morals and sex taboos and homosexuality, which convinced me that he is one of the wisest and most thoroughly sensible men I have ever met. I shall go to him once a year.

8   I arrived at Milwaukee at 3:15 and was met by Lynnie[5] and Cole. We had a peaceful evening, played my Las Vegas record, which is excellent, and I went to bed early and finished *War and Peace*. Yes, yes, yes, it is a great book but it is far too long and although all the characters are brilliantly drawn they are, most of them, bloody bores, particularly the hero and heroine, Pierre and Natasha, whom I personally find absolutely idiotic. Prince Andrei is, to me, the only sympathetic creature in the whole book and even he gets a bit fuzzy and mystic before he kicks the bucket.

9   Well, I have finished it and I am very, very proud.

VOCABULARY

excruciating (1)	ambrosia (4)	unequivocally (5)
contingency (2)	lacerate (4)	jubilation (6)
ramshackle (3)	exasperation (5)	festooned (6)
skittish (3)		

QUESTIONS FOR CRITICAL THINKING

1. Coward says that American women are the dominant sex and know it. What is your view of this opinion?
2. Do you agree with Coward that American women do not make good nurses? Why or why not?
3. How does the dietary advice given Coward by his doctor differ from present-day medical thinking?
4. Coward grudgingly admits that *War and Peace* is a great book but confesses that he also found it boring. Why do you think he persisted, then, in reading it?

[5]Lynn Fontanne (1889–1983), English-born stage actress and wife of Alfred Lunt with whom she often performed.

QUESTIONS ON THE WRITING PROCESS

1. What is the organizing focus of this excerpt?
2. Coward wrote mainly for the theatre. What elements of theatricality can you find in this excerpt?
3. What is ironic about the exchange reported in paragraph 2?
4. Based on this excerpt, do you think Coward wrote his journal entirely for private reading, or do you believe he had an audience in mind?

WRITING ASSIGNMENTS

1. Write an essay detailing the steps in any physical examination you have ever taken.
2. Write an essay on the usefulness of keeping a journal.
3. Write an essay on the regimen you follow in keeping yourself physically healthy.

HOW TO MARK A BOOK

Mortimer Adler

Mortimer Adler (1902–   ), American educator and editor, is a dynamic lecturer and discussion-group leader. His career as an editor of massive reference works was crowned in 1974 by the fifteenth edition of the Encyclopedia Britannica, *the arrangement of which he largely planned. His* How to Read a Book *(1940), excerpted below, became a best seller.*

In this essay, reprinted from the Saturday Review of Literature *(July 6, 1940), Mortimer Adler argues that marking up a book is an act of love, not of mutilation.*

1   You know you have to read "between the lines" to get the most out of anything. I want to persuade you to do something equally important in the course of your reading. I want to persuade you to "write between the lines." Unless you do, you are not likely to do the most efficient kind of reading.

2   I contend, quite bluntly, that marking up a book is not an act of mutilation but of love.

3   You shouldn't mark up a book which isn't yours. Librarians (or your friends) who lend you books expect you to keep them clean, and you should. If you decide that I am right about the usefulness of marking books, you will have to buy them. Most of the world's great books are available today, in reprint editions, at less than a dollar.

4   There are two ways in which one can own a book. The first is the property right you establish by paying for it, just as you pay for clothes and furniture. But this act of purchase is only the prelude to possession. Full ownership comes only when you have made it a part of yourself, and the best way to make yourself a part of it is by writing in it. An illustration may make the point clear. You buy a beefsteak and transfer it from the butcher's icebox to your own. But you do not own the beefsteak in the most important sense until you consume it and get it into your bloodstream. I am arguing that books, too, must be absorbed in your bloodstream to do you any good.

5   Confusion about what it means to own a book leads people to a false reverence for paper, binding, and type—a respect for the physical thing—the craft of the printer rather than the genius of the author. They forget that it is possible for a man to acquire the idea, to possess the beauty, which a great book contains, without staking his claim by pasting his bookplate inside the cover. Having a fine library doesn't prove that its owner has a

mind enriched by books; it proves nothing more than that he, his father, or his wife, was rich enough to buy them.

6   There are three kinds of book owners. The first has all the standard sets and best-sellers—unread, untouched. (This deluded individual owns wood-pulp and ink, not books.) The second has a great many books—a few of them read through, most of them dipped into, but all of them as clean and shiny as the day they were bought. (This person would probably like to make books his own, but is restrained by a false respect for their physical appearance.) The third has a few books or many—every one of them dog-eared and dilapidated, shaken and loosened by continual use, marked and scribbled in from front to back. (This man owns books.)

7   Is it false respect, you may ask, to preserve intact and unblemished a beautifully printed book, an elegantly bound edition? Of course not. I'd no more scribble all over a first edition of *Paradise Lost* than I'd give my baby a set of crayons and an original Rembrandt! I wouldn't mark up a painting or a statue. Its soul, so to speak, is inseparable from its body. And the beauty of a rare edition or of a richly manufactured volume is like that of a painting or a statue.

8   But the soul of a book *can* be separated from its body. A book is more like the score of a piece of music than it is like a painting. No great musician confuses a symphony with the printed sheets of music. Arturo Toscanini reveres Brahms, but Toscanini's score of the C-minor Symphony is so thoroughly marked up that no one but the maestro himself can read it. The reason why a great conductor makes notations on his musical scores—marks them up again and again each time he returns to study them—is the reason why you should mark your books. If your respect for magnificent binding or typography gets in the way, buy yourself a cheap edition and pay your respects to the author.

9   Why is marking up a book indispensable to reading? First, it keeps you awake. (And I don't mean merely conscious; I mean wide awake.) In the second place, reading, if it is active, is thinking, and thinking tends to express itself in words, spoken or written. The marked book is usually the thought-through book. Finally, writing helps you remember the thoughts you had, or the thoughts the author expressed. Let me develop these three points.

10   If reading is to accomplish anything more than passing time, it must be active. You can't let your eyes glide across the lines of a book and come up with an understanding of what you have read. Now an ordinary piece of light fiction, like say, *Gone with the Wind,* doesn't require the most active kind of reading. The books you read for pleasure can be read in a state of relaxation, and nothing is lost. But a great book, rich in ideas and beauty, a book that raises and tries to answer great fundamental questions, demands the most active reading of which you are capable. You don't absorb the

ideas of John Dewey[1] the way you absorb the crooning of Mr. Vallee.[2] You have to reach for them. That you cannot do while you're asleep.

11   If, when you've finished reading a book, the pages are filled with your notes, you know that you read actively. The most famous *active* reader of great books I know is President Hutchins, of the University of Chicago. He also has the hardest schedule of business activities of any man I know. He invariably reads with a pencil, and sometimes, when he picks up a book and pencil in the evening, he finds himself, instead of making intelligent notes, drawing what he calls "caviar factories" on the margins. When that happens, he puts the book down. He knows he's too tired to read, and he's just wasting time.

12   But, you may ask, why is writing necessary? Well, the physical act of writing, with your own hand, brings words and sentences more sharply before your mind and preserves them better in your memory. To set down your reaction to important words and sentences you have read, and the questions they have raised in your mind, is to preserve those reactions and sharpen those questions.

13   Even if you wrote on a scratch pad, and threw the paper away when you had finished writing, your grasp of the book would be surer. But you don't have to throw the paper away. The margins (top and bottom, as well as side), the end-papers, the very space between the lines, are all available. They aren't sacred. And, best of all, your marks and notes become an integral part of the book and stay there forever. You can pick up the book the following week or year, and there are all your points of agreement, disagreement, doubt, and inquiry. It's like resuming an interrupted conversation with the advantage of being able to pick up where you left off.

14   And that is exactly what reading a book should be: a conversation between you and the author. Presumably he knows more about the subject than you do; naturally, you'll have the proper humility as you approach him. But don't let anybody tell you that a reader is supposed to be solely on the receiving end. Understanding is a two-way operation; learning doesn't consist in being an empty receptacle. The learner has to question himself and question the teacher. He even has to argue with the teacher, once he understands what the teacher is saying. And marking a book is literally an expression of your differences, or agreements of opinion, with the author.

15   There are all kinds of devices for marking a book intelligently and fruitfully. Here's the way I do it:

16   1. *Underlining:* of major points, of important or forceful statements.

---

[1] John Dewey (1859–1952), educational philosopher who had a profound influence on learning through experimentation.

[2] Rudy Vallee was a popular singer of the 1920s, famous for his crooning high notes.

17   2. *Vertical lines at the margin:* to emphasize a statement already underlined.

18   3. *Star, asterisk, or other doo-dad at the margin:* to be used sparingly, to emphasize the ten or twenty most important statements in the book. (You may want to fold the bottom corner of each page on which you use such marks. It won't hurt the sturdy paper on which most modern books are printed, and you will be able to take the book off the shelf at any time and, by opening it at the folded-corner page, refresh your recollection of the book.)

19   4. *Numbers in the margin:* to indicate the sequence of points the author makes in developing a single argument.

20   5. *Numbers of other pages in the margin:* to indicate where else in the book the author made points relevant to the point marked; to tie up the ideas in a book, which, though they may be separated by many pages, belong together.

21   6. *Circling of key words or phrases.*

22   7. *Writing in the margin, or at the top or bottom of the page, for the sake of:* recording questions (and perhaps answers) which a passage raised in your mind; reducing a complicated discussion to a simple statement; recording the sequence of major points right through the books. I use the end-papers at the back of the book to make a personal index of the author's points in the order of their appearance.

23   The front end-papers are, to me, the most important. Some people reserve them for a fancy bookplate. I reserve them for fancy thinking. After I have finished reading the book and making my personal index on the back end-papers, I turn to the front and try to outline the book, not page by page, or point by point (I've already done that at the back), but as an integrated structure, with a basic unity and an order of parts. This outline is, to me, the measure of my understanding of the work.

24   If you're a die-hard anti-book-marker, you may object that the margins, the space between the lines, and the end-papers don't give you room enough. All right. How about using a scratch pad slightly smaller than the page-size of the book—so that the edges of the sheets won't protrude? Make your index, outlines, and even your notes on the pad, and then insert these sheets permanently inside the front and back covers of the book.

25   Or, you may say that this business of marking books is going to slow up your reading. It probably will. That's one of the reasons for doing it. Most of us have been taken in by the notion that speed of reading is a measure of our intelligence. There is no such thing as the right speed for intelligent reading. Some things should be read quickly and effortlessly, and some should be read slowly and even laboriously. The sign of intelligence in reading is the ability to read different things differently according to their worth. In the case of good books, the point is not to see how many of them

you can get through, but rather how many can get through you—how many you can make your own. A few friends are better than a thousand acquaintances. If this be your aim, as it should be, you will not be impatient if it takes more time and effort to read a great book than it does a newspaper.

26   You may have one final objection to marking books. You can't lend them to your friends because nobody else can read them without being distracted by your notes. Furthermore, you won't want to lend them because a marked copy is a kind of intellectual diary, and lending it is almost like giving your mind away.

27   If your friend wishes to read your *Plutarch's Lives, Shakespeare,* or *The Federalist Papers,* tell him gently but firmly to buy a copy. You will lend him your car or your coat—but your books are as much a part of you as your head or your heart.

VOCABULARY

mutilation (2)	typography (8)	receptacle (14)
prelude (4)	indispensable (9)	asterisk (18)
reverence (5)	fundamental (10)	recollection (18)
deluded (6)	invariably (11)	index (22)
woodpulp (6)	integral (13)	protrude (24)
dilapidated (6)	inquiry (13)	laboriously (25)
maestro (8)	presumably (14)	

QUESTIONS FOR CRITICAL THINKING

1. Teachers often complain that they cannot get students to mark their textbooks. Do you believe that this complaint is justified? Why or why not?
2. What device for marking books mentioned by Adler do you already use? Why do you find it useful?
3. Do you become attached to the textbooks you have read and studied carefully, or is it easy for you to sell them back to the bookstore? Give reasons for your answers.
4. Is it possible to judge people by the books they read? Supply examples that support your answer.
5. How do you feel about lending your books? Why?

QUESTIONS ON THE WRITING PROCESS

1. Why does the author take up fifteen paragraphs before he gets to the actual process of marking up books?
2. What word in paragraph 6 announces that a classification is about to take place?
3. In paragraph 4, what analogy does the author use to illustrate his point about owning books? How effective is the analogy?
4. What analogy does the author use in paragraph 8?
5. Why does the author refer to *Gone with the Wind* in paragraph 10?
6. In paragraph 14, how does the author define reading a book?
7. How does the author make it easier for his readers to follow his process analysis of marking a book?
8. What tone does the author use throughout his essay? What is your reaction to him?

WRITING ASSIGNMENTS

1. Write a 500-word essay in which you outline the steps for writing a research paper. Make your process so clear that someone who has never written a research paper could understand each step.
2. Write a well-developed essay in which you describe how you get yourself out of a depressed, angry, or revengeful mood. Present the process in terms of steps. Use transitions between steps.
3. Write a process description on how to keep a romance going. Your tone may be either serious or satirical.

BEHIND THE FORMALDEHYDE CURTAIN

Jessica Mitford

*Jessica Mitford (1917–   ) was born in England to Lord and Lady
Redesdale, members of the privileged gentry. But as a young woman
she moved to the United States and became a naturalized citizen of
this country. Since 1963, when she published* The American Way of
Death, *a relentless exposé of the mortuary business, she has been considered one of America's most successful muckrakers. With acerbic wit and
biting satire, she goes after the corruption and absurd traditions in certain corners of American society. Her other works are* Kind and Unusual
Punishment: The Prison Business *(1973);* Poison Penmanship *(1979),
a collection of her articles from* The Atlantic, Harper's, *and other peri-
odicals; and* A Fine Old Madness *(1977), the second volume of her
autobiography, which in 1960 began with* Daughters and Rebels.*

Taken from her book The American Way of Death, *the essay below is
typical of Mitford's muckraking technique, used here to expose mercilessly the hypocrisy behind one of America's most profitable businesses—the mortuary.*

1   The drama begins to unfold with the arrival of the corpse at the mortuary.

2   Alas, poor Yorick! How surprised he would be to see how his counter-
part of today is whisked off to a funeral parlor and is in short order sprayed,
sliced, pierced, pickled, trussed, trimmed, creamed, waxed, painted, rouged
and neatly dressed—transformed from a common corpse into a Beautiful
Memory Picture. This process is known in the trade as embalming and
restorative art, and is so universally employed in the United States and
Canada that the funeral director does it routinely, without consulting
corpse or kin. He regards as eccentric those few who are hardy enough to
suggest that it might be dispensed with. Yet no law requires embalming, no
religious doctrine commends it, nor is it dictated by considerations of
health, sanitation, or even of personal daintiness. In no part of the world
but in Northern America is it widely used. The purpose of embalming is to
make the corpse presentable for viewing in a suitably costly container; and
here too the funeral director routinely, without first consulting the family,
prepares the body for public display.

3   Is all this legal? The processes to which a dead body may be subjected
are after all to some extent circumscribed by law. In most states, for instance, the signature of next of kin must be obtained before an autopsy may
be performed, before the deceased may be cremated, before the body may
be turned over to a medical school for research purposes; or such provision
must be made in the decedent's will. In the case of embalming, no such

206

permission is required nor is it ever sought. A textbook, *The Principles and Practices of Embalming,* comments on this: "There is some question regarding the legality of much that is done within the preparation room." The author points out that it would be most unusual for a responsible member of a bereaved family to instruct the mortician, in so many words, to "embalm" the body of a deceased relative. The very term "embalming" is so seldom used that the mortician must rely upon custom in the matter. The author concludes that unless the family specifies otherwise, the act of entrusting the body to the care of a funeral establishment carries with it an implied permission to go ahead and embalm.

4   Embalming is indeed a most extraordinary procedure, and one must wonder at the docility of Americans who each year pay hundreds of millions of dollars for its perpetuation, blissfully ignorant of what it is all about, what is done, how it is done. Not one in ten thousand has any idea of what actually takes place. Books on the subject are extremely hard to come by. They are not to be found in most libraries or bookshops.

5   In an era when huge television audiences watch surgical operations in the comfort of their living rooms, when, thanks to the animated cartoon, the geography of the digestive system has become familiar territory even to the nursery school set, in a land where the satisfaction of curiosity about almost all matters is a national pastime, the secrecy surrounding embalming can, surely, hardly be attributed to the inherent gruesomeness of the subject. Custom in this regard has within this century suffered a complete reversal. In the early days of American embalming, when it was performed in the home of the deceased, it was almost mandatory for some relative to stay by the embalmer's side and witness the procedure. Today, family members who might wish to be in attendance would certainly be dissuaded by the funeral director. All others, except apprentices, are excluded by law from the preparation room.

6   A close look at what does actually take place may explain in large measure the undertaker's intractable reticence concerning a procedure that has become his major *raison d'être.* Is it possible he fears that public information about embalming might lead patrons to wonder if they really want this service? If the funeral men are loath to discuss the subject outside the trade, the reader may, understandably, be equally loath to go on reading at this point. For those who have the stomach for it, let us part the formaldehyde curtain. . . .

7   The body is first laid out in the undertaker's morgue—or rather, Mr. Jones is reposing in the preparation room—to be readied to bid the world farewell.

8   The preparation room in any of the better funeral establishments has the tiled and sterile look of a surgery, and indeed the embalmer-restorative artist who does his chores there is beginning to adopt the term "derma-surgeon" (appropriately corrupted by some mortician-writers as "demi-

surgeon") to describe his calling. His equipment, consisting of scalpels, scissors, augers, forceps, clamps, needles, pumps, tubes, bowls and basins, is crudely imitative of the surgeon's, as is his technique, acquired in a nine- or twelve-month post-high-school course in an embalming school. He is supplied by an advanced chemical industry with a bewildering array of fluids, sprays, pastes, oils, powders, creams, to fix or soften tissue, shrink or distend it as needed, dry it here, restore the moisture there. There are cosmetics, waxes and paints to fill and cover features, even plaster of Paris to replace entire limbs. There are ingenious aids to prop and stabilize the cadaver: a Vari-Pose Head Rest, the Edwards Arm and Hand Positioner, the Repose Block (to support the shoulders during the embalming), and the Throop Foot Positioner, which resembles an old-fashioned stocks.

9   Mr. John H. Eckels, president of the Eckels College of Mortuary Science, thus describes the first part of the embalming procedure: "In the hands of a skilled practitioner, this work may be done in a comparatively short time and without mutilating the body other than by slight incision— so slight that it scarcely would cause serious inconvenience if made upon a living person. It is necessary to remove the blood, and doing this not only helps in the disinfecting, but removes the principal cause of disfigurements due to discoloration."

10   Another textbook discusses the all-important time element: "The earlier this is done, the better, for every hour that elapses between death and embalming will add to the problems and complications encountered...." Just how soon should one get going on the embalming? The author tells us, "On the basis of such scanty information made available to this profession through its rudimentary and haphazard system of technical research, we must conclude that the best results are to be obtained if the subject is embalmed before life is completely extinct—that is, before cellular death has occurred. In the average case, this would mean within an hour after somatic death." For those who feel that there is something a little rudimentary, not to say haphazard, about this advice, a comforting thought is offered by another writer. Speaking of fears entertained in early days of premature burial, he points out, "One of the effects of embalming by chemical injection, however, has been to dispel fears of live burial." How true; once the blood is removed, chances of live burial are indeed remote.

11   To return to Mr. Jones, the blood is drained out through the veins and replaced by embalming fluid pumped in through the arteries. As noted in *The Principles and Practices of Embalming,* "every operator has a favorite injection and drainage point—a fact which becomes a handicap only if he fails or refuses to forsake his favorites when conditions demand it." Typical favorites are the carotid artery, femoral artery, jugular vein, subclavian vein. There are various choices of embalming fluid. If Flextone is used, it will produce a "mild, flexible rigidity. The skin retains a velvety softness, the tissues are rubbery and pliable. Ideal for women and children." It may

be blended with B. and G. Products Company's Lyf-Lyk tint, which is guaranteed to reproduce "nature's own skin texture . . . the velvety appearance of living tissue." Suntone comes in three separate tints: Suntan; Special Cosmetic Tint, a pink shade "especially indicated for young female subjects"; and Regular Cosmetic Tint, moderately pink.

12   About three to six gallons of a dyed and perfumed solution of formaldehyde, glycerin, borax, phenol, alcohol and water is soon circulating through Mr. Jones, whose mouth has been sewn together with a "needle directed upward between the upper lip and gum and brought out through the left nostril," with the corners raised slightly "for a more pleasant expression." If he should be bucktoothed, his teeth are cleaned with Bon Ami and coated with colorless nail polish. His eyes, meanwhile, are closed with flesh-tinted eye caps and eye cement.

13   The next step is to have at Mr. Jones with a thing called a trocar. This is a long, hollow needle attached to a tube. It is jabbed into the abdomen, poked around the entrails and chest cavity, the contents of which are pumped out and replaced with "cavity fluid." This done, and the hole in the abdomen sewn up, Mr. Jones's face is heavily creamed (to protect the skin from burns which may be caused by leakage of the chemicals), and he is covered with a sheet and left unmolested for a while. But not for long—there is more, much more, in store for him. He has been embalmed, but not yet restored, and the best time to start the restorative work is eight to ten hours after embalming, when the tissues have become firm and dry.

14   The object of all this attention to the corpse, it must be remembered, is to make it presentable for viewing in an attitude of healthy repose. "Our customs require the presentation of our dead in the semblance of normality . . . unmarred by the ravages of illness, disease or mutilation," says Mr. J. Sheridan Mayer in his *Restorative Art*. This is rather a large order since few people die in the full bloom of health, unravaged by illness and unmarked by some disfigurement. The funeral industry is equal to the challenge: "In some cases the gruesome appearance of a mutilated or disease-ridden subject may be quite discouraging. The task of restoration may seem impossible and shake the confidence of the embalmer. This is the time for intestinal fortitude and determination. Once the formative work is begun and affected tissues are cleaned or removed, all doubts of success vanish. It is surprising and gratifying to discover the results which may be obtained."

15   The embalmer, having allowed an appropriate interval to elapse, returns to the attack, but now he brings into play the skill and equipment of sculptor and cosmetician. Is a hand missing? Casting one in plaster of Paris is a simple matter. "For replacement purposes, only a cast of the back of the hand is necessary; this is within the ability of the average operator and is quite adequate." If a lip or two, a nose or an ear should be missing, the embalmer has at hand a variety of restorative waxes with which to model replacements. Pores and skin texture are simulated by stippling with a little

brush, and over this cosmetics are laid on. Head off? Decapitation cases are rather routinely handled. Ragged edges are trimmed, and head joined to torso with a series of splints, wires and sutures. It is a good idea to have a little something at the neck—a scarf or a high collar—when time for viewing comes. Swollen mouth? Cut out tissue as needed from inside the lips. If too much is removed, the surface contour can easily be restored by padding with cotton. Swollen necks and cheeks are reduced by removing tissue through vertical incisions made down each side of the neck. "When the deceased is casketed, the pillow will hide the suture incisions . . . as an extra precaution against leakage, the suture may be painted with liquid sealer."

16   The opposite condition is more likely to present itself—that of emaciation. His hypodermic syringe now loaded with massage cream, the embalmer seeks out and fills the hollowed and sunken areas by injection. In this procedure the backs of the hands and fingers and the under-chin area should not be neglected.

17   Positioning the lips is a problem that recurrently challenges the ingenuity of the embalmer. Closed too tightly, they tend to give a stern, even disapproving expression. Ideally, embalmers feel, the lips should give the impression of being ever so slightly parted, the upper lip protruding slightly for a more youthful appearance. This takes some engineering, however, as the lips tend to drift apart. Lip drift can sometimes be remedied by pushing one or two straight pins through the inner margin of the lower lip and then inserting them between the two front upper teeth. If Mr. Jones happens to have no teeth, the pins can just as easily be anchored in his Armstrong Face Former and Denture Replacer. Another method to maintain lip closure is to dislocate the lower jaw, which is then held in its new position by a wire run through holes which have been drilled through the upper and lower jaws at the midline. As the French are fond of saying, *il faut souffrir pour être belle.*[1]

18   If Mr. Jones has died of jaundice, the embalming fluid will very likely turn him green. Does this deter the embalmer? Not if he has intestinal fortitude. Masking pastes and cosmetics are heavily laid on, burial garments and casket interiors are color-correlated with particular care, and Jones is displayed beneath rose-colored lights. Friends will say "How *well* he looks." Death by carbon monoxide, on the other hand, can be rather a good thing from the embalmer's viewpoint: "One advantage is the fact that this type of discoloration is an exaggerated form of a natural pink coloration." This is nice because the healthy glow is already present and needs but little attention.

19   The patching and filling completed, Mr. Jones is now shaved, washed and dressed. Cream-based cosmetic, available in pink, flesh, suntan, brunette and blond, is applied to his hands and face, his hair is shampooed and combed (and, in the case of Mrs. Jones, set), his hands manicured. For the

[1]You have to suffer to be beautiful.

horny-handed son of toil special care must be taken; cream should be applied to remove ingrained grime, and the nails cleaned. "If he were not in the habit of having them manicured in life, trimming and shaping is advised for better appearance—never questioned by kin."

20   Jones is now ready for casketing (this is the present participle of the verb "to casket"). In this operation his right shoulder should be depressed slightly "to turn the body a bit to the right and soften the appearance of lying flat on the back." Positioning the hands is a matter of importance, and special rubber positioning blocks may be used. The hands should be cupped slightly for a more lifelike, relaxed appearance. Proper placement of the body requires a delicate sense of balance. It should lie as high as possible in the casket, yet not so high that the lid, when lowered, will hit the nose. On the other hand, we are cautioned, placing the body too low "creates the impression that the body is in a box."

21   Jones is next wheeled into the appointed slumber room where a few last touches may be added—his favorite pipe placed in his hand or, if he was a great reader, a book propped into position. (In the case of little Master Jones a Teddy bear may be clutched.) Here he will hold open house for a few days, visiting hours 10 A.M. to 9 P.M.

22   All now being in readiness, the funeral director calls a staff conference to make sure that each assistant knows his precise duties. Mr. Wilber Kriege writes: "This makes your staff feel that they are a part of the team, with a definite assignment that must be properly carried out if the whole plan is to succeed. You never heard of a football coach who failed to talk to his entire team before they go on the field. They have drilled on the plays they are to execute for hours and days, and yet the successful coach knows the importance of making even the bench-warming third-string substitute feel that he is important if the game is to be won." The winning of *this* game is predicated upon glass-smooth handling of the logistics. The funeral director has notified the pallbearers whose names were furnished by the family, has arranged for the presence of clergyman, organist, and soloist, has provided transportation for everybody, has organized and listed the flowers sent by friends. In *Psychology of Funeral Service* Mr. Edward A. Martin points out: "He may not always do as much as the family thinks he is doing, but it is his helpful guidance that they appreciate in knowing they are proceeding as they should. . . . The important thing is how well his services can be used to make the family believe they are giving unlimited expression to their own sentiment."

23   The religious service may be held in a church or in the chapel of the funeral home; the funeral director vastly prefers the latter arrangement, for not only is it more convenient for him but it affords him the opportunity to show off his beautiful facilities to the gathered mourners. After the clergyman has had his say, the mourners queue up to file past the casket for a last look at the deceased. The family is *never* asked whether they want an open-casket ceremony; in the absence of their instruction to the contrary, this is

taken for granted. Consequently well over 90 per cent of all American funerals feature the open casket—a custom unknown in other parts of the world. Foreigners are astonished by it. An English woman living in San Francisco described her reaction in a letter to the writer:

> I myself have attended only one funeral here—that of an elderly fellow worker of mine. After the service I could not understand why everyone was walking towards the coffin (sorry, I mean casket), but thought I had better follow the crowd. It shook me rigid to get there and find the casket open and poor old Oscar lying there in his brown tweed suit, wearing a suntan makeup and just the wrong shade of lipstick. If I had not been extremely fond of the old boy, I have a horrible feeling that I might have giggled. Then and there I decided that I could never face another American funeral—even dead.

24   The casket (which has been resting throughout the service on a Classic Beauty Ultra Metal Casket Bier) is now transferred by a hydraulically operated device called Porto-Lift to a balloon-tired, Glide Easy casket carriage which will wheel it to yet another conveyance, the Cadillac Funeral Coach. This may be lavender, cream, light green—anything but black. Interiors, of course, are color-correlated, "for the man who cannot stop short of perfection."

25   At graveside, the casket is lowered into the earth. This office, once the prerogative of friends of the deceased, is now performed by a patented mechanical lowering device. A "Lifetime Green" artificial grass mat is at the ready to conceal the sere earth, and overhead, to conceal the sky, is a portable Steril Chapel Tent ("resists the intense heat and humidity of summer and the terrific storms of winter . . . available in Silver Grey, Rose or Evergreen"). Now is the time for the ritual scattering of earth over the coffin, as the solemn words "earth to earth, ashes to ashes, dust to dust" are pronounced by the officiating cleric. This can today be accomplished "with a mere flick of the wrist with the Gordon Leak-Proof Earth Dispenser. No grasping of a handful of dirt, no soiled fingers. Simple, dignified, beautiful, reverent! The modern way!" The Gordon Earth Dispenser (at $5) is of nickel-plated brass construction. It is not only "attractive to the eye and long wearing"; it is also "one of the 'tools' for building better public relations" if presented as "an appropriate non-commercial gift" to the clergyman. It is shaped something like a saltshaker.

26   Untouched by human hand, the coffin and the earth are now united.

27   It is in the function of directing the participants through this maze of gadgetry that the funeral director has assigned to himself his relatively new role of "grief therapist." He has relieved the family of every detail, he has revamped the corpse to look like a living doll, he has arranged for it to nap for a few days in a slumber room, he has put on a well-oiled performance in which the concept of *death* has played no part whatsoever—unless it was inconsiderately mentioned by the clergyman who conducted the religious

service. He has done everything in his power to make the funeral a real pleasure for everybody concerned. He and his team have given their all to score an upset victory over death.

VOCABULARY

trussed (1)	rudimentary (10)	emaciation (16)
decedent (3)	somatic (10)	predicated (22)
intractable (6)	decapitation (15)	cleric (25)
stocks (8)		

QUESTIONS FOR CRITICAL THINKING

1. What tone does the author use throughout much of the essay? What purpose does this tone serve? What is your reaction to the tone?
2. In much of the essay, Mitford treats the embalmer with irreverent irony. What are some typical examples? What is the effect? Point out two or three specific passages.
3. Much of Mitford's anger is directed toward the secrecy surrounding the embalming process. Why does the secrecy evoke such anger?
4. Do you consider the essay entirely muckraking? Or is there imbedded in the relentless criticism also some advice to Americans with respect to their handling of funerals? Give reasons for your answer.
5. According to Mitford, what is the mortician's primary purpose when doing his job? How do you feel about this purpose?

QUESTIONS ON THE WRITING PROCESS

1. What are the *major* steps by which this process analysis is divided? List each step.
2. The reader of this essay needs to have a strong stomach. Is the author aware of the gruesomeness of her description? What is the reason for so many grisly details?
3. What is the meaning of the allusion to Yorick in paragraph 2?
4. What does the letter from the English woman living in San Francisco contribute to the essay? (See paragraph 23.)
5. With little subtlety, Mitford also satirizes the mortuary industry for using euphemisms associated with death. What are some of these euphemisms? List two or three. Do you approve of them or would you prefer direct language? What other euphemisms has our society invented in order to mask unpleasant aspects of our society?

WRITING ASSIGNMENTS

1. In a 500-word essay, support the American custom of embalming. Begin with a clear proposition and support your position with facts and examples. Expert testimony will also help your position.

2. Following Mitford's model, choose another American custom that you consider loathsome or unnecessary and argue for its abolition or replacement. If you have the ability, use satire as your way of making the custom look ridiculous.

3. Write a 500-word essay in which you describe the action behind the scenes of some common activity, such as cooking the food in an elegant restaurant, pulling a tooth at a dentist's office, getting ready for a wedding, making a movie or television show.

HOW TO MAKE A PINWHEEL

Jacob Fairchild

When I was five years old, my mother taught me how to make a pinwheel. I was so thrilled and proud of this accomplishment that during my elementary school years I taught many of my friends how to make pinwheels. Here are the steps involved.

First of all, make sure that the following materials are handy: a sheet of paper, a straight pin, a pencil with an eraser, a ruler, and a pair of scissors. The paper that makes a pinwheel must be square. You can make sure that it is square by folding it. (See drawing A.)

A

Next, draw lines from corner to corner of the paper with a ruler. Then, draw a small circle about the size of a penny in the center of the paper where the lines from corner to corner cross. (See drawing B.) Cut the paper on the lines, but do not cut into the circle. By doing this, you are cutting each corner into two others, making a total of eight corners. Next, bend every other corner into the center of the pennysized circle. Four bent corners should result. Now, put a straight pin through the four corners and the center of the paper. Finally, stick the pin into the eraser on the end of a pencil.

B

The pinwheel should proudly spin in the wind when you blow on it or run with it. Sometimes when the paper that makes the pinwheel is pinned tightly to the eraser, the pinwheel is unable to spin. But when given a little additional room, the pinwheel should spin easily. Different decorations, such as red dots, multicolored lines, or geometric figures, produce fascinating patterns as the pinwheel spins.

SIX

CLASSIFICATION

Anyone old enough to read this book has surely engaged in classification. It occurs whenever one attempts to break down a thing, an idea, or a process into its principal parts. There is almost no limit to the number of categories our ingenuity for classifying has produced. Some of these are formal attempts at classification, as when biologists group flora and fauna into phyla, classes, and species. Others are informal distinctions that we make every day. We speak of baseball games that are no-hitters, one-hitters, or slugfests; novels that are gothics, romances, or mysteries; people who are heroes, villains, or fools.

Most of the classifications attempted in the essay are merely interesting observations someone has made about something. They are not intended as formal, ironclad distinctions, and are useful only because they provide insight into the writer's subject. Take, for example, the first paragraph in this chapter, "The Three New Yorks," by E. B. White. It would be fruitless to quibble that White is mistaken, that there are not three New Yorks, but actually a hundred. In fact, one could argue that there is probably at least one New York for every inhabitant of the city. But White's classification of New York gives us an insightful way to grasp the idea of this vast city. Without this kind of shorthand thinking, a subject as vast as New York would remain incomprehensible to the single mind.

It is much the same with "Poetic People" by Max Eastman. A literal-minded reader might protest that surely there are other kinds of people in this world than simply the practical and the poetic. No doubt there are. Indeed, one would think it almost foolish to attempt to find categories into which all the people of the world can fit. Yet Eastman's two types are readily recognizable to any people-watcher. They are surely not absolute; but they provide a useful way of looking at people.

If the way to approach classification, then, is to regard it merely as a useful way of organizing a subject, that is the spirit in which you must write one. For example, if your teacher asks you to write an essay classifying the kinds of friendships you have experienced, the assignment is intended mainly to force you to think deeply about the friendships in your life. It is not meant to provoke you into writing a scientific treatise on friendship. You are obviously the best judge of the categories your friends fall into, and other students will no doubt mention categories you didn't even think of. In short, with many classification essays it is less a question of whether you have got the categories right, and more a question of whether you can make a convincing case for the ones you invent.

It is possible, of course, to invent a classification that is dead wrong. It is possible that the categories you come up with will simply not match the subject, especially for a subject that is divisible into universally recognizable categories. For example, if you were asked to write an essay classifying the techniques of teaching used in the college classroom and you omitted the lecture method, you would obviously have overlooked an important category. Indeed, incompleteness in the division is a common error in student classification essays. Yet it is one that can be made only when the subject being classified is divisible into categories that everyone should know.

The basic idea behind classifying any subject is to make your selection of types according to a single principle. Indeed, a writer will usually begin this kind of essay by explaining the classification principle on which it is based. Theodore H. White, for example, begins his short essay by explaining that he is writing about a system of self-classification used by students during his school days. Lewis Thomas begins his essay by explaining that he is going to do a technology assessment of the methods of managing disease. If a reader is to follow what you intend to do in a classification essay, this sort of revelation is generally indispensable.

To write a useful classification, then, you need to observe these practices: make your categories mutually exclusive, base your classification on a single principle, and explain that principle to your reader. You must also try to use intelligence and originality in constructing a classification, bearing in mind that this kind of essay is really an exercise in creative thinking.

THE THREE NEW YORKS

E. B. White

Elwyn Brooks White (1899–   ) is an American writer noted for his witty, satiric style. He has written some seven books of essays, much light verse, and three well-known children's books, Stuart Little *(1945),* Charlotte's Web *(1952), and* The Trumpet of the Swan *(1970).*

In this paragraph, taken from Here Is New York *(1949), E. B. White classifies the city of New York into three categories according to the people who live there.*

There are roughly three New Yorks. There is, first, the New York of the man or woman who was born here, who takes the city for granted and accepts its size and its turbulence as natural and inevitable. Second, there is the New York of the commuter—the city that is devoured by locusts each day and spat out each night. Third, there is the New York of the person who was born somewhere else and came to New York in quest of something. Of these three trembling cities the greatest is the last—the city of final destination, the city that is a goal. It is this third city that accounts for New York's high-strung disposition, its poetical deportment, its dedication to the arts, and its incomparable achievements. Commuters give the city its tidal restlessness, natives give it solidity and continuity, but the settlers give it passion. And whether it is a farmer arriving from Italy to set up a small grocery store in a slum, or a young girl arriving from a small town in Mississippi to escape the indignity of being observed by her neighbors, or a boy arriving from the Corn Belt with a manuscript in his suitcase and a pain in his heart, it makes no difference: each embraces New York with the intense excitement of first love, each absorbs New York with the fresh eyes of an adventurer, each generates heat and light to dwarf the Consolidated Edison Company.

VOCABULARY

turbulence	disposition	deportment

QUESTIONS FOR CRITICAL THINKING

1. What are your impressions of New York? How have you formed them?
2. In his examples of new arrivals to the city, the author cites the case of "a young girl arriving from a small town in Mississippi to escape the indignity of being observed." What do you think are the main differences between life in a small Mississippi town and life in a big city such as New York?

QUESTIONS ON THE WRITING PROCESS

1. Every division must be based on a single principle. On what single principle is this division based?
2. The author classifies New York into three cities and briefly discusses each of them. What transition does he use to introduce and separate his discussion of each "city"?
3. In the first half of the paragraph, the author explains what he means by "three New Yorks." What does he deal with in the second half of the paragraph? How does he move the discussion from the three New Yorks to the new topic?

WRITING ASSIGNMENTS

1. Write a paragraph dividing the people in your hometown into at least two categories.
2. Write an essay that classifies the various towns and communities in which you have lived.

POETIC PEOPLE

Max Eastman

Max Eastman (1883–1969), American writer and poet, was for many years an avowed Communist and leader of the American left. Eventually he became disenchanted with Communism and wrote several books critical of the system, such as Reflections on the Failure of Socialism *(1955).*

The following paragraph is taken from his Enjoyment of Poetry *(1913). In it Eastman proposes an ingenious experiment to distinguish between two types of human temperament.*

A simple experiment will distinguish two types of human nature. Gather a throng of people and pour them into a ferry-boat. By the time the boat has swung into the river you will find that a certain proportion have taken the trouble to climb upstairs in order to be out on deck and see what is to be seen as they cross over. The rest have settled indoors to think what they will do upon reaching the other side, or perhaps lose themselves in apathy or tobacco smoke. But leaving out those apathetic, or addicted to a single enjoyment, we may divide all the alert passengers on the boat into two classes: those who are interested in crossing the river, and those who are merely interested in getting across. And we may divide all the people on the earth, or all the moods of people, in the same way. Some of them are chiefly occupied with attaining ends, and some with receiving experiences. The distinction of the two will be more marked when we name the first kind practical, and the second poetic, for common knowledge recognizes that a person poetic or in a poetic mood is impractical, and a practical person is intolerant of poetry.

VOCABULARY

apathy   attaining

QUESTIONS FOR CRITICAL THINKING

1. What are the characteristics of poetry that would cause practical people to dislike it?
2. The author claims that "common knowledge recognizes that a person poetic or in a poetic mood is impractical, and a practical person is intolerant of poetry." Has this assertion been borne out by your own experience? Into which group would you classify yourself?
3. How would you define "practicalness" as a personality trait?

QUESTIONS ON THE WRITING PROCESS

1. Examine the third sentence of the paragraph. What pronoun does the author use to refer to the reader? What effect does his use of this pronoun have on the writing?
2. How does the author refer to himself in the paragraph? By what name is this form of self-reference commonly known?
3. Classifications may be formal or informal depending on the purpose and method of the author. Into which category would you place this one? What is its ultimate purpose?

WRITING ASSIGNMENTS

1. Write a brief essay classifying the kinds of moods you often seem to be in.
2. Are you primarily poetic or practical? Describe yourself in one or the other of these terms in a brief essay. Be sure to give examples.

SHORT ESSAYS

TYPES OF COLLEGE STUDENTS

Theodore H. White

Theodore Harold White (1913–   ) was born in Boston and educated at Harvard. He has been a bureau chief for Time *and an editor of the* New Republic. *He is the author of several books, including* The Making of a President, 1964 *(1965) and* Breach of Faith *(1975).*

The author describes the classifications in which Harvard students of his day chose to sort themselves, and places himself in one of the categories.

1 Students divide themselves by their own discriminations in every generation, and the group I ran with had a neat system of classification. Harvard, my own group held, was divided into three groups—white men, gray men and meatballs. I belonged to the meatballs, by self-classification. White men were youngsters of great name; my own class held a Boston Saltonstall, a New York Straus, a Chicago Marshall Field, two Roosevelts (John and Kermit), a Joseph P. Kennedy, Jr. The upper classes had another Roosevelt (Franklin, Jr.), a Rockefeller (David, with whom I shared a tutor in my sophomore year), a Morgan, and New York and Boston names of a dozen different fashionable pedigrees. Students of such names had automobiles; they went to Boston deb parties, football games, the June crew race against Yale; they belonged to clubs. At Harvard today, they are called "preppies," the private-school boys of mythical "St. Grottlesex."

2 Between white men above and meatballs at the bottom came the gray men. The gray men were mostly public-high-school boys, sturdy sons of America's middle class. They went out for football and baseball, manned the *Crimson* and the *Lampoon,* ran for class committees and, later in life, for school committees and political office. They came neither of the aristocracy nor of the deserving poor, as did most meatballs and scholarship boys. Caspar Weinberger, of my class of 1938, for example, was president of the *Crimson* and graduated magna cum laude; he later became Secretary of Health, Education and Welfare, but as an undergraduate was a gray man from California. John King, of the same class of 1938, was another gray man; he became governor of New Hampshire. Wiley Mayne, an earnest student of history, who graduated with us, was a gray man from Iowa, later becoming congressman from Sioux City. He served on the House Judiciary Committee that voted to impeach Richard Nixon—with Wiley Mayne voting to support the President. The most brilliant member of the class was probably Arthur M. Schlesinger, Jr., who defied categorization. Definitely no meatball, Schlesinger lacked then either the wealth or the savoir-faire of the white men. Indeed, Schlesinger, who was to go on to a fame surpassing that of his scholar father, was one who could apparently mingle with both

white men *and* meatballs. In his youth, Schlesinger was a boy of extraordinary sweetness and generosity, one of the few on campus who would be friendly to a Jewish meatball, not only a liberal by heredity, but a liberal in practice. Since Wiley Mayne, Arthur Schlesinger and I were all rivals, in an indistinct way, in the undergraduate rivalry of the History Department, I followed their careers with some interest. Mayne was a conservative, tart-tongued and stiff. I remember on the night of our Class Day dance, as we were all about to leave, he unburdened himself to me on "Eastern liberals who look down their long snob noses on people like me from the Midwest." Over the years Mayne grew into a milder, gentler, warmer person until in his agony over Nixon, wrestling with his conscience on whether to impeach or not, he seemed to be perhaps the most sensitive and human member of the Judiciary Committee. Schlesinger, by contrast, developed a certainty about affairs, a public tartness of manner associated with the general liberal rigidity of the late sixties that offended many—and yet, for all that, he remained as kind and gentle to old friends like myself, with whose politics he came profoundly to disagree, as he had been in boyhood. Both Schlesinger and Mayne, the liberal and the conservative, were always absolutely firm in their opinions. I, in the years starting at Harvard, and continuing in later life, wandered all through the political spectrum, and envied them both for their certainties.

3   I find some difficulty in describing what a "meatball" was. Meatballs were usually day students or scholarship students. We were at Harvard not to enjoy the games, the girls, the burlesque shows of the Old Howard, the companionship, the elms, the turning leaves of fall, the grassy banks of the Charles. We had come to get the Harvard badge, which says "Veritas," but really means a job somewhere in the future, in some bureaucracy, in some institution, in some school, laboratory, university or law firm.

VOCABULARY

discriminations (1)	surpassing (2)	Veritas (3)
savoir-faire (2)	heredity (2)	

QUESTIONS FOR CRITICAL THINKING

1. Is there an American aristocracy, as the author seems to imply? What are the implications of such a class in a democratic society?
2. How do you account for so many of the author's classmates' achieving political and social prominence? What possible contribution do you think the "Harvard badge" might have made to the careers of these men?
3. The author describes Arthur M. Schlesinger, Jr., as having "the general liberal rigidity of the late sixties." What was the nature of this liberal rigidity? What were its premises and beliefs?
4. The author says that he envied both Schlesinger and Mayne for their certainties. What do you suppose he means by that? Why would certainty be an enviable thing?

QUESTIONS ON THE WRITING PROCESS

1. How does the author support his contention that "white men" were youngsters of great name?
2. What common rhetorical device does the author use throughout in describing the three categories of Harvard students?
3. The second paragraph, though continuing with the division, attempts to perform at least two different rhetorical functions. What are they? Identify where one function ends and the other begins.
4. The author's description of "meatballs" relies on an indirect contrast. With what is he contrasting the life of the "meatball"? In which sentence is the indirect contrast drawn?
5. The excerpt consists of three paragraphs with no transitions between them. Why are transitions unnecessary in this particular case?

WRITING ASSIGNMENTS

1. Write an essay classifying the students at your own school.
2. Write an essay classifying the teachers you have had.
3. Is there an aristocracy in America? Write an essay discussing this idea.

LEARNED WORDS AND POPULAR WORDS

J. B. Greenough and G. L. Kittredge

J. B. Greenough (1833–1901) was a professor of Latin at Harvard and author of a series of classical textbooks. George Lyman Kittredge (1860–1941) was a Harvard-educated scholar and teacher. He was the author and editor of many books, including the popular Complete Works of Shakespeare *(1936).*

The authors describe two broad categories into which most words of any language can be sorted.

1   In every cultivated language there are two great classes of words which, taken together, comprise the whole vocabulary. First, there are those words with which we become acquainted in ordinary conversation, which we learn, that is to say, from the members of our own family and from our familiar associates, and which we should know and use even if we could not read or write. They concern the common things of life, and are the stock in trade of all who speak the language. Such words may be called "popular," since they belong to the people at large and are not the exclusive possession of a limited class.

2   On the other hand, our language includes a multitude of words which are comparatively seldom used in ordinary conversation. Their meanings are known to every educated person, but there is little occasion to employ them at home or in the market-place. Our first acquaintance with them comes not from our mother's lips or from the talk of our schoolmates, but from books that we read, lectures that we hear, or the more formal conversation of highly educated speakers who are discussing some particular topic in a style appropriately elevated above the habitual level of everyday life. Such words are called "learned," and the distinction between them and "popular" words is of great importance to a right understanding of linguistic process.

3   The difference between popular and learned words may be easily seen in a few examples. We may describe a girl as "lively" or as "vivacious." In the first case, we are using a native English formation from the familiar noun *life.* In the latter, we are using a Latin derivative which has precisely the same meaning. Yet the atmosphere of the two words is quite different. No one ever got the adjective *lively* out of a book. It is a part of everybody's vocabulary. We cannot remember a time when we did not know it, and we feel sure that we learned it long before we were able to read. On the other hand, we must have passed several years of our lives before learning the word *vivacious.* We may even remember the first time that we saw it in

print or heard it from some grown-up friend who was talking over our childish heads. Both *lively* and *vivacious* are good English words, but *lively* is popular and *vivacious* is learned.

4   From the same point of view we may contrast the following pairs of synonyms:[1] *the same, identical; speech, oration; fire, conflagration; choose, select; brave, valorous; swallowing, deglutition; striking, percussion; building, edifice; shady, umbrageous; puckery, astringent; learned, erudite; secret, cryptic; destroy, annihilate; stiff, rigid; flabby, flaccid; queer, eccentric; behead, decapitate; round, circular; thin, emaciated; fat, corpulent; truthful, veracious; try, endeavor; bit, modicum; piece, fragment; sharp, acute; crazy, maniacal; king, sovereign; book, volume; lying, mendacious; beggar, mendicant; teacher, instructor; play, drama; air, atmosphere; paint, pigment.*

5   The terms "popular" and "learned," as applied to words, are not absolute definitions. No two persons have the same stock of words, and the same word may be "popular" in one man's vocabulary and "learned" in another's. There are also different grades of "popularity"; indeed there is in reality a continuous gradation from infantile words like *mama* and *papa* to such erudite derivatives as *concatenation* and *cataclysm*. Still, the division into "learned" and "popular" is convenient and sound. Disputes may arise as to the classification of any particular word, but there can be no difference of opinion about the general principle. We must be careful, however, to avoid misconception. When we call a word "popular," we do not mean that it is a favorite word, but simply that it belongs to the people as a whole—that is, it is everybody's word, not the possession of a limited number. When we call a word "learned" we do not mean that it is used by scholars alone, but simply that its presence in the English vocabulary is due to books and the cultivation of literature rather than to the actual needs of ordinary conversation.

VOCABULARY

comprise (1)	concatenation (5)
gradation (5)	cataclysm (5)

---

[1]Not all the words are exact synonyms, but that is of no importance in the present discussion.

QUESTIONS FOR CRITICAL THINKING

1. This excerpt comes from a book originally published in 1901. How applicable are the observations of the authors to the way we use words today?
2. Which class of words do you think is growing faster today? Why?
3. How do we adapt the vocabulary we use to suit the social circumstances of the moment? How does this obvious adapting, which most people do, affect our sincerity?
4. Which class of words are we most likely to use in the classroom setting? Why, and to whom, would we habitually use such words?
5. Some people claim that the cultivation of literature and scholarship is diminishing today. If true, what effect is this likely to have on the vocabulary of the language?

QUESTIONS ON THE WRITING PROCESS

1. Apart from the obvious attempt at dividing words into two classes, what other rhetorical function are the authors trying to accomplish?
2. Examine the first sentence of paragraph 2. What is the purpose of the initial phrase in this sentence?
3. In the third and fourth paragraphs, the authors try to make clear the distinction between the two classes of words. What rhetorical strategy do they rely on to do this?
4. What is the purpose of the fifth paragraph of this excerpt?
5. In the third paragraph, the authors rely heavily on the use of transition words and phrases to hold their argument together. What are these words and phrases? Identify at least three of them.

WRITING ASSIGNMENTS

1. Write two brief essays about any hobby that you enjoy. In the first essay, use only common, everyday words. In the second, try to use as many learned words as you can in place of the common ones. Contrast the two pieces.
2. Write an essay in which you analyze your vocabulary and give examples of both the learned and popular words in it.

DIFFERENT TYPES OF COMPOSERS

Aaron Copland

American composer Aaron Copland (1900–　) is widely known for his many ballet scores and major orchestral works. He has lectured extensively and has written many books that attempt to explain classical music to uninitiated audiences. This brief excerpt is taken from his What to Listen For in Music *(1957).*

Copland classifies composers into four primary types based on their different approaches to the art of composing.

1　I can see three different types of composers in musical history, each of whom conceives music in a somewhat different fashion.

2　The type that has fired public imagination most is that of the spontaneously inspired composer—the Franz Schubert type, in other words. All composers are inspired, of course, but this type is more spontaneously inspired. Music simply wells out of him. He can't get it down on paper fast enough. You can almost tell this type of composer by his prolific output. In certain months, Schubert wrote a song a day. Hugo Wolf did the same.

3　In a sense, men of this kind begin not so much with a musical theme as with a completed composition. They invariably work best in the shorter forms. It is much easier to improvise a song than it is to improvise a symphony. It isn't easy to be inspired in that spontaneous way for long periods at a stretch. Even Schubert was more successful in handling the shorter forms of music. The spontaneously inspired man is only one type of composer, with his own limitations.

4　Beethoven symbolizes the second type—the constructive type, one might call it. This type exemplifies my theory of the creative process in music better than any other, because in this case the composer really does begin with a musical theme. In Beethoven's case there is no doubt about it, for we have the notebooks in which he put the themes down. We can see from his notebooks how he worked over his themes—how he would not let them be until they were as perfect as he could make them. Beethoven was not a spontaneously inspired composer in the Schubert sense at all. He was the type that begins with a theme; makes it a germinal idea; and upon that constructs a musical work, day after day, in painstaking fashion. Most composers since Beethoven's day belong to this second type.

5　The third type of creator I can only call, for lack of a better name, the traditionalist type. Men like Palestrina and Bach belong in this category. They both exemplify the kind of composer who is born in a particular period of musical history, when a certain musical style is about to reach its fullest development. It is a question at such a time of creating music in a well-known and accepted style and doing it in a way that is better than anyone has done it before you.

6   Beethoven and Schubert started from a different premise. They both had serious pretensions to originality: After all, Schubert practically created the song form single-handed; and the whole face of music changed after Beethoven lived. But Bach and Palestrina simply improved on what had gone before them.

7   The traditionalist type of composer begins with a pattern rather than with a theme. The creative act with Palestrina is not the thematic conception so much as the personal treatment of a well-established pattern. And even Bach, who conceived forty-eight of the most varied and inspired themes in his *Well Tempered Clavichord,* knew in advance the general formal mold that they were to fill. It goes without saying that we are not living in a traditionalist period nowadays.

8   One might add, for the sake of completeness, a fourth type of composer—the pioneer type: men like Gesualdo in the seventeenth century, Moussorgsky and Berlioz in the nineteenth, Debussy and Edgar Varese in the twentieth. It is difficult to summarize the composing methods of so variegated a group. One can safely say that their approach to composition is the opposite of the traditionalist type. They clearly oppose conventional solutions of musical problems. In many ways, their attitude is experimental—they seek to add new harmonies, new sonorities, new formal principles. The pioneer type was the characteristic one at the turn of the seventeenth century and also at the beginning of the twentieth century, but it is much less evident today.

VOCABULARY

prolific (2)   germinal(4)

improvise (3)   sonorities (8)

QUESTIONS FOR CRITICAL THINKING

1. What are your general impressions of classical music? How do you account for its longevity?
2. Why do you suppose the spontaneously inspired composer is so widely admired?
3. Classical music is sometimes referred to as long-hair music. How do you suppose it got this nickname? Why is this nickname appropriate or not appropriate?
4. Is music a classless art form? What inference can you draw about someone from knowing the kind of music he likes? Are such inferences justified?

QUESTIONS ON THE WRITING PROCESS

1. What is the function of the first paragraph?
2. How does the author make clear the characteristic musical style and method of each type of composer?
3. What is the purpose of paragraph 6?
4. Writers frequently use transition words and phrases within and between paragraphs to help hold the progressing argument together. Identify at least three phrases used in this article whose obvious function is to smooth the transition from one idea to another.
5. The author writes in short, direct paragraphs. What can you deduce about his intended audience from these paragraphs?

WRITING ASSIGNMENTS

1. Write a brief essay describing your favorite kind of music and explaining why you like it.
2. Who is your favorite composer? Write an appreciation of him/her.
3. Write an essay in which you classify the work of any musician or musical group into different composing styles or periods.

SOME AMERICAN TYPES

Max Lerner

Max Lerner (1902–   ), author and lecturer, was born in Minsk, Russia and brought to the United States at an early age. He was educated at Yale University and Washington University in St. Louis. In 1927 he earned a Ph.D. from the Robert Brookings Graduate School of Economics and Government. His best-known work is America as a Civilization *(1957) from which this short selection was excerpted.*

1 Seventeenth-century England produced a number of books on *Characters* depicting English society through the typical personality patterns of the era. Trying something of the same sort for contemporary America, the first fact one encounters is the slighter emphasis on a number of character types than stand out elsewhere in Western society: to be sure, they are to be found in America as well, but they are not characteristically American. One thinks of the scholar, the aesthete, the priest or "parson," the "aristocratic" Army officer, the revolutionary student, the civil servant, the male schoolteacher, the marriage broker, the courtesan, the mystic, the saint. Anyone familiar with European literature will recognize these characters as stock literary types and therefore as social types. Each of them represents a point of convergence for character and society. Anyone familiar with American literature will know that it contains stock portraits of its own which express social types. I want to use these traditional types as backdrops and stress some of the social roles that are new and still in process of formation.

2 Thus there is the *fixer*, who seems an organic product of a society in which the middleman function eats away the productive one. He may be public-relations man or influence peddler; he may get your traffic fine settled, or he may be able—whatever the commodity—to "get it for you wholesale." He is contemptuous of those who take the formal rules seriously; he knows how to cut corners—financial, political, administrative, or moral. At best there is something of the iconoclast in him, an unfooled quality far removed from the European personality types that always obey authority. At worst he becomes what the English call a "spiv" or cultural procurer.

3 Related to the fixer is the *inside dopester*, as Riesman[1] has termed him. He is oriented not so much toward getting things fixed as toward being "in the know" and "wised up" about things that innocents take at face value. He is not disillusioned because he has never allowed himself the luxury of illusions. In the 1920s and 1930s he consumed the literature of "debunking"; in the current era he knows everything that takes place in the financial

---

[1] David Riesman, American sociologist, author of *The Lonely Crowd* and other works.

centers of Wall Street, the political centers of Capitol Hill, and the communications centers of Madison Avenue—yet among all the things he knows there is little he believes in. His skepticism is not the wisdom which deflates pretentiousness but that of the rejecting man who knows ahead of time that there is "nothing in it" whatever the "it" may be. In short, he is "hep."

4   Another link leads to the *neutral* man. He expresses the devaluing tendency in a culture that tries to avoid commitments. Fearful of being caught in the crosscurrents of conflict that may endanger his safety or status, he has a horror of what he called "controversial figures"—and anyone becomes "controversial" if he is attacked. As the fixer and the inside dopester are the products of a middleman's society, so the neutral man is the product of a technological one. The technician's detachment from everything except effective results becomes—in the realm of character—an ethical vacuum that strips the results of much of their meaning.

5   From the neutral man to the *conformist* is a short step. Although he is not neutral—in fact, he may be militantly partisan—his partisanship is on the side of the big battalions. He lives in terror of being caught in a minority where his insecurity will be conspicuous. He gains a sense of stature by joining the dominant group, as he gains security by making himself indistinguishable from that group. Anxious to efface any unique traits of his own, he exacts conformity from others. He fears ideas whose newness means they are not yet accepted, but once they are firmly established he fights for them with a courage born of the knowledge that there is no danger in championing them. He hates foreigners and immigrants. When he talks of the "American way," he sees a world in which other cultures have become replicas of his own.

6   It is often hard to distinguish the conformist from the *routineer*. Essentially he is a man in uniform, sometimes literally, always symbolically. The big public-service corporations—railroads, air lines, public utilities—require their employees to wear uniforms that will imprint a common image of the enterprise as a whole. City employees, such as policemen and firemen, wear uniforms. Gas-station attendants, hotel clerks, bellhops, must similarly keep their appearance within prescribed limits. Even the sales force in big department stores or the typists and stenographers in big corporations tend toward the same uniformity. There are very few young Americans who are likely to escape the uniform of the Armed Services. With the uniform goes an urge toward pride of status and a routineeering habit of mind. There is the confidence that comes of belonging to a large organization and sharing symbolically in its bigness and power. There is a sense of security in having grooves with which to move. This is true on every level of corporate business enterprise, from the white-collar employee to "the man in the gray flannel suit," although it stops short of the top executives who create the uniforms instead of wearing them. Even

outside the government and corporate bureaus there are signs of American life becoming bureaucratized, in a stress on forms and routines, on "going through channels."

7   Unlike the conformist or routineer, the *status seeker* may possess a resourceful energy and even originality, but he directs these qualities toward gaining status. What he wants is a secure niche in a society whose men are constantly being pulled upward or trodden down. Scott Fitzgerald has portrayed a heartbreaking case history of this character type in *The Great Gatsby,* whose charm and energy are invested fruitlessly in an effort to achieve social position. The novels of J. P. Marquand are embroideries of a similar theme, narrated through the mind of one who already has status and is confronted by the risk of losing it. At various social levels the status seeker becomes a "joiner" of associations which give him symbolic standing.

VOCABULARY

aesthete (1)	skepticism (3)	efface (5)
courtesan (1)	pretentiousness (3)	replicas (5)
convergence (1)	militantly (5)	bureaucratized (6)
iconoclast (2)	partisan (5)	niche (7)
procurer (2)		

QUESTIONS FOR CRITICAL THINKING

1. What are stock social types? What value do these types have for a society?
2. What is the relationship of a role to the self? Is the self knowable outside of the role it plays?
3. What is your attitude towards the "middleman"? What connotations do you attach to this word?
4. What meaning do you attach to the phrase "the American way"?
5. What effect can job roles have on one's sense of self?

QUESTIONS ON THE WRITING PROCESS

1. In the first paragraph the author announces his intention to discuss social types. How does he subsequently use the types to tie together the entire excerpt?

2. In the first paragraph, how does the author emphasize his assertion that social types are common to both European and American literature?

3. How does Lerner make his individual types clear to the reader?

4. The author sprinkles his discussion of types with quoted terms and phrases. Why?

5. What transition device is used to link paragraphs 3 and 4?

WRITING ASSIGNMENTS

1. Write an essay discussing one of the social types with whom you might be personally acquainted.

2. Write an essay defining what you mean by "self."

3. Write an essay discussing any one of these social types in literature.

TECHNOLOGY IN MEDICINE

Lewis Thomas, M.D.

Dr. Lewis Thomas (1913–   ) is president of the Memorial Sloan-Kettering Cancer Center in New York. He has served as professor of Pediatric Research at the University of Minnesota and has held other appointments at various major medical schools. His first book of essays, The Lives of a Cell (1974), from which this excerpt was taken, won the National Book Award.

In the essay that follows, a medical researcher writes frankly about the promise and limitations of modern medicine. Classifying all medical treatment into three types, "nontechnology, halfway-technology, and true technology," he evaluates the effectiveness of each.

1   Technology assessment has become a routine exercise for the scientific enterprises on which the country is obliged to spend vast sums for its needs. Brainy committees are continually evaluating the effectiveness and cost of doing various things in space, defense, energy, transportation, and the like, to give advice about prudent investments for the future.

2   Somehow medicine, for all the $80-odd billion that it is said to cost the nation, has not yet come in for much of this analytical treatment. It seems taken for granted that the technology of medicine simply exists, take it or leave it, and the only major technologic problem which policy-makers are interested in is how to deliver today's kind of health care, with equity, to all the people.

3   When, as is bound to happen sooner or later, the analysts get around to the technology of medicine itself, they will have to face the problem of measuring the relative cost and effectiveness of all the things that are done in the management of disease. They make their living at this kind of thing, and I wish them well, but I imagine they will have a bewildering time. For one thing, our methods of managing disease are constantly changing—partly under the influence of new bits of information brought in from all corners of biologic science. At the same time, a great many things are done that are not so closely related to science, some not related at all.

4   In fact, there are three quite different levels of technology in medicine, so unlike each other as to seem altogether different undertakings. Practitioners of medicine and the analysts will be in trouble if they are not kept separate.

5   1. First of all, there is a large body of what might be termed "nontechnology," impossible to measure in terms of its capacity to alter either the natural course of disease or its eventual outcome. A great deal of money is spent on this. It is valued highly by the professionals as well as the patients.

It consists of what is sometimes called "supportive therapy." It tides patients over through diseases that are not, by and large, understood. It is what is meant by the phrases "caring for" and "standing by." It is indispensable. It is not, however, a technology in any real sense, since it does not involve measures directed at the underlying mechanism of disease.

6   It includes the large part of any good doctor's time that is taken up with simply providing reassurance, explaining to patients who fear that they have contracted one or another lethal disease that they are, in fact, quite healthy.

7   It is what physicians used to be engaged in at the bedside of patients with diphtheria, meningitis, poliomyelitis, lobar pneumonia, and all the rest of the infectious diseases that have since come under control.

8   It is what physicians must now do for patients with intractable cancer, severe rheumatoid arthritis, multiple sclerosis, stroke, and advanced cirrhosis. One can think of at least twenty major diseases that require this kind of supportive medical care because of the absence of an effective technology. I would include a large amount of what is called mental disease, and most varieties of cancer, in this category.

9   The cost of this nontechnology is very high, and getting higher all the time. It requires not only a great deal of time but also very hard effort and skill on the part of physicians; only the very best of doctors are good at coping with this kind of defeat. It also involves long periods of hospitalization, lots of nursing, lots of involvement of nonmedical professionals in and out of the hospital. It represents, in short, a substantial segment of today's expenditures for health.

10   2. At the next level up is a kind of technology best termed "halfway technology." This represents the kinds of things that must be done after the fact, in efforts to compensate for the incapacitating effects of certain diseases whose course one is unable to do very much about. It is a technology designed to make up for disease, or to postpone death.

11   The outstanding examples in recent years are the transplantations of hearts, kidneys, livers, and other organs, and the equally spectacular inventions of artificial organs. In the public mind, this kind of technology has come to seem like the equivalent of the high technologies of the physical sciences. The media tend to present each new procedure as though it represented a breakthrough and therapeutic triumph, instead of the makeshift that it really is.

12   In fact, this level of technology is, by its nature, at the same time highly sophisticated and profoundly primitive. It is the kind of thing that one must continue to do until there is a genuine understanding of the mechanisms involved in disease. In chronic glomerulonephritis, for example, a much clearer insight will be needed into the events leading to the destruction of glomeruli by the immunologic reactants that now appear to govern this

disease, before one will know how to intervene intelligently to prevent the process, or turn it round. But when this level of understanding has been reached, the technology of kidney replacement will not be much needed and should no longer pose the huge problems of logistics, cost, and ethics that it poses today.

13 An extremely complex and costly technology for the management of coronary heart disease has evolved—involving specialized ambulances and hospital units, all kinds of electronic gadgetry, and whole platoons of new professional personnel—to deal with the end results of coronary thrombosis. Almost everything offered today for the treatment of heart disease is at this level of technology, with the transplanted and artificial hearts as ultimate examples. When enough has been learned to know what really goes wrong in heart disease, one ought to be in a position to figure out ways to prevent or reverse the process, and when this happens the current elaborate technology will probably be set to one side.

14 Much of what is done in the treatment of cancer, by surgery, irradiation, and chemotherapy, represents halfway technology, in the sense that these measures are directed at the existence of already established cancer cells, but not at the mechanisms by which cells become neoplastic.

15 It is a characteristic of this kind of technology that it costs an enormous amount of money and requires a continuing expansion of hospital facilities. There is no end to the need for new, highly trained people to run the enterprise. And there is really no way out of this, at the present state of knowledge. If the installation of specialized coronary-care units can result in the extension of life for only a few patients with coronary disease (and there is no question that this technology is effective in a few cases), it seems to me an inevitable fact of life that as many of these as can be will be put together, and as much money as can be found will be spent. I do not see that anyone has much choice in this. The only thing that can move medicine away from this level of technology is new information, and the only imaginable source of this information is research.

16 3. The third type of technology is the kind that is so effective that it seems to attract the least public notice; it has come to be taken for granted. This is the genuinely decisive technology of modern medicine, exemplified best by modern methods for immunization against diphtheria, pertussis, and the childhood virus diseases, and the contemporary use of antibiotics and chemotherapy for bacterial infections. The capacity to deal effectively with syphilis and tuberculosis represents a milestone in human endeavor, even though full use of this potential has not yet been made. And there are, of course, other examples: the treatment of endocrinologic disorders with appropriate hormones, the prevention of hemolytic disease of the newborn, the treatment and prevention of various nutritional disorders, and perhaps just around the corner the management of Parkinsonism and sickle-cell anemia. There are other examples, and everyone will have his favorite

candidates for the list, but the truth is that there are nothing like as many as the public has been led to believe.

17   The point to be made about this kind of technology—the real high technology of medicine—is that it comes as the result of a genuine understanding of disease mechanisms, and when it becomes available, it is relatively inexpensive, relatively simple, and relatively easy to deliver.

18   Offhand, I cannot think of any important human disease for which medicine possesses the outright capacity to prevent or cure where the cost of the technology is itself a major problem. The price is never as high as the cost of managing the same diseases during the earlier stages of nontechnology or halfway technology. If a case of typhoid fever had to be managed today by the best methods of 1935, it would run to a staggering expense. At, say, around fifty days of hospitalization, requiring the most demanding kind of nursing care, with the obsessive concern for details of diet that characterized the therapy of that time, with daily laboratory monitoring, and, on occasion, surgical intervention for abdominal catastrophe, I should think $10,000 would be a conservative estimate for the illness, as contrasted with today's cost of a bottle of chloramphenicol and a day or two of fever. The halfway technology that was evolving for poliomyelitis in the early 1950s, just before the emergence of the basic research that made the vaccine possible, provides another illustration of the point. Do you remember Sister Kenny, and the cost of those institutes for rehabilitation, with all those ceremonially applied hot fomentations, and the debates about whether the affected limbs should be totally immobilized or kept in passive motion as frequently as possible, and the masses of statistically tormented data mobilized to support one view or the other? It is the cost of that kind of technology, and its relative effectiveness, that must be compared with the cost and effectiveness of the vaccine.

19   Pulmonary tuberculosis had similar episodes in its history. There was a sudden enthusiasm for the surgical removal of infected lung tissue in the early 1950s, and elaborate plans were being made for new and expensive installations for major pulmonary surgery in tuberculosis hospitals, and then INH and streptomycin came along and the hospitals themselves were closed up.

20   It is when physicians are bogged down by their incomplete technologies, by the innumerable things they are obliged to do in medicine when they lack a clear understanding of disease mechanisms, that the deficiencies of the health-care system are most conspicuous. If I were a policy-maker, interested in saving money for health care over the long haul, I would regard it as an act of high prudence to give high priority to a lot more basic research in biologic science. This is the only way to get the full mileage that biology owes to the science of medicine, even though it seems, as used to be said in the days when the phrase still had some meaning, like asking for the moon.

VOCABULARY

equity (2)	profoundly (12)	neoplastic (14)
intractable (8)	immunologic (12)	obsessive (18)
segment (9)	reactants (12)	catastrophe (18)
compensate (10)	logistics (12)	fomentations (18)
incapacitating (10)	coronary thrombosis (13)	conspicuous (20)
makeshift (11)	ultimate (13)	prudence (20)

QUESTIONS FOR CRITICAL THINKING

1. The author of this article has been much praised for his style of writing. How would you characterize his writing style?
2. How effective do you think doctors are at dispensing what the author calls "medical nontechnology"?
3. What is your attitude toward so-called socialized medicine? Should health care be dispensed equally to all, without regard to ability to pay? Why or why not?
4. The author admits that most varieties of cancer are being treated by medical nontechnology. What is your attitude toward so-called alternative cancer treatments? Should cancer patients be allowed to use a drug such as laetrile even if the medical establishment regards it as worthless?
5. Experts predict a glut of doctors in the near future. What effect on the practice of American medicine do you think this is likely to have?
6. What is your attitude towards advertising by doctors and other medical people? Would you submit yourself to the care of a heavily advertised doctor? Why or why not?
7. It is often said that medical people are lionized in the United States to a degree unequalled in other countries. Why? What does this say about our attitude towards medicine?

QUESTIONS ON THE WRITING PROCESS

1. Where is the thesis of this essay stated?
2. What lead-ins does the author use to introduce each of the major types of technology? Identify each lead-in along with the paragraph in which it is used.
3. Examine paragraphs 6, 7, and 8. How does the author link these three paragraphs together?
4. Examine paragraph 9. Three sentences in it begin with the identical pronoun. Why? What is the author attempting to do?
5. In classifying medical treatment into three technologies, how does the author clarify the nature and function of each kind of technology? What simple rhetorical strategy does he repeatedly use throughout the essay?
6. What kind of audience do you think the essay was written for? How do you know?

WRITING ASSIGNMENTS

1. Write an essay describing a visit to a doctor or a stay in a hospital. Try to analyze what kind of medical technology was used to treat you.
2. Write a brief essay classifying the childhood illnesses you have had.
3. Write a description of the characteristics you think the ideal medical person should have.

THE FACE IN THE MIRROR

Gilbert Highet

Gilbert Highet (1906–1978) was a Scottish born classicist highly respected for his scholarly and critical writing. He was educated at the University of Glasgow and at Oxford. From 1938 to 1950 he was a Professor of Greek and Latin at Columbia University. Highet, who became a naturalized American citizen in 1951, was married to popular novelist Helen MacInnes. Among his best known works are The Classical Tradition *(1949) and* The Anatomy of Satire *(1962).*

Classification in the liberal arts is often an informal attempt at thinking originally about a subject. This essay exemplifies that tack. Highet surveys the field of autobiography and proposes a classification of the genre into three primary types: "What I Did"; "What I Saw"; and "What I Felt."

1   They say that every man and every woman has one book inside him or her. Some have more, but everybody has at least one. This is a volume of autobiography. We have all been talked almost to death by bores who attached themselves to us in a club car or a ship's smoking room, and insisted on giving us a play-by-play account of their marital troubles, or their complete medical history. I once met one who carried a set of his own x-rays. Yet even these people might be interesting if they could tell the whole truth. They are boring not because they talk about themselves, but because they talk about only one aspect of themselves, that phase of their lives which fascinates and worries them personally. If they were really to tell us everything, we should listen with amazement.

2   Most of us cannot tell the whole truth, or even the important parts of the truth. This is one reason why there are not many good autobiographies. People cannot, or will not, put down the facts. The wife of the philosopher Carlyle said that the story of her life, written down without falsification or disguise, would have been a priceless record for other women to read, but that "decency forbade her to do any such thing." Think how many millions of people have told secrets to their wives or husbands, to their psychiatrists, to their doctors, their lawyers, or their priests—secrets which they would rather die than see printed in a book and published under their own names. And the other reason for the dearth of readable autobiographies is simply that most people cannot write. Writing an interesting story, a fictional story, is difficult enough. Writing eloquently about oneself is still more difficult; it needs a style even more subtle and a finer sense of balance.

3   Apparently there are three kinds of autobiography: three different ways of telling the story of one's life. (We can leave out journals like Pepys's

242

Diary, which was not meant to be published, and collections of letters, and disguised autobiographies, which so many modern novels are.)

4   The first group could all be issued under the same title. They could all be called 'What I Did.' They are essentially success stories. In them, a man who has achieved something of wide importance explains how he did it, what were the obstacles in his way, how they were overcome, and what was the effect on the world. Self-made men often write such books—or have such books written for them. There is a splendid one by Ben Franklin, and an equally good one by his English opposite number, William Cobbett: these are optimistic works, a good tonic for anyone who despairs of solving his own problems.

5   Sir Winston Churchill's six-volume work *The Second World War* (published by Houghton Mifflin) is really an autobiographical record. He himself says it is "the story as I knew and experienced it as Prime Minister and Minister of Defense of Great Britain." Therefore it cannot be called anything like a complete history of the war. For example, Churchill tells the story of one of the crucial events of the war, one of the crucial events of this century—the reduction of Japan to impotence and surrender by intensive bombardment culminating in what he calls the "casting" of two atomic bombs—in only eight pages, while a greater amount of wordage is devoted to a reprint of the broadcast which he made to British listeners on VE day.

6   A similar personalized history of the last twenty years is *The Secret Diary of Harold L. Ickes* (issued by Simon & Schuster). This is a view of the New Deal and of the war years, as experienced and interpreted by a single, rather lonely politician. It is not a traditional success story. Ickes was so fantastically vain and ambitious that he saw the world as a conspiracy designed to deprive him of his rights; he would scarcely have been content with anything less than the perpetual presidency of the entire solar system. Therefore he accepted, and recorded in his diary, every piece of flattery which was offered to him—however blatant or insincere—and, while freely and gladly delivering cruelly effective attacks on his rivals and enemies, he bitterly resented any personal slight to himself. There is one very funny chapter in the latest volume, in which Ickes explains why he stopped going to the Gridiron Club dinners in Washington. At the last one he attended, a reporter dressed up as Donald Duck caricatured Secretary Ickes: 'crowing like a rooster, he strutted and patted himself on the chest, and indicated by sound and action that evidently he thought that Secretary Ickes was the greatest man in the world.' Ickes goes on to comment, 'I have completely fooled myself if I give the impression to anyone that I am conceited and possess a feeling of superiority over other men.' Obviously he did give just that impression, and every entry in his diary confirms it; but he refuses to face the fact. On the very same page he describes Governor Thomas Dewey as 'a political streetwalker,' and similar delicacies occur throughout the book. Still, there is no doubt that Ickes conceived of himself as a cham-

pion fighting alone against tremendous odds, and for that reason his diary is a success story.

7   One instructive contrast between the autobiographies of Churchill and Ickes is in the matter of discretion. Churchill has often been charged with talking out of turn, and dropping rash remarks to provoke the opposition, but anyone who reads his book carefully will be surprised to see how much is tactfully omitted. For example, he spends a page on describing his meeting with King Ibn-Sa'ud just after Yalta. His account is full of vivid and interesting details—such as the fact that the king's cupbearer gave Churchill a glass of water from the sacred well at Mecca, 'the most delicious' (he says) 'that I had ever tasted'—and probably the first such drink he had had for a very long time. It is only when we reread the episode that we realize how discreet the old statesman has been: he has not said a single word about the purpose of the meeting, and not a single word about its results, although his book purports to be a history of the war. On the other hand, Ickes seems to have attended confidential meetings of the Cabinet and of other bodies, at which data of great importance and secrecy were given out, and then to have come straight home and dictated a verbatim report to his secretaries, who then typed it up and kept it in a folder. No doubt it was relief for him to do so, and certainly it makes interesting reading now, but surely it was a shocking piece of indiscretion for a man in a position of confidence to betray everything to his employees, particularly secrets which were not his to keep or to disclose.

8   So much for the first type of autobiography: 'What I Did.' The second type might be called 'What I Saw.' Here the emphasis is not on the achievements of the narrator, but rather on the strange sights he saw and the strange experiences through which he lived. Most good books of exploration are like this. Both the book *Kon-Tiki* and the film were absorbingly interesting, not because the author was an unusual man, but because he could describe to us some unique adventures. We shall never cross New Guinea on foot, or spend a whole year alone with two companions on the Arctic ice, or climb Mount Everest; therefore we are delighted when a man who has done such a thing can tell us about it clearly—and modestly. The greatest of all such books in the English language is probably Doughty's *Travels in Arabia Deserta*. Some good adventure autobiographies have been written by ordinary soldiers and sailors. Many of our finest descriptions of the Napoleonic wars come from such books as the *Recollections of Rifleman Harris*, and there are similar documents from the American Civil War. Such also are the pathetic and marvelous books of reminiscence written by men and women who have survived long terms in prison. It would be virtually impossible for us to tell how the German and Russian prison camps worked, if we did not possess such books as Christopher Burney's *Dungeon Democracy*, Tadeusz Wittlin's *A Reluctant Traveller in Russia*, Seweryna Szmaglewska's *Smoke Over Birkenau*, and Odd Nansen's *From*

Day to Day. Finally, a great deal of social history is best conveyed through autobiography. At or near the top of the ladder there is a rather snobbish but delightfully written work by Sir Osbert Sitwell, in five volumes, which came out at intervals during the last decade, and which he himself describes as 'a portrait of an age and person.' At the bottom of the ladder, there is a painful but unforgettable description of the life of tramps and outcasts by George Orwell, called *Down and Out in Paris and London.* What Orwell tells us about the filth and calculated vileness of the kitchens in smart Parisian restaurants (where he himself worked as a dishwasher) is enough to sicken the strongest stomach, and I know that I personally have never enjoyed a meal in Paris since I read his book. One paragraph about the handling of food in the smart hotel kitchens ends, "Roughly speaking, the more one pays for food [in Paris], the more sweat and spittle one is obliged to eat with it." A good book of this kind has a perfectly unequaled impact: if its author can write at all, it is very hard to forget what he says.

9   Then there is a third kind of autobiography. It does not describe "What I Did," or "What I Saw," but "What I Felt," "What I Endured." These are the books of inner adventure. In them there is achievement, yes, but it is a struggle and a victory within the spirit. In them there are dangerous explorations, and the discovery of unknown worlds, but the explorer is making his way through the jungles of the soul. Such are the books of failure, disaster, and regeneration which are now so popular: for example, Lillian Roth's *I'll Cry Tomorrow,* which tells how a woman wrecked her life with drink and then rebuilt it. Such also are the books which describe one of the most dangerous of all adventures: the process of growing up. My own favorite among them is Edward Gibbon's autobiography, partly because it is unconsciously funny. More famous perhaps are the self-studies of John Stuart Mill, Herbert Spencer, and Henry Adams—all of which seem to me excruciatingly pompous and dull. There is also an exquisite little book, now out of print and very hard to procure, which tells how a little boy brought up in a sternly intellectual and narrowly religious family fought his way out and remade his character. This is *Father and Son,* by Edmund Gosse. I wish it could be reprinted. It is both very sad and very amusing. The famous records of religious suffering and conversion could all be subtitled "What I Felt": the *Confessions* St. Augustine, the journals of John Bunyan and of the first Quaker, George Fox. And many of the most famous autobiographers have concentrated on reporting the events which happened during their lifetime, not as objective facts, but simply as occurrences which impinged upon their own personalities: in books like the reminiscences of Benvenuto Cellini, of Rousseau, of Boswell, Yeats, and André Gide, we see the world as in an elaborate distorting mirror.

10   "What I Did," "What I Saw," "What I Felt." . . . Really, it is difficult to make a sharp division between the three types of autobiographical writing. The emphasis in one book is more toward reporting of external happen-

ings, in another toward self-analysis, but a man can scarcely describe what he did without also letting us know what he felt and saw. Even the most egoistic of men, like St. Augustine and James Boswell, do from time to time give us valuable information about their outer as well as their inner worlds. The most interesting of these books give us something of all three kinds of experience. For a time, while we read them, it is possible to enjoy one of the rarest artistic pleasures—complete escape: escape into another sphere of action and perception. From that escape we return—with what relief!— to the real center of the universe, which is our own self.

VOCABULARY

dearth (2)	conceived (6)	exquisite (9)
impotence (4)	discretion (7)	procure (9)
culminating (5)	verbatim (7)	impinged (9)
perpetual (6)	reminescence (8)	distorting (9)
blatant (6)	regeneration (9)	perception (10)
caricatured (6)	excruciatingly (9)	

QUESTIONS FOR CRITICAL THINKING

1. Why would writing about oneself require, as Highet puts it, "a style even more subtle and a finer sense of balance" than writing fiction? What elements might make autobiography more difficult to write than fiction?

2. What logical approach does Highet seem to recommend for reading autobiography?

3. Highet says that one reason for a scarcity of good autobiographies is that most of us cannot tell the whole truth. Can anyone know the whole truth about himself or herself?

4. The author says that a book like *Kon-Tiki* is interesting to read not because the author is an unusual person, but because he has had unique adventures. What relationship, if any, do you think exists between the person and the deed?

5. Highet calls the process of growing up "the most dangerous of all adventures." What do you think he means by this? What makes growing up such a dangerous adventure?

6. From this article, what important differences do you think exist between autobiography and biography?

7. If autobiography presents another "sphere of perception," how accurate a source can it be for history?

QUESTIONS ON THE WRITING PROCESS

1. Who are the "they" with whose opinion the first paragraph of the essay begins? What does this use of "they" immediately establish for the essay?
2. An essay, even one faithful to one mode of development, will often develop side issues in other modes. What is one example of this?
3. If you were hunting for the thesis or controlling statement of this essay, in which paragraph would you find it? What is significant about this placement?
4. How does Highet clarify his categories?
5. In moving from the first to the second kind of autobiography, what transition does Highet use?
6. What internal transitions does Highet employ in paragraph 6 in presenting his complicated discussion about the "What I Saw" genre of autobiography?
7. Aside from summing up the discussion, what point do you think Highet is also making in his final paragraph?

WRITING ASSIGNMENTS

1. Assume that humans can be informally classified into those who do, those who see, and those who feel. Write an essay classifying your acquaintances and friends into these three categories. Be sure to give examples.
2. Write an essay about the autobiography you enjoyed reading the most.
3. Write an essay informally classifying the characters of any genre of fiction (e.g. romances, westerns, detective stories) you regularly read.

COLORS AND PEOPLE

Anh U Diec

There are three primary colors: red, yellow, and blue. Certain psychologists have categorized people who love these three colors into different groups.

The group of people who love red are those who have self-confidence enough to be heroes and winners of competitions. The members of this group are optimistic. If someone's favorite color is red, that person is sure to be a leader or an active member in society who enjoys getting involved in clubs, politics, or church organizations. People who love the color red usually believe that everything will end up the way they have planned. They spend no time agonizing over errors made or catastrophes that might happen.

The yellow color is commonly loved by cowardly people. Lovers of yellow get along easily with others because they are afraid of friction and argument. However, in secret, despite their cowardice, they thrive on excitement. Lovers of yellow fantasize being lovers of red; only they lack the nerve to make their fantasies come true. They may daydream about leading a ticker-tape parade, being adored by a movie star, or managing millions of dollars. Lovers of yellow tend to betray their friends and loved ones. The reason for their lack of integrity is probably that they prefer lying or cheating to taking any hard stand. One surprising characteristic of this group is that they seem more cheerful and more relaxed than most people—perhaps because they don't view evil from a strong puritanical perspective.

The color blue is the color loved commonly by sad people who have a low self-esteem, who have no confidence, and who probably often suffer from depression. Lovers of blue believe in others rather than in themselves. "Mr. X is so much better than I am" is a typical comment made by one who loves blue. One who chooses blue is probably more quiet and shy than one who prefers red or yellow. He is often drawn to sad movies, gloomy philosophies, and woebegone memories. This group of people would rather follow than lead. Arrogant commanders like Napoleon, Genghis Khan, and Alexander the Great most likely avoided blues of any shade. Those who adore blue will tend to be pessimists with no hope for tomorrow.

Color psychology can be an interesting field in which to do some studies, but there is no proof to indicate that its findings are reliable.

SEVEN

COMPARISON/CONTRAST

The comparison/contrast may be the most familiar of all the modes of writing. It is habitually assigned at all grade levels in school. It is the sort of operation everyone does in daily life. Strictly speaking, the comparison searches for likenesses between items, and the contrast for differences. But usually the one is done in conjunction with the other. When we ask how one thing is similar to another, we also wonder how the two things differ.

There are two main patterns used to draw a comparison/contrast, and they are known by a variety of names. First, there is the alternating pattern, which is done *within* a paragraph. This kind of pattern is also known as the intraparagraph pattern, since it takes place within, rather than between, paragraphs.

The second pattern is known variously as the block pattern or the interparagraph pattern, depending on whom you ask. It means that the comparison/contrast is conducted between, rather than within, paragraphs. Here, from "Ross and Tom," is an example:

Ross was an oak of prudence and industry. He rarely drank and he never smoked. He excelled at everything he did. He had married his hometown sweetheart, was proudly faithful to her and produced four fine children. After a sampling of success on both coasts he had gone home to the Indiana of his parents and childhood friends.

Tom Heggen had a taste for low life. He had been divorced, had no children and shared bachelor quarters in New York with an ex-actor and screenwriter, Dorothy Parker's estranged husband, Alan Campbell. Tom was a drinker and a pill addict. He turned up regularly at the fashionable restaurant "21," usually bringing along a new girl, a dancer or an actress.

The use of one pattern or the other is dictated by the writer's style and by the complexity of the subject. Most writers freely combine the two patterns in their essays. Elsewhere in "Ross and Tom," for example, both patterns are used. The same is true of "On The Difference Between Wit and Humor."

A few commonsense observations can be made about writing a good comparison/contrast essay. First, the treatment of the compared/contrasted items should be balanced and fair. This simply means that you should cover both items on the same points. For example, if you are comparing the poetry of Keats with the poetry of Tennyson and you discuss Keats's use of imagery, fairness obliges you to also discuss Tennyson's. Indeed, a mechanical way of writing a comparison/contrast, and one often recommended for beginners, is simply to list the points on which you will compare/contrast your subjects, and then to cover them successively for both. Most of the essays in this chapter faithfully observe the rule of fairness and balance. A good writer can sometimes get away with writing an unbalanced comparison/contrast, but not in freshman English.

The second rule is to be generous in your use of expressions that illustrate either comparison or contrast. Most of these expressions are well known to everyone, but they still need to be used. Expressions of comparison include such solid standbys as "like," "similar to," and "the same as." The arsenal of contrasting expressions is just as rich and includes "in contrast to," "unlike," and "dissimilar." Both kinds of expressions do more than simply fill in the chinks between your comparisons and contrasts. They tell the reader what you are going to do or what you have done.

Sometimes no expression is needed, but only when a prefatory remark has made the writer's purpose abundantly clear. Take, for example, the two paragraphs we quoted from "Ross and Tom." No expression of contrast intervenes between them because the writer had prefaced the two paragraphs with this one:

> Tom and Ross were similar in that neither had any previous notoriety and they came from obscure, middle-class, Midwest backgrounds. *Yet as men they could not have been more different.*

This italicized sentence makes it clear that contrasting information will follow.

The third rule in writing a comparison/contrast is to match your subjects on important, not trivial points. For example, if you were contrasting the classroom styles of two teachers, the physical appearance of each does not deserve mention unless it is somehow related to their styles of teaching. The point is to mention and cover the *essential* similarities and differences between your subjects, not the unimportant ones.

SINGLE PARAGRAPHS

LENIN AND GLADSTONE

Bertrand Russell

The grandson of a prime minister, Bertrand Arthur William Russell (1872-1970) was a British philosopher, mathematician, and social reformer. Throughout his long life he advocated pacificism, and was twice jailed for his unpopular political views. His most important works in philosophy and mathematics, The Principles of Mathematics *(1903) and, with Alfred North Whitehead,* Principia Mathematica *(3 vols., 1910-1913), were written during his early years at Trinity College, Cambridge. In 1950 he received the Nobel Prize in literature.*

Russell contrasts two eminent men of an earlier time, William E. Gladstone (1809-1898), the British prime minister, and Vladimir Ilyich Lenin (1870-1924), the Russian revolutionary and founder of Bolshevism.

Lenin, with whom I had a long conversation in Moscow in 1920, was, superficially, very unlike Gladstone, and yet, allowing for the difference of time and place and creed, the two men had much in common. To begin with the differences: Lenin was cruel, which Gladstone was not; Lenin had no respect for tradition, whereas Gladstone had a great deal; Lenin considered all means legitimate for securing the victory of his party, whereas for Gladstone politics was a game with certain rules that must be observed. All these differences, to my mind, are to the advantage of Gladstone, and accordingly Gladstone on the whole had beneficent effects, while Lenin's effects were disastrous. In spite of all these dissimilarities, however, the points of resemblance were quite as profound. Lenin supposed himself to be an atheist, but in this he was mistaken. He thought that the world was governed by the dialectic, whose instrument he was; just as much as Gladstone, he conceived of himself as the human agent of a superhuman Power. His ruthlessness and unscrupulousness were only as to means, not as to ends; he would not have been willing to purchase personal power at the expense of apostasy. Both men derived their personal force from this unshakable conviction of their own rectitude. Both men, in support of their respective faiths, ventured into realms in which, from ignorance, they could only cover themselves with ridicule—Gladstone in Biblical criticism, Lenin in philosophy.

VOCABULARY

beneficent   unscrupulousness   rectitude
dialectic   apostasy   ridicule
ruthlessness

QUESTIONS FOR CRITICAL THINKING

1. Is your opinion of politics closer to Gladstone's than to Lenin's? Do the ends in politics justify the means?
2. What is Communism? What are its principles and main ideas? How do you account for the explosive popularity of this doctrine?
3. What is your theory of "great people"? Do people become great because of time and opportunity, or for some other reason?

QUESTIONS ON THE WRITING PROCESS

1. What phrase does the author use to announce his intention of drawing a contrast?
2. Halfway through the paragraph, the author shifts from drawing a contrast to making a comparison. What transition does he use in order to accomplish this switch?
3. What common words of contrast and comparison does the author repeatedly use?

WRITING ASSIGNMENTS

1. Write a paragraph comparing and contrasting the two most influential figures in your life.
2. Write a short essay contrasting the person you like most with the person you like least.

WOMEN'S FEATURES IN AN INSECURE AGE

Cecil Beaton

Cecil Beaton (1904–1980) was a photographer, costume and stage designer, painter, and writer. He was born in London, where he became the favorite photographer of the royal family. He won Academy Awards for costume design in two movies, Gigi *(1959) and* My Fair Lady *(1965), and was the author of several best-selling diaries.*

This paragraph presents a contrast between the way women used to look and the way they look today.

Our pace of life has quickened so that women's features now reflect the frenzied, insecure age in which they live. Women's eyes used to be wistful. Today few possess serene eyes; they do not mind creases in their brows and often wear a frown on their foreheads. Young girls are proud of their high cheekbones and a flat hollow in their cheeks, whereas fifty years ago cheeks were fully rounded. Latterly the rather prehensile mouths have replaced the rosebud of yesterday. Whereas make-up was used only by *cocottes* in the Victorian and Edwardian heydays (ladies used to slap their cheeks and bite their lips before entering a ballroom to obtain a higher colour), any woman without lipstick today appears anaemic. Hair dyeing has become so general that it is not kept a guarded secret. Eyebrows, instead of being arched or wearing the old-fashioned startled look or the look of pained surprise, are slightly raised towards the outer edges, even acquiring a mongolian look. After twenty years of eyebrow plucking, eyebrows do not grow as thickly as they did.

VOCABULARY

frenzied	prehensile	anaemic
wistful	cocottes	mongolian
latterly	heydays	

QUESTIONS FOR CRITICAL THINKING

1. Why have women's looks changed over the years? Has the change, in your opinion, been for the better or the worse?
2. What effect on women's looks and fashion has the feminist movement had?
3. How have the looks and fashions of men changed over the years? Has the change been for the better or for the worse?
4. What effect do a person's looks have on his/her success with the opposite sex?

QUESTIONS ON THE WRITING PROCESS

1. What is the topic sentence of this paragraph?
2. On what points are women of yesterday and today contrasted in this paragraph? Enumerate the successive points of contrast.
3. What common word of contrast does the author use throughout the paragraph?

WRITING ASSIGNMENTS

1. Write a paragraph describing the way you think the ideal man or woman should look.
2. Write a brief essay contrasting the dress styles and looks of an older and younger relative.

ACCEPTING MEN AS THEY ARE

Albert Ellis

Albert Ellis (1913-   ) is a clinical psychologist who was educated at Columbia University. He has taught at Rutgers and N.Y.U., and has been director of the Institute for Rational Living since 1968. He is the author of numerous popular books, including The Intelligent Woman's Guide to Mating and Dating *(1979), from which this excerpt was taken.*

The contrast presented in this brief excerpt is more oblique than direct, the author arguing that men are significantly different from women in their approach to love, sex, and marriage.

1   For both biological and social reasons, there are definite differences between males and females. And if you're going to get along well, or at least gracefully, with men, you'd better accept these differences. *Accept* is the key word here—nobody's asking you to wax highly enthusiastic about them.

2   This means, in plain English, that you'd better deal with the fact that most males are much more interested in sex than love, that they love *after* being sexually satisfied rather than *before* going to bed, as females often do, and that even their best loving (or indeed vital absorption in any person or thing) tends to be considerably less romantic and single-minded (read: monogamous) than that of the opposite gender. This also means that there is nothing *insulting* or intrinsically *nasty* about how the male feels about sex, you, or his outside interests. You may never greatly *like* the way he behaves in these respects, but it is pointless for you to fight him for being the way he is. Remember, at best, you're probably only going to be able to change him slightly.

3   You may, then, be perfectly correct when leveling certain charges, such as: "Men are interested in only one thing—sex," or "Men only care about their work and don't give enough to their homes or families," or "All men are selfish." There is considerable, if not total truth in all these statements. So what! I don't really see the *horror* of men being interested in sex, in their work, or in themselves. It might, perhaps, be a much better world if this were not so (though it might be a much worse world, too!). But it *is* so. And all the wishing on your part and all the bitter demanding that men be different from the way they are is not going to change things very much. Except for the worse!

4   If, then, you are interested in finding a man for your true, true love, seek exactly that: a *man*. Not a mouse, not an angel, not a female, not a little boy, but a man. And fully expect, if you find such a man, that he will have, for

better *and* for worse, some distinctly *manly* traits. For the most part, in all likelihood, he *will* be more sexually demanding, less devoted to the children, more fickle, more absorbed in outside affairs, less warm and romantic, less sociable, and more interested in some silly sporting events than you. Tough! That's the way the sonofagun is. After all, he's a *man*. And isn't that why you wanted him in the first place?

VOCABULARY

wax (1)   intrinsically (2)

monogamous (2)   fickle (4)

QUESTIONS FOR CRITICAL THINKING

1. What does this article imply about the biological and social behavior of women?
2. What is your opinion of the author's statements about the nature of men? Do you agree with him? Why, or why not?
3. If men are the way the author says they are, how did they get this way? What effect on the behavior of both sexes is the women's movement likely to have?

QUESTIONS ON THE WRITING PROCESS

1. For what kind of audience was this article obviously written? How can you tell?
2. What is the author contrasting in this article? Where is the intention to draw a contrast stated?
3. In paragraph 3, the author summarizes in quotation marks various charges made against men. What is implied by the use of quotation marks here?
4. In the fourth paragraph, the author advises his readers to seek a man, "not a mouse, not an angel, not a female, not a little boy." What is the implication of this sentence?
5. Who are men contrasted with in the final paragraph of the article?

WRITING ASSIGNMENTS

1. Write a 300-word essay describing the kind of person you think would make a perfect husband or wife.
2. Compare and contrast the behavior of your closest male and female friend.
3. Write an essay arguing either for or against the author's thesis about the differences between men and women.

ONE VOTE FOR THIS AGE OF ANXIETY

Margaret Mead

American anthropologist Margaret Mead (1901–1978) was known both for her work in anthropology and for her prominence in public affairs. A student of the anthropologist Ruth Benedict, Mead did most of her field work among the peoples of Oceania. She wrote several books, among them Coming of Age in Samoa (1928), Sex and Temperament in Three Primitive Societies (1935), and the autobiography of her early years, Blackberry Winter (1972).

A comparison/contrast may be either direct or implied. In the essay that follows, we have an example of an implied contrast between our own so-called age of anxiety and the lives of primitive peoples.

1   When critics wish to repudiate the world in which we live today, one of their familiar ways of doing it is to castigate modern man because anxiety is his chief problem. This, they say, in W. H. Auden's phrase, is the age of anxiety. This is what we have arrived at with it, our vaunted progress, our great technological advances, our great wealth—everyone goes about with a burden of anxiety so enormous that, in the end, our stomachs and our arteries and our skins express the tension under which we live. Americans who have lived in Europe come back to comment on our favorite farewell which, instead of the old goodbye (God be with you), is now "Take it easy," each American admonishing the other not to break down from the tension and strain of modern life.

2   Whenever an age is characterized by a phrase, it is presumably in contrast to other ages. If we are the age of anxiety, what were other ages? And here the critics and carpers do a very amusing thing. First, they give us lists of the opposites of anxiety: security, trust, self-confidence, self-direction. Then without much further discussion, they let us assume that other ages, other periods of history, were somehow the ages of trust or confident direction.

3   The savage who, on his South Sea island, simply sat and let bread fruit fall into his lap, the simple peasant, at one with the fields he ploughed and the beasts he tended, the craftsman busy with his tools and lost in the fulfillment of the instinct of workmanship—these are the counter-images conjured up by descriptions of the strain under which men live today. But no one who lived in those days has returned to testify how paradisaical they really were.

4   Certainly if we observe and question the savages or simple peasants in the world today, we find something quite different. The untouched savage

in the middle of New Guinea isn't anxious; he is seriously and continually *frightened*—of black magic, of enemies with spears who may kill him or his wives and children at any moment, while they stoop to drink from a spring, or climb a palm tree for a coconut. He goes warily, day and night, taut and fearful.

5   As for the peasant populations of a great part of the world, they aren't so much anxious as hungry. They aren't anxious about whether they will get a salary raise, or which of the three colleges of their choice they will be admitted to, or whether to buy a Ford or Cadillac, or whether the kind of TV set they want is too expensive. They are hungry, cold and, in many parts of the world, they dread that local warfare, bandits, political coups may endanger their homes, their meager livelihoods and their lives. But surely they are not anxious.

6   For anxiety, as we have come to use it to describe our characteristic state of mind, can be contrasted with the active fear of hunger, loss, violence and death. Anxiety is the appropriate emotion when the immediate personal terror—of a volcano, an arrow, the sorcerer's spell, a stab in the back and other calamities, all directed against one's self—disappears.

7   This is not to say that there isn't plenty to worry about in our world of today. The explosion of a bomb in the streets of a city whose name no one had ever heard before may set in motion forces which end up ruining one's carefully planned education in law school, half a world away. But there is still not the personal, immediate, active sense of impending disaster that the savage knows. There is rather the vague anxiety, the sense that the future is unmanageable.

8   The kind of world that produces anxiety is actually a world of relative safety, a world in which no one feels that he himself is facing sudden death. Possibly sudden death may strike a certain number of unidentified other people—but not him. The anxiety exists as an uneasy state of mind, in which one has a feeling that something unspecified and undeterminable may go wrong. If the world seems to be going well, this produces anxiety— for good times may end. If the world is going badly—it may get worse. Anxiety tends to be without locus; the anxious person doesn't know whether to blame himself or other people. He isn't sure whether it is 1956 or the Administration or a change in climate or the atom bomb that is to blame for this undefined sense of unease.

9   It is clear that we have developed a society which depends on having the *right* amount of anxiety to make it work. Psychiatrists have been heard to say, "He didn't have enough anxiety to get well," indicating that, while we agree that too much anxiety is inimical to mental health, we have come to rely on anxiety to push and prod us into seeing a doctor about a symptom which may indicate cancer, into checking up on that old life insurance policy which may have out-of-date clauses in it, into having a conference with Billy's teacher even though his report card looks all right.

10   People who are anxious enough keep their car insurance up, have the brakes checked, don't take a second drink when they have to drive, are careful where they go and with whom they drive on holidays. People who are too anxious either refuse to go into cars at all—and so complicate the ordinary course of life—or drive so tensely and overcautiously that they help cause accidents. People who aren't anxious enough take chance after chance, which increases the terrible death toll of the roads.

11   On balance, our age of anxiety represents a large advance over savage and peasant cultures. Out of a productive system of technology drawing upon enormous resources, we have created a nation in which anxiety has replaced terror and despair, for all except the severely disturbed. The specter of hunger means something only to those Americans who can identify themselves with the millions of hungry people on other continents. The specter of terror may still be roused in some by a knock at the door in a few parts of the South, or in those who have just escaped from a totalitarian regime or who have kin still behind the Curtains.

12   But in this twilight world which is neither at peace nor at war, and where there is insurance against certain immediate, down-right, personal disasters, for most Americans there remains only anxiety over what may happen, might happen, could happen.

13   This is the world out of which grows the hope, for the first time in history, of a society where there will be freedom from want and freedom from fear. Our very anxiety is born of our knowledge of what is now possible for each and for all. The number of people who consult psychiatrists today is not, as is sometimes felt, a symptom of increasing mental ill health, but rather the precursor of a world in which the hope of genuine mental health will be open to everyone, a world in which no individual feels that he needs to be hopelessly brokenhearted, a failure, a menace to others or a traitor to himself.

14   But if, then, our anxieties are actually signs of hope, why is there such a voice of discontent abroad in the land? I think this comes perhaps because our anxiety exists without an accompanying recognition of the tragedy which will always be inherent in human life, however well we build our world. We may banish hunger, and fear of sorcery, violence or secret police; we may bring up children who have learned to trust life and who have the spontaneity and curiosity necessary to devise ways of making trips to the moon; we cannot—as we have tried to do—banish death itself.

15   Americans who stem from generations which left their old people behind and never closed their parents' eyelids in death, and who have experienced the additional distance from death provided by two world wars fought far from our shores are today pushing away from them both a recognition of death and a recognition of the tremendous significance—for the future—of the way we live our lives. Acceptance of the inevitability of death, which, when faced, can give dignity to life, and acceptance of

our inescapable role in the modern world, might transmute our anxiety about making the right choices, taking the right precautions, and the right risks into the sterner stuff of responsibility, which ennobles the whole face rather than furrowing the forehead with the little anxious wrinkles of worry.

16   Worry in an empty context means that men die daily little deaths. But good anxiety—not about the things that were left undone long ago, that return to haunt and harry men's minds, but active, vivid anxiety about what must be done and that quickly—binds men to life with an intense concern.

17   This is still a world in which too many of the wrong things happen somewhere. But this is a world in which we now have the means to make a great many more of the right things happen everywhere. For Americans, the generalization which a Swedish social scientist made about our attitudes on race relations is true in many other fields: anticipated change which we feel is right and necessary but difficult makes us unduly anxious and apprehensive, but such change, once consummated, brings a glow of relief. We are still a people who—in the literal sense—believe in making good.

VOCABULARY

repudiate (1)	taut (4)	precursor (13)
castigate (1)	coups (5)	inherent (14)
vaunted (1)	impending (7)	spontaneity (14)
admonishing (1)	undeterminable (8)	transmute (15)
carpers (2)	locus (8)	ennobles (15)
conjured (3)	inimical (9)	consummated (17)
paradisaical (3)	specter (11)	literal (17)
warily (4)	totalitarian (11)	

QUESTIONS FOR CRITICAL THINKING

1. Our age has been called the age of anxiety. In what ways is anxiety evident in our daily lives?
2. The author gives examples of stereotypes about the lives of simpler peoples. What are some other stereotypes about the lives of simpler peoples?
3. The author remarks that our way of saying goodbye, "Take it easy," is a reminder of how anxious we are. What other ways of saying goodbye do we use, and what might we infer from them about our life-style?
4. What is your idea of the good life? How does it compare with the life you live now?

5. What useful effect has anxiety had in your own life? What harmful effect?
6. What thing or event are you most anxious about?
7. How do you feel about death? Do you agree with the author that people are unable to accept its inevitability?

QUESTIONS ON THE WRITING PROCESS

1. With what is the author contrasting our own age? Where does the author announce her intention to draw a contrast?
2. What pattern of contrast does this essay mainly use? Point out specific examples.
3. What is the purpose of the scenario sketched in paragraph 3?
4. Examine the final sentence in paragraph 5. What tone is the author using here?
5. What is the author contrasting in the final two sentences of paragraph 7?
6. What is the purpose of paragraph 8?
7. The thesis of the author's argument is summed up in paragraph 11. What is it?
8. Examine paragraphs 14 and 15. What rhetorical mode are these paragraphs written in?

WRITING ASSIGNMENTS

1. Write a 300-word essay about your own bouts with anxiety, giving examples of what you most fear.
2. Compare and contrast your life today with the way you imagine it would be in a primitive place such as New Guinea.
3. Write an essay describing an ideal world, one that lives up to your every expectation.

ON THE DIFFERENCE BETWEEN
WIT AND HUMOR

Charles Brooks

Charles Brooks (1878–1934), essayist, was a native of Cleveland, where he was one of the founders of the Cleveland Playhouse. Among his many essay collections are There's Pippins and Cheese to Come *(1917),* Chimney-Pot Papers *(1919), and* Roundabout to Canterbury *(1926).*

This essay draws a detailed contrast between two similar yet vastly different characteristics: wit and humor.

1   I am not sure that I can draw an exact line between wit and humor. Perhaps the distinction is so subtle that only those persons can decide who have long white beards. But even an ignorant man, so long as he is clear of Bedlam, may have an opinion.

2   I am quite positive that of the two, humor is the more comfortable and more liveable quality. Humorous persons, if their gift is genuine and not a mere shine upon the surface, are always agreeable companions and they sit through the evening best. They have pleasant mouths turned up at the corners. To these corners the great Master of marionettes has fixed the strings, and he holds them in his nimblest fingers to twitch them at the slightest jest. But the mouth of a merely witty man is hard and sour until the moment of its discharge. Nor is the flash from a witty man always comforting, whereas a humorous man radiates a general pleasure and is like another candle in the room.

3   I admire wit, but I have no real liking for it. It has been too often employed against me, whereas humor is always an ally. It never points an impertinent finger into my defects. Humorous persons do not sit like explosives on a fuse. They are safe and easy comrades. But a wit's tongue is as sharp as a donkey driver's stick. I may gallop the faster for its prodding, yet the touch behind is too persuasive for any comfort.

4   Wit is a lean creature with sharp inquiring nose, whereas humor has a kindly eye and comfortable girth. Wit, if it be necessary, uses malice to score a point—like a cat it is quick to jump—but humor keeps the peace in an easy chair. Wit has a better voice in a solo, but humor comes into the chorus best. Wit is as sharp as a stroke of lightning, whereas humor is diffuse like sunlight. Wit keeps the season's fashions and is precise in the phrases and judgments of the day, but humor is concerned with homely eternal things. Wit wears silk, but humor in homespun endures the wind. Wit sets a snare, whereas humor goes off whistling without a victim in its

mind. Wit is sharper company at table, but humor serves better in mischance and in the rain. When it tumbles, wit is sour, but humor goes uncomplaining without its dinner. Humor laughs at another's jest and holds its sides, while wit sits wrapped in study for a lively answer. But it is a workaday world in which we live, where we get mud upon our boots and come weary to the twilight—it is a world that grieves and suffers from many wounds in these years of war: and therefore as I think of my acquaintance, it is those who are humorous in its best and truest meaning rather than those who are witty who give the more profitable companionship.

5   And then, also, there is wit that is not wit. As someone has written:

> Nor ever noise for wit on me could pass,
> When thro' the braying I discern'd the ass.

6   I sat lately at dinner with a notoriously witty person (a really witty man) whom our hostess had introduced to provide the entertainment. I had read many of his reviews of books and plays, and while I confess their wit and brilliancy, I had thought them to be hard and intellectual and lacking in all that broader base of humor which aims at truth. His writing—catching the bad habit of the time—is too ready to proclaim a paradox and to assert the unusual, to throw aside in contempt the valuable haystack in a fine search for a paltry needle. His reviews are seldom right—as most of us see the right—but they sparkle and hold one's interest for their perversity and unexpected turns.

7   In conversation I found him much as I had found him in his writing— although, strictly speaking, it was not a conversation, which requires an interchange of word and idea and is turn about. A conversation should not be a market where one sells and another buys. Rather, it should be a bargaining back and forth, and each person should be both merchant and buyer. My rubber plant for your victrola, each offering what he has and seeking his deficiency. It was my friend B—— who fairly put the case when he said that he liked so much to talk that he was willing to pay for his audience by listening in his turn.

8   But this was a speech and a lecture. He loosed on us from the cold spigot of his intellect a steady flow of literary allusion—a practice which he professes to hold in scorn—and wit and epigram. He seemed torn from the page of Meredith.[1] He talked like ink. I had believed before that only people in books could talk as he did, and then only when their author had blotted and scratched their performance for a seventh time before he sent it to the printer. To me it was an entirely new experience, for my usual acquaintances are good common honest daytime woollen folk and they seldom average better than one bright thing in an evening.

---

[1]George Meredith (1828–1909), English novelist who wrote complex and comic novels.

9   At first I feared that there might be a break in his flow of speech which I should be obliged to fill. Once, when there was a slight pause—a truffle was engaging him—I launched a frail remark; but it was swept off at once in the renewed torrent. And seriously it does not seem fair. If one speaker insists—to change the figure—on laying all the cobbles of a conversation, he should at least allow another to carry the tarpot and fill in the chinks. When the evening was over, although I recalled two or three clever stories, which I shall botch in the telling, I came away tired and dissatisfied, my tongue dry with disuse.

10   Now I would not seek that kind of man as a companion with whom to be becalmed in a sailboat, and I would not wish to go to the country with him, least of all to the North Woods or any place outside of civilization. I am sure that he would sulk if he were deprived of an audience. He would be crotchety at breakfast across his bacon. Certainly for the woods a humorous man is better company, for his humor in mischance comforts both him and you. A humorous man—and here lies the heart of the matter—a humorous man has the high gift of regarding an annoyance in the very stroke of it as another man shall regard it when the annoyance is long past. If a humorous person falls out of a canoe, he knows the exquisite jest while his head is still bobbing in the cold water. A witty man, on the contrary, is sour until he is changed and dry: but in a week's time when company is about, he will make a comic story of it.

11   My friend A—— with whom I went once into the Canadian woods has genuine humor, and no one can be a more satisfactory comrade. I do not recall that he said many comic things, and at bottom he was serious as the best humorists are. But in him there was a kind of joy and exaltation that lasted throughout the day. If the duffle were piled too high and fell about his ears, if the dinner was burned or the tent blew down in a driving storm at night, he met these mishaps as though they were the very things he had come north to get, as though without them the trip would have lacked its spice. This is an easy philosophy in retrospect but hard when the wet canvas falls across you and the rain beats in. A—— laughed at the very moment of disaster as another man will laugh later in an easy chair. I see him now swinging his axe for firewood to dry ourselves when we were spilled in a rapids; and again, while pitching our tent on a sandy beach when another storm had drowned us. And there is a certain cry of his (dully, *Wow!* on paper) expressive to the initiated of all things gay, which could never issue from the mouth of a merely witty man.

12   Real humor is primarily human—or divine, to be exact—and after that the fun may follow naturally in its order. Not long ago I saw Louis Jouvet of the French Company play Sir Andrew Ague-Cheek.[2] It was a most humorous performance of the part, and the reason is that the actor made no

[2]Sir Andrew Ague-Cheek is a comic character in Shakespeare's *Twelfth Night*.

primary effort to be funny. It was the humanity of his playing, making his audience love him first of all, that provoked the comedy. His long thin legs were comical and so was his drawling talk, but the very heart and essence was this love he started in his audience. Poor fellow! How delightfully he smoothed the feathers in his hat! How he feared to fight the duel! It was easy to love such a dear silly human fellow. A merely witty player might have drawn as many laughs, but there would not have been the catching at the heart.

13   As for books and the wit or humor of their pages, it appears that wit fades, whereas humor lasts. Humor uses permanent nutgalls. But is there anything more melancholy than the wit of another generation? In the first place, this wit is intertwined with forgotten circumstance. It hangs on a fashion—on the style of a coat. It arose from a forgotten bit of gossip. In the play of words the sources of the pun are lost. It is like a local jest in a narrow coterie, barren to an outsider. Sydney Smith[3] was the most celebrated wit of his day, but he is dull reading now. *Blackwood's* at its first issue was a witty daring sheet, but for us the pages are stagnant. I suppose that no one now laughs at the witticisms of Thomas Hood.[4] Where are the wits of yester-year? Yet the humor of Falstaff and Lamb and Fielding[5] remains and is a reminder to us that humor, to be real, must be founded on humanity and on truth.

VOCABULARY

Bedlam (1)	perversity (6)	mishaps (11)
marionettes (2)	allusion (8)	retrospect (11)
nimblest (2)	epigram (8)	initiated (11)
malice (4)	botch (9)	nutgalls (13)
diffuse (4)	sulk (10)	melancholy (13)
homespun (4)	crotchety (10)	coterie (13)
mischance (4)	exquisite (10)	stagnant (13)
paradox (6)	exaltation (11)	witticisms (13)

[3]Sydney Smith (1771-1845), English clergyman, writer, and notable wit.

[4]Thomas Hood (1799-1845), English poet who wrote mainly in a humorous vein. His work is noted for its clever puns.

[5]Falstaff, a comic character in Shakespeare's *King Henry IV*, parts I and II. Charles Lamb (1775-1834) was an English essayist, and Henry Fielding (1707-1754), an English novelist and dramatist.

QUESTIONS FOR CRITICAL THINKING

1. Which of the two qualities seems the more artificial—wit or humor? Why?
2. Why do you think the author pictures the humorous person as being fat, and the witty person as being thin? Why are fat people so often regarded as humorous?
3. Is wit or humor more dominant in our day? Why?
4. Which of these two traits is more likely to be displayed by a modern comedian or talk show host? Why?
5. The author's preference is for the humorous person over the witty one. Which would you prefer to be becalmed in a sailboat with? Why?
6. Which of the two sexes is more likely to be the more humorous? The more witty? Why?
7. Which of these two traits is more likely to be found in the comic antics of children—wit or humor? Why?

QUESTIONS ON THE WRITING PROCESS

1. What is the basis of the contrast developed in the second paragraph?
2. Paragraph 4 contains this sentence: "Wit is a lean creature with sharp inquiring nose, whereas humor has a kindly eye and comfortable girth." What is the author attempting to do in this figure of speech?
3. What two common words of contrast are repeatedly used in the fourth paragraph?
4. Why is paragraph 5 so short? What effect is the author trying to achieve in this short paragraph?
5. What is the purpose of the anecdote related in paragraphs 6 through 9?
6. What is the author attempting to do in paragraph 11?
7. What two patterns of contrast are used in this essay? Where is the one mainly used, and where the other?

WRITING ASSIGNMENTS

1. In a 300-word essay, compare and contrast any humorous person with any witty person of your acquaintance.
2. Write a 300-word essay analyzing the humor/wit of your favorite comic.
3. Are you primarily witty or humorous? Write a brief essay describing and giving examples of your humor and/or wit.

DOCTOR-AS-GOD IS DEAD, OR DYING

Ellen Goodman

Ellen Goodman (1941–   ) is a nationally syndicated columnist whose work appears in more than 200 newspapers every week. She was edu-cated at Radcliffe and has been a reporter for Newsweek *and the* Detroit Free Press. *Since 1971 she has been attached to the Boston Globe as a full-time columnist. Her books include* Turning Points *(1979), a study of changes in the lives of over 150 people, and* At Large *(1981), a collec-tion of her essays.*

Anyone who has lately gone into a doctor's office may have noticed a subtle change in the practitioner in the white suit. Few of the younger medicos give off the aura of infallibility commonly assumed by their older peers. Instead, many of the new generation make an effort to re-gard and treat their patients as equals. Goodman analyzes and humor-ously comments on this latest trend.

1   My friend went to the doctor's office expecting to find God. The doctors whom she knew always played God, except on Wednesday afternoons, when they played golf.

2   But what she discovered was that Doctor-God-Sir, the professional keeper of the Temple of the Body, was not available. Instead, a new doctor sat down before her, opened up her chart, met her eyes sincerely and asked her to think of him as her "junior partner in health care."

3   This somewhat abrupt transfer from God to the junior partner had a startling effect on my friend's blood pressure. But she had discovered the latest trend of the medical profession: God is dead, or at least dying out.

4   The whole history of Doctor-as-God began way back when medicine men were merely priests. Eventually they got academic degrees and de-manded a promotion, although there were some who thought that God was a little high.

5   Medicine still remained a profound mystery to the laity. Such is the way with all religions. It was conducted in Latin or Medicalese, which was Greek to the average person. The patient-supplicant was required to have faith, hope and a little something to put on the plate when it was passed.

6   We were expected to submit to such rituals as the knife and to such magic as pills. Few of us ever saw the appendix that was removed or under-stood how antibiotics work. But we took penicillin as a kind of oral penance for illness: four times a day for ten days, and bow to the east three times.

7   Somewhere along the way in this skeptical secular era the medical laity became less worshipful. The best and brightest of the young apprentices were also less willing to pretend omniscience.

8   And so we have now entered the era of the junior partner in health care.

9   What are the characteristics of a junior partner? First of all, an aura of humility. You can tell a junior partner by precisely how many times he or she uses the expression "We really don't know. . . ." Junior partners believe in sharing—especially in sharing doubts.

10   You can also identify junior partners by their passion for education. This friend called her J.P. recently when a bee sting had blown her arm up to the size of a large thigh. "What do I do"? she asked. He answered, "First let me tell you something about bee stings."

11   All junior partners have been educated by the full-disclosure, informed-consent school of medicine. Gods give out proclamations; J.P.s give odds. The odds that you will get better, the odds that you will get worse. Along with every prescription comes a description of side effects. If just one Manchurian lost an ear lobe or a belly button from this cream, you will hear about it.

12   Consider the true story of a woman who discussed the possibility of surgery with her J.P. After listening to his explanations she tried to recap the pros and cons. "So," she said, "the worst that can happen. . . ." "Oh, no," he interrupted. "The worst that can happen is that you'll die from the anesthesia." After peeling her off the floor he admitted that this possibility was fairly remote—one in 30,000. This is called overinformed consent.

13   The most basic thing to remember for your next encounter with a J.P. is that he or she will not tell you what to do. Gods give commandments, but J.P.s only lay out options. It is up to you, the Senior Partner, to take responsibility for your health decisions. (This fact is on a poster in the J.P.'s waiting room, near stacks of pamphlets on fiber in the diet.)

14   It is still possible, of course, to find God. But he is likely to be (1) he, (2) older or (3) a specialist in heart or brain surgery. The life-and-death stuff still seems to fall into the hands of you-know-Who.

15   Should we be surprised by the takeover of the junior partners? After all, isn't this what we all wanted? We wanted doctors to stop treating us like children. We wanted them to talk to us, tell us the whole story. We wanted them to stop acting like gods. We wanted them to admit their fallibility.

16   Isn't that right? Absolutely. Positively. I swear to God.

VOCABULARY

laity (5)	skeptical (7)	omniscience (7)
supplicant (5)	secular (7)	fallibility (15)
penance (6)		

QUESTIONS FOR CRITICAL THINKING

1. What value, if any, can you see in the Doctor-as-God? What price do we pay for this kind of doctor?
2. What factors do you think have caused the demotion of the doctor from God to the junior partner?
3. Medicine in America has traditionally been a male dominated field. What effect do you think the woman's movement has had on the demotion of the Doctor-as-God?
4. What advantage, if any, is there in the junior-partner's approach to medicine?
5. What effect does consumer demand have on changes in medical treatment? What effect should it have?

QUESTIONS ON THE WRITING PROCESS

1. What method of contrast is employed throughout this article?
2. What transition device does the author use to move the discussion from the Godlike doctor to the junior partner?
3. What main use does the author make of the interrogative throughout this essay?
4. What is the point of the repetition in paragraph 15?
5. Aside from the diction and humor, what single feature of this essay identifies it as coming from a journalistic source?

WRITING ASSIGNMENTS

1. Write an essay comparing and contrasting the treatment you might have received from any man or woman in the medical profession.
2. Write an essay comparing/contrasting the bedside manner of any two physicians who've treated you.
3. Argue for or against the feminization of medicine.

ROSS AND TOM

John Leggett

John Leggett (1917–   ) was born in New York City and educated at Yale. He has worked as an editor at Houghton Mifflin and Harper & Row publishers, and is currently director of the University of Iowa Writers Workshop. Among his books are Wilder Stone *(1960),* Who Took the Gold Away? *(1969), and* Gulliver House *(1979), a novel about the publishing business.*

In the excerpt that follows, taken from Ross and Tom: Two American Tragedies *(1974), the writer is trying to determine what two young, successful writers, both of whom died tragically, had in common.*

1 Taking my life is inconceivable to me. I shall lose it soon enough. To abandon even one of my allotted minutes might be to miss some important or funny thing, perhaps even the point.

2 Also—and there is a connection—I am ambitious. I have been bred to "getting ahead," to the belief that if I fall behind, shame and starvation will catch me, but if I achieve some thing I will be looked after, admired and loved in perpetuity. Long ago I accepted these as the rules of the game. I only quarrel with them when the score is running against me.

3 Sometime during World War II I decided to have my achievement as a writer. It took me five years and a fat swatch of rejection slips to find out how hard that was and, in frustration, to take a job with a book publisher.

4 Thus it was in Houghton Mifflin's warren overlooking Boston Common that I learned about a dark side of achievement—how, a few years earlier, two young novelists, just my age and no more promising in background, had been published so successfully that their first books made them rich and famous. Then, at the peak of their acclaim, they died.

5 The first, Ross Lockridge, took his own life, locking his new garage doors behind his new Kaiser and asphyxiating himself. The second, Thomas Heggen, drowned in his bathwater—an accident, it was claimed, but it was the accident of a desperate man.

6 Tom and Ross were similar in that neither had any previous notoriety and they came from obscure, middle-class, Midwest backgrounds. Yet as men they could not have been more different.

7 Ross was an oak of prudence and industry. He rarely drank and he never smoked. He excelled at everything he did. He had married his hometown sweetheart, was proudly faithful to her and produced four fine children. After a sampling of success on both coasts he had gone home to the Indiana of his parents and childhood friends.

8 Tom Heggen had a taste for low life. He had been divorced, had no children and shared bachelor quarters in New York with an ex-actor and

screenwriter, Dorothy Parker's estranged husband, Alan Campbell. Tom was a drinker and a pill addict. He turned up regularly at the fashionable restaurant "21," usually bringing along a new girl, a dancer or an actress.

9   After the success of their first novels, neither Ross nor Tom had been able to start a new book. At the time of their deaths neither had written anything in months.

10   What had happened to them? There were grumblings that some villainy of Houghton Mifflin's had done Ross Lockridge in, that in publishing his huge novel, *Raintree County,* the firm had exploited him, somehow threatened both his income and his privacy. (There had been a quarrel and Ross had made unpleasant accusations.)

11   Could it have been fatigue—had the two novelists written themselves out, found they had nothing more to say? Or was it disappointment: had the finished book—or in Heggen's case the dramatic version of *Mister Roberts* which was then playing on Broadway—fallen short of some original notion of perfection? There are always spoilers. *Raintree County*'s first reviews had called it a masterpiece and compared its author to Thomas Wolfe, but these were followed by some contemptuous ones, and there had been a denouncement by a Jesuit priest which struck at Ross's own self-doubts.

12   Still, none of these sounded as likely an explanation as that of the bitch-goddess herself—the writers spoiled by success, his need to write smothered in a surfeit of reward. Clearly there is something disillusioning in attainment. Many writers (such as J. D. Salinger and James Gould Cozzens, among others) drift into unproductivity after a big, popular success, just as the very productive ones such as Henry James are often those who pursue, yet never quite attain, an enthusiastic public embrace.

13   There is still another area for conjecture. Suppose that Tom Heggen's and Ross Lockridge's final act was not one of surrender at all, but defiance. Perhaps success had brought them to some promontory from which they could see the whole of their path and from there they had made this appalling comment about it. What could so disillusion them about that view? I needed to know. If they were rejecting their own incentives, they were, so far as I knew, rejecting mine.

14   Searching for an entryway to their spirits, I drew a professional comparison. Lockridge was a Vesuvius. When he was at work, twenty or thirty pages spewed from his typewriter each day, some on their way to the wastebasket, others to be revised, endlessly before they were satisfactory, but always expanding. Progress toward a desired shape was by laying on more material.

15   Heggen was the reverse, a distiller. The molding was a prelude to writing and was done in his head. He would sit by the hour, staring out a window, so that a passerby would think him daydreaming. But then he would turn to his typewriter and strike a flawless passage, each word and inflection so precisely chosen there was no need for revision.

16   But in spite of this difference in the way they worked, Ross and Tom appeared to be equally single-minded about writing, each compelled to it with a force that dwarfed the other elements of his life. Thus the common experience preceding their deaths, of wanting to write again and not being able to, is significant. The being able to—the energy—is the essential part of incentive and I had the impression they had lost that, knew they had lost it and knew that without it they were useless men.

17   What *is* a writer's incentive? That he has a gift for expression in words can be taken for granted; but I suspect that gift doesn't contribute half so much to motivation as social failure. I know that my own feelings of inadequacy and shyness were first routed when, in the third grade, my piece on tadpoles appeared in the school paper, and I suspect that only a man who doubts the persuasiveness of his tongue and fists would sit alone dirtying good paper when he could be in company.

18   Wanting to write fiction has even more elaborate roots and these reach not just into a writer's present reveries but back into his childhood. When he is read to, when he is sick and is brought an adventure book with his medicine, a child gets a first set of furnishings for his dream world. When he graduates to adult novels his debt to fiction is increased by a more utilitarian, though still romantic, vision of himself and a way to behave. If he chooses wisely and is lucky in the library he can find dream enough to sustain him for a lifetime.

19   But the path of a writer is too lonely and discouraging for any kind of propulsion but the hugest. In an essay on Willa Cather, Leon Edel notes that for her novel about an ambitious opera singer, *The Song of the Lark,* she chose the epigraph "It was a wondrous lovely storm that drove me," and that this was not only appropriate for Thea, the heroine, but for the author.

20   "It was a wondrous, lovely storm that drove Willa Cather," he says, "and what she cared for above all was the storm. With success achieved . . . she felt depressed. She didn't know what to do with success; or rather, she seems to have experienced a despair altogether out of proportion to the actual circumstances of her achievement. . . . Success, by the very testimony of the tales she wrote, created for Willa Cather a deep despair and even a wish for death. . . ."

21   Willa Cather's experience of depression in achievement makes a striking parallel with Ross's and Tom's. And I cannot find a better description for the kind of force a novelist wants to contain than "the wondrous lovely storm." It is vague, yet so evocative of the emotion and energy that can bring forth a significant book—wondrous in its mysterious origin and awesome power, lovely because it is not terrifying at all, but blissful, as though it is love itself.

22   When I first looked into Tom Heggen's and Ross Lockridge's lives, seeking some clues to their deaths, I found myself in barren country. Neither had the nature for casual confessions nor the kind of apprenticeships which called for public self-examinations. An even bigger difficulty lay

with those who had known them best. They suffered from having been present at, yet unable to prevent, a tragedy. Understandably the families were wary of talking about the darker, human parts of the natures and experiences of the two writers.

23 Still, inconsequential, even irrelevant details about them intrigued me. Instead of flagging, my interest grew. Occasionally I felt I might be guilty of dancing on their graves, a jig for my own compensating survival. But what most absorbed me was self-discovery.

24 Ross, Tom and I grew up to the same music, worshiping the same idols, suffering from the same inhibitions. It was remarkably easy for me to slip into their adolescent skins. As an adult and a writer, I could recognize in those highs of self-certainty, in those plunging lows of self-doubt, my own emotional weather. Finally, in each of their natures—one black, reckless; the other a marching band of virtues—I saw two halves of my own.

VOCABULARY

inconceivable (1)	surfeit (12)	reveries (18)
allotted (1)	attainment (12)	utilitarian (18)
in perpetuity (2)	conjecture (13)	epigraph (19)
warren (4)	defiance (13)	evocative (21)
acclaim (4)	appalling (13)	irrelevant (23)
asphyxiating (5)	Vesuvius (14)	flagging (23)
notoriety (6)	prelude (15)	compensating (23)
prudence (7)	preceding (16)	inhibitions (24)
denouncement (11)	routed (17)	

QUESTIONS FOR CRITICAL THINKING

1. What effect do you think success is likely to have on doers in other fields?
2. Leggett says that Lockridge, the novelist, was a Vesuvius who wrote and rewrote endlessly, whereas Heggen, the playwright, spun out flawless passages without need for revision. What effect do you think their respective literary forms—the novel and the play—had on their methods of composing?
3. Robert Browning wrote, "A man's reach must exceed his grasp, or what's heaven for"? How could this line be related to the histories of Ross and Tom?
4. What justification exists, if any, for suicide?
5. What role do you think incentive plays in artistic creations?
6. The author implies in paragraph 17 that there is something effete in the makeup of the man who becomes a writer. What relationship do you think exists between masculinity and literary creativity?
7. Which of the literary forms do you think the most useful, and which the least? Why?.

QUESTIONS ON THE WRITING PROCESS

1. What is the purpose of the first four paragraphs of this essay?
2. Examine paragraphs 7 and 8. What method of contrast does the author use in these two paragraphs?
3. What common method of transition does the author use in paragraphs 10 and 11?
4. Although the author's primary intent is to compare and contrast Ross and Tom, he frequently writes paragraphs that accomplish other, necessary functions. For example, how are paragraphs 12 and 13 developed? What is the author attempting to do in these paragraphs?
5. What is the basis of the contrast drawn in paragraphs 14 and 15?
6. What is the purpose of the anecdote about Willa Cather in paragraphs 19 and 20?
7. In paragraph 20, why does the writer quote Leon Edel on Willa Cather?

WRITING ASSIGNMENTS

1. Write a 500-word essay that contrasts your ideas of success and failure in life.
2. Write an essay describing a favorite book, poem, or play, explaining in detail why you are so fond of it.
3. What kind of college classes do you like most, and what kind do you like least? Write an essay contrasting the two.

LOVERS VERSUS WORKERS

Sam Keen

Theologian and writer Sam Keen (1932–   ) did his undergraduate work at Harvard Divinity School and earned a Ph.D. from the Department of Religion, Princeton University in 1962. He is the author of numerous books, among them To A Dancing God *(1970),* Voices and Visions *(1974) and* Beginnings Without End *(1975).*

For some Americans, says the writer, the Great God Work is Dead. What killed this idol and what has taken its place in the theology of the new workers are discussed in this essay, which presents a subtle contrast between those who continue to worship work, and those who have found a different theology.

1   Jay, a carpenter who has worked for me on several occasions, is a barrel of a man, stout as an oak log. Though not yet 30 years old, his convictions are well seasoned; he is true to the grain of his own wood. On good days he shows up for work between 9 and 10 a.m. If it is raining, or his dog needs to go to the veterinarian, or he has promised to help a friend, or there is an exhibit of Zen art at the museum, he may not get here at all. As yet he hasn't called to say the day is too beautiful to spend working. But I wouldn't be surprised if he did. When he arrives, he unwraps his bundles of Japanese woodworking tools, removes the fine saws and chisels from their mahogany cases, puts some shakuhachi flute music on his tape deck, and begins methodically to sculpt the elaborate joints in the beams that will form the structure of the studio we are building. He works slowly, pausing to watch a hawk circle overhead, to tell a joke, to savor the smell of the wood. Occasionally I try to hurry him. "That looks close enough, Jay," I say. "May as well take the time to do it right the first time," he replies and goes on working at his own pace. After several days he announces that the beams are ready to be hoisted into place. We lift and tug and push. Notch joins notch. Tongue slips into groove. The puzzle fits together. We sigh with relief. A satisfying day.

2   Some would say Jay is an underachiever, a dropout, that he lacks ambition. A college graduate with honors in football, he works sporadically, for carpenters' wages. He has no pension, no health insurance, no fringe benefits. He drives an old truck and lives in a funky neighborhood near the industrial district of Oakland. When he doesn't need money, he tends his garden, writes poetry, paints, and studies Japanese and wood joinery. "I get by," he says. "It doesn't make any sense to sell your soul for security and have no time left to do the things you love."

3   I say Jay is one of a new breed of Americans who are refusing to make work the central value in their lives. These light-hearted rebels have

paused to consider the lilies of the field (executive coronaries and the pollution of the Love Canal) and have decided neither to toil nor to spin. They are turning everything upside down, creating what Nietzsche called "a transvaluation of values," and calling into question the traditional, orthodox virtues of the Protestant work ethic and American dream. They are inventing new "life-styles," forging new myths and visions of the good life, new definitions of happiness.

4   The rebellion is directed *against* the long-reigning secular theology of work that is best summed up in the words of Ayn Rand, whose popular philosophy romanticized capitalism and sanctified selfishness: "... your work is the process of achieving your values ... your body is a machine, but your mind is its driver ... your work is the purpose of your life, and you must speed past any killer who assumes the right to stop you ... any value you might find outside your work, any other loyalty or love, can be only travelers you choose to share your journey with and must be travelers going on their own power in the same direction." The rebels reject the sacred symbol $ and refuse to judge the worth of their lives by the economic equivalent of the last judgment—The Bottom Line. Disillusioned with the ideal of Progress, they are no longer willing to sacrifice present happiness for the promise of future economic security. In short, they have declared: the great God Work is dead.

5   A revolution in cultural values, like a storm front, is difficult to chart. Our values, self-images, myths, heroes, goals, visions of the good life, shift like the weather. The best computers and statistics give us only a fair to middling account of what's happening and why. To have any hope of predicting the emerging trends that will shape tomorrow's climate we need intuition, the latest reports from the barometer, Grandma's rheumatism, and a good deal of what an irreverent engineer friend of mine calls S.W.A.G. (Scientific Wild Ass Guess). By assembling a collage of statistics, events, ideas, and social movements we may construct a weather map of our times—a profile of a revolution in process.

6   Items:

• Discontent with the world of work is widespread. Yankelovich surveys report that only 40 percent of all adults now believe "hard work always pays off." As many as 75 percent of adult Americans are involved in some way in a search for new meanings, for self-fulfillment. More men in their prime working years are dropping out of the work force. Some, tired of the unrewarding jobs and professions for which they were trained, are undergoing the now nearly obligatory "mid-life crisis," retiring early and taking up a second life. Alan, for instance, "retired" from a high-stress, high-paying job in a Silicone Valley computer industry at age 47 and moved to Prescott, Arizona, where he sells real estate, rides his horses, and enjoys the immense silence of the desert.

• The vast majority of Americans endure their work because they see no other way to make a living. But even among those faithful to organized business, there is an increasing demand to make the rules of work more flexible. Businesses are gradually yielding to the pressure for humanizing and personalizing the office and factory. Flex-time and job-sharing are being tried in many progressive industries. The most adventurous are trying to find ways to coordinate changing individual body rhythms and work schedules. It is even rumored that in some far-out establishments—in where else but California—job descriptions are being matched with astrological types: Sagittarians for the long-range, wide-arching planning tasks, Virgos for bookkeeping detail.

8   • An undetermined number of Americans are discovering ways to make a living or improve their financial circumstances that do not involve job, work, or employment. A thriving outlaw economy exists, unreported to the IRS and uncounted in our estimates of the GNP. Edgar Feige, an economist at the University of Wisconsin in Madison, estimates that the underground economy consists of as much as 30 percent of the Gross National Product, an economy of $700 billion (larger than France's entire GNP). This figure includes an estimate of the value of all those transactions not involving the exchange of money—such as bartering, trading, goods and services—in which wealth is created. Flea markets and garage sales have made merchants and economic outlaws of us all. Millions of Americans are learning the skill of what maverick economist Paul Hawken calls "disintermediation," cutting out the middleman. When you repair your car, grow a garden, can food, have your baby at home, refinish your furniture, design or build your own house, care for your own health, you join the revolution, you sign the emancipation proclamation that frees you from economic bondage to yet more specialists and experts.

9   *The Next Whole Earth Catalog* is the new bible and dream book for those who long for or practice a life-style high in self-sufficiency and low in high technology. Its display of "tools" for living—these "tools" being books that contain information on anything from Swiss Army knives to underground houses—encourages a do-it-yourself ethic. Shovels and rakes and seeds are an invitation to a garden. And with a crop of fresh tomatoes, apples, or squash, a man or woman can eat well, barter the surplus, and thumb a nose at the supermarket. According to Scott Burns, in an article charting the "Shift from a Market Economy to a Household Economy" (in *CoEvolution Quarterly,* Fall 1976), in 1974 an astounding 47 percent of American families ate (or perhaps smoked) something grown in their own gardens.

10   The philosophical spokesman who provided the creed of the revolution and its motto, "Small is Beautiful," was E. F. Schumacher. His "Buddhist" economics rejects the ideal of exponential growth, the ethic of more is

better, the technological hope of those he calls the "people of the forward stampede" (whose slogan is "A breakthrough a day keeps the crisis at bay"). Notice, he says, that excessive complexity and specialization produce constant agitation and strain that crowd out the spirit. "The amount of time people have is in inverse proportion to the amount of labor-saving machinery they employ." The people Schumacher calls "home-comers" remember what life is really about and trade the lust for more goods and the compulsion to work for bags of time, silence, and simplicity. Schumacher and his followers have popularized the Buddhist principle of discovering a right livelihood—a socially creative, ecologically appropriate, and kindly way of working.

11   Duane Elgin, in his book *Voluntary Simplicity,* reports that as many as five percent of all Americans are consciously exploring a life-style of voluntary simplicity—and right livelihood—with more emphasis on self-sufficiency, conservation, cooperation, and community.

12   There is no doubt that the revolution in values we are experiencing includes much nostalgia for simpler times, rural virtue, and an agricultural way of life. The forerunners of the present revolution, following the example of Thoreau, went to the woods and the farms in the 1970s to create a rural renaissance. The back-to-the-land movement is still alive and well though largely ignored by the media, hiding out in coves in Tennessee and mountain valleys in Oregon and Washington. Although some call it romanticism, it is really a dream that animates many of us. In the years I have been working with groups of people struggling to define their hopes and dreams for the future, I have encountered few persons who did not dream of eventually settling down in a small town or rural area with trees, mountains, streams, or an ocean. No clocks or deadlines.

13   But city living and right livelihood are quite compatible. In San Francisco, for instance, a group of vest-pocket capitalists and entrepreneurs calling themselves the Briarpatch Community have banded together, pooling their resources and know-how to create a network of small businesses designed to serve people and provide a modest living for their proprietors rather than amass a large monetary surplus.

14   The cloud of witnesses to the changing status and value of work might continue. But the time has come to ask: "Why"?

15   Hard work, honest sweat, and entrepreneurial imagination made America the strongest and most envied kingdom on earth. Why the revolution in paradise? Why the search for new life-styles, new values? Why are we abandoning the virtues and world view that made us great and prosperous?

16   The quick and easy answers are economic.

17   The right-wing priests of the status quo say our problem is that the privileged sons and daughters of the affluent, like welfare recipients, never had to work and are lazy. They want it all now. The "me" generation is spoiled: since they never had to worry about the wolf at the door, they have

the luxury of turning inward and meditating on the dove of the spirit or the navel of their own experience. The solution is to get tough, get busy, expand the economy, and get America back to work.

18   The apocalyptic left says the problem is that we are running out of resources. Energy and materials are more expensive, and economies everywhere are slowing down. No amount of resourcefulness will allow us to continue our pattern of economic expansion. Our only solution is to learn to live small, cut our wants, trim our budgets, produce less, consume less, work less.

19   Fluctuations in the economy from affluence to stagflation certainly affect the way we think about work. But the deepest motives animating our revolution in work are psychological, or perhaps spiritual.

20   Yesterday's gods have become today's demons. The Greeks invented the idea of nemesis to show how a single virtue, stubbornly maintained, gradually changes into a destructive vice. Our success, our industry, our habit of work have all produced our economic nemesis. We were the first nation to dream the materialist dream of plenty for all, and to come close to making it a reality. Even in our present moment of economic crisis we are driving to the poorhouse in new automobiles, spending our inflated dollars for calorie-free food, and lamenting our falling productivity in an environment polluted by our industry. Work made us great but now threatens to usurp our soul, to inundate the earth in goods and trash, to destroy our capacity to wonder and to love. The rebels who are trying to overthrow the tyranny of work are, in effect, asking us to meditate on the wisdom of the Greeks, who claimed that Hephaestus (Vulcan) the Blacksmith, the only Olympian god who worked, was born lame.

21   As Western culture, and America in particular, became increasingly industrialized, gradually the meaning and purpose—the reason for which people worked—did a flip-flop. The stages in this process were roughly as follows:

(1.)   In the beginning work was a means, never an end in itself. People worked to provide the necessities of life for themselves, and to create leisure to contemplate and enjoy life. Only slaves existed to work.

(2.)   The invention of machines allowed us to produce the necessities of life more easily and, according to Herbert Marcuse, might have freed us from excessive work to enjoy a more erotic and pleasurable way of life.

(3.)   However, to keep the machines busy, production increasing and the economy expanding, we invented a new set of needs. Advertising convinced us that we "needed" and wouldn't be happy without those commodities our factories were producing—cars, radios, TV, hula-hoops, appliances, and more. To keep artificial needs stimulated, style and model changes were created: it is this year's new thing you need. Before we knew what was happening, all the luxuries became defined as psychological necessities.

(4.)   Our ethic changed from one of production to one of consumption. Our worth gradually became associated with what could be purchased, possessed, and consumed. The size of the toys separated the men from the boys. The important people (who, of course, were defined as "the happy" or fortunate ones) were those with the most expensive things.

(5.)   For the middle class, work became that activity that men (and later women) increasingly engaged in to provide themselves not only with food, clothing, and shelter, but also with the new "necessities"—the large automobile, the suburban home, and the symbolic things that had to be conspicuously consumed to gain status.

(6.)   Our loyalties were gradually shifted from family, friends, and community to work. Identity, especially for the male, became rooted in one's job. The first question men asked each other were: What do you do? Where do you work? The affluent managers and semi-affluent white-collar workers began to gain their identity, their sense of worth, from that work.

(7.)   The job and the corporation colonized and governed our psyches. They determined our dress, our conduct, where we lived, when we moved, how we measured success, and our friends (or acquaintances and associates). They dictated that we would live in obedience to the clock. They turned us into a nation of what Drs. Friedman and Rosenman called Type A personalities—stressed, chronically struggling, driven.

(8.)   And in the end—the final tyranny—we came to love our chains. According to a *Psychology Today* survey (May 1978) only 29 percent of us would place enjoyment of the work we do as a priority in continuing to work at all. And yet—as Yankelovich found—80 percent of us would go right on working for money even if we didn't have to! As work has come to occupy the center of our identity, to turn the imagination into a factory, we have forgotten that it was for leisure and love that we originally agreed to labor.

22   No one better articulates and illustrates the problem than Freud. When asked what a mature person should be able to do he replied: "To love and to work." In fact, however, Freud honored work and was skeptical of love. For all his efforts to free sexuality from Victorian prudery, the center of his life was labor, not eros. He wrote a long shelf of books yet had an "active" sex life that may have lasted a bare 10 years. Power, cigars, and theory were more important to him than the flesh. He was, in his own words, a "conquistador"—an intellectual worker and warrior. His patriarchial, autocratic temperament cast out as heretics from the psychoanalytic movement all who were his spiritual sons and might have been his friends—Jung, Reich, and Adler. Like most power-hungry men, he was a failure at *philia,* that form of brotherly love or friendship that the Greeks considered of equal dignity with eros. In theory, Freud trusted the executive, the "reality principle" within the psyche, more than the playful child. Psychoanalysis seeks to strengthen the ego against the infantile demands of the id, the pleasure

principle. Work first and then love, if there is enough time and energy. There won't be.

23   The hostility toward work that has developed in this generation comes largely from sons of fathers who, like Freud, were workaholics. The fathers of today's middle-class children lived through and were wounded by the great Depression. Anyone who grew up in the 1940s lives with the fear that the tide of prosperity might recede again, as it did in 1931, and then there would be no jobs. As a result, most of the men who have risen to middle-management positions devoted themselves to their work and their corporations with religious zeal: the job was the center of their lives. And so a generation of sons and daughters identify "work" as the villain who took Daddy away from them and returned him tired and used-up at the end of the day. A thousand times in the average middle-class home a child eager to play with Daddy was told, "Not now, Daddy's tired" or "Daddy has to go to work." "Work" was the excuse that covered a multitude of sins.

24   The poet Robert Bly offers a clue to some of the psychological motives behind our hostility toward work: "The boy and his father . . . are the love-unit most damaged by the Industrial Revolution." In primitive cultures fathers initiated their sons into manhood, guided their hands in the use of a bow and arrow or a digging stick, shared the excitement of the hunt, taught them the myths and mysteries of the tribe. In the last two decades the work of the fathers has become so abstract, so remote from the home, so routinized that, for the first time in history, men have abandoned the task and joy of initiating their children.

25   Instead of time, tenderness, and tacit knowledge of the world, they have given their children the trinkets of affluence. Often in groups I have conducted, I have heard a man break down and sob: "Dad, I never knew you. Where were you? Who were you? You never let me in on your life." The sons have seen the fathers swallowed by the world of work. They have watched as work stole from them the thing they wanted most—Father as the living presence, model, and guide for manhood. As Earl Shorris shows in The Oppressed Middle, the corporation man increasingly surrendered his consciousness, his moral autonomy, his private values, to serve the aims of the totalitarian corporation. And the sons lost respect when the fathers sold their souls for the illusion of security.

26   And the daughters? Daddy was also absent from their lives (which taught them early that they couldn't expect much from men). But little girls had Mother as a companion and role model. She touched them, held them when they cried, tended them when they were sick, taught them to bake a cherry pie or make a dress. But they also learned that Mother's task of keeping the hearth was not as valuable as Father's work. His was the kingdom, the power, and the superior dignity. Value was created in the factory, the corporation, and the marketplace, not in the home—the real action was in business. Only inferior beings took care of children, raised gardens, and

practiced the ancient art of managing a household (the original definition of economics). If you wanted to be important you had to be involved with the new value-creating process—economics as the production, distribution, and consumption of commodities.

27   By the 1970s women were becoming dissatisfied. Traditionally, the center of their identity had been in love relationships. As work became more important than love, women experienced a crisis in identity. What Maggie Scarf called "the more sorrowful sex" (*Psychology Today,* April 1979) suffered depression two to five times more often than men. Thirty-two percent of women in the prime of life (30–44) were using prescription drugs for mood elevation. As the desacralization and devaluing of home and hearth continued, a majority of women decided to enter that valuable world of paid work. In the '70s they won the right to measure their worth by money and position in a professional hierarchy and gained equal access with men to the diseases of stress—ulcers and heart attacks.

28   There are already signs that many women who were liberated in the '70s to enjoy the male prerogatives of sex without love and identities centered around work are coming full circle. The sexual revolution is cooling. The joy of commitment is re-emerging. Many women now in their mid-thirties who are seasoned workers are deciding that their anatomy might have something to do with their destiny and are having children.

29   Our changing valuation of work is a symptom of our changing view of all of reality. The new iconoclasm is directed against the idolatry of economics, the myth of money, the assumptions that more is better, work makes free (the motto that was emblazoned on the gate over Auschwitz), technology can make us all healthy, wealthy, and wise. Many Americans have reached the top of the success ladder but are beginning to suspect it may be leaning against the wrong wall.

30   It is too soon to say where the questions and the new quest will lead. It is clear that a civil war may be developing between two philosophies of life, two value systems. And in the chaos that is bound to result from this clash we might best be guided by the words, but not the example, of Freud. It may help us to remember that in his prescription of love and work—*lieben und arbeiten*—he designated love as the first among equals.

A Conflict of Values

Workers	Lovers
• Their psychological center is in: profession, job, work, doing, accomplishment, possessions, consuming, productivity, competition.	• Their psychological center is in: amateur activities, being, experiencing, relationships, enjoying, creativity, cooperation.

- They value: winning, efficiency, tough-mindedness, pragmatism, material comfort, progress, experts, quantitative measurements. Motto: More is better.

- Their metaphors for understanding life are taken from machines. The body is a machine, the mind a computer, a product of conditioning, a stimulus-response mechanism.

- Workers nearly always wear watches, live by measured, chronological time. Type A consciousness.

- Nature is seen as the source of raw materials, as parks for recreation, or as factories for agribusiness. Land is property that I have a right to own and exploit as I please. It is a form of capital that may be accumulated, and utilized for private profit.

- Their tribe is the corporation. They belong with their associates, tend to move often, and have few close friends but many acquaintances. Often lonely and isolated.

- They dream of a technological future, an information society with computerized communication networks, a planned expanding economy, a brave new world without illness or poverty.

- The value: sharing, openness, a path with heart, mysticism, "spiritual" experience, growth, generalists—disintermediation, qualitative measurements. Motto: Small is beautiful.

- Their metaphors for understanding life are taken from agriculture. The body is humus, the mind a part of the pattern that connects all of nature in a single ecological system.

- Lovers are tuned in to their body rhythms, feelings, moods, the movements of stars and seasons. Type B consciousness.

- Nature is seen as our matrix, a sacred, living environment that we must respect, as a web of kinship. Land is a trust we must husband, the soil is a part of the definition of human beings; place and person are joined in a synergistic union.

- They are rooted within their friendships, their families, their communities, their locales. Thus they are sometimes engulfed and stifled and unable to break ties that could lead to positive changes.

- They dream of establishing an ecologically sound, decentralized society with appropriate small-scale technologies and regional independence. Ecotopia.

VOCABULARY

sporadically (2)	affluent (17)	heretics (22)
orthodox (3)	apocalyptic (18)	zeal (23)
secular (4)	fluctuations (19)	initiated (24)
sanctified (4)	stagflation (19)	routinized (24)
obligatory (6)	nemesis (20)	tacit (25)
exponential (10)	usurp (20)	autonomy (25)
agitation (10)	inundate (20)	totalitarian (25)
inverse (10)	pragmatism (21)	desacralization (28)
nostalgia (12)	matrix (21)	hierarchy (27)
renaissance (12)	synergistic (21)	prerogatives (27)
animates (12)	prudery (22)	iconoclasm (29)
entrepreneurial (15)	patriarchial (22)	emblazoned (29)

QUESTIONS FOR CRITICAL THINKING

1. What do you think about Jay and his philosophy?
2. What are the characteristics of the "obligatory mid-life crisis" to which the author refers?
3. What relationship do you suppose exists between affluence and mid-life crises? Do you suppose that impoverished people in third-world countries also suffer them?
4. What does economic bondage to experts and specialists entail?
5. What relationship, if any, can be said to exist between lovers and workers? Could lovers exist in a society that contained no workers?
6. Who or what has taken the father's place in our society?
7. What are your own views on the relationship between enjoyment and meaningful work?

QUESTIONS ON THE WRITING PROCESS

1. What is the author really contrasting in this essay?
2. What method of contrast is used throughout this essay?
3. Writers can make their points either by showing or telling. In the first paragraph, how does the writer make his point about the new kind of worker?
4. The writer says in paragraph 2 that some would call Jay an underachiever. Whom do you suppose he means by "some"?
5. What point is the author making in paragraph 5? What does it contribute to his discussion?
6. What is the function of paragraph 16?
7. What mode of development does the author use in paragraphs 17 through 20?

WRITING ASSIGNMENTS

1. Which are you: a lover or a worker? Write an essay outlining and defending your view of work.

2. Have you encountered any evidence to support the author's thesis that our values about work are changing? Write an essay in which you give examples of people you know who embody the revolution against the work ethic.

3. Compare and contrast the job you hated most with the one you loved best.

HOBBITS AND ELVES

Liane Frost

The elves and the hobbits, or the "fair folks" and the "halflings," as they are sometimes referred to in their land of Middle Earth, are as different in nature as the texture of fine silk is different from cheesecloth.

The elves are tall, slender, and exquisitely beautiful. Their movements are so quick and graceful that one motion appears to melt into the next. Their speech is like the sound of the wind caressing the leaves and has a very soothing, enchanting effect on all who hear it. Unlike the elves, the hobbits are short and rather round in appearance (the latter feature being due to their habit of enjoying several meals a day). They also have an abundance of dark curly hair upon their heads and feet and move as slowly and infrequently as possible, being somewhat lazy by nature. Their speech is simple and common, but they are quite in love with the sound of it and are known for their fondness for story-telling.

The elves, unlike the hobbits, dwell in the golden boughs of the Elora trees hundreds of feet above the earth, on carved wooden platforms. Their shelter is the silver leaves of the trees that form a lacy ceiling through which the stars can be seen, but by some magic no rain can penetrate. On the other hand, the hobbits live in "hobbit holes," which are raised mounds of earth that have been hollowed on the inside. The "hobbit holes" usually contain many rooms, with plain comfortable furniture and little round doors and windows. The thought of living in any home that is above the ground is not only ridiculous to the hobbits but actually distasteful.

The elves are a wise race, skilled in the ways of the forest and in the arts of magic. Everything that they craft has been endowed with a magical power to endure through time and to be of utmost benefit to its user. On the other hand, the hobbits are plain and simple folk. They rarely give thought to anything other than a comfortable meal and a pipeful of the best tobacco.

Needless to say, the elves and the hobbits rarely have dealings with each other. On the few occasions that they do, the hobbits regard the elves with awe and a little fear, whereas the elves regard the hobbits with a gentle tolerance.

EIGHT

CAUSAL ANALYSIS

Causal analysis is really an exercise in thinking. One must search for cause, weigh it, and pass judgment on its validity. Or one must analyze effect, separating and relating the strands of consequence. Causal analysis is the kind of exercise most suitable for a person with a logical turn of mind. Probably for this reason, it is by far the hardest of all the expository modes to write well.

The whole notion of causation is deeply bound up with personal philosophy. One person may believe that astrological forces are the root cause of the world's miseries; another may hold that crime is caused mainly by the devil. Neither explanation, however, is likely to be sympathetically received in a college essay. *Cause,* as most teachers understand the word, refers to that which is verifiable and reasonable. It does not include the idiosyncratic or the proposition that must be accepted on intuition or faith.

Your analysis of cause must therefore contain explanations that appeal to reasonable people. It must not rely on special belief or on mystical thinking. It is not good enough, for example, to say that the steamship *Titanic,* which sank in 1912 after striking an iceberg, did so because God wanted to teach humankind a lesson. Such an assertion belongs in the pulpit, not in a college essay.

Collected in this chapter are essays that illustrate the analysis of both cause and effect. Cause refers to antecedent events, to what has gone before; effect refers to consequences, to what will come after. If you write to explain what made a particular thin man gain weight, you are analyzing cause (overeating). But if you write an essay predicting what is likely to happen to a man who eats more than his body needs for sustenance, you are analyzing effect.

You might find it useful to think of causation as occurring in three categories. First, there is contributory cause, which may help an event happen but cannot make it happen by itself. For example, the panel investigating the cause of the *Titanic* disaster heard testimony that a pair of binoculars usually left in the crow's nest had been removed by a transferred officer shortly before the ship sailed. The lookout testified that had the glasses been in their usual place, he might have seen the iceberg sooner and sounded the alarm early enough for the collision to be avoided. Yet the missing glasses only contributed to the ship's collision with the iceberg, and cannot be said to be the only cause. Had the ship been steaming slower, she might have avoided the iceberg altogether; had she heeded the ice warnings radioed to her, she might have maintained a greater vigilance and averted the disaster.

A *necessary* cause is one that must be present for an event to occur but cannot cause the event by itself. For example, some catastrophe such as the collision with the iceberg was a necessary cause of the *Titanic*'s sinking, but the collision alone did not cause her to sink. Indeed, the ship was thought to be unsinkable because she had been engineered and designed to withstand such an impact. However, had the collision not occurred, the ship would not have sunk.

A *sufficient* cause is one that by itself can produce a given effect. In the case of the *Titanic* the ripping of a 300-foot gash under her waterline was sufficient cause for her sinking. It is interesting to note that after the *Titanic* disaster her sister ship, the *Olympic,* underwent modifications to her hull that made her able to withstand the kind of damage that sunk the *Titanic.* A 300-foot gash under her waterline would not have been sufficient cause to sink her.

In analyzing cause, it is easy enough to confuse the contributory with the necessary and the necessary with the sufficient. Most complex events have not one but many causes. Students often go wrong in their causal analysis essays by writing simplistically about complex events. In other words, they assume that the single cause they ascribe to an event is always sufficient to bring it about.

This kind of simple causation is hardly ever the case, especially with a complex event. You will notice, in this regard, that the tone of all the essays presented in this chapter is essentially cautious. In "Making Babies," Anne Taylor Fleming seems to be grappling with trying to explain why women are reluctant to have children. Nora Ephron, in "Fantasies," puzzles about why a liberated woman such as herself could have such unliberated fantasies. Neither writer is trying to be mysterious; each is simply being cautious because causation is hard to fathom and difficult to write about.

Sufficient causes may be readily enough found for simple events, such as a person dropping dead after eating food contaminated with botulism toxin. But for a more complex event, such as the cause of violent crime, it is difficult to pinpoint a sole sufficient cause. Poverty is certainly a contributory cause; breakdown in the family unit may be another; a third may be little-understood personality factors in criminals. The writer who simply assumes that all violent crime is caused by violence on television and bases an essay on that one proposition is mistaking a contributory cause for a sufficient one. With a complex event such as violent crime, there is hardly ever a single sufficient cause that can account for it.

In writing about causation, then, caution is the customary tone that reasonable people employ. And it is one that students would also be advised to adopt in their own essays. This is not to say that you should be wishy-washy; none of the writers presented in this chapter is that. But you should not assume that there are simple reasons for everything. Generally, the simple answer is the one that relies more on faith than on intelligent analysis.

SINGLE PARAGRAPHS

WHY THE RADIO PROGRAM
"THE WAR OF THE WORLDS"
CAUSED PANIC

John Houseman

John Houseman (1902–) is a well-known producer, director, and actor. He was born in Bucharest and educated at Clifton College, England. Co-founder of the Mercury Theater, which produced "The War of the Worlds," Houseman is best known for his role in the movie Paper Chase *(1974), for which he won an Academy Award, and for his part in the television series of the same name.*

On October 30, 1938, the Mercury Theater on the Air presented a radio play of H. G. Wells's classic science fiction novel, The War of the Worlds. *The result was an unprecedented panic among listeners, who thought that an actual invasion from Mars had taken place. In this paragraph, Houseman tries to explain the cause of all the furor.*

At least one book and quite a pile of sociological literature has appeared on the subject of "The Invasion from Mars." Many theories have been put forward to explain the "tidal wave" of panic that swept the nation. I know of two factors that largely contributed to the broadcast's extraordinarily violent effect. First, its historical timing. It came within thirty-five days of the Munich crisis. For weeks, the American people had been hanging on their radios, getting most of their news no longer from the press, but over the air. A new technique of "on-the-spot" reporting had been developed and eagerly accepted by an anxious and news-hungry world. The Mercury Theater on the Air by faithfully copying every detail of the new technique—including its imperfections—found an already enervated audience ready to accept its wildest fantasies. The second factor was the show's sheer technical brilliance. To this day it is impossible to sit in a room and hear the scratched, worn, off-the-air recording of the broadcast, without feeling in the back of your neck some slight draft left over from that great wind of terror that swept the nation. Even with the element of credibility totally removed it remains a surprisingly frightening show.

VOCABULARY

enervated

289

QUESTIONS FOR CRITICAL THINKING

1. What other famous actor was associated with the Mercury Theater on the Air?
2. Some diehards claim that radio drama at its best was far better than the drama seen on television. What are your impressions of radio drama? How is it likely to differ from television drama in its effect on an audience?
3. What famous events took place at Munich that so frightened the world?

QUESTIONS ON THE WRITING PROCESS

1. What lead-ins does the author use in introducing the two factors that made the show so frightening?
2. The author writes, "First, its historical timing." What kind of construction is this? Is its usage here appropriate?
3. Why do you think the author chose to arrange the two factors in the order that they are in? What would be the effect of reversing their order?

WRITING ASSIGNMENTS

1. What is the most frightening movie you have ever seen? Write a paragraph explaining why you found it so frightening.
2. Write a brief essay on your favorite actor or actress, explaining why you like him/her so well.

THE EFFECT OF TALKING TO A BABY

Richard E. Leakey

Richard Erksine Leakey (1944–   ), anthropologist, is director of the National Museums of Kenya. He is the leader of an excavation project in search of early man at Lake Turkana in northern Kenya. Leakey is also the author of two books, Origins *(1978) and* People of the Lake *(1979).*

This brief paragraph illustrates the analysis of effect, specifically the stimulus effect of talking to a baby.

When you talk to a very young baby, a curious thing is happening. Along with the arm-waving, the gurgling, and the engaging stare that can coax a smile from even the most solemn adult, the baby's body ripples with tiny coordinated muscular movements that can be detected only with specially sensitive electronic equipment. This extraordinary response, only recently discovered, is a powerful demonstration of just how firmly language is rooted in the human brain. In that baby the whole constellation of tiny, almost imperceptible movements have been generated by the brain as a result of the sound uttered by the admiring adult. More astonishing still— but also, on reflection, inevitable—is the discovery that exactly the same phenomenon occurs, whatever the permutation of nationality in baby and adult: that is, an American infant responds to the sounds of Chinese, Russian, and French exactly as it does to those of the English language.

VOCABULARY

constellation   imperceptible   permutation

QUESTIONS FOR CRITICAL THINKING

1. What similar effect does language exert on an adult?
2. In what ways do you adapt language to suit your audience?

QUESTIONS ON THE WRITING PROCESS

1. The paragraph analyzes effect rather than cause. Where is the intent of the writer first made clear?
2. The article mentions two astonishing effects of talking to a baby. What transition does the writer use to move the discussion from one effect to the other?
3. Repetition of a key word is one technique writers frequently use to achieve coherence in a paragraph. What key word is repeatedly used in this paragraph?

WRITING ASSIGNMENTS

1. In a paragraph, enumerate some obvious effects that certain kinds of language (say, slang or baby talk) have on you.
2. Do you have any bad language habits you would like to be rid of? Write an essay explaining what they are and how you acquired them.

FANTASIES

Nora Ephron

Nora Ephron (1941–   ), a freelance writer, was born in New York City and educated at Wellesley College. She has been a reporter for the New York Post *and a contributing editor for* Esquire *magazine. She has written three books,* Wallflower at the Orgy *(1970),* Crazy Salad *(1975), and* Scribble, Scribble *(1978).*

A self-described feminist admits to having sexual fantasies of being domi-nated by faceless males, and tries to explain why, in spite of her political beliefs, she is still haunted by "unliberated" fantasies.

1   One of the trump cards that men who are threatened by women's liberation are always dredging up is the question of whether there is sex after liber-ation. I have heard at least five or six experts or writers or spokesmen or some such stand up at various meetings and wonder aloud what happens to sex between men and women when the revolution comes. These men are always hooted down by the women present; in fact, I am usually one of the women present hooting them down, sniggering snide remarks to whoever is next to me like well-we-certainly-know-how-sure-of-himself-he-is. This fall, at the *Playboy* Writers' Convocation, an author named Morton Hunt ut-tered the magic words at a panel on The Future of Sex, and even in that room, full of male chauvinism and *Playboy* philosophers, the animosity against him was audible.

2   I spend a great deal of my energy these days trying to fit feminism into marriage, or vice versa—I'm never sure which way the priorities lie; it depends on my mood—but as truly committed as I am to the movement and as violent as I have become toward people who knock it, I think it is unfair to dismiss these men. They deserve some kind of answer. Okay. The answer is, nobody knows what happens to sex after liberation. It's a big mystery. And now that I have gotten that out of the way, I can go on to what really interests and puzzles me about sex and liberation—which is that it is difficult for me to see how sexual behavior and relations between the sexes can change at all unless our sexual fantasies change. So many of the conscious and unconscious ways men and women treat each other have to do with romantic and sexual fantasies that are deeply ingrained, not just in society but in literature. The movement may manage to clean up the mess in society, but I don't know whether it can ever clean up the mess in our minds.

3   I am somewhat liberated by current standards, but I have in my head this dreadful unliberated sex fantasy. One of the women in my consciousness-raising group is always referring to her "rich fantasy life," by which I sup-pose she means that in her fantasies she makes it in costume, or in exotic

places, or with luminaries like Mao Tse-tung in a large bowl of warm Wheatena. My fantasy life is unfortunately nowhere near that interesting.

4   Several years ago, I went to interview photographer Philippe Halsman, whose notable achievements include a charming book containing photographs of celebrities jumping. The jumps are quite revealing in a predictable sort of way—Richard Nixon with his rigid, constricted jump, the Duke and Duchess of Windsor in a deeply dependent jump. And so forth. In the course of the interview, Halsman asked me if I wanted to jump for him; seeing it as a way to avoid possible years of psychoanalysis, I agreed. I did what I thought was my quintessential jump. "Do it again," said Halsman. I did, attempting to duplicate exactly what I had done before. "Again," he said, and I did. "Well," said Halsman, "I can see from your jump that you are a very determined, ambitious, directed person, but you will never write a novel." "Why is that?" I asked. "Because you have only one jump in you," he said.

5   At the time, I thought that was really unfair—I had, after all, thought he wanted to see the *same* jump, not a different one every time; but I see now that he was exactly right. I have only one jump in me. I see this more and more every day. I am no longer interested in thirty-one flavors; I stick with English toffee. More to the point, I have had the same sex fantasy, with truly minor variations, since I was about eleven years old. It is really a little weird to be stuck with something so crucially important for so long; I have managed to rid myself of all the other accoutrements of being eleven—I have pimples more or less under control, I can walk fairly capably in high heels—but I find myself with this appalling fantasy that has burrowed in and has absolutely nothing to do with my life.

6   I have never told anyone the exact details of my particular sex fantasy: it is my only secret and I am not going to divulge it here. I once told *almost* all of it to my former therapist; he died last year, and when I saw his obituary I felt a great sense of relief: the only person in the world who almost knew how crazy I am was gone and I was safe. Anyway, without giving away any of the juicy parts, I can tell you that in its broad outlines it has largely to do with being dominated by faceless males who rip my clothes off. That's just about all they have to do. Stare at me in this faceless way, go mad with desire, and rip my clothes off. It's terrific. In my sex fantasy, nobody ever loves me for my mind.

7   The fantasy of rape—of which mine is in a kind of prepubescent subcategory—is common enough among women and (in mirror image) among men. And what I don't understand is that with so many of us stuck with these clichéd feminine/masculine, submissive/dominant, masochistic/ sadistic fantasies, how are we ever going to adjust fully to the less thrilling but more desirable reality of equality? A few months ago, someone named B. Lyman Steward, a urologist at Cedars of Lebanon Hospital in Los Angeles, attributed the rising frequency of impotence among his male patients to

the women's movement, which he called an effort to dominate men. The movement is nothing of the kind; but it and a variety of other events in society have certainly brought about a change in the way women behave in bed. A young man who grows up expecting to dominate sexually is bound to be somewhat startled by a young woman who wants sex as much as he does, and multi-orgasmic sex at that. By the same token, I suspect that a great deal of the difficulty women report in achieving orgasm is traceable—sadly—to the possibility that a man who is a tender fellow with implicit capabilities for impotence hardly fits into classic fantasies of big brutes with implicit capabilities for violence. A close friend who has the worst marriage I know—her husband beats her up regularly—reports that her sex life is wonderful. I am hardly suggesting that women ask their men to beat them—nor am I advocating the course apparently preferred by one of the most prominent members of the women's movement, who makes it mainly with blue-collar workers and semiliterates. But I wonder how we will ever break free from all the nonsense we grew up with; I wonder if our fantasies can ever catch up to what we all want for our lives.

8   It is possible, through sheer willpower, to stop having unhealthy sex fantasies. I have several friends who did just that. "What do you have instead?" I asked. "Nothing," they replied. Well, I don't know. I'm not at all sure I wouldn't rather have an unhealthy sex fantasy than no sex fantasy at all. But my real question is whether it is possible, having discarded the fantasy, to discard the thinking and expectations it represents. In my case, I'm afraid it wouldn't be. I have no desire to be dominated. Honestly I don't. And yet I find myself becoming angry when I'm not. My husband has trouble hailing a cab or flagging a waiter, and suddenly I feel a kind of rage; ball-breaking anger rises to my T-zone. I wish he were better at hailing taxis than I am; on the other hand, I realize that expectation is culturally conditioned, utterly foolish, has nothing to do with anything, is exactly the kind of thinking that ought to be got rid of in our society; on still another hand, having that insight into my reaction does not seem to calm my irritation.

9   My husband is fond of reminding me of the story of Moses, who kept the Israelites in the desert for forty years because he knew a slave generation could not found a new free society. The comparison with the women's movement is extremely apt, I think; I doubt that it will ever be possible for the women of my generation to escape from our own particular slave mentality. For the next generation, life may indeed be freer. After all, if society changes, the fantasies will change; where women are truly equal, where their status has nothing to do with whom they marry, when the issues of masculine/feminine cease to exist, some of this absurd reliance on role playing will be eliminated. But not all of it. Because even after the revolution, we will be left with all the literature. "What will happen to the literature"? Helen Dudar of the New York *Post* once asked Ti-Grace Atkinson.

"What does it matter what happens?" Ms. Atkinson replied. But it does. You are what you eat. After liberation, we will still have to reckon with the Sleeping Beauty and Cinderella. Granted there will also be a new batch of fairy tales about princesses who refuse to have ladies-in-waiting because it is exploitative of the lower classes—but that sounds awfully tedious, doesn't it? Short of a mass book burning, which no one wants, things may well go on as they are now: women being pulled between the intellectual attraction of liberation and the emotional, psychological, and cultural mishmash it's hard to escape growing up with; men trying to cope with these two extremes, and with their own ambivalence besides. It's not much fun this way, but at least it's not boring.

VOCABULARY

sniggering (1)	accoutrements (5)	multi-orgasmic (7)
snide (1)	appalling (5)	implicit (7)
chauvinism (1)	burrowed (5)	advocating (7)
animosity (1)	divulge (6)	semiliterates (7)
ingrained (2)	prepubescent (7)	conditioned (8)
luminaries (3)	masochistic (7)	exploitative (9)
constricted (4)	urologist (7)	mishmash (9)
quintessential (4)	impotence (7)	ambivalence (9)

QUESTIONS FOR CRITICAL THINKING

1. The author claims that in spite of her sexual fantasy about being dominated, and in spite of her anger at her husband when he is not dominant, she honestly has no desire to be dominated. What do you think of this apparent contradiction?
2. The author regards her fantasy as an unliberated one. Should one's fantasies necessarily conform to one's ideological beliefs? If so, what should the liberated fantasy of a feminist be like?
3. What is your opinion of the view that the women's movement is the cause of much male impotence?
4. How would you characterize the author's attitude toward her own sexual fantasy?
5. The author implies that by abandoning their own sexual fantasies her friends have made their sex lives poorer. What part do fantasies play in a normal sex life?
6. What are the goals and aims of the women's movement? How are men affected by the movement?

QUESTIONS ON THE WRITING PROCESS

1. In the first sentence, the author writes that "one of the trump cards" men are always "dredging up" is the question of sex after liberation. What is odd about this figure of speech?
2. In the first paragraph, why does the author hyphenate the phrase "well-we-certainly-know-how-sure-of-himself-*he*-is"?
3. In the second paragraph, the author does two things: first, she answers the question about sex after liberation; then she talks about how sexual fantasies affect the relations between the sexes. What transition does she use to move the discussion from the first point to the second?
4. Paragraph 3 is the shortest paragraph in the essay. What is its primary function?
5. What rhetorical mode is paragraph 4 written in?
6. What transition does the author use in paragraph 5 to shift the discussion from her experience with photographer Halsman to her sexual fantasy?
7. How would you characterize the tone of the last sentence in paragraph 6?
8. In paragraph 7, the author writes that "a man who is a tender fellow with implicit capabilities for impotence hardly fits into classic fantasies about big brutes with implicit capabilities for violence." What characteristic does the sentence have?
9. In which paragraphs does the author actually analyze the cause of her unliberated sexual fantasy?

WRITING ASSIGNMENTS

1. Write a 300-word essay analyzing the effects of the women's movement on the relations between the sexes.
2. Write an essay describing what the world would be like if men and women were considered absolutely equal in every respect.
3. Write a brief essay defining fantasy.

MAKING BABIES

Anne Taylor Fleming

Anne Taylor Fleming is a West Coast writer. She is co-author of The First Time *(1975), written with her husband Karl.*

This article is a poignant analysis of the dislocation of roles caused by the feminist revolution, as one woman tries to explain why her generation is afraid of motherhood.

1 Four years ago, when I was 21 and newly school-sprung, many of the women I knew—myself included—were agonizing about whether to marry. Most of us finally did. Now a lot of my friends and other women of my generation are agonizing about whether to get pregnant. Many of us haven't so far. And the troubling thought has crept into our souls or our wombs (presuming they are separate places, and sometimes I'm not so sure they are) that we just might never make babies, that we might enter middle age alone—perhaps divorced or widowed—childless, womb-tight and woe-begone. Why, if women face this almost certain aloneness later on, are so many of us so strangely steeled against pregnancy?

2 Some non-baby-making women will explain it by saying something like: "The world's in a hell of a mess and I don't want to bring a baby into it"; or, "There are too many babies around already." I myself give lip service to answers like those; but I don't really buy them. After all, the world has always seemed a treacherous place to a prospective mother. As for over-population, it is a serious concern to serious-minded young women but I just don't believe it ever stopped one specific woman from having one specific baby.

3 The other most oft-given answer, and one I give more credence to, is: "Well, I have a career to pursue and I can't risk dividing my energies and loyalties between work and a baby." How stern and unlovely and downright corny that sounds. Yet I myself have said it many a time and will undoubt-edly say it many more. I believe it. I believe that I am not put together enough right now to cope with dishes and diapers and postpartum depres-sions while trying to carry on what I imagine to be a life's work.

4 A baby was never going to fill my me-need, my what-am-I-going-to-do-when-I-grow-up-need. I always knew that. And then the women's move-ment came along and firmed up my resolve to work and the resolves of women like me. Also, many of us had watched our mothers try, at 40, to pick up the pieces of some long-abandoned life and work when our fathers had left them. Their example was not lost on us. I have many times said to myself and heard other women say: "That won't happen to me. I'll always have my work. Nobody—but nobody—can take that away from me."

5   And so, rather fiercely, we cling to our work as to a life raft, hoping that it will keep us afloat in good times and bad. Though we might in private moments yearn sometimes to trade back in our full heads and empty wombs for empty heads and full wombs, we cannot now. Having committed ourselves so early and so firmly to our so-called careers, we are afraid to commit also to a baby. We're afraid to risk failing twice. It is, in fact, precisely because we take motherhood so seriously—as, God help us, we seem to take everything these days—that we're staying away from it, at least for the moment.

6   There is something, though, deeper than our work that is keeping many of us from making babies, something to do with sex. What has happened to many young women, I think, is that effective contraceptives—which we have used faithfully for a decade—are now so much a part of our bodies, and of our consciousnesses, that we are scared to set them aside, scared to get pregnant, not physically scared, some other kind of scared, a bigger kind. Before the recent arrival of fail-safe contraceptives, lovemaking for women was always baby-making, pure and simple. But these new contraceptives put women on an equal footing—rather, on an equal bedding—with men, so that for us, sexual pleasure is now no longer an accidental by-product of procreation, just as a baby is now no longer the by-product of accidental afternoon lust. The very urges themselves, the lovemaking urge and the baby-making urge, have become separated in women. Now we can, like men, bed at will, without being physically or psychologically penalized, without having the moment complicated, or dignified, by the possibility of procreation. What a relief! What a joy!

7   So we are very reluctant to set aside the contraceptives, and are unwilling to have sex become so serious again so soon, and are afraid to have one moment of pleasure become something so tangible and so permanent as a baby. We are ready to be true sex objects at last!

8   But—and the irony is obvious—many men I listen to these days don't seem quite ready for women's newly liberated libidos. They are already greatly scared and greatly weary of our fierce wakefulness. In the marriages I know, in fact, it is the men, not the women, who nowadays want to make babies, perhaps as a way of holding on to us, just as women were forever having babies to try to hold on to men. And when women refuse to get pregnant, men have in their eyes a hint of what for so long they saw in ours: that fear of being left or, worse, of being cuckolded.

9   This kind of fear is not pretty to me. Like many women, I have had too much of that kind of sexual fear myself all too recently. When the women's movement was in first bloom a few years ago, women, in their exhilaration, could not resist gloating a bit over male sexual insecurities. But now the movement is in its revisionist stage and men and women seem to want to be tender with one another again and to honor each other's needs, old and new. In that spirit, many of the women I know long to tumble easily and

hopefully into pregnancy, like their mothers and grandmothers before them, with no agony aforethought, long to pledge allegiance with their wombs to the men they love. But they can't. They're stuck in a holding pattern. So am I. I'm feeling willful and wobbly and—oh, why do we women feel the need to soft-peddle it?—I'm competitive and ambitious and confused a lot and I don't think any baby ought to be subjected to me right now. At least no baby of mine.

VOCABULARY

agonizing (1)	resolve (4)	cuckolded (8)
woebegone (1)	procreation (6)	exhilaration (9)
credence (3)	tangible (7)	gloating (9)
postpartum (3)	libidos (8)	revisionist (9)

QUESTIONS FOR CRITICAL THINKING

1. What finally emerges as the author's reason for not wanting to have children?
2. The population of the rest of the world is growing much faster than the population of the United States. What possible consequences can this have for the United States?
3. What is your attitude toward so-called recreational sex?
4. The author talks about "full heads and empty wombs," implying that if the one is full the other must be empty. Is it possible for women to have both full heads and full wombs? Why or why not?
5. Why should, or why shouldn't, a constitutional amendment banning abortions be passed?
6. What is your own attitude toward child-bearing?

QUESTIONS ON THE WRITING PROCESS

1. The author writes that four years ago many women of her generation were "agonizing about whether to marry," but many are now "agonizing about whether to get pregnant." Why are these sentences so similarly phrased?
2. What is the thesis of this article? Where is it stated, and how is it worded?
3. What two points are dealt with in paragraph 4? What transition does the author use between them?
4. What transition does the author use between the fourth and fifth paragraphs?
5. How would you characterize the tone of the last sentence of paragraph 8?
6. The author writes that she is "stuck in a holding pattern." What is the origin of this phrase? What kind of figure of speech is it?

WRITING ASSIGNMENTS

1. Do you intend to have children? Write a 300-word essay explaining why you will, or why you will not.

2. The author mentions that many women of her generation have watched their 40-year-old mothers try to pick up the pieces of their lives after being deserted by their husbands. In an essay, explain why you think so many marriages break down at this critical stage, when the husbands and wives have reached mid-life.

3. Some people are now pressing for a constitutional amendment limiting abortions. In a brief essay, take a stand for or against this issue.

THE DECLARATION OF INDEPENDENCE

Thomas Jefferson

Thomas Jefferson (1743–1826), 3rd President of the United States and author of the Declaration of Independence, was born at "Shadwell" in Maryland and educated at the College of William and Mary. He served successively as Governor of Virginia, minister to France, Secretary of State, Vice President, and President. Jefferson was a scientist, architect, philosopher, and founder of the University of Virginia with wide-ranging interests in nearly every sphere of human effort. His collected writings comprise over 50 volumes.

The Declaration of Independence, along with the Constitution and the Bill of Rights, is numbered among the few sacred secular documents. Its historical significance has been studied from every conceivable angle by historians of every imaginable stripe. But it is also a powerful statement of cause: of why a young nation rebelled and overthrew a colonial master it regarded as tyrannical.

In CONGRESS, July 4, 1776.
The Unanimous Declaration of the Thirteen United States of America.

1   When in the Course of human events, it becomes necessary for one people to dissolve the political bands which have connected them with another, and to assume among the powers of the earth, the separate and equal station to which the Laws of Nature and of Nature's God entitle them, a decent respect to the opinions of mankind requires that they should declare the causes which impel them to the separation.

2   We hold these truths to be self-evident, that all men are created equal, that they are endowed by their Creator with certain unalienable Rights, that among these are Life, Liberty and the pursuit of Happiness.

3   That to secure these rights, Governments are instituted among Men, deriving their just powers from the consent of the governed.

4   That whenever any Form of Government becomes destructive of these ends, it is the Right of the People to alter or to abolish it, and to institute new Government, laying its foundation on such principles and organizing its powers in such form, as to them shall seem most likely to effect their Safety and Happiness. Prudence, indeed, will dictate that Governments long established should not be changed for light and transient causes; and accordingly all experience hath shewn, that mankind are more disposed to suffer, while evils are sufferable, than to right themselves by abolishing the forms to which they are accustomed. But when a long train of abuses and usurpations, pursuing invariably the same Object evinces a design to re-

duce them under absolute Despotism, it is their right, it is their duty, to throw off such Government, and to provide new Guards for their future security.

5 Such has been the patient sufferance of these Colonies; and such is now the necessity which constrains them to alter their former Systems of Government. The history of the present King of Great Britain is a history of repeated injuries and usurpations, all having in direct object the establishment of an absolute Tyranny over these States. To prove this, let Facts be submitted to a candid world.

6 He has refused his Assent to Laws, the most wholesome and necessary for the public good.

7 He has forbidden his Governors to pass Laws of immediate and pressing importance, unless suspended in their operation till his Assent should be obtained; and when so suspended, he has utterly neglected to attend to them.

8 He has refused to pass other Laws for the accommodation of large districts of people, unless those people would relinquish the right of Representation in the Legislature, a right inestimable to them and formidable to tyrants only.

9 He has called together legislative bodies at places unusual, uncomfortable, and distant from the depository of their public Records for the sole purpose of fatiguing them into compliance with his measures.

10 He has dissolved Representative Houses repeatedly, for opposing with manly firmness his invasions on the rights of people.

11 He has refused for a long time, after such dissolutions, to cause others to be elected; whereby the Legislative powers, incapable of Annihilation, have returned to the People at large for their exercise the State remaining in the mean time exposed to all the dangers of invasion from without, and convulsions within.

12 He has endeavoured to prevent the population of these States; for that purpose obstructing the Laws of Naturalization of Foreigners; refusing to pass others to encourage their migrations hither, and raising the conditions of new Appropriations of Lands.

13 He has obstructed the Administration of Justice, by refusing his Assent to Laws for establishing Judiciary powers.

14 He has made Judges dependent on his Will alone, for the tenure of their offices, and the amount and payment of their salaries.

15 He has erected a multitude of New Offices, and sent hither swarms of Officers to harass our people, and eat out their substance.

16 He has kept among us, in times of peace, Standing Armies without the Consent of our legislatures.

17 He has affected to render the Military independent of and superior to the Civil power.

18   He has combined with others to subject us to a jurisdiction foreign to our constitution, and unacknowledged by our laws; giving his Assent to their Acts of pretended Legislation:

For Quartering large bodies of armed troops among us:

For Protecting them, by a mock Trial, from punishment for any Murders which they should commit on the Inhabitants of these States:

For cutting off our Trade with all parts of the world:

For imposing Taxes on us without our Consent:

For depriving us in many cases, of the benefits of Trial by Jury:

For transporting us beyond Seas to be tried for pretended offenses:

For abolishing the free System of English Laws in a neighbouring Province, establishing therein an Arbitrary government, and enlarging its Boundaries so as to render it at once an example and fit instrument for introducing the same absolute rule into these Colonies:

For taking away our Charters, abolishing our most valuable Laws, and altering fundamentally the Forms of our Governments:

For suspending our own Legislatures, and declaring themselves invested with power to legislate for us in all cases whatsoever.

19   He has abdicated Government here, by declaring us out of his Protection and waging War against us:

20   He has plundered our seas, ravaged our Coasts, burnt our towns, and destroyed the lives of our people.

21   He is at this time transporting large Armies of foreign Mercenaries to compleat the works of death, desolation and tyranny, already begun with circumstances of Cruelty & perfidy scarcely paralleled in the most barbarous ages, and totally unworthy the Head of a civilized nation.

22   He has constrained our fellow Citizens taken Captive on the high Seas to bear Arms against their Country, to become the executioners of their friends and Brethren, or to fall themselves by their Hands.

23   He has excited domestic insurrections amongst us, and has endeavoured to bring on the inhabitants of our frontiers, the merciless Indian Savages, whose known rule of warfare, is an undistinguished destruction of all ages, sexes and conditions. In every stage of these Oppressions We have Petitioned for Redress in the most humble terms: Our repeated Petitions have been answered only by repeated injury. A Prince, whose character is thus marked by every act which may define a Tyrant, is unfit to be the ruler of a free people. Nor have We been wanting in attentions to our British brethren. We have warned them from time to time of attempts by their legislature to extend an unwarrantable jurisdiction over us. We have reminded them of the circumstances of our emigration and settlement here. We have appealed to their native justice and magnanimity, and we have conjured them by the ties of our common kindred to disavow these usurpations, which, would inevitably interrupt our connections and correspondence.

They too have been deaf to the voice of justice and of consanguinity. We must, therefore, acquiesce in the necessity, which denounces our Separation, and hold them, as we hold the rest of mankind, Enemies in War, in Peace Friends.

24   We, THEREFORE the Representatives of the UNITED STATES OF AMERICA, in General Congress Assembled, appealing to the Supreme Judge of the world for the rectitude of our intentions, do, in the Name and by Authority of the good People of these Colonies, solemnly publish and declare, That these United Colonies are, and of Right ought to be FREE AND INDEPENDENT STATES: that they are Absolved from all Allegiance to the British Crown, and that all political connection between them and the State of Great Britain, is and ought to be totally dissolved; and that as Free and Independent States, they have full Power to levy War, conclude Peace, contract Alliances, establish Commerce, and to do all other Acts and Things which Independent States may of right do.

25   And for the support of this Declaration, with a firm reliance on the protection of divine Providence, we mutually pledge to each other our Lives, our Fortunes and our sacred Honor.

VOCABULARY

unalienable (2)	formidable (8)	magnanimity (23)
transient (4)	annihilation (11)	conjured (23)
usurpations (4)	abdicated (19)	consanguinity (23)
evinces (4)	perfidy (21)	acquiesce (23)
despotism (4)	insurrections (23)	rectitude (24)
inestimable (8)	redress (23)	

QUESTIONS FOR CRITICAL THINKING

1. In what sense can it be truly said that "all men are created equal"?
2. The Declaration of Independence stresses that governments derive their just powers from the consent of the governed. To what extent does this principle apply to the individual who objects to the policies of a state?
3. What, in your view, should be the purpose and aim of good government?
4. What can government do to promote the end of "happiness"?
5. Imagine that the American revolution is occurring today and that both colony and colonist possess nuclear arsenals. How would you view the Declaration of Independence under such circumstances?

QUESTIONS ON THE WRITING PROCESS

1. What does paragraphing add to the charges against the king listed in the Declaration of Independence?
2. What part do parallelism and balance play in the framing of the sentences in the Declaration?
3. Climax in writing refers to the arranging of ideas in their order of importance. Examine the final sentence of the Declaration. How would a modern writer most likely order the threesome of "lives, fortunes, and honor"? What does this order say about Jefferson's values?
4. As an example of changes in the style of punctuation, examine the first sentence of paragraph 23. How would a modern writer punctuate this sentence?
5. For what audience was the Declaration of Independence intended? How does its language reflect this intent?

WRITING ASSIGNMENTS

1. Write an essay clarifying the meaning of the phrase, "all men are created equal."
2. Write a definition of "happiness" as you think it is meant in the Declaration of Independence.
3. Write an essay arguing for the superiority of either a republican or monarchical system of government.

SUPERSTITION*

Robert Lynd

*Robert Lynd (1879–1949), Irish essayist, was born in Belfast and edu-
cated at Queen's College. Living most of his life in London, he worked
as the literary editor for the* London News Chronicle *and as an editorial
writer for the* New Statesman and Nation. *His many published works
include* The Pleasures of Ignorance *(1921) and* Solomon in All His
Glory *(1923).*

*This article analyzes the causes of superstition—a trait to which most of
us would only secretly confess. The author cleverly reconstructs a likely
beginning for superstition and makes the point that it is closer to
rationality than we might think.*

1   It was announced shortly before the production of *The Golden Moth* that
the name of the play was to be changed because the company believe that
the presence of the word "golden" in a title is unlucky. A little later the
management of the theatre decided to defy superstition and the play was
produced with the original title after all. The stage is perhaps the most
superstitious institution in England, after the racecourse. The latter is so
superstitious that to wish a man luck when on his way to a racemeeting is
considered unlucky. Instead of saying "Good luck!" you should say something insulting, such as, "May you break your leg!" Actors and actresses
have not only all the ordinary superstitions about picking up of pins, breaking looking-glasses, and the unluckiness of certain numbers. They have also
a number of professional superstitions. It is unlucky, they say, for instance,
to quote *Macbeth*. Actors dare not say to each other at parting: "When
shall we three meet again?" No good actress would advise a nervous fellow-
artist to "screw her courage to the sticking-place." It is unlucky during
rehearsals to quote the catchword of a forthcoming play in casual conversation. It is unlucky to carry a make-up box, like an amateur actress. Then
there are certain theatres that are regarded as unlucky, and the superstitious actor is depressed at the prospect of having to appear at one of them.
The luck may turn, we are told, if the name of the theatre is changed; this
was probably the cause of the change of the name of one London theatre
which has since been successful.

2   Most of us are accustomed to regard superstitious people as unenlight-
ened, and there is no one who feels more eminently wise than the man who
rises first from a table at which thirteen guests have sat down. So far as I

have discovered, however, the dividing line between those who are superstitious and those who are not is not at all the same as the line that divides
enlightenment from unenlightenment. Some of the world's wisest men
have been superstitious. Some of the world's greatest dunderheads have
been free from superstition. Plutarch was a wise man, not only for his own
age, but for any age, yet he believed in superstitions that a modern bus-
conductor would laugh at. Many of those who laugh at superstitions do so
from narrowness of mind. They are incredulous of everything that their
eyes have not seen. They cannot imagine anything outside the day's work
and the football results. Their unbelief in black cats is simply a form of dull
materialism. I do not, I may say, contend that the superstitious man is wiser
than the unsuperstitious. All I contend is that freedom from superstition is
not necessarily a form of wisdom, but that it frequently results from
thoughtlessness. Perfect wisdom, I believe, gives perfect freedom from superstition, but it probably involves belief in a good many things that will
seem superstitious to a thoughtless man.

3   Consider, for a moment, how the first superstition came into the world.
Man found himself cast into a chaos of drifting phenomena without the
slightest notion of what they meant or whether they meant anything. He
could not distinguish between things and their shadows. He was as ignorant
as a child as to how children were born. He did not know what was happening to his friends when they died. He was frightened of many things, because some things hurt him, and he did not know which did and which did
not. All that he knew was that queer things were constantly happening, but
they happened, not according to any rule that he could see, but in a confused and terrifying jumble. One day, in the forest, however, he casually
picked up a pin—or, let us say, a sharp pine-needle—and immediately afterwards he came on the most delightful bunch of bananas he had ever tasted.
This did not at the moment strike him as being remarkable. But the next
day he noticed the same sort of pine-needle lying on the ground and picked
it up. Immediately afterwards he discovered another bunch of bananas even
more delightful than the first. His brain swam with the sense of discovery.
He beat his forehead with his hands—hairy, prehensile hands—for the
birth of something absolutely new in his mind was making his head ache.
He muttered: "I pick up pine-needles and find sweet bananas! I pick up
pine-needles and find sweet bananas!" It was some time before even this
conveyed a clear message to a brain unaccustomed to act. But as he repeated the words in a sort of trance, the truth suddenly flashed upon him.
When he uncovered his face he was looking ten years older, but he was
wearing a smile that was almost human. He did not exactly say to himself,
"I have found a pattern in the universe," but he had made the first move
towards the happiest of all Eurekas. He was never quite simian again. He
was like a child who, after long contemplation of the stars in the night sky,
that seem to lie about haphazard like fallen apples, suddenly picks out the

certain pattern of a constellation. He, too, has seen a pattern: the stars are no longer an abracadabra to him, but reveal meaning to him in a speech that he continually learns to understand better. In the same way, primitive man in his superstitions was slowly learning to put two and two together. What matter if they often came to five? It is better to put two and two together wrong than to believe that they cannot be put together at all.

4   This, it may be said, may account for the reign of superstition, but it does not therefore justify the superstitions of civilized men and women. We have surer means nowadays of discovering the pattern in life. We cannot be content with apparent cause and effect, but we employ intelligent tests for the discovery of the real cause. The child in arms may believe that the watch flies open because it blows hard on its back, but a grown-up man would be an imbecile to imagine that this is the real reason why the watch flies open. This is true enough. When the real pattern of cause and effect is known, there is no room for fantastic explanations. We have not the right to believe that the crowing of cocks causes the sun to rise, or that railway trains are propelled, not by steam, but by the waving of a green flag or a green light. One might as well doubt the pattern of the Seven Stars. Such patterns are established once for all. On the other hand, the greater part of the universe is undiscovered and uncharted, as the greater part of the sky is. Our lives are still a voyage amid chance and confusion, and there are many things of which we know as little as the first monkey. While this continues, men will go on being superstitious—casting their fancies into the unknown in search of signs. For superstition is mainly a belief in signs. The superstitious man does not believe that bringing blackthorn in flower into a house actually causes a death in the house; what he believes is that it announces a death. It is the same with telling fortunes with the cards. The cards are not supposed to control events but only to prophesy them. I know that the superstitious do not always adopt this comparatively philosophical attitude. Some of them will put the blame of their misfortunes on a friend, for instance, who has sent them a gift of white flowers without a mixture of other colours. But this is unreasonable. The only reasonable defence of modern superstition I have ever heard was that certain signs show the direction of events as a weather-cock shows the direction in which the wind is blowing.

5   Even so, in practice, it is at times almost impossible to distinguish between the prophet of bad news and the causer of bad events. In the old days the prophets were stoned because they were hated as a woman hates a broken mirror. I have heard superstitious people arguing gravely as to whether President Wilson's downfall was caused by his association with the number thirteen, or whether his association with the number thirteen was a prophecy of his downfall. It will be remembered that on his arrival in France he was entertained at a dinner at which thirteen persons sat down, because he had announced that he regarded thirteen as a lucky number. It

will also be remembered that, though he originally published his Fourteen points, they were afterwards reduced to Thirteen, owing to the objections of the Allies to the "Freedom of the Seas." The superstitious find it difficult to think that this was only an omen. They half believe at the back of their minds that another guest and another point might have made the world safe for democracy.

6   The ordinary man's reply to superstitions of the kind is seldom based on reason. He is content to say "Rot!" and will no more argue about it than if you told him that a runner duck in your back-yard had been heard quoting *Paradise Lost*. As a matter of fact, neither the attack on superstition nor the defence of it has very much to do with reason. We believe or disbelieve according to our temperaments. Two men, equal in brain and courage, will behave quite differently when it comes to walking under a ladder or lighting a cigarette from a match from which two cigarettes have been already lit. Parnell was eminent for moral courage, but he believed that green was an unlucky colour, and was horror-stricken—and not on aesthetic grounds—when he was presented with a green smoking-cap by a too patriotic lady. During the war the men who carried mascots were not noticeably inferior to the men who did not. By a curious irony, it was in the country which instituted the worship of reason that mascots were most popular. An interesting essay could be written on the theme that an increase of rationalism leads automatically to an increase of superstition. I doubt whether the religious Victorians, who sneered at ghosts and picked up pins only on grounds of economy, were quite so superstitious as their irreligious successors. After all, the human mind cannot be content to accept the unknown as unknowable. Life is a mystery, but most of us feel that, like a jigsaw puzzle, it may yield a solution if only we keep trying to put the apparently incoherent pieces together. Superstition will never give us the whole pattern, but is a pardonable attempt to unite two or three of the pieces in a sub-pattern. All science and art is but the piecing together of a sub-pattern out of chaos. Be not censorious if an inhabitant of chaos finds a meaning you do not in two magpies or a dog's howl or a slice of bread-and-butter that falls with its face in the dust.

VOCABULARY

catchword (1)	simian (3)	irreligious (6)
eminently (2)	haphazard (3)	incoherent (6)
dunderheads (2)	aesthetic (6)	censorious (6)
prehensile (3)	rationalism (6)	

QUESTIONS FOR CRITICAL THINKING

1. The author says that theatre people are extraordinarily superstitious. What explanation can you give for this?
2. Why would a materialist tend to be unsuperstitious?
3. What is the relationship between cause and effect and sequence? What does the author imply about this relationship?
4. Which is more important: the process of thinking or the answer it produces? Justify your answer.
5. How is science similar to superstition? How is it different?

QUESTIONS ON THE WRITING PROCESS

1. The author does not actually begin to present his views on superstition until the second paragraph. What is he trying to do in the first?
2. What can you deduce about the audience for whom this essay was intended by its diction, syntax, and paragraphs?
3. How does the author stress in the first paragraph the importance of superstitions to theatrical people?
4. What lead-in does the author use in presenting his view of how superstition may have begun?
5. What simile does the author use in paragraph 3 to describe the ignorance of primitive man? Why is it effective?

WRITING ASSIGNMENTS

1. Write an essay about any superstition you may have, explaining the cause of it.
2. Argue against the author's view that superstition is a necessary and useful beginning in a search for patterns.
3. In their search for patterns in life, how do art and science mainly differ? Write an essay comparing and contrasting the method of searching implicit in each.

MORALS AND WEAPONS

Konrad Z. Lorenz

Konrad Z. Lorenz (1903–   ) is an Austrian zoologist and ethologist. He was awarded the Nobel Prize in physiology and medicine in 1973 for his work in establishing the science of ethology. Lorenz, along with Oscar Heinroth, is credited with the discovery of imprinting—rapid and irreversible learning that occurs early in an animal's life.

Taken from King Solomon's Ring *(1952), this essay is Lorenz's attempt to explain why some species of animals fight to the death and others do not.*

1   It is early one Sunday morning at the beginning of March, when Easter is already in the air, and we are taking a walk in the Vienna forest whose wooded slopes of tall beeches can be equalled in beauty by few and surpassed by none. We approach a forest glade. The tall smooth trunks of the beeches soon give place to the Hornbeam which are clothed from top to bottom with pale green foliage. We now tread slowly and more carefully. Before we break through the last bushes and out of cover on to the free expanse of the meadow, we do what all wild animals and all good naturalists, wild boars, leopards, hunters and zoologists would do under similar circumstances: we reconnoitre, seeking, before we leave our cover, to gain from it the advantage which it can offer alike to hunter and hunted, namely, to see without being seen.

2   Here, too, this age-old strategy proves beneficial. We do actually see someone who is not yet aware of our presence, as the wind is blowing away from him in our direction: in the middle of the clearing sits a large fat hare. He is sitting with his back to us, making a big V with his ears, and is watching intently something on the opposite edge of the meadow. From this point, a second and equally large hare emerges and with slow, dignified hops, makes his way towards the first one. There follows a measured encounter, not unlike the meeting of two strange dogs. This cautious mutual taking stock soon develops into sparring. The two hares chase each other round, head to tail, in minute circles. This giddy rotating continues for quite a long time. Then suddenly, their pent-up energies burst forth into a battle royal. It is just like the outbreak of war, and happens at the very moment when the long mutual threatening of the hostile parties has forced one to the conclusion that neither dares to make a definite move. Facing each other, the hares rear up on their hind legs and, straining to their full height, drum furiously at each other with their fore pads. Now they clash in flying leaps and, at last, to the accompaniment of squeals and grunts, they discharge a volley of lightning kicks, so rapidly that only a slow motion camera could help us to discern the mechanism of these hostilities. Now,

312

for the time being, they have had enough, and they recommence their circling, this time much faster than before; then follows a fresh, more embittered bout. So engrossed are the two champions, that there is nothing to prevent myself and my little daughter from tiptoeing nearer, although that venture cannot be accomplished in silence. Any normal and sensible hare would have heard us long ago, but this is March and March Hares are mad! The whole boxing match looks so comical that my little daughter, in spite of her iron upbringing in the matter of silence when watching animals, cannot restrain a chuckle. That is too much even for March Hares—two flashes in two different directions and the meadow is empty, while over the battlefield floats a fistful of fluff, light as a thistledown.

3   It is not only funny, it is almost touching, this duel of the unarmed, this raging fury of the meek in heart. But are these creatures really so meek? Have they really got softer hearts than those of the fierce beasts of prey? If, in a zoo, you ever watched two lions, wolves or eagles in conflict, then, in all probability, you did not feel like laughing. And yet, those sovereigns come off no worse than the harmless hares. Most people have the habit of judging carnivorous and herbivorous animals by quite inapplicable moral criteria. Even in fairy-tales, animals are portrayed as being a community comparable to that of mankind, as though all species of animals were beings of one and the same family, as human beings are. For this reason, the average person tends to regard the animal that kills animals in the same light as he would the man that kills his own kind. He does not judge the fox that kills a hare by the same standard as the hunter who shoots one for precisely the same reason, but with that severe censure that he would apply to the gamekeeper who made a practice of shooting farmers and frying them for supper! The "wicked" beast of prey is branded as a murderer, although the fox's hunting is quite as legitimate and a great deal more necessary to his existence than is that of the gamekeeper, yet nobody regards the latter's "bag" as his prey, and only one author,[1] whose own standards were indicted by the severest moral criticism, has dared to dub the fox-hunter "the unspeakable in pursuit of the uneatable!" In their dealing with members of their own species, the beasts and birds of prey are far more restrained than many of the "harmless" vegetarians.

4   Still more harmless than a battle of hares appears the fight between turtle- or ring-doves. The gentle pecking of the frail bill, the light flick of the fragile wing seems, to the uninitiated, more like a caress than an attack. Some time ago I decided to breed a cross between the African blond ring-dove and our own indigenous somewhat frailer turtle-dove, and, with this object, I put a tame, home-reared male turtle-dove and a female ring-dove together in a roomy cage. I did not take their original scrapping seriously. How could these paragons of love and virtue dream of harming one an-

[1]Oscar Wilde

other? I left them in their cage and went to Vienna. When I returned, the next day, a horrible sight met my eyes. The turtle-dove lay on the floor of the cage; the top of his head and neck, as also the whole length of his back, were not only plucked bare of feathers, but so flayed as to form a single wound dripping with blood. In the middle of this gory surface, like an eagle on his prey, stood the second harbinger of peace. Wearing that dreamy facial expression that so appeals to our sentimental observer, this charming lady pecked mercilessly with her silver bill in the wounds of her prostrated mate. When the latter gathered his last resources in a final effort to escape, she set on him again, struck him to the floor with a light clap of her wing and continued with her slow pitiless work of destruction. Without my interference she would undoubtedly have finished him off, in spite of the fact that she was already so tired that she could hardly keep her eyes open. Only in two other instances have I seen similar horrible lacerations inflicted on their own kind by vertebrates: once, as an observer of the embittered fights of cichlid fishes who sometimes actually skin each other, and again as a field surgeon, in the late war, where the highest of all vertebrates perpetrated mass mutilations on members of his own species. But to return to our "harmless" vegetarians. The battle of the hares which we witnessed in the forest clearing would have ended in quite as horrible a carnage as that of the doves, had it taken place in the confines of a cage where the vanquished could not flee the victor.

5   If this is the extent of the injuries meted out to their own kind by our gentle doves and hares, how much greater must be the havoc wrought amongst themselves by those beasts to whom nature has relegated the strongest weapons with which to kill their prey? One would certainly think so, were it not that a good naturalist should always check by observation even the most obvious-seeming inferences before he accepts them as truth. Let us examine that symbol of cruelty and voraciousness, the wolf. How do these creatures conduct themselves in their dealings with members of their own species? At Whipsnade, that zoological country paradise, there lives a pack of timber wolves. From the fence of a pine-wood of enviable dimensions we can watch their daily round in an environment not so very far removed from conditions of real freedom. To begin with, we wonder why the antics of the many woolly, fat-pawed whelps have not led them to destruction long ago. The efforts of one ungainly little chap to break into a gallop have landed him in a very different situation from that which he intended. He stumbles and bumps heavily into a wicked-looking old sinner. Strangely enough, the latter does not seem to notice it, he does not even growl. But now we hear the rumble of battle sounds! They are low, but more ominous than those of a dog-fight. We were watching the whelps and have therefore only become aware of this adult fight now that it is already in full swing.

6   An enormous old timber wolf and a rather weaker, obviously younger

one are the opposing champions and they are moving in circles round each other, exhibiting admirable "footwork." At the same time, the bared fangs flash in such a rapid exchange of snaps that the eye can scarcely follow them. So far, nothing has really happened. The jaws of one wolf close on the gleaming white teeth of the other who is on the alert and wards off the attack. Only the lips have received one or two minor injuries. The younger wolf is gradually being forced backwards. It dawns upon us that the older one is purposely manoeuvring him towards the fence. We wait with breathless anticipation what will happen when he "goes to the wall." Now he strikes the wire netting, stumbles . . . and the old one is upon him. And now the incredible happens, just the opposite of what you would expect. The furious whirling of the grey bodies has come to a sudden standstill. Shoulder to shoulder they stand, pressed against each other in a stiff and strained attitude, both heads now facing in the same direction. Both wolves are growling angrily, the elder in a deep bass, the younger in higher tones, suggestive of the fear that underlies his threat. But notice carefully the position of the two opponents; the older wolf has his muzzle close, very close against the neck of the younger, and the latter holds away his head, offering unprotected to his enemy the bend of his neck, the most vulnerable part of his whole body! Less than an inch from the tensed neck-muscles, where the jugular vein lies immediately beneath the skin, gleam the fangs of his antagonist from beneath the wickedly retracted lips. Whereas, during the thick of the fight, both wolves were intent on keeping only their teeth, the one invulnerable part of the body, in opposition to each other, it now appears that the discomfited fighter proffers intentionally that part of his anatomy to which a bite must assuredly prove fatal. Appearances are notoriously deceptive, but in his case, surprisingly, they are not!

7   This same scene can be watched any time wherever street-mongrels are to be found. I cited wolves as my first example because they illustrate my point more impressively than the all-too familiar domestic dog. Two adult male dogs meet in the street. Stiff-legged, with tails erect and hair on end, they pace towards each other. The nearer they approach, the stiffer, higher and more ruffled they appear, their advance becomes slower and slower. Unlike fighting cocks they do not make their encounter head to head, front against front, but make as though to pass each other, only stopping when they stand at last flank to flank, head to tail, in close juxtaposition. Then a strict ceremonial demands that each should sniff the hind regions of the other. Should one of the dogs be overcome with fear at this juncture, down goes his tail between his legs and he jumps with a quick, flexible twist, wheeling at an angle of 180 degrees thus modestly retracting his former offer to be smelt. Should the two dogs remain in an attitude of self-display, carrying their tails as rigid as standards, then the sniffing process may be of a long protracted nature. All may be solved amicably and there is still the chance that first one tail and then the other may begin to wag with small

but rapidly increasing beats and then this nerve-racking situation may develop into nothing worse than a cheerful canine romp. Failing this solution the situation becomes more and more tense, noses begin to wrinkle and to turn up with a vile, brutal expression, lips begin to curl, exposing the fangs on the side nearer the opponent. Then the animals scratch the earth angrily with their hind feet, deep growls rise from their chests, and, in the next moment, they fall upon each other with loud piercing yells.

8 But to return to our wolves, whom we left in a situation of acute tension. This was not a piece of inartistic narrative on my part, since the strained situation may continue for a great length of time which is minutes to the observer, but very probably seems hours to the losing wolf. Every second you expect violence and await with bated breath the moment when the winner's teeth will rip the jugular vein of the loser. But your fears are groundless, for it will not happen. In this particular situation, the victor will definitely not close on his less fortunate rival. You can see that he would like to, but he just cannot! A dog or wolf that offers its neck to its adversary in this way will never be bitten seriously. The other growls and grumbles, snaps with his teeth in the empty air and even carries out, without delivering so much as a bite, the movement of shaking something to death in the empty air. However, this strange inhibition from biting persists only so long as the defeated dog or wolf maintains his attitude of humility. Since the fight is stopped so suddenly by this action, the victor frequently finds himself straddling his vanquished foe in anything but a comfortable position. So to remain, with his muzzle applied to the neck of the "under-dog" soon becomes tedious for the champion, and, seeing that he cannot bite anyway, he soon withdraws. Upon this, the under-dog may hastily attempt to put distance between himself and his superior. But he is not usually successful in this, for, as soon as he abandons his rigid attitude of submission, the other again falls upon him like a thunderbolt and the victim must again freeze into his former posture. It seems as if the victor is only waiting for the moment when the other will relinquish his submissive attitude, thereby enabling him to give vent to his urgent desire to bite. But, luckily for the "under-dog," the top-dog at the close of the fight is overcome by the pressing need to leave his trade-mark on the battlefield, to designate it as his personal property—in other words, he must lift his leg against the nearest upright object. This right-of-possession ceremony is usually taken advantage of by the under-dog to make himself scarce.

9 By this commonplace observation, we are here, as so often, made conscious of a problem which is actual in our daily life and which confronts us on all sides in the most various forms. Social inhibitions of this kind are not rare, but so frequent that we take them for granted and do not stop to think about them. An old German proverb says that one crow will not peck out the eye of another and for once the proverb is right. A tame crow or raven

will no more think of pecking at your eye than he will at that of one of his own kind. Often when Roah, my tame raven, was sitting on my arm, I purposely put my face so near to his bill that my open eye came close to its wickedly curved point. Then Roah did something positively touching. With a nervous, worried movement he withdrew his beak from my eye, just as a father who is shaving will hold back his razor blade from the inquisitive fingers of his tiny daughter. Only in one particular connection did Roah ever approach my eye with his bill during this facial grooming. Many of the higher, social birds and mammals, above all monkeys, will groom the skin of a fellow-member of their species in those parts of his body to which he himself cannot obtain access. In birds, it is particularly the head and the region of the eyes which are dependent on the attentions of a fellow. In my description of the jackdaw, I have already spoken of the gestures with which these birds invite one another to preen their head feathers. When, with half-shut eyes, I held my head sideways towards Roah, just as corvine birds do to each other, he understood this movement in spite of the fact that I have no head feathers to ruffle, and at once began to groom me. While doing so, he never pinched my skin, for the epidermis of birds is delicate and would not stand such rough treatment. With wonderful precision, he submitted every attainable hair to a dry-cleaning process by drawing it separately through his bill. He worked with the same intensive concentration that distinguishes the "lousing" monkey and the operating surgeon. This is not meant as a joke: the social grooming of monkeys, and particularly of anthropoid apes has not the object of catching vermin—these animals usually have none—and is not limited to the cleaning of this skin, but serves also more remarkable operations, for instance the dexterous removal of thorns and even the squeezing-out of small carbuncles.

10   The manipulations of the dangerous-looking corvine beak round the open eye of a man naturally appear ominous and, of course, I was always receiving warnings from onlookers at this procedure. "You never know—a raven is a raven—" and similar words of wisdom. I used to respond with the paradoxical observation that the warner was for me potentially more dangerous than the raven. It has often happened that people have been shot dead by madmen who have masked their condition with the cunning and pretence typical of such cases. There was always a possibility, though admittedly a very small one, that our kind adviser might be afflicted with such a disease. But a sudden and unpredictable loss of the eye-pecking inhibition in a healthy, mature raven is more unlikely by far than an attack by a well-meaning friend.

11   Why has the dog the inhibition against biting his fellow's neck? Why has the raven an inhibition against pecking the eye of his friend? Why has the ring-dove no such "insurance" against murder? A really comprehensive

answer to these questions is almost impossible. It would certainly involve a *historical* explanation of the process by which these inhibitions have been developed in the course of evolution. There is no doubt that they have arisen side by side with the development of the dangerous weapons of the beast of prey. However, it is perfectly obvious why these inhibitions are necessary to all weapon-bearing animals. Should the raven peck, without compunction, at the eye of his nest-mate, his wife or his young, in the same way as he pecks at any other moving and glittering object, there would, by now, be no more ravens in the world. Should a dog or wolf unrestrainedly and unaccountably bite the neck of his pack-mates and actually execute the movement of shaking them to death, then his species also would certainly be exterminated within a short space of time.

12   The ring-dove does not require such an inhibition since it can only inflict injury to a much lesser degree, while its ability to flee is so well developed that it suffices to protect the bird even against enemies equipped with vastly better weapons. Only under the unnatural conditions of close confinement which deprive the losing dove of the possibility of flight does it become apparent that the ring-dove has no inhibitions which prevent it from injuring or even torturing its own kind. Many other "harmless" herbivores prove themselves just as unscrupulous when they are kept in narrow captivity. One of the most disgusting, ruthless and blood-thirsty murderers is an animal which is generally considered as being second only to the dove in the proverbial gentleness of its nature, namely the roe-deer. The roe-buck is about the most malevolent beast I know and is possessed, into the bargain, of a weapon, its antlers, which it shows mighty little restraint in putting into use. The species can "afford" this lack of control since the fleeing capacity even of the weakest doe is enough to deliver it from the strongest buck. Only in very large paddocks can the roe-buck be kept with females of his own kind. In smaller enclosures, sooner or later he will drive his fellows, females and young ones included, into a corner and gore them to death. The only "insurance against murder" which the roe-deer possesses, is based on the fact that the onslaught of the attacking buck proceeds relatively slowly. He does not rush with lowered head at his adversary as, for example, a ram would do, but he approaches quite slowly, cautiously feeling with his antlers for those of his opponent. Only when the antlers are interlocked and the buck feels firm resistance does he thrust with deadly earnest. According to the statistics given by W. T. Hornaday, the former director of the New York Zoo, tame deer cause yearly more serious accidents than captive lions and tigers, chiefly because an uninitiated person does not recognize the slow approach of the buck as an earnest attack, even when the animal's antlers have come dangerously near. Suddenly there follows, thrust upon thrust, the amazingly strong stabbing movement of the sharp weapon, and you will be lucky if you have time

enough to get a good grip on the aggressor's antlers. Now there follows a wrestling-match in which the sweat pours and the hands drip blood, and in which even a very strong man can hardly obtain mastery over the roe-buck unless he succeeds in getting to the side of the beast and bending his neck backwards. Of course, one is ashamed to call for help—until one has the point of an antler in one's body! So take my advice and if a charming, tame roe-buck comes playfully towards you, with a characteristic prancing step and flourishing his antlers gracefully, hit him, with your walking stick, a stone or the bare fist, as hard as you can, on the side of his nose, before he can apply his antlers to your person.

13   And now, honestly judged: who is really a "good" animal, my friend Roah to whose social inhibitions I could trust the light of my eyes, or the gentle ring-dove that in hours of hard work nearly succeeded in torturing its mate to death? Who is a "wicked" animal, the roe-buck who will slit the bellies even of females and young of his own kind if they are unable to escape him, or the wolf who cannot bite his hated enemy if the latter appeals to his mercy?

14   Now let us turn our mind to another question. Wherein consists the essence of all the gestures of submission by which a bird or animal of a social species can appeal to the inhibitions of its superior? We have just seen, in the wolf, that the defeated animal actually facilitates his own destruction by offering to the victor those very parts of his body which he was most anxious to shield as long as the battle was raging. All submissive attitudes with which we are so far familiar, in social animals, are based on the same principle: The supplicant always offers to his adversary the most vulnerable part of his body, or, to be more exact, that part *against which every killing attack is inevitably directed!* In most birds, this area is the base of the skull. If one jackdaw wants to show submission to another, he squats back on his hocks, turns away his head, at the same time drawing in his bill to make the nape of his neck bulge, and, leaning towards his superior, seems to invite him to peck at the fatal spot. Seagulls and herons present to their superior the top of their head, stretching their neck forward horizontally, low over the ground, also a position which makes the supplicant particularly defenceless.

15   With many gallinaceous birds, the fights of the males commonly end by one of the combatants being thrown to the ground, held down and then scalped as in the manner described in the ring-dove. Only one species shows mercy in this case, namely the turkey: and this one only does so in response to a specific submissive gesture which serves to forestall the intent of the attack. If a turkey-cock has had more than his share of the wild and grotesque wrestling-match in which these birds indulge, he lays himself with outstretched neck upon the ground. Whereupon the victor behaves exactly as a wolf or dog in the same situation, that is to say, he evidently

wants to peck and kick at the prostrated enemy, but simply cannot: he would if he could but he can't! So, still in threatening attitude, he walks round and round his prostrated rival, making tentative passes at him, but leaving him untouched.

16 This reaction—though certainly propitious for the turkey species—can cause a tragedy if a turkey comes to blows with a peacock, a thing which not infrequently happens in captivity, since these species are closely enough related to "appreciate" respectively their mutual manifestations of virility. In spite of greater strength and weight the turkey nearly always loses the match, for the peacock flies better and has a different fighting technique. While the red-brown American is muscling himself up for the wrestling-match, the blue East-Indian has already flown above him and struck at him with his sharply pointed spurs. The turkey justifiably considers this infringement of his fighting code as unfair and, although he is still in possession of his full strength, he throws in the sponge and lays himself down in the above depicted manner now. And a ghastly thing happens: the peacock does not "understand" this submissive gesture of the turkey, that is to say, it elicits no inhibition of his fighting drives. He pecks and kicks further at the helpless turkey, who, if nobody comes to his rescue, is doomed, for the more pecks and blows he receives, the more certainly are his escape reactions blocked by the psycho-physiological mechanism of the submissive attitude. It does not and cannot occur to him to jump up and run away.

17 The fact that many birds have developed special "signal organs" for eliciting this type of social inhibition, shows convincingly the blind instinctive nature and the great evolutionary age of these submissive gestures. The young of the water-rail, for example, have a bare red patch at the back of their head which, as they present it meaningly to an older and stronger fellow, takes on a deep red colour. Whether, in higher animals and man, social inhibitions of this kind are equally mechanical, need not for the moment enter into our consideration. Whatever may be the reasons that prevent the dominant individual from injuring the submissive one, whether he is prevented from doing so by a simple and purely mechanical reflex process or by a highly philosophical moral standard, is immaterial to the practical issue. The essential behaviour of the submissive as well as of the dominant partner remains the same: the humbled creature suddenly seems to lose his objections to being injured and removes all obstacles from the path of the killer, and it would seem that the very removal of these outer obstacles raises an insurmountable inner obstruction in the central nervous system of the aggressor.

18 And what is a human appeal for mercy after all? Is it so very different from what we have just described? The Homeric warrior who wishes to yield and plead mercy, discards helmet and shield, falls on his knees and inclines his head, a set of actions which should make it easier for the enemy

to kill, but, in reality, hinders him from doing so. As Shakespeare makes Nestor say of Hector:

> Thou hast hung thy advanced sword i' the air,
> Not letting it decline on the declined.

19 Even to-day, we have retained many symbols of such submissive attitudes in a number of our gestures of courtesy: bowing, removal of the hat, and presenting arms in military ceremonial. If we are to believe the ancient epics, an appeal to mercy does not seem to have raised an "inner obstruction" which was entirely insurmountable. Homer's heroes were certainly not as soft-hearted as the wolves of Whipsnade! In any case, the poet cites numerous instances where the supplicant was slaughtered with or without compunction. The Norse heroic sagas bring us many examples of similar failures of the submissive gesture and it was not till the era of knight-errantry that it was no longer considered "sporting" to kill a man who begged for mercy. The Christian knight is the first who, for reasons of traditional and religious morals, is as chivalrous as is the wolf from the depth of his natural impulses and inhibitions. What a strange paradox!

20 Of course, the innate, instinctive, fixed inhibitions that prevent an animal from using his weapons indiscriminately against his own kind are only a functional analogy, at the most a slight foreshadowing, a genealogical predecessor of the social morals of man. The worker in comparative ethology does well to be very careful in applying moral criteria to animal behaviour. But here, I must myself own to harbouring sentimental feelings: I think it a truly magnificent thing that one wolf finds himself unable to bite the proffered neck of the other, but still more so that the other relies upon him for this amazing restraint. Mankind can learn a lesson from this, from the animal that Dante calls "la bestia senza pace."[2] I at least have extracted from it a new and deeper understanding of a wonderful and often misunderstood saying from the Gospel which hitherto had only awakened in me feelings of strong opposition: "And unto him that smiteth thee on the one cheek offer also the other." (St. Luke VI, 26). A wolf has enlightened me: not so that your enemy make strike you again do you turn the other cheek toward him, but to make him unable to do it.

21 When, in the course of its evolution, a species of animals develops a weapon which may destroy a fellow-member at one blow, then, in order to survive, it must develop, along with the weapon, a social inhibition to prevent a usage which could endanger the existence of the species. Among the predatory animals, there are only a few which lead so solitary a life that they can, in general, forgo such restraint. They come together only at the

---

[2]"The beast without peace."

mating season when the sexual impulse outweighs all others, including that of aggression. Such unsociable hermits are the polar bear and the jaguar and, owing to the absence of these social inhibitions, animals of these species, when kept together in zoos, hold a sorry record for murdering their own kind. The system of special inherited impulses and inhibitions, together with the weapons with which a social species is provided by nature, form a complex which is carefully computed and self-regulating. All living beings have received their weapons through the same process of evolution that moulded their impulses and inhibitions; for the structural plan of the body and the system of behaviour of a species are parts of the same whole.

> If such be Nature's holy plan,
> Have I not reason to lament
> What man has made of man?

Wordsworth is right: there is only one being in possession of weapons which do not grow on his body and of whose working plan, therefore, the instincts of his species know nothing and in the usage of which he has no correspondingly adequate inhibition. That being is man. With unarrested growth his weapons increase in monstrousness, multiplying horribly within a few decades. But innate impulses and inhibitions, like bodily structures, need time for their development, time on a scale in which geologists and astronomers are accustomed to calculate, and not historians. We did not receive our weapons from nature. We made them ourselves, of our own free will. Which is going to be easier for us in the future, the production of the weapons or the engendering of the feeling of responsibility that should go along with them, the inhibitions without which our race must perish by virtue of its own creations? We must build up these inhibitions purposefully for we cannot rely upon our instincts. Fourteen years ago, in November 1935, I concluded an article on "Morals and Weapons of Animals" which appeared in a Viennese journal, with the words, "The day will come when two warring factions will be faced with the possibility of each wiping the other out completely. The day may come when the whole of mankind is divided into two such opposing camps. Shall we then behave like doves or like wolves? The fate of mankind will be settled by the answer to this question." We may well be apprehensive.

VOCABULARY

surpassed (1)	inferences (5)	flourishing (12)
reconnoitre (1)	voraciousness (5)	facilitates (14)
engrossed (2)	whelps (5)	supplicant (14)
carnivorous (3)	vulnerable (6)	forestall (15)
herbivorous (3)	antagonist (6)	tentative (15)
criteria (3)	discomfited (6)	propitious (16)
censure (3)	juxtaposition (7)	manifestations (16)
indicted (3)	protracted (7)	infringement (16)
uninitiated (4)	amicably (7)	depicted (16)
caress (4)	adversary (8)	elicits (16)
indigenous (4)	inhibition (8)	psycho-physiological (16)
paragons (4)	submission (8)	insurmountable (17)
harbinger (4)	relinquish (8)	chivalrous (19)
prostrated (4)	dexterous (9)	innate (20)
lacerations (4)	carbuncles (9)	indiscriminately (20)
mutilations (4)	paradoxical (10)	analogy (20)
carnage (4)	compunction (11)	foreshadowing (20)
vanquished (4)	unscrupulous (12)	ethology (20)
havoc (5)	proverbial (12)	forgo (21)
relegated (5)	malevolent (12)	engendering (21)

QUESTIONS FOR CRITICAL THINKING

1. According to the author, the dove, far from being a peaceful bird, can be savage and vicious to its own kind. Why do you think the dove has universally become the symbol of peace?

2. What connotations does the word "wolf" suggest? Are these justified by what we know about the wolf?

3. In the light of this article, what explanation can you give for small-talk?

4. What do writers mean when they attribute an event or development to "nature"? What is your definition of "nature"?

5. An earlier age believed that man lay halfway between the animals and the angels. What is your own view? Is man strictly an animal, subjected to the same blind forces of nature as any other species? Or is man more than this?

6. The author says that wolves are frequently more merciful to their own kind than are people. What is your view of this? Is an animal's mercy, deriving entirely from blind instinct, comparable to the mercy humans might show from free choice?

QUESTIONS ON THE WRITING PROCESS

1. What verb tense does the author begin his essay with? Why?
2. How are the first two paragraphs of this essay developed?
3. What is the purpose of the two questions at the beginning of paragraph 3?
4. In paragraph 4, why does the author put "harmless" in quotation marks?
5. Frequently, the author will stray from the scene he is describing, or the point he is making, only to come back to it later. What sentence does he use in paragraph 4 to bring the discussion back to its original topic?
6. By implication, what is the relationship between the paragraphs in which the fight between the two doves is described, and the paragraphs that describe the fight between the two wolves?
7. In paragraph 7, the author describes the fight between two street mongrels. What lead-in does he use in paragraph 8 to return the discussion to the combat between the two timber wolves?
8. In which paragraphs does the author actually analyze the cause of the seemingly paradoxical fighting behavior of the different animal species? What typical lead-in does he use to introduce his analysis of cause?
9. What transition sentence does the author use at the beginning of paragraph 14?
10. What specific detail does the author use in paragraph 14 to explain the essence of submissive gestures?
11. What ironic contrast forms the basis of paragraph 19?

WRITING ASSIGNMENTS

1. Is there such a thing as animal morality? Write an essay defining animal morality and giving examples of it.
2. Write an essay comparing and contrasting the moral ways of humans and animals.
3. The author says that humans also display submissive gestures when faced with certain defeat. Write a narration about any human conflict you witnessed in which one of the combatants displayed submissive gestures. Be sure to explain the outcome.

THE EFFECTS OF NUCLEAR WEAPONS

Jonathan Schell

Jonathan Schell (1943–   ) was born in New York City and has been a writer for New Yorker *magazine since 1968. His works include* The Village of Ben Suc *(1967),* The Time of Illusion *(1976), and his latest,* The Fate of the Earth *(1982) from which the following excerpt was taken.*

Nuclear war, humankind's latest and most appalling nightmare, looms over the fate of the earth with terrifying reality. Drawing from the best of what is known and has been written about the aftermath of a nuclear holocaust, this excerpt, with chilling realism, analyzes the spectrum of lethal effects that a nuclear war would bring in its wake.

1   Whereas most conventional bombs produce only one destructive effect—the shock wave—nuclear weapons produce many destructive effects. At the moment of the explosion, when the temperature of the weapon material, instantly gasified, is at the superstellar level, the pressure is millions of times the normal atmospheric pressure. Immediately, radiation, consisting mainly of gamma rays, which are a very high-energy form of electromagnetic radiation, begins to stream outward into the environment. This is called the "initial nuclear radiation," and is the first of the destructive effects of a nuclear explosion. In an air burst of a one-megaton bomb—a bomb with the explosive yield of a million tons of TNT, which is a medium-sized weapon in present-day nuclear arsenals—the initial nuclear radiation can kill unprotected human beings in an area of some six square miles. Virtually simultaneously with the initial nuclear radiation, in a second destructive effect of the explosion, an electromagnetic pulse is generated by the intense gamma radiation acting on the air. In a high-altitude detonation, the pulse can knock out electrical equipment over a wide area by inducing a powerful surge of voltage through various conductors, such as antennas, overhead power lines, pipes, and railroad tracks. The Defense Department's Civil Preparedness Agency reported in 1977 that a single multi-kiloton nuclear weapon detonated one hundred and twenty-five miles over Omaha, Nebraska, could generate an electromagnetic pulse strong enough to damage solid-state electrical circuits throughout the entire continental United States and in parts of Canada and Mexico, and thus threaten to bring the economies of these countries to a halt. When the fusion and fission reactions have blown themselves out, a fireball takes shape. As it expands, energy is absorbed in the form of X rays by the surrounding air, and then the air re-radiates a portion of that energy into the environment in the form of the thermal pulse—a wave of blinding light and intense heat—

which is the third of the destructive effects of a nuclear explosion. (If the burst is low enough, the fireball touches the ground, vaporizing or incinerating almost everything within it.) The thermal pulse of a one-megaton bomb lasts for about ten seconds and can cause second-degree burns in exposed human beings at a distance of nine and a half miles, or in an area of more than two hundred and eighty square miles, and that of a twenty-megaton bomb (a large weapon by modern standards) lasts for about twenty seconds and can produce the same consequences at a distance of twenty-eight miles, or in an area of two thousand four hundred and sixty square miles. As the fireball expands, it also sends out a blast wave in all directions, and this is the fourth destructive effect of the explosion. The blast wave of an air-burst one-megaton bomb can flatten or severely damage all but the strongest buildings within a radius of four and a half miles, and that of a twenty-megaton bomb can do the same within a radius of twelve miles. As the fireball burns, it rises, condensing water from the surrounding atmosphere to form the characteristic mushroom cloud. If the bomb has been set off on the ground or close enough to it so that the fireball touches the surface, in a so-called ground burst, a crater will be formed, and tons of dust and debris will be fused with the intensely radioactive fission products and sucked up into the mushroom cloud. This mixture will return to earth as radioactive fallout, most of it in the form of fine ash, in the fifth destructive effect of the explosion. Depending upon the composition of the surface, from forty to seventy per cent of this fallout—often called the "early" or "local" fallout—descends to earth within about a day of the explosion, in the vicinity of the blast and downwind from it, exposing human beings to radiation disease, an illness that is fatal when exposure is intense. Air bursts may also produce local fallout, but in much smaller quantities. The lethal range of the local fallout depends on a number of circumstances, including the weather, but under average conditions a one-megaton ground burst would, according to the report by the Office of Technology Assessment, lethally contaminate over a thousand square miles. (A lethal dose, by convention, is considered to be the amount of radiation that, if delivered over a short period of time, would kill half the able-bodied young adult population.)

2   The initial nuclear radiation, the electromagnetic pulse, the thermal pulse, the blast wave, and the local fallout may be described as the local primary effects of nuclear weapons. Naturally, when many bombs are exploded the scope of these effects is increased accordingly. But in addition these primary effects produce innumerable secondary effects on societies and natural environments, some of which may be even more harmful than the primary ones. To give just one example, nuclear weapons, by flattening and setting fire to huge, heavily built-up areas, generate mass fires, and in some cases these may kill more people than the original thermal pulses and

blast waves. Moreover, there are—quite distinct from both the local primary effects of individual bombs and their secondary effects—global primary effects, which do not become significant unless thousands of bombs are detonated all around the earth. And these global primary effects produce innumerable secondary effects of their own throughout the ecosystem of the earth as a whole. For a full-scale holocaust is more than the sum of its local parts; it is also a powerful direct blow to the ecosphere. In that sense, a holocaust is to the earth what a single bomb is to a city. Three grave direct global effects have been discovered so far. The first is the "delayed," or "worldwide," fallout. In detonations greater than one hundred kilotons, part of the fallout does not fall to the ground in the vicinity of the explosion but rises high into the troposphere and into the stratosphere, circulates around the earth, and then, over months or years, descends, contaminating the whole surface of the globe—although with doses of radiation far weaker than those delivered by the local fallout. Nuclear-fission products comprise some three hundred radioactive isotopes, and though some of them decay to relatively harmless levels of radioactivity within a few hours, minutes, or even seconds, others persist to emit radiation for up to millions of years. The short-lived isotopes are the ones most responsible for the lethal effects of the local fallout, and the long-lived ones are responsible for the contamination of the earth by stratospheric fallout. The energy released by all fallout from a thermonuclear explosion is about five per cent of the total. By convention, this energy is not calculated in the stated yield of a weapon, yet in a ten-thousand-megaton attack the equivalent of five hundred megatons of explosive energy, or forty thousand times the yield of the Hiroshima bomb, would be released in the form of radioactivity. This release may be considered a protracted afterburst, which is dispersed into the land, air, and sea, and into the tissues, bones, roots, stems, and leaves of living things, and goes on detonating there almost indefinitely after the explosion. The second of the global effects that have been discovered so far is the lofting, from ground bursts, of millions of tons of dust into the stratosphere; this is likely to produce general cooling of the earth's surface. The third of the global effects is a predicted partial destruction of the layer of ozone that surrounds the entire earth in the stratosphere. A nuclear fireball, by burning nitrogen in the air, produces large quantities of oxides of nitrogen. These are carried by the heat of the blast into the stratosphere, where, through a series of chemical reactions, they bring about a depletion of the ozone layer. Such a depletion may persist for years. The 1975 N.A.S. report has estimated that in a holocaust in which ten thousand megatons were detonated in the Northern Hemisphere the reduction of ozone in this hemisphere could be as high as seventy per cent and in the Southern Hemisphere as high as forty per cent, and that it could take as long as thirty years for the ozone level to return to normal. The ozone layer is crucial to life on earth, because it shields the surface of the earth from lethal levels of ultraviolet radiation, which is present in sunlight. Glasstone[1] remarks simply, "If it were not for the absorption of much of the solar ultraviolet radiation by the ozone, life as currently known could not exist except possibly in the ocean." Without the ozone shield, sunlight, the life-giver, would become a life-extinguisher. In judging the global effects of a holocaust, therefore, the primary question is not how many people would be irradiated, burned, or crushed to death by the immediate effects of the bombs but how well the ecosphere, regarded as a single living entity, on which all forms of life depend for their continued existence, would hold up. The issue is the habitability of the earth, and it is in this context, not in the context of the direct slaughter of hundreds of millions of people by the local effects, that the question of human survival arises.

3   Usually, people wait for things to occur before trying to describe them. (Futurology has never been a very respectable field of inquiry.) But since we cannot afford under any circumstances to let a holocaust occur, we are forced in this one case to become the historians of the future—to chronicle and commit to memory an event that we have never experienced and must never experience. This unique endeavor, in which foresight is asked to perform a task usually reserved for hindsight, raises a host of special difficulties. There is a categorical difference, often overlooked, between trying to describe an event that has already happened (whether it is Napoleon's invasion of Russia or the pollution of the environment by acid rain) and trying to describe one that has yet to happen—and one, in addition, for which there is no precedent, or even near-precedent, in history. Lacking experience to guide our thoughts and impress itself on our feelings, we resort to speculation. But speculation, however brilliantly it may be carried out, is at best only a poor substitute for experience. Experience gives us facts, whereas in pure speculation we are thrown back on theory, which has never been a very reliable guide to future events. Moreover, experience engraves its lessons in our hearts through suffering and the other consequences that it has for our lives; but speculation leaves our lives untouched, and so gives us leeway to reject its conclusions, no matter how well argued they may be. (In the world of strategic theory, in particular, where strategists labor to simulate actual situations on the far side of the nuclear abyss, so that generals and statesmen can prepare to make their decisions in case the worst happens, there is sometimes an unfortunate tendency to mistake pure ratiocination for reality, and to pretend to a knowledge of the future that it is not given to human beings to have.) Our knowledge of the local primary effects of the bombs, which is based both on the physical principles that made their construction possible and on experience gathered from

---

[1] Samuel Glasstone, co-author of a classic text "The Effects of Nuclear Weapons" published by the Department of Defense and the Energy Research and Development Administration.

the bombings of Hiroshima and Nagasaki and from testing, is quite solid. And our knowledge of the extent of the local primary effects of many weapons used together, which is obtained simply by using the multiplication table, is also solid: knowing that the thermal pulse of a twenty-megaton bomb can give people at least second-degree burns in an area of two thousand four hundred and sixty square miles, we can easily figure out that the pulses of a hundred twenty-megaton bombs can give people at least second-degree burns in an area of two hundred and forty-six thousand square miles. Nevertheless, it may be that our knowledge even of the primary effects is still incomplete, for during our test program new ones kept being discovered. One example is the electromagnetic pulse, whose importance was not recognized until around 1960, when, after more than a decade of tests, scientists realized that this effect accounted for unexpected electrical failures that had been occurring all along in equipment around the test sites. And it is only in recent years that the Defense Department has been trying to take account strategically of this startling capacity of just one bomb to put the technical equipment of a whole continent out of action.

4   When we proceed from the local effects of single explosions to the effects of thousands of them on societies and environments, the picture clouds considerably, because then we go beyond both the certainties of physics and our slender base of experience, and speculatively encounter the full complexity of human affairs and of the biosphere. Looked at in its entirety, a nuclear holocaust can be said to assail human life at three levels: the level of individual life, the level of human society, and the level of the natural environment—including the environment of the earth as a whole. At none of these levels can the destructiveness of nuclear weapons be measured in terms of firepower alone. At each level, life has both considerable recuperative powers, which might restore it even after devastating injury, and points of exceptional vulnerability, which leave it open to sudden, wholesale, and permanent collapse, even when comparatively little violence has been applied. Just as a machine may break down if one small part is removed, and a person may die if a single artery or vein is blocked, a modern technological society may come to a standstill if its fuel supply is cut off, and an ecosystem may collapse if its ozone shield is depleted. Nuclear weapons thus do not only kill directly, with their tremendous violence, but also kill indirectly, by breaking down the man-made and the natural systems on which individual lives collectively depend. Human beings require constant provision and care, supplied both by their societies and by the natural environment, and if these are suddenly removed people will die just as surely as if they had been struck by a bullet. Nuclear weapons are unique in that they attack the support systems of life at every level. And these systems, of course, are not isolated from each other but are parts of a single whole: ecological collapse, if it goes far enough, will bring about social collapse, and social collapse will bring about individual deaths. Fur-

thermore, the destructive consequences of a nuclear attack are immeasurably compounded by the likelihood that all or most of the bombs will be detonated within the space of a few hours, in a single huge concussion. Normally, a locality devastated by a catastrophe, whether natural or manmade, will sooner or later receive help from untouched outside areas, as Hiroshima and Nagasaki did after they were bombed; but a nuclear holocaust would devastate the "outside" areas as well, leaving the victims to fend for themselves in a shattered society and natural environment. And what is true for each city is also true for the earth as a whole: a devastated earth can hardly expect "outside" help. The earth is the largest of the support systems for life, and the impairment of the earth is the largest of the perils posed by nuclear weapons.

5   The incredible complexity of all these effects, acting, interacting, and interacting again, precludes confident detailed representation of the events in a holocaust. We deal inevitably with approximations, probabilities, even guesses. However, it is important to point out that our uncertainty pertains not to *whether* the effects will interact, multiplying their destructive power as they do so, but only to *how*. It follows that our almost built-in bias, determined by the limitations of the human mind in judging future events, is to underestimate the harm. To fear interactive consequences that we cannot predict, or even imagine, may not be impossible, but it is very difficult. Let us consider, for example, some of the possible ways in which a person in a targeted country might die. He might be incinerated by the fireball or the thermal pulse. He might be lethally irradiated by the initial nuclear radiation. He might be crushed to death or hurled to his death by the blast wave or its debris. He might be lethally irradiated by the local fallout. He might be burned to death in a firestorm. He might be injured by one or another of these effects and then die of his wounds before he was able to make his way out of the devastated zone in which he found himself. He might die of starvation, because the economy had collapsed and no food was being grown or delivered, or because existing local crops had been killed by radiation, or because the local ecosystem had been ruined, or because the ecosphere of the earth as a whole was collapsing. He might die of cold, for lack of heat and clothing, or of exposure, for lack of shelter. He might be killed by people seeking food or shelter that he had obtained. He might die of an illness spread in an epidemic. He might be killed by exposure to the sun if he stayed outside too long following serious ozone depletion. Or he might be killed by any combination of these perils. But while there is almost no end to the ways to die in and after a holocaust, each person has only one life to lose: someone who has been killed by the thermal pulse can't be killed again in an epidemic. Therefore, anyone who wishes to describe a holocaust is always at risk of depicting scenes of devastation that in reality would never take place, because the people in them would already have been killed off in some earlier scene of devastation. The

task is made all the more confusing by the fact that causes of death and destruction do not exist side by side in the world but often encompass one another, in widening rings. Thus, if it turned out that a holocaust rendered the earth uninhabitable by human beings, then all the more immediate forms of death would be nothing more than redundant preliminaries, leading up to the extinction of the whole species by a hostile environment. Or if a continental ecosystem was so thoroughly destroyed by a direct attack that it could no longer sustain a significant human population, the more immediate causes of death would again decline in importance. In much the same way, if an airplane is hit by gunfire, and thereby caused to crash, dooming all the passengers, it makes little difference whether the shots also killed a few of the passengers in advance of the crash. On the other hand, if the larger consequences, which are less predictable than the local ones, failed to occur, then the local ones would have their full importance again.

6   Faced with uncertainties of this kind, some analysts of nuclear destruction have resorted to fiction, assigning to the imagination the work that investigation is unable to do. But then the results are just what one would expect: fiction. An approach more appropriate to our intellectual circumstances would be to acknowledge a high degree of uncertainty as an intrinsic and extremely important part of dealing with a possible holocaust. A nuclear holocaust is an event that is obscure because it is future, and uncertainty, while it has to be recognized in all calculations of future events, has a special place in calculations of a nuclear holocaust, because a holocaust is something that we aspire to keep in the future forever, and never to permit into the present. You might say that uncertainty, like the thermal pulses or the blast waves, is one of the features of a holocaust. Our procedure, then, should be not to insist on a precision that is beyond our grasp but to inquire into the rough probabilities of various results insofar as we can judge them, and then to ask ourselves what our political responsibilities are in the light of these probabilities. This embrace of investigative modesty—this acceptance of our limited ability to predict the consequences of a holocaust— would itself be a token of our reluctance to extinguish ourselves.

7   There are two further aspects of a holocaust which, though they do not further obscure the factual picture, nevertheless vex our understanding of this event. The first is that although in imagination we can try to survey the whole prospective scene of destruction, inquiring into how many would live and how many would die and how far the collapse of the environment would go under attacks of different sizes, and piling up statistics on how many square miles would be lethally contaminated, or what percentage of the population would receive first-, second-, or third-degree burns, or be trapped in the rubble of its burning houses, or be irradiated to death, no one actually experiencing a holocaust would have any such overview. The news of other parts necessary to put together that picture would be one of the things that were immediately lost, and each surviving person, his vision

drastically foreshortened by the collapse of his world, and his impressions clouded by his pain, shock, bewilderment, and grief, would see only as far as whatever scene of chaos and agony happened to lie at hand. For it would not be only such abstractions as "industry" and "society" and "the environment" that would be destroyed in a nuclear holocaust; it would also be, over and over again, the small collections of cherished things, known landscapes, and beloved people that made up the immediate contents of individual lives.

8   The other obstacle to our understanding is that when we strain to picture what the scene would be like after a holocaust we tend to forget that for most people, and perhaps for all, it wouldn't be *like* anything, because they would be dead. To depict the scene as it would appear to the living is to that extent a falsification, and the greater the number killed, the greater the falsification. The right vantage point from which to view a holocaust is that of a corpse, but from that vantage point, of course, there is nothing to report.

VOCABULARY

superstellar (1)	ecosphere (2)	assail (4)
inducing (1)	protracted (2)	recuperative (4)
incinerating (1)	habitability (2)	impairment (4)
ecosystem (2)	simulate (3)	intrinsic (6)
holocaust (2)	ratiocination (3)	foreshortened (7)

QUESTIONS FOR CRITICAL THINKING

1. Which of the effects of nuclear weapons do you think the worst? Why?
2. What cause or causes do you think worth the risk of nuclear war?
3. What is the presumed aim of any war? What paradox in the attainment of this aim do nuclear weapons present?
4. Since nuclear war would probably put an end to all humankind, to whom should the responsibility of starting or waging it be entrusted?
5. What can be done to prevent nuclear war? What can any single human being do?
6. Assuming that the effects of a nuclear war were as calamitous as the author describes them, would you like to be the survivor of such a war? Why or why not?
7. In what ways have nuclear weapons redefined the concept of a "combatant"?

QUESTIONS ON THE WRITING PROCESS

1. What can you deduce about the intended audience of this excerpt from its diction, syntax, and paragraphs?
2. How does the author keep track of the complicated series of effects described in the first paragraph?
3. What transition does the author use to link the discussion in paragraphs 1 and 2?
4. What is the point of the cautionary discussion to which paragraph 3 is devoted?
5. What does the author's use of specific detail contribute to the discussion?
6. How does the author personalize the discussion of the killing effects of nuclear weapons in paragraph 5?
7. What rhetorical device does the author use in paragraph 6 to make his discussion emphatic and coherent?

WRITING ASSIGNMENTS

1. Write an essay on the way you feel when you think about a nuclear holocaust.
2. Write an essay arguing for or against the notion that any alternative is better than a nuclear war.
3. What do you think are the prospects for avoiding a nuclear holocaust? Write an essay, organized any way you wish, on this theme.

RUNNING FOR LIFE

Pat Svetich

The effects of long-distance running are psychologically uplifting. Because many people live in a world full of suffering, cruelty, and chaos, tensions build up, causing neurosis. In such a world, running helps reinforce the view that life is good and that man can accomplish what he sets his mind to. Each hill is approached as a positive challenge, causing the runner to grow stronger with each stride and leading him to tranquility and harmony.

Long-distance running helps a person forget pressing family problems as well as job-related annoyances. An example comes quickly to mind. One day I had a terrible fight with my landlady over some foolish incident. I screamed and yelled at her; she screamed and yelled at me and very nearly threw me out. A few minutes later, I set out on my daily run. By the end of the first mile, the argument seemed like a bad dream. At the end of the second, the reason for it seemed trivial. By the end of the fourth mile, I was filled with feelings of remorse and positive benign forgiveness toward the landlady. It might have been the influence of the endomorphins that psychologists say the exertion of running produces in a runner's brain, but I saw how unreasonable I had been. I stopped at a curbside flower seller and bought my landlady a beautiful rose, which I immediately gave her as I stepped inside the house. All was quickly forgiven and well again between us. Running has that kind of effect on most runners. It makes us feel benign and serene.

Incorporating long-distance running into a daily routine will significantly change a runner's life-style. After I had been running for a while I found that I had more energy and could do more. My days grew longer, because I seemed to need less sleep; what sleep I did get seemed more restful. My body became thinner, smoother, firmer. Where there had been flab, suddenly there was beautiful, graceful, sinewy muscle. Running also produces a healthful feeling of euphoria. Whether it comes from adherence to a strict routine, which psychologists say is beneficial, or because of the improved physical condition of the runner, I don't know. I only know that running makes me feel good, about myself and about the world.

There are other long-term effects of running which are beneficial, especially to males of the so-called coronary age. I happen not to be in that age group, and so these benefits mean less to me than they might to others. But what benefits running does offer me are already enough to make me addicted to the sport for the rest of my life.

NINE

ARGUMENTATION

Persuasion is the ultimate goal of the argumentation essay. The writer hopes to sway his readers—to reaffirm the views of those who share his convictions or to change the views of those who do not. To this end, the effective argument will use logic, cite evidence, and quote the testimony of authorities. Some arguments will rely more heavily on one tactic than another, and some will contain an equal blend of all three. But it is difficult to see how any argument can persuade if it does not use at least one of these tactics.

Anthologized in this chapter are examples that demonstrate the use of these various tactics. The single-paragraph example "The Use of an Effective Opposition" illustrates the argument that tries to persuade by pure logic. Beginning with a series of premises—reasonable assumptions that serve as the starting point for his argument—the author proceeds to construct a logical argument. "How to Make People Smaller Than They Are" uses logic to argue against the spreading vocationalization of colleges.

On the other hand, Robert Jastrow's "The Case for UFOs" is an argument that uses a balance of logic, evidence, and authority. Jastrow argues that in the vastness of outer space it is illogical to suppose that only one planet—Earth—has the conditions necessary to support life. He mentions the studies of Dr. Allen Hynek, who concluded that several of the reported UFO sightings were unmistakably authentic and were therefore acceptable evidence of the existence of UFOs. He cites the testimony of the Book of Ezekiel and wonders if the author may not have witnessed the landing of a UFO.

As an example of an argument that relies heavily on personal experience to support its thesis, we have included Jack Connor's "Will Spelling Count?" Written in a narrative vein, this piece describes the early experiences of a novice teacher in the classroom and how he gradually became more orthodox in his approach to teaching English. It is not an argument in the classical sense, but it is a persuasive piece of writing that uses personal experience as convincing evidence. And although the author does not come right out and argue for stricter classroom discipline and rigid enforcement of academic standards, this conclusion is implicit at the end of the narrative.

Irrelevancy is the most common error of the argumentation essay. Logic demands that a writer not only stick to the point in an argument, but also observe certain ground rules of fair play. Logicians have catalogued violations of these ground rules under a variety of names. For example, the writer who directs his thunder against an opponent rather than the opponent's ideas is said to be guilty of an *ad hominem* argument, meaning that he is directing his argument against the man, rather than against the issue. Another example is the writer who tries to divert attention from the weakness of his own position by introducing some lurid but secondary issue, called a *red herring.* There is also the *ad populum* irrelevancy, which is an appeal to popular feelings and prejudices. All three examples represent a straying from the point, the cardinal sin of most bad arguments.

Above all else, the argumentation essay must be logical. It must proceed from premise to conclusion in a traceable and obvious way. It should not leap from one point to another without blazing a well-marked trail that can be seen and followed by any reader. Writers do this by including words and phrases which indicate their reasoning. For example, having discussed the age of the Earth in relation to the age of the universe, Jastrow writes in "The Case for UFOs":

> Thus, many planets circling distant stars are 5, 10, and even 15 billion years older than the Earth. It follows that the Earth is a very recent arrival in the cosmic family of planets, and man is among the youngest denizens of the Universe.

The "thus" and "it follows" are there to show that the writer is drawing a conclusion. All writing will contain occasional well-placed words and phrases that indicate the writer's train of thought. But in an argumentation essay such words are indispensable to signify turns in the writer's reasoning.

The argumentation essay is different, though more in degree than in kind, from any other type of essay you will have to write. All essays, for example, require logical thinking, but the argumentation essay especially so. All essays require the use of supporting detail, and so does the argumentation essay, where it is marshaled as evidence. The difference between writing an argumentation essay and writing, say, a descriptive essay is that the first is generally more complex than the second. A writer is more likely to use the techniques of description to shape an argument than to use the techniques of argumentation to write a description. To write an effective argumentation essay, in short, you may have to draw on what you have learned from all the other modes of writing already discussed in this book.

SINGLE PARAGRAPHS

THE USE OF AN EFFECTIVE OPPOSITION

Walter Lippmann

Walter Lippmann (1889–1974) was an American essayist and editor. Born in New York City, he was associated with the New Republic, *the* New York World, *and the* New York Herald Tribune. *While with the* Tribune, *he began writing an influential syndicated column that lasted for over thirty years. He was the author of several books, among them* A Preface to Politics *(1913),* The Good Society *(1937), and* The Communist World and Ours *(1959). In 1958 he won a special Pulitzer Prize citation for his insightful analysis of the news.*

In the paragraph below Lippmann argues persuasively that democracy cannot succeed without an effective, credible opposition.

The democratic system cannot be operated without effective opposition. For, in making the great experiment of governing people by consent rather than by coercion, it is not sufficient that the party in power should never outrage the minority. That means that it must listen to the minority and be moved by the criticisms of the minority. That means that its measures must take account of the minority's objections, and that in administering measures it must remember that the minority may become the majority. The opposition is indispensable. A good statesman, like any other sensible human being, always learns more from his opponents than from his fervent supporters. For his supporters will push him to disaster unless his opponents show him where the dangers are. So if he is wise he will often pray to be delivered from his friends, because they will ruin him. But, though it hurts, he ought also to pray never to be left without opponents; for they keep him on the path of reason and good sense. The national unity of a free people depends upon a sufficiently even balance of political power to make it impracticable for the administration to be arbitrary and for the opposition to be revolutionary and irreconcilable. Where that balance no longer exists, democracy perishes. For unless all the citizens of a state are forced by circumstances to compromise, unless they feel that they can affect policy but that no one can wholly dominate it, unless by habit and necessity they have to give and take, freedom cannot be maintained.

VOCABULARY

coercion	fervent	irreconcilable
indispensable	impracticable	

337

QUESTIONS FOR CRITICAL THINKING

1. What can any sensible human being learn about himself from an opponent?
2. What part do friends play in your life? What part do enemies play?
3. What function in formulating government policy do citizens play in a democracy?

QUESTIONS ON THE WRITING PROCESS

1. What key word does the author repeat several times throughout the first part of the paragraph? What is the purpose of this repetition?
2. In explaining what he means when he writes that the majority should not outrage the minority, how does the author emphasize his point?
3. Examine the final sentence of the paragraph. Why does the author repeat *unless* three times in it?

WRITING ASSIGNMENTS

1. Write a single paragraph about the value of friendship to you.
2. Argue in a single paragraph the merits of listening to the criticism of someone who dislikes you.

IT'S TIME TO BAN HANDGUNS

Lance Morrow

Lance Franzbert Morrow (1944–   ) is a senior writer for Time *maga-zine. He received a Ph.D. from Duke University in 1975 and is the author of* Minnesota, a State That Works *(1973).*

On April 13, 1981, the week following an assassination attempt on Presi-dent Reagan, Time *magazine took an editorial stand in favor of banning handguns. The paragraph that follows was taken from this editorial.*

The post-assassination sermon, an earnest lamentation about the "sickness of American society," has become a notably fatuous genre that blames everyone and then, after 15 minutes of earnestly empty regret, absolves everyone. It is true that there is a good deal of evil in the American air; television and the sheer repetitiousness of violence have made a lot of the country morally weary and dull and difficult to shock. Much of the vio-lence, however, results not from the sickness of the society but the stupid-ity and inadequacy of its laws. The nation needs new laws to put at least some guns out of business. Mandatory additional punishments for anyone using a gun in a crime—the approach that Ronald Reagan favors—would help. But a great deal more is necessary. Because of the mobility of guns, only federal laws can have any effect upon them. Rifles and shotguns—long guns—are not the problem; they make the best weapons for defending the house anyway, and they are hard for criminals to conceal. Most handguns are made to fire at people, not at targets or game. Such guns should be banned. The freedoms of an American individualism bristling with small arms must yield to the larger communal claim to sanity and safety—the "pursuit of happiness."

VOCABULARY

fatuous   genre   mandatory

QUESTIONS FOR CRITICAL THINKING

1. What is your attitude toward gun control?
2. Polls have repeatedly shown that a vast majority of people favor the legislative control of handguns. Why has such a law not been passed?

QUESTIONS ON THE WRITING PROCESS

1. What is the topic sentence of this paragraph?
2. What transition does the author use to shift the discussion from the "sickness of American society" to the need for gun control?
3. In putting the phrase "pursuit of happiness" in quotation marks in the final sentence, what point of the opposition is the author implicitly arguing against?

WRITING ASSIGNMENTS

1. Write a paragraph arguing for or against gun control laws.
2. Write an essay analyzing the logic of the slogan "When guns are outlawed, only outlaws will have guns."

SHORT ESSAYS

WE HAVE NO "RIGHT TO HAPPINESS"

C. S. Lewis

Born in Belfast, Ireland, Clive Staples Lewis (1898–1963) was a scholar, writer, and witty advocate of the Christian point of view. He was the author of numerous books and articles on medieval and Renaissance literature, chief among them being The Allegory of Love *(1936), a study of the literary evolution of romantic love. From 1954 until his death he was professor of Medieval and Renaissance English at Cambridge University, England. His many other published works include* The Screwtape Letters *(1942),* That Hideous Strength *(1945) and an autobiography,* Surprised By Joy *(1954).*

In this essay Lewis argues with characteristic logic and style against the notion that we have a right to sexual happiness even at the expense of old spouses and relationships.

1 "After all," said Clare, "they had a right to happiness." We were discussing something that once happened in our own neighborhood. Mr. A. had deserted Mrs. A. and got his divorce in order to marry Mrs. B., who had likewise got her divorce in order to marry Mr. A. And there was certainly no doubt that Mr. A. and Mrs. B. were very much in love with one another. If they continued to be in love, and if nothing went wrong with their health or their income, they might reasonably expect to be very happy.

2 It was equally clear that they were not happy with their old partners. Mrs. B. had adored her husband at the outset. But then he got smashed up in the war. It was thought he had lost his virility, and it was known that he had lost his job. Life with him was no longer what Mrs. B. had bargained for. Poor Mrs. A., too. She had lost her looks—and all her liveliness. It might be true, as some said, that she consumed herself by bearing his children and nursing him through the long illness that overshadowed their earlier married life.

3 You mustn't, by the way, imagine that A. was the sort of man who nonchalantly threw a wife away like the peel of an orange he'd sucked dry. Her suicide was a terrible shock to him. We all knew this, for he told us so himself. "But what could I do?" he said. "A man has a right to happiness. I had to take my chance when it came."

4 I went away thinking about the concept of a "right to happiness."

5 At first this sounds to me as odd as a right to good luck. For I believe—whatever one school of moralists may say—that we depend for a very great deal of our happiness or misery on circumstances outside all human control. A right to happiness doesn't, for me, make much more sense than a right to be six feet tall, or to have a millionaire for your father, or to get good weather whenever you want to have a picnic.

6   I can understand a right as a freedom guaranteed me by the laws of the society I live in. Thus, I have a right to travel along the public roads because society gives me that freedom; that's what we mean by calling the roads "public." I can also understand a right as a claim guaranteed me by the laws, and correlative to an obligation on someone else's part. If I have a right to receive £100 from you, this is another way of saying that you have a duty to pay me £100. If the laws allow Mr. A. to desert his wife and seduce his neighbor's wife, then, by definition, Mr. A. has a legal right to do so, and we need bring in no talk about "happiness."

7   But of course that was not what Clare meant. She meant that he had not only a legal but a moral right to act as he did. In other words, Clare is— or would be if she thought it out—a classical moralist after the style of Thomas Aquinas, Grotius, Hooker and Locke. She believes that behind the laws of the state there is a Natural Law.

8   I agree with her. I hold this conception to be basic to all civilization. Without it, the actual laws of the state become an absolute, as in Hegel. They cannot be criticized because there is no norm against which they should be judged.

9   The ancestry of Clare's maxim, "They have a right to happiness," is august. In words that are cherished by all civilized men, but especially by Americans, it has been laid down that one of the rights of man is a right to "the pursuit of happiness." And now we get to the real point.

10   What did the writers of that august declaration mean?

11   It is quite certain what they did not mean. They did not mean that man was entitled to pursue happiness by any and every means—including, say, murder, rape, robbery, treason and fraud. No society could be built on such a basis.

12   They meant "to pursue happiness by all lawful means"; that is, by all means which the Law of Nature eternally sanctions and which the laws of the nation shall sanction.

13   Admittedly this seems at first to reduce their maxim to the tautology that men (in pursuit of happiness) have a right to do whatever they have a right to do. But tautologies, seen against their proper historical context, are not always barren tautologies. The declaration is primarily a denial of the political principles which long governed Europe: a challenge flung down to the Austrian and Russian empires, to England before the Reform Bills, to Bourbon France. It demands that whatever means of pursuing happiness are lawful for any should be lawful for all; that "man," not men of some particular caste, class, status or religion, should be free to use them. In a century when this is being unsaid by nation after nation and party after party, let us not call it a barren tautology.

14   But the question as to what means are "lawful"—what methods of pursuing happiness are either morally permissible by the Law of Nature or should be declared legally permissible by the legislature of a particular

nation—remains exactly where it did. And on that question I disagree with Clare. I don't think it is obvious that people have the unlimited "right of happiness" which she suggests.

15   For one thing, I believe that Clare, when she says "happiness," means simply and solely "sexual happiness." Partly because women like Clare never use the word "happiness" in any other sense. But also because I never heard Clare talk about the "right" to any other kind. She was rather leftist in her politics, and would have been scandalized if anyone had defended the actions of a ruthless man-eating tycoon on the ground that his happiness consisted in making money and he was pursuing his happiness. She was also a rabid teetotaler; I never heard her excuse an alcoholic because he was happy when he was drunk.

16   A good many of Clare's friends, and especially her female friends, often felt—I've heard them say so—that their own happiness would be perceptibly increased by boxing her ears. I very much doubt if this would have brought her theory of a right to happiness into play.

17   Clare, in fact, is doing what the whole western world seems to me to have been doing for the last forty-odd years. When I was a youngster, all the progressive people were saying, "Why all this prudery? Let us treat sex just as we treat all our other impulses." I was simple-minded enough to believe they meant what they said. I have since discovered that they meant exactly the opposite. They meant that sex was to be treated as no other impulse in our nature has ever been treated by civilized people. All the others, we admit, have to be bridled. Absolute obedience to your instinct for self-preservation is what we call cowardice; to your acquisitive impulse, avarice. Even sleep must be resisted if you're a sentry. But every unkindness and breach of faith seems to be condoned provided that the object aimed at is "four bare legs in a bed."

18   It is like having a morality in which stealing fruit is considered wrong—unless you steal nectarines.

19   And if you protest against this view you are usually met with chatter about the legitimacy and beauty and sanctity of "sex" and accused of harboring some Puritan prejudice against it as something disreputable or shameful. I deny the charge. Foam-born Venus . . . golden Aphrodite . . . Our Lady of Cyprus . . . I never breathed a word against you. If I object to boys who steal my nectarines, must I be supposed to disapprove of nectarines in general? Or even of boys in general? It might, you know, be stealing that I disapproved of.

20   The real situation is skillfully concealed by saying that the question of Mr. A.'s "right" to desert his wife is one of "sexual morality." Robbing an orchard is not an offense against some special morality called "fruit morality." It is an offense against honesty. Mr. A.'s action is an offense against good faith (to solemn promises), against gratitude (toward one to whom he was deeply indebted) and against common humanity.

21   Our sexual impulses are thus being put in a position of preposterous privilege. The sexual motive is taken to condone all sorts of behavior which, if it had any other end in view, would be condemned as merciless, treacherous and unjust.

22   Now though I see no good reason for giving sex this privilege, I think I see a strong cause. It is this.

23   It is part of the nature of a strong erotic passion—as distinct from a transient fit of appetite—that it makes more towering promises than any other emotion. No doubt all our desires make promises, but not so impressively. To be in love involves the almost irresistible conviction that one will go on being in love until one dies, and that possession of the beloved will confer, not merely frequent ecstasies, but settled, fruitful, deep-rooted, lifelong happiness. Hence all seems to be at stake. If we miss this chance we shall have lived in vain. At the very thought of such a doom we sink into fathomless depths of self-pity.

24   Unfortunately these promises are found often to be quite untrue. Every experienced adult knows this to be so as regards all erotic passions (except the one he himself is feeling at the moment). We discount the world-without-end pretensions of our friends' amours easily enough. We know that such things sometimes last—and sometimes don't. And when they do last, this is not because they promised at the outset to do so. When two people achieve lasting happiness, this is not solely because they are great lovers but because they are also—I must put it crudely—good people; controlled, loyal, fairminded, mutually adaptable people.

25   If we establish a "right to (sexual) happiness" which supersedes all the ordinary rules of behavior, we do so not because of what our passion shows itself to be in experience but because of what it professes to be while we are in the grip of it. Hence, while the bad behavior is real and works miseries and degradations, the happiness which was the object of the behavior turns out again and again to be illusory. Everyone (except Mr. A. and Mrs. B.) knows that Mr. A. in a year or so may have the same reason for deserting his new wife as for deserting his old. He will feel again that all is at stake. He will see himself again as the great lover, and his pity for himself will exclude all pity for the woman.

26   Two further points remain.

27   One is this. A society in which conjugal infidelity is tolerated must always be in the long run a society adverse to women. Women, whatever a few male songs and satires may say to the contrary, are more naturally monogamous than men; it is a biological necessity. Where promiscuity prevails, they will therefore always be more often the victims than the culprits. Also, domestic happiness is more necessary to them than to us. And the quality by which they most easily hold a man, their beauty, de-

creases every year after they have come to maturity, but this does not happen to those qualities of personality—women don't really care two-pence about our *looks*—by which we hold women. Thus in the ruthless war of promiscuity women are at a double disadvantage. They play for higher stakes and are also more likely to lose. I have no sympathy with moralists who frown at the increasing crudity of female provocativeness. These signs of desperate competition fill me with pity.

28   Secondly, though the "right to happiness" is chiefly claimed for the sexual impulse, it seems to me impossible that the matter should stay there. The fatal principle, once allowed in that department, must sooner or later seep through our whole lives. We thus advance toward a state of society in which not only each man but every impulse in each man claims *carte blanche*. And then, though our technological skill may help us survive a little longer, our civilization will have died at heart, and will—one dare not even add "unfortunately"—be swept away.

VOCABULARY

virility (2)	prudery (17)	transient (23)
correlative (6)	bridled (17)	supersedes (25)
august (9)	acquisitive (17)	degradations (25)
sanctions (12)	avarice (17)	illusory (25)
tautology (13)	disreputable (19)	adverse (27)
teetotaler (15)	condone (21)	promiscuity (27)
perceptibly (16)		

QUESTIONS FOR CRITICAL THINKING

1. What is a Natural Law? How can a Natural Law be defined?
2. Given the situation between Mr. A. and Mrs. A. as described in the opening paragraph, on whom do you blame her suicide?
3. How is a moral right different from a legal one?
4. Lewis claims that women are more naturally monogamous than men, and hints that there is biological necessity behind this. What is your attitude towards his view? If you believe he is right, how did women become more naturally monogamous?
5. What is your view of the author's contention that a promiscuous society is harder on women than on men?

QUESTIONS ON THE WRITING PROCESS

1. How would you characterize the beginning of this essay? Why is this an effective opening?
2. How would you characterize the tone of paragraph 3?
3. What is the writer's aim in paragraph 6?
4. What do paragraphs 4, 10, 18, and 26 have in common?
5. In paragraph 15, Lewis tries to clarify what "Clare" means by "happiness." What techniques does he use to narrow and debunk her meaning?

WRITING ASSIGNMENTS

1. Write an essay defending the right to sexual happiness even at the cost of old spouses and relationships.
2. Write an essay analyzing the causes of any bad marriage you know about.
3. Compare and contrast moral right with legal right.

HOW TO MAKE PEOPLE SMALLER
THAN THEY ARE

Norman Cousins

Norman Cousins (1915–   ) is an influential editor and essayist who has been associated with the New York Post, Current History, *and* Saturday Review. *Among his many books are* Modern Man Is Obsolete *(1945),* Dr. Schweitzer of Lambarene *(1960), and* Anatomy of an Illness *(1979).*

With the emphasis today on career training in education, many colleges have cut back on courses in the humanities and increased their vocational offerings. The author of this essay argues that this trend toward practicality in education is demeaning to the individual and dangerous to a democratic society.

1   Three months ago in this space we wrote about the costly retreat from the humanities on all the levels of American education. Since that time, we have had occasion to visit a number of campuses and have been troubled to find that the general situation is even more serious than we had thought. It has become apparent to us that one of the biggest problems confronting American education today is the increasing vocationalization of our colleges and universities. Throughout the country, schools are under pressure to become job-training centers and employment agencies.

2   The pressure comes mainly from two sources. One is the growing determination of many citizens to reduce taxes—understandable and even commendable in itself, but irrational and irresponsible when connected to the reduction or dismantling of vital public services. The second source of pressure comes from parents and students who tend to scorn courses of study that do not teach people how to become attractive to employers in a rapidly tightening job market.

3   It is absurd to believe that the development of skills does not also require the systematic development of the human mind. Education is being measured more by the size of the benefits the individual can extract from society than by the extent to which the individual can come into possession of his or her full powers. The result is that the life-giving juices are in danger of being drained out of education.

4   Emphasis on "practicalities" is being characterized by the subordination of words to numbers. History is seen not as essential experience to be transmitted to new generations, but as abstractions that carry dank odors. Art is regarded as something that calls for indulgence or patronage and that has no place among the practical realities. Political science is viewed more

as a specialized subject for people who want to go into politics than as an opportunity for citizens to develop a knowledgeable relationship with the systems by which human societies are governed. Finally, literature and philosophy are assigned the role of add-ons—intellectual adornments that have nothing to do with "genuine" education.

5   Instead of trying to shrink the liberal arts, the American people ought to be putting pressure on colleges and universities to increase the ratio of the humanities to the sciences. Most serious studies of medical-school curricula in recent years have called attention to the stark gaps in the liberal education of medical students. The experts agree that the schools shouldn't leave it up to students to close those gaps.

6   We must not make it appear, however, that nothing is being done. In the past decade, the National Endowment for the Humanities has been a prime mover in infusing the liberal arts into medical education and other specialized schools. During this past year alone, NEH has given 108 grants to medical schools and research organizations in the areas of ethics and human values. Some medical schools, like the one at Pennsylvania State University, have led the way in both the number and the depth of courses offered in the humanities. Penn State has been especially innovative in weaving literature and philosophy into the full medical course of study. It is ironical that the pressure against the humanities should be manifesting itself at precisely the time when so many medical schools are at long last moving in this direction.

7   The irony of the emphasis being placed on careers is that nothing is more valuable for anyone who has had a professional or vocational education than to be able to deal with abstractions or complexities, or to feel comfortable with subtleties of thought or language, or to think sequentially. The doctor who knows only disease is at a disadvantage alongside the doctor who knows at least as much about people as he does about pathological organisms. The lawyer who argues in court from a narrow legal base is no match for the lawyer who can connect legal precedents to historical experience and who employs wide-ranging intellectual resources. The business executive whose competence in general management is bolstered by an artistic ability to deal with people is of prime value to his company. For the technologist, the engineering of consent can be just as important as the engineering of moving parts. In all these respects, the liberal arts have much to offer. Just in terms of career preparation, therefore, a student is shortchanging himself by shortcutting the humanities.

8   But even if it could be demonstrated that the humanities contribute nothing directly to a job, they would still be an essential part of the educational equipment of any person who wants to come to terms with life. The humanities would be expendable only if human beings didn't have to make decisions that affect their lives and the lives of others; if the human past

never existed or had nothing to tell us about the present; if thought processes were irrelevant to the achievement of purpose; if creativity was beyond the human mind and had nothing to do with the joy of living; if human relationships were random aspects of life; if human beings never had to cope with panic or pain, or if they never had to anticipate the connection between cause and effect; if all the mysteries of mind and nature were fully plumbed; and if no special demands arose from the accident of being born a human being instead of a hen or a hog.

9   Finally, there would be good reason to eliminate the humanities if a free society were not absolutely dependent on a functioning citizenry. If the main purpose of a university is job training, then the underlying philosophy of our government has little meaning. The debates that went into the making of American society concerned not just institutions or governing principles but the capacity of humans to sustain those institutions. Whatever the disagreements were over other issues at the American Constitutional Convention, the fundamental question sensed by everyone, a question that lay over the entire assembly, was whether the people themselves would understand what it meant to hold the ultimate power of society, and whether they had enough of a sense of history and destiny to know where they had been and where they ought to be going.

10   Jefferson was prouder of having been the founder of the University of Virginia than of having been President of the United States. He knew that the educated and developed mind was the best assurance that a political system could be made to work—a system based on the informed consent of the governed. If this idea fails, then all the saved tax dollars in the world will not be enough to prevent the nation from turning on itself.

VOCABULARY

vocationalization (1)	infusing (6)	sequentially (7)
subordination (4)	innovative (6)	pathological (7)
dank (4)	manifesting (6)	expendable (8)
indulgence (4)	subtleties (7)	irrelevant (8)
adornments (4)		

QUESTIONS FOR CRITICAL THINKING

1. What have the humanities contributed to your own growth and development as a person?
2. What is the value of poetry to someone who wants only to be a mechanic?
3. Should general elective courses in college be eliminated or should they be expanded?
4. What is the point of teaching a foreign language to someone who never intends to use it?
5. Which of all the humanities courses do you think has the least practical value? Why?

QUESTIONS ON THE WRITING PROCESS

1. How is the second paragraph developed?
2. What specific details does the author cite in the fourth paragraph to demonstrate the effects of "practicalities" on the educational system?
3. In which paragraph does the author state what he thinks ought to be done?
4. What transition does the author use between paragraphs 5 and 6?
5. In paragraph 7, how does the author illustrate the superiority of a humanities education over a merely technical one?
6. What is the author attempting to do in mentioning Jefferson's connection with the University of Virginia?

WRITING ASSIGNMENTS

1. Write a 300-word essay arguing for or against the author's thesis that vocationalization of colleges and universities is undesirable.
2. Write a 300-word essay in defense of the teaching of your favorite humanities course.

THE CASE FOR UFOs

Robert Jastrow

Robert Jastrow was born in New York and educated at Columbia University. He is the founder and director of the Goddard Institute for Space Studies of NASA, professor of astronomy and geology at Columbia, and professor of earth science at Dartmouth. He is the author of several books, among them Until the Sun Dies *(1977).*

A noted astronomer argues that statistical evidence alone strongly suggests that life exists in other galaxies—life far superior to our own.

1 Can you imagine a form of life as far beyond man as man is beyond the worm? Science assures us that such highly evolved beings must exist on the stars and planets around us, if life is common in the Universe.

2 These extraterrestrials are not like the flower children in *Close Encounters of the Third Kind* or the cowboys of *Star Wars*. They are creatures whom we will judge to be possessed of magical powers when we see them. By our standards, they will be immortal, omniscient and omnipotent. They are the kinds of creatures who would be capable of a trip to the Earth from another star.

3 How can these bizarre notions be supported by science? Here is the evidence. One hundred billion stars like the Sun surround us in our galaxy alone; according to indirect but solid astronomical evidence, many have planets made of the same ingredients as the Earth; these planets have water and air and the same vicissitudes of climate as the Earth; the molecules on their surfaces enter into the same chemical combinations, subject to the same laws of chemistry and physics, as molecules on our planet. All the necessary elements for the evolution of life are present—simple, unthinking life at first and complex, intelligent life later on.

4 On the basis of these considerations, I believe that life is common on the many planetary systems in the cosmos.

5 Moreover, recent discoveries in astronomy prove that *if* life exists on other planets in the Universe, most of this life is far older than life on the Earth. The discoveries relate to the so-called Big Bang theory, which holds that the Universe began with a gigantic explosion. The Big Bang theory has now been proved to be a fact by the Nobel Prize-winning work of Arno Penzias and Robert Wilson, who discovered the remnant of the primordial flash of light and heat that filled the Universe at the time of the great explosion. In other words, they discovered a relic of events that actually took place shortly after the beginning of the world. Although many astronomers had resisted the Big Bang theory, the Penzias-Wilson discovery has convinced very nearly the last doubting Thomas.

6   The importance of the Big Bang in a discussion of UFOs and life on other worlds is that it tells us *when* the world began; it tells us the age of the Universe. An astronomer can calculate on the back of an envelope how long ago the Big Bang occurred. That moment marked the birth of the Universe. The result of the calculation is that the Universe came into being *20 billion years ago.*

7   The Earth, on the other hand, was born only 4.6 billion years ago. That result comes from measurements of the ages of meteorites and from the ages of the moon rocks brought back by the Apollo astronauts. Since meteorites and the moon are relatively unchanged samples of solar-system material, dating back to the birth of the planets, their age is thought to give a good estimate of the age of the Earth.

8   Thus, many planets circling distant stars are 5, 10 and even 15 billion years older than the Earth. It follows that the Earth is a very recent arrival in the cosmic family of planets, and man is among the youngest denizens of the Universe.

9   Of course, the fact that life elsewhere is older than man does not necessarily mean that this life is more intelligent. However, other scientific evidence suggests that this is likely to be the case. Throughout the last 300 million years of life on Earth, only one seemingly universal trend can be discerned in evolution; this is the trend toward greater intelligence. Since before the fishes left the water, the most intelligent form of life present on Earth in each era has been the rootstock out of which new and still more intelligent forms have evolved. The line of increasing intelligence stretches unbroken from the fishes to the reptiles to the mammals, the primates and man. Apparently, intelligence—which permits a flexible response to changing conditions—has a greater survival value than any other single trait.

10   Now we come to a critical point. Why should a line of evolution that has proceeded unchecked for hundreds of millions of years suddenly stop at the particular level of intelligence that we call "human"? Homo erectus had less brain power than Homo sapiens has; the successors to Homo sapiens should have more. If the past is any guide to the future, our descendants a billion years from now will surpass us in intelligence. And if the Earth is typical of planets in the cosmos—and everything we know in astronomy and geology tells us that it is—intelligent beings who live on planets billions of years older than the Earth have already reached that advanced level of intelligence that our successors will only achieve in the distant future.

11   This argument, proceeding step by step on the basis of evidence acquired in the basic scientific disciplines, leads to the conclusion that life on other worlds is not only billions of years *older* than man, but also billions of years beyond him in intelligence.

12   What does a billion years mean in the evolution of intelligence? For an answer, look again at the fossil record. One billion years ago, the highest form of life on the Earth was a simple, wormlike animal. The creatures who

dwell on planets a billion years older than the Earth must possess an intelligence that surpasses ours by as much as we surpass the mindless, soft-bodied creatures who burrow through the soil of our gardens.

13   These considerations bring me full circle to my opening statement: According to the best scientific evidence, intelligent life on other worlds is likely to be as far beyond man as man is beyond the worm.

14   Why is it so important, in a discussion of UFOs, to establish a scientific foundation for the existence of races more intelligent than man? The answer is related to the fact that the distances between the stars are so enormously great. If a UFO reaches the Earth, its crew must have covered those enormous distances somehow; they must have started out from someplace beyond the edge of our solar system. They cannot come from the Earth's sister planets, because no intelligent life exists in this solar system except on our own planet. All the evidence acquired by NASA spacecraft in the past few years regarding Venus, Mars and Jupiter points to that conclusion. It follows that UFOs, if they arrive here, have come from another star.

15   There is the rub. The closest star to the Sun is 25 trillion miles away, and it would take one million years to cover that enormous distance with the fastest rockets known to man. Our science and engineering are not adequate to meet that challenge; a trip to the stars is beyond our reach at the present time. But in another billion years, our descendants—possessed of highly evolved minds and with a science and engineering far beyond ours—should be able to undertake an interstellar voyage. And what our descendants can do a billion years in the future, other races, a billion years older and more evolved than man, should be able to do today.

16   My conclusion is that UFOs—visitors from another star—are a scientifically sound concept because science tells us that it is reasonable to believe in the existence of forms of life older and far more intelligent than man.

17   Has the Earth already been visited by these older, more advanced beings? The first chapter of the Book of Ezekiel records a remarkable incident that took place several thousand years ago. After an account of what seems to be a landing and an exploration by unusual beings, apparently metallic in construction, verse 24 describes their departure: "And when they went, I heard the noise of their wings, like the noise of great waters. . . ." Anyone who saw a Saturn V rocket take off will remember that the thunderous roar sounded like Niagara Falls. Nothing man-made except the launch of a rocket sounds like that.

18   Are such visits occurring at this moment? Dr. Allen Hynek has made a study of reported UFO sightings and concludes that several are unmistakably UFOs—Unidentified *Flying* Objects. He cannot say whether these unidentified objects have come from another star, but there are good reasons for believing that such extraterrestrial contacts—either visitors or messages—are more probable today than ever before in the history of our planet. Since about 1960, television stations scattered across the Earth have

been spraying their signals into space at a million-watt level. In the course of the last 20 years, that expanding shell of television signals, moving away from the Earth at the speed of light, has traveled 240 trillion miles; it has now swept past more than 40 stars in the neighborhood of the Sun. Old Jack Paar programs, moving away from the Earth at the speed of light, have carried the message to these stars that intelligent life exists on this planet. These television signals make the Earth the brightest radio star in our neighborhood of the galaxy at TV frequencies. For the first time in 4.6 billion years, our planet is a notable object in the heavens.

19   If any of those 40 nearby stars harbor intelligent beings, our presence is now known to them. As it took 20 years for our signals to reach these stars, it must take 20 years for their reply, traveling at the same speed, to get back. Unless man is alone in the cosmos, we can expect to receive a message—or a visit—by the end of this century.

20   And would these superior beings bother to talk to us? "In their eyes," one observer notes, "Einstein would qualify as a waiter and Thomas Jefferson as a busboy."

21   I think they would. They are jaded; they have lived a billion years; they have done nearly everything; they are eager for fresh experiences. After all, where else in the galaxy have they seen a creature like man before?

VOCABULARY

omniscient (2)	primordial (5)	surpass (12)
omnipotent (2)	denizens (8)	interstellar (15)
vicissitudes (3)	discerned (9)	

QUESTIONS FOR CRITICAL THINKING

1. How do you think the world would react to the discovery of extraterrestrial life far superior to our own?
2. If extraterrestrial life should be found to exist, what effect would this discovery have on our religious beliefs?
3. What is your opinion of UFOs?
4. What conceptions of human life are extraterrestrials likely to form from old Jack Paar programs?
5. What do you think intelligent extraterrestrial beings look like?

QUESTIONS ON THE WRITING PROCESS

1. This article was originally published in a popular science magazine. In light of this fact, how would you characterize its opening sentence?
2. Because this article was written for popular consumption and primarily to entertain, the author obviously does not observe a strict scientific method in presenting his arguments for extraterrestrial life. How would you expect a scientist to argue a similar topic before a panel of other scientists? How would the style and manner of argument of a professional scientist differ from this presentation?
3. What lead-in does the author use to introduce the evidence supporting the existence of life on other planets?
4. What is the function of paragraph 4?
5. In paragraph 5, the author writes, "Although many astronomers had resisted the Big Bang theory, the Penzias-Wilson discovery has convinced very nearly the last doubting Thomas." What is the implication of labeling those who doubt the Big Bang theory as doubting Thomases? What logical fallacy is evident in this kind of labeling?
6. In paragraphs 10 and 12, the author uses a similar rhetorical ploy to advance his argument. What is this ploy?
7. What is the purpose of paragraph 13?
8. In paragraph 15, the author writes, "There is the rub." What is the meaning and origin of this sentence?
9. How would you characterize the argument presented in paragraph 17? What is the obvious weakness of this argument?

WRITING ASSIGNMENTS

1. Pretend you are a student on the planet Crixx. Write a 300-word essay arguing that the messages your planet has received from the distant planet Earth (game shows, talk shows, or _____) indicate beyond a doubt that there is no intelligent life on Earth.
2. Using any viewpoint you like, philosophical or religious, write a counterargument to the author's thesis that extraterrestrial life probably exists. Offer alternative explanations to the deductions and conclusions drawn by the author.
3. Pretend that you are an extraterrestrial being seeing Earth and humans for the first time. Write a letter to your spouse on your own planet giving your first impressions of what you have seen.

WILL SPELLING COUNT?

Jack Connor

Jack Connor grew up in Elizabeth, N.J., and received his Ph.D. from the University of Florida. He teaches English in the Department of Humanities and Communications at Drexel University, Philadelphia.

The article that follows implicitly advocates a toughening of standards in the classroom by telling the amusing story of how a young teacher gradually changed his methods of teaching.

1   "Will spelling count?" In my first year of teaching freshman composition I had a little act I performed whenever a student asked that inevitable question. Frowning, taking my pipe out of my mouth, and hesitating, I would try to look like a man coming down from some higher mental plane. Then, with what I hoped sounded like a mixture of confidence and disdain, I would answer, "No. Of course it won't."

2   In that first year, I was convinced that to have a significant effect on my students' writing I had to demonstrate that I was not the stereotypical English teacher: a fussbudget who would pick through their essays in search of misspellings and trivial errors. I intended to inspire students in my classes to write the kinds of papers the unconventional teachers I had read about—John Holt, A. S. Neill, Herbert Kohl, and Ken Macrorie—had inspired: papers bristling with life, written by the students with their inner voices.

3   It was not to be. Week after week students handed in papers that had obviously been dashed off in 30 or 40 minutes. By the end of the year I realized my mistake: I had been too subtle; I had not made it clear enough that mine was a revolutionary way to teach writing.

4   So, in my second year, I answered the question with a 50-minute lecture. I quoted education theories, told several semifictional stories of my student days, and recited some entirely fictional statistics—all of which argued that people write better when they don't worry about spelling.

5   "What you have to do is write honestly about things you care about," I told them. "Don't interrupt your thoughts to check your spelling."

6   That lecture—and other strategic changes I made in my teaching style that second year—had no noticeable effect. Once again, almost all the papers were dull, predictable, and carelessly done. My students didn't understand that writing could be an act of self-exploration and discovery.

7   They wrote essays of two kinds: unorganized narratives with such titles as "My First Drunk" or "How to Roll a Joint at 70 m.p.h." and fourth-hand, insipid arguments with such titles as "Capital Punishment = Murder" or "The Space Race—What a Waste."

8   Since assigning topics or imposing organizational schemes would mark me as just another conventional English teacher, killing any chance I had to inspire my students to discover their inner voices, I tried to proceed indirectly—with class discussions on subjects I thought would make good topics: the latest editorial in the student newspaper, the problems of communicating with parents and friends, political apathy, the sights and sounds of the campus. However, although I could sometimes get a "lively" discussion going, it was obvious that the students saw these exchanges not as relevant to their writing but as a painless way to spend the 50 minutes. They sat up and took note only to ask me about the mechanical details of the next assignment: "How many words does it have to be?" "How much do you take off for late papers?" "Is it O.K. to write in blue ink?"

9   It was in that year that I began to be embarrassed by my students' course evaluations. They usually gave me top grades in every category and then wrote something such as, "This was a great class because the teacher understood that students in this university have a lot of other things to worry about besides his particular course."

10   By the start of the third year, I was wondering whether the education theorists had known what they were taking about. When the usual question came, I equivocated and told them they could decide questions about spelling for themselves.

11   It was a low point. By that time a couple of hundred freshmen had passed through my composition classes, but I could not have named one who had discovered himself as a writer because of my teaching. Of the few A+ papers in my files, half were written by students who could have written an A+ paper the first day of class; the rest were happy accidents, written by students in moments of inspiration they were unable to repeat.

12   That year, one student wrote in his evaluation, "This was a very good course because the teacher believed college students are mature enough to make their own decisions about things like whether spelling is important. It isn't important to me. I'm going to let my secretary take care of my spelling."

13   I knew it was time for a radical change. I was going to have to give up trying to teach my students that writing could be an act of self-exploration; I would have to concentrate on teaching a truth more essential to their education: Writing is hard work.

14   In the summer before my fourth year, I wrote a ten-page syllabus, two pages of which were given over to the old questions and my new answers:

Q: Is blue ink acceptable?
A: No. In fact, handwriting is unacceptable. All papers in this course must be typed.
Q: What about students who can't type?
A: This course will provide them with an opportunity to learn.

Q: Why do papers have to be typed?

A: Because in the real world adults type when they want to put serious communications in writing.

Q: What if we can't hand a paper in on time?

A: Hand it in as soon as possible. It will be marked "late."

Q: What if we have a legitimate excuse?

A: Keep it to yourself. My job is to evaluate your writing, not your excuses.

15   Knowing the eternal question would come up the first day, I had my best answer in reserve. When one of the students asked it after my introductory talk, I crossed my arms and let them have it.

16   "The best answer to that question is an analogy: Imagine a team of college basketball players meeting their coach for the first time. The coach distributes a book outlining the plays he will be teaching them, and then talks to them about how the practices will be organized, what he thinks his role should be, and what he considers their responsibilities to be. When he has finished, the first question is, 'Will dribbling count?'"

17   The student who asked the question dropped the course, as did a couple of others who didn't like their first impressions of me and my nasty syllabus. But my new tone, and the classroom style it forced me to adopt, had several excellent consequences:

18   I stopped trying to make the class interesting. No more lively discussions on the sights and sounds of the campus—or anything else that wasn't directly related to helping my students write better this week than they had last week.

19   I learned to keep oral analysis and commentary to a minimum, because it disappeared into the air over my classroom. I put all directions and suggestions in writing, and tried to note on each of the papers submitted where the writer had followed my advice and where he had not.

20   The students spent more and more time pushing their pens across paper in class: writing thesis statements, writing drafts of introductory paragraphs, listing ten concrete words (five from last week's essay, five they thought they could use in next week's), working to arrange a sentence or two from their last essay into a parallel structure.

21   I stopped hoping to find in the weekly pile of papers evidence of some student writing with his inner voice. Inspired papers continued to appear at the old rate (about one in a hundred), but I no longer looked to them for proof of my effectiveness as a teacher.

22   A new kind of paper appeared in the weekly pile: well organized, mechanically polished, and clearly a second or third draft. Although some of them were titled "My First Drunk" and "The Space Race—What a Waste," I could read them attentively and praise their strengths sincerely.

23   Finally, I received some negative comments in the course evaluations: "I did not enjoy this class. The teacher was too finicky and graded too hard."

24   After four years of teaching I had learned that, given my particular skills, I had to leave consciousness-raising to other teachers. My first three years had been unsuccessful because I had been too intent on playing the guru, and I couldn't pull it off. The role I adopted that fourth year was not one I was comfortable with—Ken Macrorie is a hero of mine, not Vince Lombardi—but I could pull it off. And, more important, the tyrannical coach was a character my students recognized, and they understood what would be expected of them.

25   Last year, on my way to a different university, I decided to modify the role a little. The new syllabus has the old rules, but—while still playing the traditional authoritarian—I have changed my tone to that of a man sure of what he wants his students to do, certain they can do it, but too cool to be nasty about it.

26   This year, I have a little act I perform whenever a student asks, "Will spelling count?" Frowning, taking my pipe out of my mouth, and hesitating a moment, I try to look like a man coming down from some higher plane. Then, with what I hope sounds like a mixture of confidence and disdain, I reply, "Yes. Of course it will."

VOCABULARY

disdain (1)	insipid (7)	analogy (16)
stereotypical (2)	apathy (8)	finicky (23)
fussbudget (2)	equivocated (10)	

QUESTIONS FOR CRITICAL THINKING

1. The implication of the author's article is that students will try to get away with as much as they can. What is your view of this suggestion?
2. How important is inspiration to good writing?
3. The author admits to adopting the role of the stern coach in the classroom. What is the relationship between teaching and role playing?
4. What are the characteristics of a good teacher?
5. Is there such a thing as an "inner voice" in writing? How can a writer develop this inner voice?

QUESTIONS ON THE WRITING PROCESS

1. Logicians classify reasoning into two types: induction and deduction. (If you do not know the meanings of these two terms, look them up.) Which method of reasoning is primarily exemplified in this article?
2. The author relates that the change in his teaching technique occurred over a period of three years. What does this revelation contribute to the author's ultimate argument against permissive teaching?
3. What is the effect of the author's beginning the article with the eternal question about spelling?
4. What dominant method of development is used throughout this essay?
5. The author does not openly repudiate the educational theories he had been trying to follow, but rather seems to blame himself for failing to be a guru. Why is this an effective tactic?
6. How would you characterize the tone of the final sentence in the third paragraph?
7. What method of development is evident in paragraph 7?

WRITING ASSIGNMENTS

1. How do you think writing ought to be taught? Develop your ideas on this in a 300-word essay.
2. Students should have more freedom in structuring their college courses. Argue for or against this idea in an essay.

LETTER TO THE HOME SECRETARY

Oscar Wilde

Oscar Wilde (1854–1900), Irish playwright, poet and writer, was born in Dublin and educated at Trinity College, Dublin, and Magdalen College, Oxford. Although Wilde wrote poetry, fairy tales, criticism and fiction, he is remembered chiefly for his witty, sophisticated comedies such as Lady Windermere's Fan (1892), A Woman of No Importance *(1893), and his masterpiece,* The Importance of Being Earnest *(1895). During his lifetime, Wilde was remarkable for his eccentricity in dress and manners. He died in poverty and bankruptcy on November 30, 1900 in Paris.*

The letter below was written by Wilde to the British Home Secretary, Sir Matthew White Ridley, begging to be released from prison where he had been sent thirteen months earlier on charges of "committing acts of gross indecency with other male persons." Wilde had been imprisoned partly because of his own rashness. In 1894, the Marquess of Queensberry, father of Wilde's constant companion, Lord Alfred Douglas, publicly insulted the playwright over his relationship with his son. Wilde filed charges of criminal libel against the Marquess. Upon dismissal of his case, Wilde was arrested on the morals charge, eventually convicted and sentenced. The letter was written from Reading Gaol and is an extreme example of the use of language to persuade.

H.M. Prison, Reading
2 July 1896

To the Right Honourable Her Majesty's Principal Secretary of State for the Home Department.

1   The Petition of the above-named prisoner humbly sheweth that he does not desire to attempt to palliate in any way the terrible offences of which he was rightly found guilty, but to point out that such offences are forms of sexual madness and are recognised as such not merely by modern pathological science but by much modern legislation, notably in France, Austria, and Italy, where the laws affecting these misdemeanours have been repealed, on the ground that they are diseases to be cured by a physician, rather than crimes to be punished by a judge. In the works of eminent men of science such as Lombroso[1] and Nordau,[2] to take merely two instances out of many, this is specially insisted on with reference to the intimate connection between madness and the literary and artistic temperament, Professor Nordau

---

[1]Cesare Lombroso (1836–1909), Italian criminologist.

[2]Max Simon Nordau (1849–1923), German author and sociologist.

in his book on "Degenerescence" published in 1894 having devoted an entire chapter to the petitioner as a specially typical example of this fatal law.

2   The petitioner is now keenly conscious of the fact that while the three years preceding his arrest were from the intellectual point of view the most brilliant years of his life (four plays from his pen having been produced on the stage with immense success, and played not merely in England, America, and Australia, but in almost every European capital, and many books that excited much interest at home and abroad having been published), still that during the entire time he was suffering from the most horrible form of erotomania, which made him forget his wife and children, his high social position in London and Paris, his European distinction as an artist, the honour of his name and family, his very humanity itself, and left him the helpless prey of the most revolting passions, and of a gang of people who for their own profit ministered to them, and then drove him to his hideous ruin.

3   It is under the ceaseless apprehension lest this insanity, that displayed itself in monstrous sexual perversion before, may now extend to the entire nature and intellect, that the petitioner writes this appeal which he earnestly entreats may be at once considered. Horrible as all actual madness is, the terror of madness is no less appalling, and no less ruinous to the soul.

4   For more than thirteen dreadful months now, the petitioner has been subject to the fearful system of solitary cellular confinement: without human intercourse of any kind; without writing materials whose use might help to distract the mind: without suitable or sufficient books, so essential to any literary man, so vital for the preservation of mental balance: condemned to absolute silence: cut off from all knowledge of the external world and the movements of life: leading an existence composed of bitter degradations and terrible hardships, hideous in its recurring monotony of dreary task and sickening privation: the despair and misery of this lonely and wretched life having been intensified beyond words by the death of his mother, Lady Wilde, to whom he was deeply attached, as well as by the contemplation of the ruin he has brought on his young wife and his two children.

5   By special permission the petitioner is allowed two books a week to read: but the prison library is extremely small and poor: it hardly contains a score of books suitable for an educated man: the books kindly added at the prisoner's request he has read and reread till they have become almost meaningless to him: he is practically left without anything to read: the world of ideas, as the actual world, is closed to him: he is deprived of everything that could soothe, distract, or heal a wounded and shaken mind: and horrible as all the physical privations of modern prison life are, they are as nothing compared to the entire privation of literature to one to whom Literature was once the first thing of life, the mode by which perfection could be realised, by which, and by which alone, the intellect could feel itself alive.

6   It is but natural that living in this silence, this solitude, this isolation from all human and humane influences, this tomb for those who are not yet dead, the petitioner should, day and night in every waking hour, be tortured by the fear of absolute and entire insanity. He is conscious that his mind, shut out artificially from all rational and intellectual interests, does nothing, and can do nothing, but brood on those forms of sexual perversity, those loathsome modes of erotomania, that have brought him from high place and noble distinction to the convict's cell and the common gaol. It is inevitable that it should do so. The mind is forced to think, and when it is deprived of the conditions necessary for healthy intellectual activity, such as books, writing materials, companionship, contact with the living world, and the like, it becomes, in the case of those who are suffering from sensual monomanias, the sure prey of morbid passions, and obscene fancies, and thoughts that defile, desecrate and destroy. Crimes may be forgotten or forgiven, but vices live on: they make their dwelling house in him who by horrible mischance or fate has become their victim: they are embedded in his flesh: they spread over him like a leprosy: they feed on him like a strange disease: at the end they become an essential part of the man: no remorse however poignant can drive them out: no tears however bitter can wash them away: and prison life, by its horrible isolation from all that could save a wretched soul, hands the victim over, like one bound hand and foot, to be possessed and polluted by the thoughts he most loathes and so cannot escape from.

7   For more than a year the petitioner's mind has borne this. It can bear it no longer. He is quite conscious of the approach of an insanity that will not be confined to one portion of the nature merely, but will extend over all alike, and his desire, his prayer is that his sentence may be remitted now, so that he may be taken abroad by his friends and may put himself under medical care so that the sexual insanity from which he suffers may be cured. He knows only too well that his career as a dramatist and writer is ended, and his name blotted from the scroll of English Literature never to be replaced: that his children cannot bear that name again, and that an obscure life in some remote country is in store for him: he knows that, bankruptcy having come upon him, poverty of a most bitter kind awaits him, and that all the joy and beauty of existence is taken from him for ever: but at least in all his hopelessness he still clings to the hope that he will not have to pass directly from the common gaol to the common lunatic asylum.

8   Dreadful as are the results of the prison system—a system so terrible that it hardens their hearts whose hearts it does not break, and brutalises those who have to carry it out no less than those who have to submit to it— yet at least amongst its aims is not the desire to wreck the human reason. Though it may not seek to make men better, yet it does not desire to drive them mad, and so, earnestly does the petitioner beg that he may be allowed to go forth while he has still some sanity left: while words have still a

meaning, and books a message: while there is still some possibility that, by medical science and humane treatment, balance may be restored to a shaken mind and health given back to a nature that once knew purity: while there is still time to rid the temperament of a revolting madness and to make the soul, even for a brief space, clean.

9 Most earnestly indeed does the petitioner beg the Home Secretary to take, if he so desires it, the opinion of any recognised medical authorities on what would be the inevitable result of solitary confinement in silence and isolation on one already suffering from sexual monomania of a terrible character.

10 The petitioner would also point out that while his bodily health is better in many respects here than it was at Wandsworth, where he was for two months in the hospital for absolute physical and mental collapse caused by hunger and insomnia, he has, since he has been in prison, almost entirely lost the hearing of his right ear through an abscess that has caused a perforation of the drum. The medical officer here has stated that he is unable to offer any assistance, and that the hearing must go entirely. The petitioner, however, feels sure that under the care of a specialist abroad his hearing might be preserved to him. He was assured by Sir William Dalby,[3] the great aurist, that with proper care there was no reason at all why he should lose his hearing. But though the abscess has been running now for the entire time of his imprisonment, and the hearing getting worse every week, nothing has been done in the way even of an attempted cure. The ear has been syringed on three occasions with plain water for the purpose of examination, that is all. The petitioner is naturally apprehensive lest, as often happens, the other ear may be attacked in a similar way, and to the misery of a shattered and debilitated mind be added the horrors of complete deafness.

11 His eyesight, of which like most men of letters he had always been obliged to take great care, has also suffered very much from the enforced living in a white-washed cell with a flaring gas-jet at night: he is conscious of great weakness and pain in the nerves of the eyes, and objects even at a short distance become blurred. The bright daylight, when taking exercise in the prison-yard, often causes pain and distress to the optic nerve, and during the past four months the consciousness of failing eyesight has been a source of terrible anxiety, and should his imprisonment be continued, blindness and deafness may in all human probability be added to the certainty of increasing insanity and the wreck of the reason.

12 There are other apprehensions of danger that the limitation of space does not allow the petitioner to enter on: his chief danger is that of madness, his chief terror that of madness, and his prayer that his long imprisonment may be considered with its attendant ruin a sufficient punishment,

[3]William Bartlett Dalby (1840–1918).

that the imprisonment may be ended now, and not uselessly or vindictively prolonged till insanity has claimed soul as well as body as its prey, and brought it to the same degradation and the same shame.

Oscar Wilde

VOCABULARY

palliate (1)	monomanias (6)	remitted (7)
erotomania (2)	defile (6)	aurist (10)
appalling (3)	desecrate (6)	debilitated (10)
degradations (4)	poignant (6)	vindictively (12)
privation (4)		

QUESTIONS FOR CRITICAL THINKING

1. What is your view of homosexuality? Is it a disease, as Wilde argues, or is it merely a chosen lifestyle as some gay advocates contend?
2. What right, if any, does society have to regulate minority sexual lifestyles?
3. Homosexuality is classified as a "victimless crime." What other kinds of victimless crime are there? What should society's stand be on victimless crimes?
4. What, in your view, is the value of imprisonment?

QUESTIONS ON THE WRITING PROCESS

1. Why do you think Wilde refers to himself in the third-person as "the petitioner"? What effect does this use have on his appeal?
2. How does Wilde portray himself in paragraph 2? What do you think he had in mind in so wording his appeal?
3. In what ways do the syntax and punctuation of paragraphs 4 and 5 underscore Wilde's plea?
4. Examine the first sentence of paragraph 5. What device of phrasing does Wilde use to emphasize his unhappiness?
5. What extended analogy does Wilde use in paragraph 6? How effective do you regard this analogy?

WRITING ASSIGNMENTS

1. Write an essay arguing for or against the notion that sexual preference should have no bearing on an applicant's fitness for a position of public responsibility.
2. Present your views on the causes of homosexuality in an essay.
3. In some countries homosexuality is still regarded as a crime punishable by imprisonment. Write an essay arguing for or against this view of homosexuality.

LONG ESSAYS

WHY THE COUNTRY NEEDS THE DRAFT

James Fallows

James Fallows (1949–   ) was educated at Harvard and at Oxford University, where he was a Rhodes Scholar. Since 1979 he has been the Washington *editor of the* Atlantic Monthly.

The author argues for an unpopular institution, the military draft, charging that without it the volunteer armed forces perpetuate a class system in which the sons of the poor are asked to fight for the sons of the rich.

I am more than angry. I did not give birth to my one and only son to have him snatched away from me 18 years later. My child has been loved and cared for and taught right from wrong and *will not* be fed into any egomaniac's war machine.

Our 18- to 25-year-olds have not brought this world to its present sorry state. Men over the age of 35, down through the centuries, have brought us here, and we women have been in silent accord.

Well, this is one woman, one mother, who says no. I did not go through the magnificent agony of childbirth to have that glorious young life snuffed out.

Until the presidents, premiers, supreme rulers, politburos, senators and congressmen of the world are ready to physically, as opposed to verbally, lead the world into combat, they can bloody well forget my child.

Unite mothers! Don't throw your sons and daughters away. Sometime, somewhere, women have just got to say no.

No. No. No. No. No. Never my child.

Louise M. Saylor

(Letter published in the Washington *Post*, January 28, 1980.)

1 Nor my child, Mrs. Saylor. Nor either of my mother's sons when, ten years ago, both were classified I-A. But *whose*, then? As our statesmen talk again of resisting aggression and demonstrating our will—as they talk, that is, of sending someone's sons (or daughters) to bear arms overseas—the only fair and decent answer to that question lies in a return to the draft.

2 I am speaking here not of the health of the military but of the character of the society the military defends. The circumstances in which that society will choose to go to war, the way its wars will be fought, and its success in absorbing the consequent suffering depend on its answer to the question Whose sons will go?

3 History rarely offers itself in lessons clear enough to be deciphered at a time when their message still applies. But of all the hackneyed "lessons" of Vietnam, one still applies with no reservations: that we wound ourselves

gravely if we flinch from honest answers about who will serve. During the five or six years of the heaviest draft calls for Vietnam, there was the starkest class division in American military service since the days of purchased draft deferments in the Civil War. Good intentions lay at the root of many of these inequities. The college-student deferment, the various "hardship" exemptions, Robert McNamara's plan to give "disadvantaged" youngsters a chance to better themselves in the military, even General Hershey's intelligence test to determine who could remain in school—all were designed to allot American talent in the most productive way. The intent was to distinguish those who could best serve the nation with their minds from those who should offer their stout hearts and strong backs. The effect was to place the poor and the black in the trenches (and later in the coffins and the rehabilitation wards), and their "betters" in colleges or elsewhere far from the sounds of war. I speak as one who took full advantage of the college-student deferment and later exploited the loopholes in the physical qualification standards that, for college students armed with a doctor's letter and advice from the campus draft counseling center, could so easily be parlayed into the "unfit for service" designation known as a I-Y. Ask anyone who went to college in those days how many of his classmates saw combat in Vietnam. Of my 1200 classmates at Harvard, I know of only two, one of them a veteran who joined the class late. The records show another fifty-five in the reserves, the stateside Army, or military service of some other kind. There may be more; the alumni lists are not complete. See how this compares with the Memorial Roll from a public high school in a big city or a West Virigina hill town.

4   For all the talk about conflict between "young" and "old" that the war caused, the lasting breach was among the young. In the protest marches on the Pentagon and the Capitol, students felt either scorn for or estrangement from the young soldiers who stood guard. What must the soldiers have felt about these, their privileged contemporaries, who taunted them so? To those who opposed the war, the ones who served were, first, animals and killers; then "suckers" who were trapped by the system, deserving pity but no respect; and finally invisible men. Their courage, discipline, and sacrifice counted for less than their collective taint for being associated with a losing war. A returned veteran might win limited redemption if he publicly recanted, like a lapsed Communist fingering his former associates before the HUAC.[1] Otherwise, he was expected to keep his experiences to himself. Most veterans knew the honor they had earned, even as they knew better than anyone else the horror of the war. They came to resent being made to suppress those feelings by students who chose not to join them and

---

[1]Acronym for the House Un-American Activities Committee, which was headed by Senator Joseph McCarthy between 1953–54. The committee held sensational public hearings on the alleged infiltration of Communists into positions of influence in public life.

who, having escaped the war without pain, now prefer to put the whole episode in the past. Perhaps no one traversed that era without pain, but pain of the psychic variety left arms, legs, life intact and did not impede progress in one's career. For people of my generation—I speak in the narrow sense of males between the ages of twenty-eight and thirty-six or thirty-seven—this wound will never fully heal. If you doubt that, sit two thirty-two-year-olds down together, one who served in Vietnam and one who did not, and ask them to talk about those years.

5   At least there was theoretical consistency between what the students of those days recommended for others and what they did themselves. Their point was that no one should go to war, starting with them. It should also be said that their objection to the war, at least in my view, was important and right. And while they—we—may have proven more effective and determined in acts of individual salvation than in anything else, they at least paid lip service to the idea of the "categorical imperative," that they should not expect others to bear a burden they considered unacceptable for themselves.

6   I hear little of that tone in the reaction to President Carter's muted call for resumption of draft registration. Within a week of his request in the State of the Union address, I spent time at two small colleges. At both, the sequence of questions was the same. Why is our defense so weak? When will we show the Russians our strength? *Isn't it terrible about the draft?*

7   Senator Kennedy, who so often decried the unfairness of the draft during Vietnam, won cheers from his college audience for his opposition to draft registration, in the same speech in which he suggested beefing up our military presence in the Persian Gulf. Kennedy did go on to argue that we should not shed blood for oil, which is more than most anti-draft groups have done to date. It would have been reassuring to hear the students say that they oppose registration *because* they oppose a military showdown in the Persian Gulf. Instead many simply say, We don't want to go. I sense that they—perhaps all of us—have come to take for granted a truth so painful that few could bear to face it during Vietnam: that there will be another class of people to do the dirty work. After seven years of the volunteer Army, we have grown accustomed to having suckers on hand.

8   That the volunteer Army is another class can hardly be denied. The Vietnam draft was unfair racially, economically, educationally. By every one of those measures, the volunteer Army is less representative still. Libertarians argue that military service should be a matter of choice, but the plain fact is that service in the volunteer force is too frequently dictated by economics. Army enlisted ranks E1 through E4—the privates and corporals, the cannon fodder, the ones who will fight and die—are 36 percent black now. By the Army's own projections, they will be 42 percent black in three years. When other "minorities" are taken into account, we will have,

for the first time, an army whose fighting members are mainly "non-major-ity," or, more bluntly, a black and brown army defending a mainly white nation. The military has been an avenue of opportunity for many young blacks. They may well be first-class fighting men. They do not represent the nation.

9   Such a selective bearing of the burden has destructive spiritual effects in a nation based on the democratic creed. But its practical implications can be quite as grave. The effect of a fair, representative draft is to hold the public hostage to the consequences of its decisions, much as children's presence in the public schools focuses parents' attention on the quality of the schools. If citizens are willing to countenance a decision that means that *someone's* child may die, they may contemplate more deeply if there is the possibility that the child will be theirs. Indeed, I would like to extend this principle even further. Young men of nineteen are rightly suspicious of the congressmen and columnists who urge them to the fore. I wish there were a practical way to resurrect the provisions of the amended Selective Service Act of 1940, which raised the draft age to forty-four. Such a gesture might symbolize the desire to offset the historic injustice of the Vietnam draft, as well as suggest the possibility that, when a bellicose columnist recommends dispatching American forces to Pakistan, he might also realize that he could end up as a gunner in a tank.

10   Perhaps the absence of a World War II-scale peril makes such a proposal unrealistic; still, the columnist or congressman should have to contemplate the possibility that his son would be there, in trench or tank. Under the vol-unteer Army that possibility will not arise, and the lack of such a prospect can affect behavior deeply. Recall how, during Vietnam, protest grew more broad-based and respectable when the graduate school deferment was elim-inated in 1968. For many families in positions of influence, the war was no longer a question of someone else's son. How much earlier would the war have ended had college students been vulnerable from the start?

11   Those newly concerned families were no better and no worse than other people at other times; they were responding to a normal human instinct, of the sort our political system is designed to channel toward constructive ends. It was an instinct that Richard Nixon and Henry Kissinger under-stood very well, as they deliberately shifted the burden of the war off draft-ees and finally off Americans, to free their hands to pursue their chosen course. Recall how fast protest ebbed with the coming of the volunteer Army and "Vietnamization" in the early 1970s. For this reason, the likes of Nixon and Kissinger might regard a return to the draft as a step in the wrong direction, for it would sap the resolve necessary for a strong foreign policy and introduce the weakening element of domestic dissent. At times leaders must take actions that seem heartless and unfair, and that an in-formed public would probably not approve. Winston Churchill let Coven-

12 try be bombed, because to sound the air-raid sirens and save its citizens would have tipped off the Germans that Britain had broken their code. But in the long run, a nation cannot sustain a policy whose consequences the public is not willing to bear. If it decides not to pay the price to defend itself, it will be defenseless. That is the risk of democracy.

12 What kind of draft? More than anything else, a fair one, with as few holes as possible to wriggle through. The 1971 Selective Service Act, passed when the heavy draft calls had already ended, theoretically closed most of the loopholes. But if real trouble should begin, those nine-year-old patches might give way before political pressures unless we concentrate again on the mechanics of an equitable draft. "Fairness" does not mean that everyone need serve. This year 4.3 million people will turn eighteen, 2.2 million women and 2.1 million men. For the last few years, the military has been taking 400,000 people annually into the volunteer Army—or, in raw figures, only one in ten of the total available pool. Using today's mental and physical standards, the military knocks off 30 percent of the manpower pool as unqualified, and it excludes women from combat positions. When these calculations are combined with the diminishing number of young men— only 1.6 million men will turn eighteen in 1993—the military projects that it will need to attract one of every three "qualified and available men" by the end of the 1980s.

13 Read another way, this means that a draft need affect *no more* than one in three—and probably far fewer. To make the draft seem—and be—fair, the pool of potential draftees should be as large as possible, even if only a few will eventually be picked. Those who are "disabled" in the common meaning of that term—the blind, paraplegics—should be excluded, but not the asthmatics and trick-back cases who are perfectly capable of performing non-combat military jobs. The military's physical requirements now assume that nearly all men must theoretically be fit for combat, even though only 14 percent of all male soldiers hold combat jobs. The proportion of draftees destined for combat would probably be higher, since those are the positions now most understrength; if actual fighting should begin it would be higher still. But combat will never represent the preponderance of military positions, and its requirements should not blindly dictate who is eligible for the draft. Instead, everyone without serious handicap should be eligible for selection by lottery—men and women, students and non-students. Once the lottery had determined *who* would serve, assignments based on physical classifications could determine where and how.

14 The question of women's service is the most emotionally troubling aspect of this generally emotional issue, but the progress of domestic politics over the last ten years suggests that the answer is clear. If any sexual distinctions that would deny a woman her place as a construction worker or a telephone pole climber have been forbidden by legislators and courts, what

possible distinction can spare women the obligation to perform similar functions in military construction units or the Signal Corps? President Carter recognized this reality in deciding to include women in his initial draft registration order. If women are drafted, they have an iron-clad case for passage of the Equal Rights Amendment. If they are not, their claim for equal treatment elsewhere becomes less compelling. At the same time, it is troubling to think of women in combat, or of mothers being drafted, and a sensible draft law would have to recognize such exceptions.

15   There should be no educational deferments except for students still in high school, and possibly in two other cases. One would be for college students who enroll in ROTC; like their counterparts in the service academies, they would be exchanging four years of protected education for a longer tour of duty as an officer after graduation. The other exception might be for doctors, possessors of a skill the military needs but cannot sensibly produce on its own. If potential doctors wanted to be spared all eligibility for the draft, they could enter a program like the Navy's V-12 during World War II, in which they could take a speeded-up college course and receive a publicly subsidized medical education, after which they would owe several years' service as military doctors. Except in the most far-fetched situations, "hardship" cases should be taken care of by compensation rather than by exemption. If these are permitted, they become an invitation to abuse: who can forget George Hamilton pleading hardship as his mother's sole supporting son? Instead, the government should offset hardship with support payments to the needy dependents.

16   One resists the idea of lottery, because it adds to the system the very element of caprice and unfairness it is so important to remove. But since only a fraction of those eligible to serve are actually required, there seems no other equitable way to distribute the burden. With a well-established lottery, every male and female might know at age eighteen whether he or she was near the top of the list and very likely to be called, or near the bottom and almost certainly protected. How far the draft calls went down the list would depend on how many people volunteered and how many more were needed.

17   None of these concerns and prescriptions would matter if the volunteer Army were what it so often seemed in the last few years—a stand-in, a symbol, designed to keep the machinery running and the troops in place, not to be sent into action for any cause less urgent than absolute survival. But now we hear from every quarter that the next decade will be a time of testing, that our will and our strategy and our manpower will be on the line. The nature of this challenge, and the style of our response, are what we should be thinking and talking about now. Our discussions will never be honest, nor our decisions just, as long as we count on "suckers" to do the job.

VOCABULARY

deciphered (3)	estrangement (4)	impede (4)
hackneyed (3)	taunted (4)	categorical imperative (5)
flinch (3)	recanted (4)	bellicose (9)
inequities (3)	suppress (4)	preponderance (13)
allot (3)	traversed (4)	caprice (16)

QUESTIONS FOR CRITICAL THINKING

1. What is your opinion of the author's claim that the volunteer army represents the starkest kind of class division?
2. The author says that he is troubled at the idea of women in combat. What is troubling about such an idea? Should women participate in military combat?
3. The author implies that his generation, even though it opposed the draft, was fairer than the current generation in recognizing the implicit class divisions of military service. What are your views of this claim?
4. What effect on the conduct of foreign policy do you think the extension of the draftable age to 44 would have?
5. Many of the children from the riotous sixties have done an about-face from their former political and social views. The author confesses himself to be one of them. How legitimate and valid do you think their current opinions are in light of their recantation of earlier, more militant views?
6. What do you think would happen if the United States disbanded all of its military with the exception of that minimum force necessary for the defense of its own soil?

QUESTIONS ON THE WRITING PROCESS

1. The author begins by quoting a letter to the editor that was published in the Washington *Post*. What is the point of doing this?
2. The author admits to taking full advantage of draft loopholes during the Vietnam war. What is the point of this admission?
3. What is the author's principal argument against the volunteer army?
4. In paragraph 4, the author compares a recanting Vietnam veteran to a lapsed Communist fingering his former associates before the HUAC. What is ironic about this comparison?
5. What is a "categorical imperative"? What is the origin of this phrase?
6. How does the author support his contention, made in paragraph 8, that the army is becoming a "black and brown army defending a mainly white nation"?
7. In the first part of the article, the author argues for restoration of the draft. What does he then attempt to do in the second part?
8. What transition does the author use at the beginning of paragraph 12 to shift the focus of his argument?

WRITING ASSIGNMENTS

1. In a 500-word essay, make a point-by-point rebuttal of the author's arguments in favor of reinstituting the draft.
2. Write a letter to the editor of your hometown newspaper stating your views on the possible reinstitution of the draft.
3. At present, the country expects its young to serve in the armed forces and fight its wars. Is this expectation fair? Write an essay arguing that if the draft is reinstituted, every able-bodied person under 50 should be required to serve.

EVOLUTION AS FACT AND THEORY

Stephen Jay Gould

*Stephen Jay Gould (1941–   ) was born in New York City and edu-
cated at Columbia University. Since 1973 he has been a Professor at
Harvard University, where he teaches geology, biology, and the history
of science. He writes a regular column for* Natural History *magazine
titled* This View of Life. *He has contributed over 100 articles to scientific journals. His books include* Ever Since Darwin *(1977) and* Hen's
Teeth and Horse's Toes *(1983), a collection of his essays.*

*The revival of anti-evolutionist sentiments under the guise of "scientific
creationism" has sparked once again the debate about Darwin's theory.
Gould has been at the center of this latest firestorm, having testified
against the beliefs and views of the creationists, whose most recent campaign is aimed at getting creationism featured side-by-side with evolution in science textbooks. In this essay, Gould argues that scientific
creationism is hokum and that Darwin's theory is not merely speculation, but also fact.*

1   Kirtley Mather,[1] who died last year at ninety-two, was a pillar of both
science and Christian religion in America and one of my dearest friends.
The difference of a half-century in our ages evaporated before our common
interests. The most curious thing we shared was a battle we each fought at
the same age. For Kirtley had gone to Tennessee with Clarence Darrow to
testify for evolution at the Scopes trial of 1925. When I think that we are
enmeshed again in the same struggle for one of the best documented, most
compelling and exciting concepts in all of science, I don't know whether to
laugh or cry.

2   According to idealized principles of scientific discourse, the arousal of
dormant issues should reflect fresh data that give renewed life to abandoned notions. Those outside the current debate may therefore be excused
for suspecting that creationists have come up with something new, or that
evolutionists have generated some serious internal trouble. But nothing has
changed; the creationists have presented not a single new fact or argument.
Darrow and Bryan were at least more entertaining than we lesser antagonists today. The rise of creationism is politics, pure and simple; it represents one issue (and by no means the major concern) of the resurgent evangelical right. Arguments that seemed kooky just a decade ago have
reentered the mainstream.

[1]Kirtley Mather (1888–1980), Professor of Geology at Harvard University 1924–1957.

3   The basic attack of modern creationists falls apart on two general counts before we even reach the supposed factual details of their assault against evolution. First, they play upon a vernacular misunderstanding of the word "theory" to convey the false impression that we evolutionists are covering up the rotten core of our edifice. Second, they misuse a popular philosophy of science to argue that they are behaving scientifically in attacking evolution. Yet the same philosophy demonstrates that their own belief is not science, and that "scientific creationism" is a meaningless and self-contradictory phrase, an example of what Orwell called "newspeak."

4   In the American vernacular, "theory" often means "imperfect fact"— part of a hierarchy of confidence running downhill from fact to theory to hypothesis to guess. Thus, creationists can (and do) argue: evolution is "only" a theory, and intense debate now rages about many aspects of the theory. If evolution is less than a fact, and scientists can't even make up their minds about the theory, then what confidence can we have in it? Indeed, President Reagan echoed this argument before an evangelical group in Dallas when he said (in what I devoutly hope was campaign rhetoric): "Well, it is a theory. It is a scientific theory only, and it has in recent years been challenged in the world of science—that is, not believed in the scientific community to be as infallible as it once was."

5   Well, evolution *is* a theory. It is also a fact. And facts and theories are different things, not rungs in a hierarchy of increasing certainty. Facts are the world's data. Theories are structures of ideas that explain and interpret facts. Facts do not go away while scientists debate rival theories for explaining them. Einstein's theory of gravitation replaced Newton's, but apples did not suspend themselves in mid-air pending the outcome. And human beings evolved from apelike ancestors whether they did so by Darwin's proposed mechanism or by some other, yet to be discovered.

6   Moreover, "fact" does not mean "absolute certainty." The final proofs of logic and mathematics flow deductively from stated premises and achieve certainty only because they are *not* about the empirical world. Evolutionists make no claim for perpetual truth, though creationists often do (and then attack us for a style of argument that they themselves favor). In science, "fact" can only mean "confirmed to such a degree that it would be perverse to withhold provisional assent." I suppose that apples might start to rise tomorrow, but the possibility does not merit equal time in physics classrooms.

7   Evolutionists have been clear about this distinction between fact and theory from the very beginning, if only because we have always acknowledged how far we are from completely understanding the mechanisms (theory) by which evolution (fact) occurred. Darwin continually emphasized the difference between his two great and separate accomplishments: establishing the fact of evolution, and proposing a theory—natural selection—to

explain the mechanism of evolution. He wrote in *The Descent of Man:* "I had two distinct objects in view; firstly, to show that species had not been separately created, and secondly, that natural selection had been the chief agent of change . . . Hence if I have erred in . . . having exaggerated its [natural selection's] power . . . I have at least, as I hope, done good service in aiding to overthrow the dogma of separate creations."

8   Thus Darwin acknowledged the provisional nature of natural selection while affirming the fact of evolution. The fruitful theoretical debate that Darwin initiated has never ceased. From the 1940s through the 1960s, Darwin's own theory of natural selection did achieve a temporary hegemony that it never enjoyed in his lifetime. But renewed debate characterizes our decade, and, while no biologist questions the importance of natural selection, many now doubt its ubiquity. In particular, many evolutionists argue that substantial amounts of genetic change may not be subject to natural selection and may spread through populations at random. Others are challenging Darwin's linking of natural selection with gradual, imperceptible change through all intermediary degrees; they are arguing that most evolutionary events may occur far more rapidly than Darwin envisioned.

9   Scientists regard debates on fundamental issues of theory as a sign of intellectual health and a source of excitement. Science is—and how else can I say it?—most fun when it plays with interesting ideas, examines their implications, and recognizes that old information may be explained in surprisingly new ways. Evolutionary theory is now enjoying this uncommon vigor. Yet amidst all this turmoil no biologist has been led to doubt the fact that evolution occurred; we are debating *how* it happened. We are all trying to explain the same thing: the tree of evolutionary descent linking all organisms by ties of genealogy. Creationists pervert and caricature this debate by conveniently neglecting the common conviction that underlies it, and by falsely suggesting that we now doubt the very phenomenon we are struggling to understand.

10   Secondly, creationists claim that "the dogma of separate creations," as Darwin characterized it a century ago, is a scientific theory meriting equal time with evolution in high school biology curricula. But a popular viewpoint among philosophers of science belies this creationist argument. Philosopher Karl Popper has argued for decades that the primary criterion of science is the falsifiability of its theories. We can never prove absolutely, but we can falsify. A set of ideas that cannot, in principle, be falsified is not science.

11   The entire creationist program includes little more than a rhetorical attempt to falsify evolution by presenting supposed contradictions among its supporters. Their brand of creationism, they claim, is "scientific" because it follows the Popperian model in trying to demolish evolution. Yet Popper's argument must apply in both directions. One does not become a

scientist by the simple act of trying to falsify a rival and truly scientific system; one has to present an alternative system that also meets Popper's criterion—it too must be falsifiable in principle.

12   "Scientific creationism" is a self-contradictory, nonsense phrase precisely because it cannot be falsified. I can envision observations and experiments that would disprove any evolutionary theory I know, but I cannot imagine what potential data could lead creationists to abandon their beliefs. Unbeatable systems are dogma, not science. Lest I seem harsh or rhetorical, I quote creationism's leading intellectual, Duane Gish, Ph.D., from his recent (1978) book, *Evolution? The Fossils Say No!* "By creation we mean the bringing into being by a supernatural Creator of the basic kinds of plants and animals by the process of sudden, or fiat, creation. We do not know how the Creator created, what processes He used, *for He used processes which are not now operating anywhere in the natural universe* [Gish's italics]. This is why we refer to creation as special creation. We cannot discover by scientific investigations anything about the creative processes used by the Creator." Pray tell, Dr. Gish, in the light of your last sentence, what then is "scientific" creationism?

13   Our confidence that evolution occurred centers upon three general arguments. First, we have abundant, direct, observational evidence of evolution in action, from both field and laboratory. This evidence ranges from countless experiments on change in nearly everything about fruit flies subjected to artificial selection in the laboratory to the famous populations of British moths that became black when industrial soot darkened the trees upon which the moths rest. (Moths gain protection from sharp-sighted bird predators by blending into the background.) Creationists do not deny these observations; how could they? Creationists have tightened their act. They now argue that God only created "basic kinds," and allowed for limited evolutionary meandering within them. Thus toy poodles and Great Danes come from the dog kind and moths can change color, but nature cannot convert a dog to a cat or a monkey to a man.

14   The second and third arguments for evolution—the case for major changes—do not involve direct observation of evolution in action. They rest upon inference, but are no less secure for that reason. Major evolutionary change requires too much time for direct observation on the scale of recorded human history. All historical sciences rest upon inference, and evolution is no different from geology, cosmology, or human history in this respect. In principle, we cannot observe processes that operated in the past. We must infer them from results that still surround us: living and fossil organisms for evolution, documents and artifacts for human history, strata and topography for geology.

15   The second argument—that the imperfection of nature reveals evolution—strikes many people as ironic, for they feel that evolution should be most elegantly displayed in the nearly perfect adaptation expressed by

some organisms—the camber of a gull's wing, or butterflies that cannot be seen in ground litter because they mimic leaves so precisely. But perfection could be imposed by a wise creator or evolved by natural selection. Perfection covers the tracks of past history. And past history—evidence of descent—is the mark of evolution.

16   Evolution lies exposed in the *imperfections* that record a history of descent. Why should a rat run, a bat fly, a porpoise swim, and I type this essay with structures built of the same bones unless we all inherited them from a common ancestor? An engineer, starting from scratch, could design better limbs in each case. Why should all the large native mammals of Australia be marsupials, unless they descended from a common ancestor isolated on this island continent? Marsupials are not "better," or ideally suited for Australia; many have been wiped out by placental mammals imported by man from other countries. This principle of imperfection extends to all historical sciences. When we recognize the etymology of September, October, November, and December (seventh, eighth, ninth, and tenth), we know that the year once started in March, or that two additional months must have been added to an original calendar of ten months.

17   The third argument is more direct: transitions are often found in the fossil record. Preserved transitions are not common—and should not be, according to our understanding of evolution (see next section)—but they are not entirely wanting, as creationists often claim. The lower jaw of reptiles contains several bones, that of mammals only one. The non-mammalian jawbones are reduced, step by step, in mammalian ancestors until they become tiny nubbins located at the back of the jaw. The "hammer" and "anvil" bones of the mammalian ear are descendants of these nubbins. How could such a transition be accomplished? the creationists ask. Surely a bone is either entirely in the jaw or in the ear. Yet paleontologists have discovered two transitional lineages of therapsids (the so-called mammal-like reptiles) with a double jaw joint—one composed of the old quadrate and articular bones (soon to become the hammer and anvil), the other of the squamosal and dentary bones (as in modern mammals). For that matter, what better transitional form could we expect to find than the oldest human, *Australopithecus afarensis*, with its apelike palate, its human upright stance, and a cranial capacity larger than any ape's of the same body size but a full 1,000 cubic centimeters below ours? If God made each of the half-dozen human species discovered in ancient rocks, why did he create in an unbroken temporal sequence of progressively more modern features—increasing cranial capacity, reduced face and teeth, larger body size? Did he create to mimic evolution and test our faith thereby?

18   Faced with these facts of evolution and the philosophical bankruptcy of their own position, creationists rely upon distortion and innuendo to buttress their rhetorical claim. If I sound sharp or bitter, indeed I am—for I have become a major target of these practices.

19   I count myself among the evolutionists who argue for a jerky, or episodic, rather than a smoothly gradual, pace of change. In 1972 my colleague Niles Eldredge and I developed the theory of punctuated equilibrium. We argued that two outstanding facts of the fossil record—geologically "sudden" origin of new species and failure to change thereafter (stasis)—reflect the predictions of evolutionary theory, not the imperfections of the fossil record. In most theories, small isolated populations are the source of new species, and the process of speciation takes thousands or tens of thousands of years. This amount of time, so long when measured against our lives, is a geological microsecond. It represents much less than 1 per cent of the average lifespan for a fossil invertebrate species—more than ten million years. Large, widespread, and well established species, on the other hand, are not expected to change very much. We believe that the inertia of large populations explains the stasis of most fossil species over millions of years.

20   We proposed the theory of punctuated equilibrium largely to provide a different explanation for pervasive trends in the fossil record. Trends, we argued, cannot be attributed to gradual transformation within lineages, but must arise from the differential success of certain kinds of species. A trend, we argued, is more like climbing a flight of stairs (punctuations and stasis) than rolling up an inclined plane.

21   Since we proposed punctuated equilibria to explain trends, it is infuriating to be quoted again and again by creationists—whether through design or stupidity, I do not know—as admitting that the fossil record includes no transitional forms. Transitional forms are generally lacking at the species level, but they are abundant between larger groups. Yet a pamphlet entitled "Harvard Scientists Agree Evolution Is a Hoax" states: "The facts of punctuated equilibrium which Gould and Eldredge . . . are forcing Darwinists to swallow fit the picture that Bryan insisted on, and which God has revealed to us in the Bible."

22   Continuing the distortion, several creationists have equated the theory of punctuated equilibrium with a caricature of the beliefs of Richard Goldschmidt, a great early geneticist. Goldschmidt argued, in a famous book published in 1940, that new groups can arise all at once through major mutations. He referred to these suddenly transformed creatures as "hopeful monsters." (I am attracted to some aspects of the non-caricatured version, but Goldschmidt's theory still has nothing to do with punctuated equilibrium.) Creationist Luther Sunderland talks of the "punctuated equilibrium hopeful monster theory" and tells his hopeful readers that "it amounts to tacit admission that anti-evolutionists are correct in asserting there is no fossil evidence supporting the theory that all life is connected to a common ancestor." Duane Gish writes, "According to Goldschmidt, and now apparently according to Gould, a reptile laid an agg from which the first bird, feathers and all, was produced." Any evolutionist who believed such nonsense would rightly be laughed off the intellectual stage; yet the only theory

that could ever envision such a scenario for the origin of birds is creationism—with God acting in the egg.

23   I am both angry at and amused by the creationists; but mostly I am deeply sad. Sad for many reasons. Sad because so many people who respond to creationist appeals are troubled for the right reason, but venting their anger at the wrong target. It is true that scientists have often been dogmatic and elitist. It is true that we have often allowed the white-coated, advertising image to represent us—"Scientists say that Brand X cures bunions ten times faster than . . ." We have not fought it adequately because we derive benefits from appearing as a new priesthood. It is also true that faceless and bureaucratic state power intrudes more and more into our lives and removes choices that should belong to individuals and communities. I can understand that school curricula, imposed from above and without local input, might be seen as one more insult on all these grounds. But the culprit is not, and cannot be, evolution or any other fact of the natural world. Identify and fight your legitimate enemies by all means, but we are not among them.

24   I am sad because the practical result of this brouhaha will not be expanded coverage to include creationism (that would also make me sad), but the reduction or excision of evolution from high school curricula. Evolution is one of the half dozen "great ideas" developed by science. It speaks to the profound issues of genealogy that fascinate all of us—the "roots" phenomenon writ large. Where did we come from? Where did life arise? How did it develop? How are organisms related? It forces us to think, ponder, and wonder. Shall we deprive millions of this knowledge and once again teach biology as a set of dull and unconnected facts, without the thread that weaves diverse material into a supple unity?

25   But most of all I am saddened by a trend I am just beginning to discern among my colleagues. I sense that some now wish to mute the healthy debate about theory that has brought new life to evolutionary biology. It provides grist for creationist mills, they say, even if only by distortion. Perhaps we should lie low and rally round the flag of strict Darwinism, at least for the moment—a kind of old-time religion on our part.

26   But we should borrow another metaphor and recognize that we too have to tread a straight and narrow path, surrounded by roads to perdition. For if we ever begin to suppress our search to understand nature, to quench our own intellectual excitement in a misguided effort to present a united front where it does not and should not exist, then we are truly lost.

VOCABULARY

idealized (2)
discourse (2)
dormant (2)
antagonists (2)
resurgent (2)
vernacular (3)
hierarchy (4)
infallible (4)
deductively (6)
empirical (6)
perverse (6)

provisional (6)
dogma (7)
hegemony (8)
ubiquity (8)
imperceptible (8)
genealogy (9)
caricature (9)
falsifiability (10)
fiat (12)
meandering (13)
artifacts (14)

temporal (17)
innuendo (18)
equilibrium (19)
inertia (19)
pervasive (20)
differential (20)
tacit (22)
brouhaha (24)
excision (24)
perdition (26)

QUESTIONS FOR CRITICAL THINKING

1. The author says that "scientific creationism" is an example of *newspeak*. What is "newspeak"? How is the term applicable to scientific creationism?
2. What is contradictory about "scientific creationism"? Why would creationists borrow the term "scientific" to describe their beliefs?
3. What conflict, if any, do you see between a belief in evolution and creation?
4. What is dogma? What part does dogma play in the ensuing debate between evolutionists and creationists?
5. Does dogma play any part in science? Why or why not?
6. Why must an idea be falsifiable to be scientific?
7. Could creationism be taught in schools without violating the separation of church and state principle? Why or why not?

QUESTIONS ON THE WRITING PROCESS

1. Many arguments are waged because of disputed definitions of basic terms. Where does Gould define some of the terms basic to his argument?
2. How does the author use rhetorical questions to present his views? How effective is this use?
3. What is the purpose of paragraph 18?
4. What is ironic about the language of paragraphs 23 and 24?
5. What allusion does the author make in paragraph 5 to underscore his argument that evolution is fact?
6. Arguments are often settled by "appeals to authority." Which authority does the author appeal to in arguing his case?
7. What three arguments does the author use to support his confidence in evolution?

WRITING ASSIGNMENTS

1. Write an essay arguing your views on whether or not both evolution and creationism should be taught in schools.
2. Does a belief in evolution necessarily lead to atheism? Write an argumentative essay on this theme.
3. Write an essay explaining what impact, if any, scientific findings have had on your faith.

APPROPRIATE HOUSING FOR THE ELDERLY

Marilyn Schuning

We cannot continue the heartless custom of shuttling our senior citizens into retirement homes or convalescent hospitals where they feel useless, isolated, and infirm. In his book, *Why Survive? Being Old in America,* Robert N. Butler, M.D., states that "old people should not be walled off in sequestered worlds, even if comfortable, but rather they should remain a part of the mainstream of life."

In 1975, there were twenty million people (or ten percent of the population) over the age of sixty-five, which shows the enormity of the problem of finding desirable homes for senior citizens. In her book *Growing Old in America,* Beth B. Hess states, "It is not only a problem of the gross neglect and low standards in many of these facilities, but also the lack of creativity in connection with them." This was certainly true in the case of Barbara Bruce, who entered a convalescent hospital at the age of ninety after breaking her hip. Up until that time she had led an active life, maintaining a small home, enjoying her children and grandchildren. Now her life seemed to stand still as the days passed very slowly, for there were no crafts, entertainment, or diversions of any kind in this sterile environment. Several weeks before she died, she confided to a visiting friend that she felt completely useless and was ready to die rather than spend the rest of her life in a place like that. There is nothing more damaging to the human spirit than boredom and inactivity.

Many elderly people feel isolated in unfamiliar surroundings, where they are cut off from their loved ones and the rest of society. They need the opportunity for a variety of social situations, such as the stimulation of young people, and a special person with whom to share thoughts. Having their children or friends visit on weekends is not enough, because the elderly need love and attention the rest of the week as well.

Robert N. Butler points to the tragic plight of many older people who are labeled senile and sent to convalescent homes even though their condition is reversible. The stark coldness of these places is not psychologically conducive to their recovery. More often than not, the old start sitting in their rooms fingering mementos of the past and gradually withdrawing from reality. In a warm and friendly atmosphere these old people might live many more years.

We must change the trend of shuttling senior citizens into retirement homes or convalesent hospitals by finding alternate ways for them to live the last part of their lives in dignity. I feel strongly that they should be allowed to remain in their own homes as long as possible, hiring part-time help, if necessary. If finances are a problem, they could share living quarters with their children, a sibling, or another adult—as long as each person has adequate privacy. A college student might be willing to do chores around an apartment or home in exchange for his room. A mobile home in a mobile home park might be the answer for some elderly people as there is little maintenance, neighbors are close by, and the age group is varied.

With appropriate housing, elderly people can continue to grow through independence, new experiences, challenges, or education. We, the younger generation, must take the responsibility for their care and happiness. After all, most of us will be following in their footsteps some day.

Index

385

Acknowledgments (*continued*)

WOMAN Excerpted from Germaine Greer, *The Female Eunuch,* published by MacGibbon and Kee, a division of Granada Publishing Company.

GAS From *The Captain's Death Bed* by Virginia Woolf, copyright 1950, 1978, by Harcourt Brace Jovanovich, Inc. Reprinted by permission of the publisher.

SHREW—THE LITTLEST MAMMAL *From Lives Around Us* by Alan Devoe. Copyright 1942 by Alan Devoe. Copyright renewed © 1970 by Mary Devoe Guinn. Reprinted by permission of Farrar, Straus and Giroux, Inc.

NAPOLEON'S RETREAT FROM RUSSIA: THE FIRST SNOWSTORM From *Napoleon's Russian Campaign* by Philippe-Paul de Segur. Copyright © 1958 by J. David Townsend. Reprinted by permission of Houghton Mifflin Company.

ON THEM From *On Nothing* by Hilaire Belloc. Reprinted by permission of A D Peters & Co. Ltd.

MARRAKECH From *Such Were the Joys* by George Orwell, copyright 1945, 1952, 1953, 1980 by Sonia Brownell Orwell; copyright 1973 by Sonia Pitt-Rivers. Reprinted by permission of Harcourt Brace Jovanovich, Inc., and A. M. Heath & Company Ltd. on behalf of the Estate of the late George Orwell and Martin Secker & Warburg.

TEACHING A STONE TO TALK From "Teaching a Stone to Talk" *Atlantic Monthly* February, 1981 Copyright © 1981 by Annie Dillard. Permission granted by the author and her agent Blanche C. Gregory, Inc.

PERINO'S Reprinted by permission.

TONNAGE From Samuel Eliot Morison, *Admiral of the Ocean Sea.* Copyright 1942 by Samuel Eliot Morison. Published by Little Brown & Company.

THE SISSY Reprinted from *The American People* by Geoffrey Gorer, with the permission of W. W. Norton & Company, Inc. Copyright 1948 by Geoffrey Gorer. Revised edition copyright © 1964 by Geoffrey Gorer.

THE PASSION OF L'AMOUR FOU From "The Passion of L'Amour Fou" by Tom Teepen, *The Atlanta Constitution* June 28, 1984. Reprinted with the permission of *The Atlanta Constitution.*

IN BED From Joan Didion, *The White Album,* 1979. Reprinted by permission of Simon & Schuster.

I WANT A WIFE From an article by Judy Syfer published in *Ms.* magazine, Dec. 31, 1971. Reprinted by permission of the author.

WILL SOMEONE PLEASE HICCUP MY PAT? From *Horizon* magazine, fall 1969. Reprinted by permission of the author, William Spooner Donald.

WHAT IS THE BIBLE? From *The Bible and the Common Reader;* copyright 1944 by Mary Ellen Chase. Reprinted by permission of MacMillan Publishing Co., Inc.

PUNK ROCK Reprinted by permission.

WOMEN'S LANGUAGE Reprinted from an article in *Ms.* magazine, July 1974.

A LAWYER'S PARAGRAPH From David S. Levine, "My Client Has Discussed Your Proposal." In Leonard Michaels and Christopher Ricks, eds., *The State of the Language.* Published by the University of California Press. Copyright 1980 by the Regents of the University of California.

GETTING DIZZY BY THE NUMBERS Copyright 1979 Time Inc. All rights reserved. Reprinted by permission from *Time.*

THREE INCIDENTS By Lee Strout White. © 1980, The New Yorker Magazine, Inc. Reprinted by permission.

SLANG ORIGINS From *Without Feathers* by Woody Allen. Copyright © 1975 by Woody Allen. Reprinted by permission of Random House, Inc.

OF WHAT USE? From Isaac Asimov, *Introduction to the Greatest Adventure,* Kone and Jordan, eds. copyright 1974, The Rockefeller University Press.

WHAT PSYCHIATRY CAN AND CANNOT DO   Originally published in *Harper's* magazine, February 1964. Reprinted by permission of the author, Thomas Szasz, M.D.

HOMO MONSTROSUS   From "Homo Monstrosus" by Annemarie de Waal Malefijt, *Scientific American,* October, 1968. Copyright © by Scientific American Inc.

MY BRÜNNHILDE   Reprinted by permission.

HOW TO START A MODEL T   From "Farewell My Lovely," by Lee Strout White; © 1936, 1964. Reprinted by permission, The New Yorker Magazine, Inc.

HOW TO HOIST SAILS   From *Sailing Technique,* © 1950 by H. A. Calahan, published by MacMillan, 1950.

THE KNIFE   From *Mortal Lessons,* © 1974, 1975, 1976 by Richard Selzer. Reprinted by permission of the publishers, Simon & Schuster.

HOW TO READ BETTER AND FASTER   Reprinted by permission of the author, Dennis Mark Doyle.

HOW DICTIONARIES ARE MADE   From *Language in Thought and Action* by S. I. Hayakawa. Reprinted by permission of the publisher, Harcourt Brace Jovanovich, Inc.

THE PHYSICAL   From *The Noel Coward Diaries,* copyright 1982 by Graham Payn. Reprinted by permission of Little, Brown and Co.

HOW TO MARK A BOOK   From "How to Mark a Book," *Saturday Review of Literature,* July 6, 1940. Copyright © 1940 by Mortimer J. Adler; copyright © renewed 1967 by Mortimer J. Adler. Reprinted by permission of the author.

BEHIND THE FORMALDEHYDE CURTAIN   From *The American Way of Death* copyright 1963, 1978 by Jessica Mitford. Reprinted by permission of SIMON & SCHUSTER, Inc.

HOW TO MAKE A PINWHEEL   Reprinted by permission.

THE THREE NEW YORKS   From "Here Is New York" from *Essays of E. B. White* by E. B. White. Copyright 1949 by E. B. White. Reprinted by permission of Harper & Row, Publishers, Inc.

POETIC PEOPLE   From Max Eastman, *Enjoyment of Poetry.* Copyright Charles Scribner's Sons, 1913.

TYPES OF COLLEGE STUDENTS   From *In Search of History* by Theodore H. White. Copyright © 1978 by Theodore H. White. Reprinted by permission of Harper & Row, Publishers, Inc.

DIFFERENT TYPES OF COMPOSERS   From *What to Listen For in Music* by Aaron Copland. Copyright 1939 by McGraw-Hill. Reprinted by permission of the publisher.

SOME AMERICAN TYPES   From *America As A Civilization* by Max Lerner Copyright © 1957 by Max Lerner. Reprinted by permission of SIMON & SCHUSTER, Inc.

TECHNOLOGY AND MEDICINE   From *The Lives of a Cell* by Lewis Thomas. Copyright © 1971 by the Massachusetts Medical Society. Originally appeared in *The New England Journal of Medicine.* Reprinted by permission of Viking Penguin, Inc.

THE FACE IN THE MIRROR   From *Talents and Geniuses* by Gilbert Highet, copyright 1957. Reprinted by permission of Curtis Brown Ltd. London.

COLORS AND PEOPLE   Reprinted by permission.

LENIN AND GLADSTONE   From "Eminent Men I Have Known," in Bertrand Russell, *Unpopular Essays.* Copyright 1950 by Bertrand Russell. Reprinted by permission.

ACCEPTING MEN AS THEY ARE   From Albert Ellis, *The Intelligent Woman's Guide to Dating & Mating.* Lyle Stuart, 1979. Reprinted by permission.

ONE VOTE FOR THIS AGE OF ANXIETY   From "One Vote for This Age of Anxiety" by Margaret Mead, *The New York Times Magazine,* May 20, 1956. Copyright © 1956 by the New York Times Company. Reprinted by permission.

ON THE DIFFERENCE BETWEEN WIT AND HUMOR   Reprinted by permission of Yale University Press from Charles S. Brooks, *Chimney-Pot Papers.* Copyright © 1919 by Yale University Press.

DOCTOR-AS-GOD IS DEAD OR DYING   From the *Atlanta Constitution* by Ellen Goodman © 1984. Boston Globe Newspaper Company/Washington Post Writers Group, reprinted with permission.

ROSS AND TOM   From John Leggett, *Ross and Tom: Two American Tragedies* (1974). Reprinted by permission of the publisher, Simon & Schuster.

LOVERS VERSUS WORKERS   From *Quest 81* by Sam Keen. Reprinted by permission of Sam Keen.

HOBBITS AND ELVES   Reprinted by permission.

WHY THE RADIO PROGRAM "THE INVASION FROM MARS" CAUSED PANIC   From *Harper's* magazine, vol. 197, no. 1183, Dec. 1948.

THE EFFECT OF TALKING TO A BABY   From *Origins.* Copyright 1977 by Richard E. Leakey and Roger Lewin. Published by E. P. Dutton.

FANTASIES   From *Crazy Salad: Some Things About Women,* by Nora Ephron. Copyright © 1975 by Nora Ephron. Reprinted by permission of Alfred A. Knopf, Inc.

MAKING BABIES   Copyright 1975 by Newsweek, Inc. All rights reserved. Reprinted by permission.

MORALS AND WEAPONS   "Morals and Weapons" from *King Solomon's Ring* by Konrad Z. Lorenz (T.Y. Crowell Company), translated by Marjorie Kerr Wilson. Copyright 1952 by Harper & Row, Publishers, Inc. Reprinted by permission of the publisher.

THE EFFECTS OF NUCLEAR WEAPONS   Originally titled "A Republic of Insects and Grass" in *The Fate of the Earth* by Jonathan Schell. Copyright © 1982 by Jonathan Schell. Reprinted by permission of Alfred A. Knopf, Inc.

RUNNING FOR LIFE   Reprinted by permission.

THE USE OF AN EFFECTIVE OPPOSITION   From Walter Lippman, "Balance of Power," *The Atlantic Monthly,* August 1939. Copyright 1939 by The Atlantic Monthly Company. Used with permission of the President and Fellows of Harvard College.

IT'S TIME TO BAN HANDGUNS   From *Time,* April 13, 1981.

WE HAVE NO RIGHT TO HAPPINESS   From *God in the Dock* Copyright © 1970 by C S Lewis Pte. Ltd., reproduced by permission of Curtis Brown Ltd. London.

HOW TO MAKE PEOPLE SMALLER THAN THEY ARE   From *Saturday Review,* Dec. 1978. Reprinted by permission.

THE CASE FOR UFOs   From *Science Digest,* Nov./Dec. 1980. © Science Digest 1980. Reprinted by permission.

WILL SPELLING COUNT?   From *Chronicle of Higher Education,* June 2, 1980. Reprinted by permission.

WHY THE COUNTRY NEEDS THE DRAFT   Copyright © 1980, by The Atlantic Monthly Company, Boston, Mass. Reprinted by permission.

EVOLUTION AS FACT AND THEORY   "Evolution as Fact and Theory" is reprinted from HEN'S TEETH AND HORSES'S TOES, Further Reflections in Natural History, by Stephen Jay Gould by permission of W. W. Norton & Company, Inc. Copyright © 1983 by Stephen Jay Gould.

APPROPRIATE HOUSING FOR THE ELDERLY   Reprinted by permission.